Mometrix
TEST PREPARATION

STAAR

Test Prep Guide Grade 3 Math

DEAR FUTURE EXAM SUCCESS STORY

First of all, **THANK YOU** for purchasing Mometrix study materials!

Second, congratulations! You are one of the few determined test-takers who are committed to doing whatever it takes to excel on your exam. **You have come to the right place.** We developed these study materials with one goal in mind: to deliver you the information you need in a format that's concise and easy to use.

In addition to optimizing your guide for the content of the test, we've outlined our recommended steps for breaking down the preparation process into small, attainable goals so you can make sure you stay on track.

We've also analyzed the entire test-taking process, identifying the most common pitfalls and showing how you can overcome them and be ready for any curveball the test throws you.

Standardized testing is one of the biggest obstacles on your road to success, which only increases the importance of doing well in the high-pressure, high-stakes environment of test day. Your results on this test could have a significant impact on your future, and this guide provides the information and practical advice to help you achieve your full potential on test day.

Your success is our success

We would love to hear from you! If you would like to share the story of your exam success or if you have any questions or comments in regard to our products, please contact us at **800-673-8175** or **support@mometrix.com**.

Thanks again for your business and we wish you continued success!

Sincerely,
The Mometrix Test Preparation Team

Written and edited by the Mometrix Exam Secrets Test Prep Team
Printed in the United States of America

TABLE OF CONTENTS

Introduction

Thank you for purchasing this resource! You have made the choice to prepare yourself for a test that could have a huge impact on your future, and this guide is designed to help you be fully ready for test day. Obviously, it's important to have a solid understanding of the test material, but you also need to be prepared for the unique environment and stressors of the test, so that you can perform to the best of your abilities.

For this purpose, the first section that appears in this guide is the **Success Strategies**. We've devoted countless hours to meticulously researching what works and what doesn't, and we've boiled down our findings to the four most impactful steps you can take to improve your performance on the test. We start at the beginning with study planning and move through the preparation process, all the way to the testing strategies that will help you get the most out of what you know when you're finally sitting in front of the test.

We recommend that you start preparing for your test as far in advance as possible. However, if you've bought this guide as a last-minute study resource and only have a few days before your test, we recommend that you skip over the first two Success Strategies since they address a long-term study plan.

If you struggle with **test anxiety**, we strongly encourage you to check out our recommendations for how you can overcome it. Test anxiety is a formidable foe, but it can be beaten, and we want to make sure you have the tools you need to defeat it.

Strategy #1 – Plan Big, Study Small

There's a lot riding on your performance. If you want to ace this test, you're going to need to keep your skills sharp and the material fresh in your mind. You need a plan that lets you review everything you need to know while still fitting in your schedule. We'll break this strategy down into three categories.

Information Organization

Start with the information you already have: the official test outline. From this, you can make a complete list of all the concepts you need to cover before the test. Organize these concepts into groups that can be studied together, and create a list of any related vocabulary you need to learn so you can brush up on any difficult terms. You'll want to keep this vocabulary list handy once you actually start studying since you may need to add to it along the way.

Time Management

Once you have your set of study concepts, decide how to spread them out over the time you have left before the test. Break your study plan into small, clear goals so you have a manageable task for each day and know exactly what you're doing. Then just focus on one small step at a time. When you manage your time this way, you don't need to spend hours at a time studying. Studying a small block of content for a short period each day helps you retain information better and avoid stressing over how much you have left to do. You can relax knowing that you have a plan to cover everything in time. In order for this strategy to be effective though, you have to start studying early and stick to your schedule. Avoid the exhaustion and futility that comes from last-minute cramming!

Study Environment

The environment you study in has a big impact on your learning. Studying in a coffee shop, while probably more enjoyable, is not likely to be as fruitful as studying in a quiet room. It's important to keep distractions to a minimum. You're only planning to study for a short block of time, so make the most of it. Don't pause to check your phone or get up to find a snack. It's also important to **avoid multitasking**. Research has consistently shown that multitasking will make your studying dramatically less effective. Your study area should also be comfortable and well-lit so you don't have the distraction of straining your eyes or sitting on an uncomfortable chair.

The time of day you study is also important. You want to be rested and alert. Don't wait until just before bedtime. Study when you'll be most likely to comprehend and remember. Even better, if you know what time of day your test will be, set that time aside for study. That way your brain will be used to working on that subject at that specific time and you'll have a better chance of recalling information.

Finally, it can be helpful to team up with others who are studying for the same test. Your actual studying should be done in as isolated an environment as possible, but the work of organizing the information and setting up the study plan can be divided up. In between study sessions, you can discuss with your teammates the concepts that you're all studying and quiz each other on the details. Just be sure that your teammates are as serious about the test as you are. If you find that your study time is being replaced with social time, you might need to find a new team.

Strategy #2 – Make Your Studying Count

You're devoting a lot of time and effort to preparing for this test, so you want to be absolutely certain it will pay off. This means doing more than just reading the content and hoping you can remember it on test day. It's important to make every minute of study count. There are two main areas you can focus on to make your studying count.

Retention

It doesn't matter how much time you study if you can't remember the material. You need to make sure you are retaining the concepts. To check your retention of the information you're learning, try recalling it at later times with minimal prompting. Try carrying around flashcards and glance at one or two from time to time or ask a friend who's also studying for the test to quiz you.

To enhance your retention, look for ways to put the information into practice so that you can apply it rather than simply recalling it. If you're using the information in practical ways, it will be much easier to remember. Similarly, it helps to solidify a concept in your mind if you're not only reading it to yourself but also explaining it to someone else. Ask a friend to let you teach them about a concept you're a little shaky on (or speak aloud to an imaginary audience if necessary). As you try to summarize, define, give examples, and answer your friend's questions, you'll understand the concepts better and they will stay with you longer. Finally, step back for a big picture view and ask yourself how each piece of information fits with the whole subject. When you link the different concepts together and see them working together as a whole, it's easier to remember the individual components.

Finally, practice showing your work on any multi-step problems, even if you're just studying. Writing out each step you take to solve a problem will help solidify the process in your mind, and you'll be more likely to remember it during the test.

Modality

Modality simply refers to the means or method by which you study. Choosing a study modality that fits your own individual learning style is crucial. No two people learn best in exactly the same way, so it's important to know your strengths and use them to your advantage.

For example, if you learn best by visualization, focus on visualizing a concept in your mind and draw an image or a diagram. Try color-coding your notes, illustrating them, or creating symbols that will trigger your mind to recall a learned concept. If you learn best by hearing or discussing information, find a study partner who learns the same way or read aloud to yourself. Think about how to put the information in your own words. Imagine that you are giving a lecture on the topic and record yourself so you can listen to it later.

For any learning style, flashcards can be helpful. Organize the information so you can take advantage of spare moments to review. Underline key words or phrases. Use different colors for different categories. Mnemonic devices (such as creating a short list in which every item starts with the same letter) can also help with retention. Find what works best for you and use it to store the information in your mind most effectively and easily.

Strategy #3 – Practice the Right Way

Your success on test day depends not only on how many hours you put into preparing, but also on whether you prepared the right way. It's good to check along the way to see if your studying is paying off. One of the most effective ways to do this is by taking practice tests to evaluate your progress. Practice tests are useful because they show exactly where you need to improve. Every time you take a practice test, pay special attention to these three groups of questions:

- The questions you got wrong
- The questions you had to guess on, even if you guessed right
- The questions you found difficult or slow to work through

This will show you exactly what your weak areas are, and where you need to devote more study time. Ask yourself why each of these questions gave you trouble. Was it because you didn't understand the material? Was it because you didn't remember the vocabulary? Do you need more repetitions on this type of question to build speed and confidence? Dig into those questions and figure out how you can strengthen your weak areas as you go back to review the material.

Additionally, many practice tests have a section explaining the answer choices. It can be tempting to read the explanation and think that you now have a good understanding of the concept. However, an explanation likely only covers part of the question's broader context. Even if the explanation makes perfect sense, **go back and investigate** every concept related to the question until you're positive you have a thorough understanding.

As you go along, keep in mind that the practice test is just that: practice. Memorizing these questions and answers will not be very helpful on the actual test because it is unlikely to have any of the same exact questions. If you only know the right answers to the sample questions, you won't be prepared for the real thing. **Study the concepts** until you understand them fully, and then you'll be able to answer any question that shows up on the test.

It's important to wait on the practice tests until you're ready. If you take a test on your first day of study, you may be overwhelmed by the amount of material covered and how much you need to learn. Work up to it gradually.

On test day, you'll need to be prepared for answering questions, managing your time, and using the test-taking strategies you've learned. It's a lot to balance, like a mental marathon that will have a big impact on your future. Like training for a marathon, you'll need to start slowly and work your way up. When test day arrives, you'll be ready.

Start with the strategies you've read in the first two Success Strategies—plan your course and study in the way that works best for you. If you have time, consider using multiple study resources to get different approaches to the same concepts. It can be helpful to see difficult concepts from more than one angle. Then find a good source for practice tests. Many times, the test website will suggest potential study resources or provide sample tests.

Test-Taking Strategies

This section contains a list of test-taking strategies that you may find helpful as you work through the test. By taking what you know and applying logical thought, you can maximize your chances of answering any question correctly!

It is very important to realize that every question is different and every person is different: no single strategy will work on every question, and no single strategy will work for every person. That's why we've included all of them here, so you can try them out and determine which ones work best for different types of questions and which ones work best for you.

Question Strategies

☑ Read Carefully

Read the question and the answer choices carefully. Don't miss the question because you misread the terms. You have plenty of time to read each question thoroughly and make sure you understand what is being asked. Yet a happy medium must be attained, so don't waste too much time. You must read carefully and efficiently.

☑ Contextual Clues

Look for contextual clues. If the question includes a word you are not familiar with, look at the immediate context for some indication of what the word might mean. Contextual clues can often give you all the information you need to decipher the meaning of an unfamiliar word. Even if you can't determine the meaning, you may be able to narrow down the possibilities enough to make a solid guess at the answer to the question.

☑ Prefixes

If you're having trouble with a word in the question or answer choices, try dissecting it. Take advantage of every clue that the word might include. Prefixes can be a huge help. Usually, they allow you to determine a basic meaning. *Pre-* means before, *post-* means after, *pro-* is positive, *de-* is negative. From prefixes, you can get an idea of the general meaning of the word and try to put it into context.

☑ Hedge Words

Watch out for critical hedge words, such as *likely, may, can, often, almost, mostly, usually, generally, rarely*, and *sometimes*. Question writers insert these hedge phrases to cover every possibility. Often an answer choice will be wrong simply because it leaves no room for exception. Be on guard for answer choices that have definitive words such as *exactly* and *always*.

☑ Switchback Words

Stay alert for *switchbacks*. These are the words and phrases frequently used to alert you to shifts in thought. The most common switchback words are *but, although*, and *however*. Others include *nevertheless, on the other hand, even though, while, in spite of, despite*, and *regardless of*. Switchback words are important to catch because they can change the direction of the question or an answer choice.

⊘ Face Value

When in doubt, use common sense. Accept the situation in the problem at face value. Don't read too much into it. These problems will not require you to make wild assumptions. If you have to go beyond creativity and warp time or space in order to have an answer choice fit the question, then you should move on and consider the other answer choices. These are normal problems rooted in reality. The applicable relationship or explanation may not be readily apparent, but it is there for you to figure out. Use your common sense to interpret anything that isn't clear.

Answer Choice Strategies

⊘ Answer Selection

The most thorough way to pick an answer choice is to identify and eliminate wrong answers until only one is left, then confirm it is the correct answer. Sometimes an answer choice may immediately seem right, but be careful. The test writers will usually put more than one reasonable answer choice on each question, so take a second to read all of them and make sure that the other choices are not equally obvious. As long as you have time left, it is better to read every answer choice than to pick the first one that looks right without checking the others.

⊘ Answer Choice Families

An answer choice family consists of two (in rare cases, three) answer choices that are very similar in construction and cannot all be true at the same time. If you see two answer choices that are direct opposites or parallels, one of them is usually the correct answer. For instance, if one answer choice says that quantity *x* increases and another either says that quantity *x* decreases (opposite) or says that quantity *y* increases (parallel), then those answer choices would fall into the same family. An answer choice that doesn't match the construction of the answer choice family is more likely to be incorrect. Most questions will not have answer choice families, but when they do appear, you should be prepared to recognize them.

⊘ Eliminate Answers

Eliminate answer choices as soon as you realize they are wrong, but make sure you consider all possibilities. If you are eliminating answer choices and realize that the last one you are left with is also wrong, don't panic. Start over and consider each choice again. There may be something you missed the first time that you will realize on the second pass.

⊘ Avoid Fact Traps

Don't be distracted by an answer choice that is factually true but doesn't answer the question. You are looking for the choice that answers the question. Stay focused on what the question is asking for so you don't accidentally pick an answer that is true but incorrect. Always go back to the question and make sure the answer choice you've selected actually answers the question and is not merely a true statement.

⊘ Extreme Statements

In general, you should avoid answers that put forth extreme actions as standard practice or proclaim controversial ideas as established fact. An answer choice that states the "process should be used in certain situations, if..." is much more likely to be correct than one that states the "process should be discontinued completely." The first is a calm rational statement and doesn't even make a definitive, uncompromising stance, using a hedge word *if* to provide wiggle room, whereas the second choice is far more extreme.

⊘ BENCHMARK

As you read through the answer choices and you come across one that seems to answer the question well, mentally select that answer choice. This is not your final answer, but it's the one that will help you evaluate the other answer choices. The one that you selected is your benchmark or standard for judging each of the other answer choices. Every other answer choice must be compared to your benchmark. That choice is correct until proven otherwise by another answer choice beating it. If you find a better answer, then that one becomes your new benchmark. Once you've decided that no other choice answers the question as well as your benchmark, you have your final answer.

⊘ PREDICT THE ANSWER

Before you even start looking at the answer choices, it is often best to try to predict the answer. When you come up with the answer on your own, it is easier to avoid distractions and traps because you will know exactly what to look for. The right answer choice is unlikely to be word-for-word what you came up with, but it should be a close match. Even if you are confident that you have the right answer, you should still take the time to read each option before moving on.

General Strategies

⊘ TOUGH QUESTIONS

If you are stumped on a problem or it appears too hard or too difficult, don't waste time. Move on! Remember though, if you can quickly check for obviously incorrect answer choices, your chances of guessing correctly are greatly improved. Before you completely give up, at least try to knock out a couple of possible answers. Eliminate what you can and then guess at the remaining answer choices before moving on.

⊘ CHECK YOUR WORK

Since you will probably not know every term listed and the answer to every question, it is important that you get credit for the ones that you do know. Don't miss any questions through careless mistakes. If at all possible, try to take a second to look back over your answer selection and make sure you've selected the correct answer choice and haven't made a costly careless mistake (such as marking an answer choice that you didn't mean to mark). This quick double check should more than pay for itself in caught mistakes for the time it costs.

⊘ DON'T RUSH

It is very easy to make errors when you are in a hurry. Maintaining a fast pace in answering questions is pointless if it makes you miss questions that you would have gotten right otherwise. Test writers like to include distracting information and wrong answers that seem right. Taking a little extra time to avoid careless mistakes can make all the difference in your test score. Find a pace that allows you to be confident in the answers that you select.

⊘ KEEP MOVING

Panicking will not help you pass the test, so do your best to stay calm and keep moving. Taking deep breaths and going through the answer elimination steps you practiced can help to break through a stress barrier and keep your pace.

Final Notes

The combination of a solid foundation of content knowledge and the confidence that comes from practicing your plan for applying that knowledge is the key to maximizing your performance on test day. As your foundation of content knowledge is built up and strengthened, you'll find that the strategies included in this chapter become more and more effective in helping you quickly sift through the distractions and traps of the test to isolate the correct answer.

Now that you're preparing to move forward into the test content chapters of this book, be sure to keep your goal in mind. As you read, think about how you will be able to apply this information on the test. If you've already seen sample questions for the test and you have an idea of the question format and style, try to come up with questions of your own that you can answer based on what you're reading. This will give you valuable practice applying your knowledge in the same ways you can expect to on test day.

Good luck and good studying!

Number and Operations

Place Value

Numbers can be broken apart and composed based on their **place value**. For example, the number 129,548 can be expressed in **expanded form** as 100,000 + 20,000 + 9,000 + 500 + 40 + 8. You should also be comfortable going from expanded form to standard form. For example, what number is represented by 30,000 + 400 + 80 + 2? Notice 3 groups of ten-thousands, 0 groups of thousands, 4 groups of hundreds, 8 groups of tens, and 2 groups of ones. This becomes 30,482.

Sometimes you will be asked to compose and decompose numbers that are presented in **picture** or **model** form. This usually includes base-10 blocks. For example, consider the model below. How many groups of thousands, hundreds, tens, and ones are there? There is 1 group of 1,000, 2 groups of 100, 4 groups of 10, and 7 ones. This forms the number 1,247.

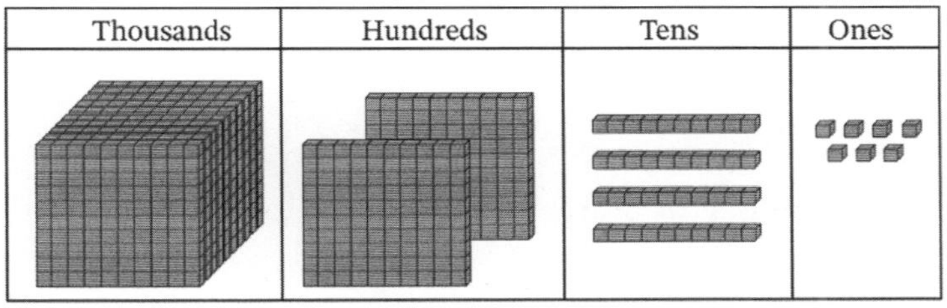

Example

Decompose the number 452,837 into expanded form.

The number 452,837 can be decomposed based on its place value. The 4 in the hundred-thousands place represents 400,000. The 5 in the ten-thousands place represents 50,000. The 2 in the thousands place represents 2,000. The 8 in the hundreds place represents 800. The 3 in the tens place represents 30. The 7 in the ones place represents 7. Altogether, 452,837 in expanded form is 400,000 + 50,000 + 2,000 + 800 + 30 + 7.

EXAMPLE

What is the combined value of all of the base ten blocks below? Express the number in expanded form.

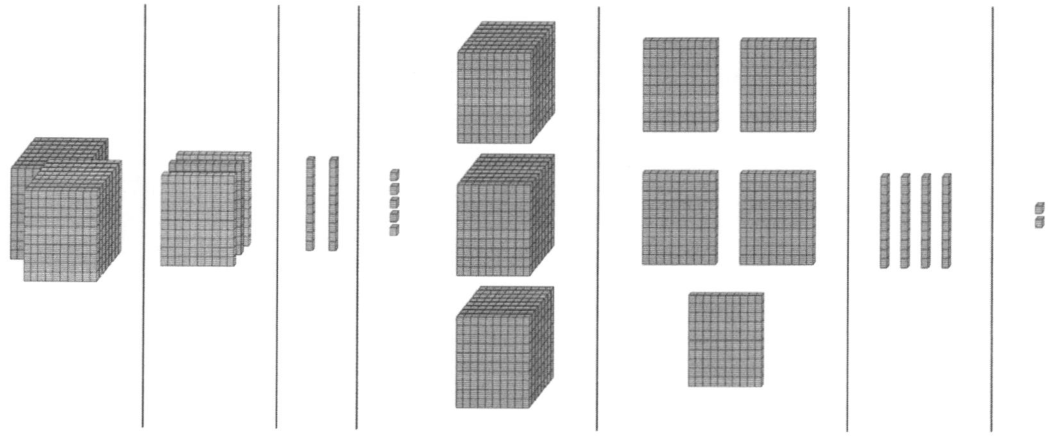

There are 5 blocks of 1,000. There are 8 plates of 100. There are 6 rods of 10. There are 7 cubes of 1. $5{,}000 + 800 + 60 + 7$ represents the amount in expanded form. In standard form the value is 5,867.

THE BASE-10 NUMBER SYSTEM

Consider the numbers 3, 30, 300, and 3,000. What happens from one number to the next? Each number is **10 times** the previous number. The great thing about the **base-10 number system** is the **consistent pattern** regarding place value. As you move from left to right, place value increases by a factor of 10. As you noticed in the previous example, 30 is 10 times as large as 3, 300 is 10 times as large as 30, 3,000 is 10 times as large as 300. This concept can be applied when you jump from a small place value to a large place value. For example, consider 45 and 450,000. How do we get from 45 to 450,000?

$$45 \times 10 = 450$$

$$45 \times 100 = 4{,}500$$

$$45 \times 1{,}000 = 45{,}000$$

$$45 \times 10{,}000 = 450{,}000$$

The important thing to remember is that each place value increases by a factor of 10. Another way to think about this is $45 \times 10 \times 10 \times 10 \times 10 = 450{,}000$.

Review Video: Number Place Value
Visit mometrix.com/academy and enter code: 205433

Rounding

There are many ways to round numbers. For example, when the number 89 is rounded to the nearest ten it becomes 90. When 89 is rounded to the nearest hundred it becomes 100.

A **number line** is a great tool to use when **rounding** numbers.

When rounding to the nearest ten, set up a number line with intervals of 10. Plot the number on the number line and look for the multiple of 10 that the number is closest to. For example, notice how 18 is closer to 20 than to 10. This means that 18 rounded to the nearest ten is 20.

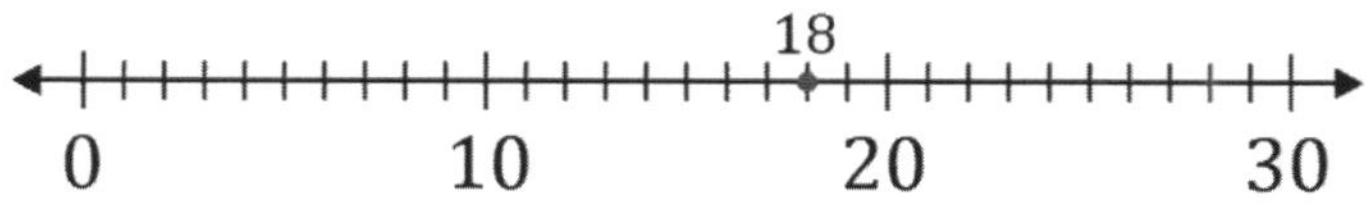

The same process works for numbers with larger place values. Consider the number 341. Create a number line with intervals of 100. Plot 341 on the number line. Notice that it is closer to 300 than 400. This means 341 rounded to the nearest hundred is 300.

Let's look at one more. Consider the number 1,627. Plot the point on a number line that has intervals of 1,000. Notice how 1,627 is closer to 2,000 than 1,000. This means that 1,627 rounded to the nearest thousand, which is 2,000.

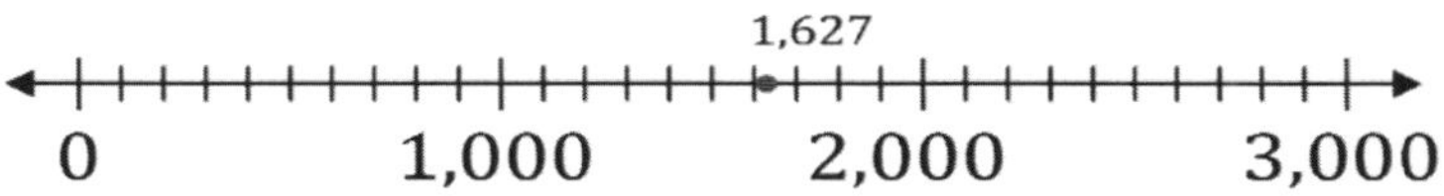

Comparing Numbers

Two important symbols are the **inequality symbols** for **greater than** (>) and **less than** (<). For example, 45 > 35 means 45 is greater than 35, and 26 < 62 means 26 is less than 62. We can now build on this skill to compare and order whole numbers up to 100,000. The important thing to remember is place value. Remember, when comparing numbers, start by comparing the **farthest left digit**. For example, when comparing 452,987 and 455,798, start by comparing the hundred-thousands place.

452,987 and 455,798

In this case, both values are 4. Since they are the same, move to the ten-thousands place.

452,987 and 455,798

Both values are both 5, so move to the thousands place.

452,987 and 455,798

2 is less than 5, so 452,987 is less than 455,798.

This can be expressed using an inequality symbol: 452,987 < 455,798.

EXAMPLE

Order the three values from least to greatest using the symbols < and >:

65,033; 65,300; 65,030.

When comparing numbers, start with the farthest left digit and move right until the digits differ. All three numbers have the same digit in the ten-thousands place (6). Move right. All three numbers have the same digit in the thousands place (5). Move right. 65,300 has the largest digit in the hundreds place (3), therefore it is the largest number. Move right. Two numbers remain. Both 65,030 and 65,033 have the same digit in the tens place (3). Move right. 65,033 has a larger digit in the ones place, therefore it is larger than 65,030. The numbers from least to greatest are 65,030 < 65,033 < 65,300.

EXAMPLE

Use an inequality symbol to compare 905,532 and 905,600.

Compare the numbers by comparing each digit from left to right. The digits in the hundred-thousands, ten-thousands, and thousands place are all the same (905). Keep moving right. The hundreds digits differ. One says 6 and one says 5. This means that 905,600 is larger than 905,532. 905,600 > 905,532, or 905,532 < 905,600.

Fractions

Values that are greater than 0 but less than or equal to 1 can be represented as a **fraction**. For example, the pizza, watermelon, and lemon are each sliced into equal pieces. The pizza has 6 equal pieces, the watermelon has 4 equal pieces, and the lemon has 8 equal pieces. These values represent the denominator of a fraction. Remember, the **denominator** is the bottom number in a fraction, which represents the **total number of pieces**.

$\frac{?}{6}$ $\frac{?}{4}$ $\frac{?}{8}$

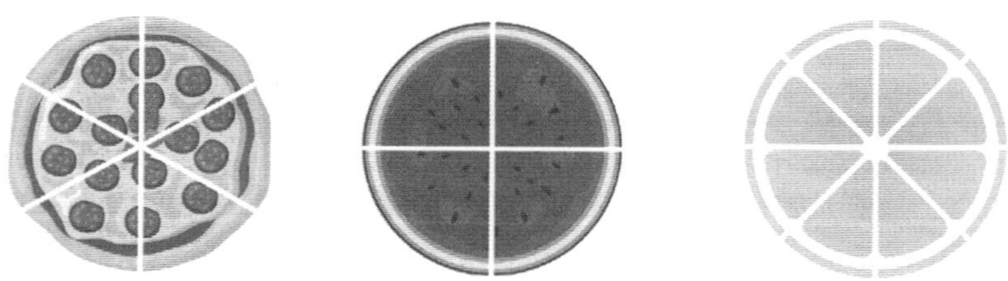

If 3 slices of each food are eaten, 3 would be the **numerator**.

$\frac{3}{6}$ of the pizza is eaten. $\frac{3}{4}$ of the watermelon is eaten. $\frac{3}{8}$ of the lemon is eaten.

Fractions can also be modeled using number lines or **fraction strips**.

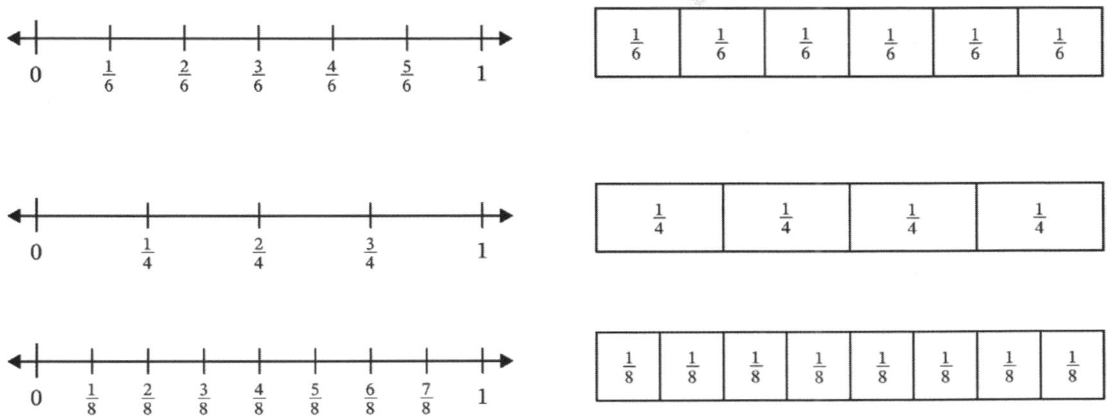

Fractions and Number Lines

Fractions are often displayed using models, fraction strips, pictures, or number lines. When determining a fraction from a number line, check to see how many **parts** there are within **one whole**. For example, consider the number line below. Notice how there are 4 **equal parts** from 0 to 1. This means each hash mark represents 1 out of 4, or $\frac{1}{4}$. Count up by $\frac{1}{4}$ to determine the missing value. $\frac{1}{4}, \frac{2}{4}, \frac{3}{4}$... The missing value is $\frac{3}{4}$.

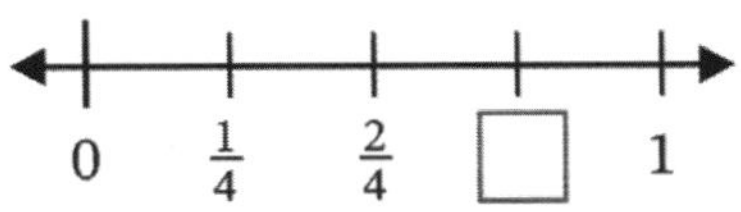

Consider the number line below. To identify the fraction that the green dot represents, first figure out the interval. The **interval** is essentially how many equal parts are shown to be within one whole number. In this case, there are 10 equal parts from 0 to 1. This means the interval is tenths. Starting from 0, or $\frac{0}{10}$, each hop to the right increases by $\frac{1}{10}$. The dot represents 8 hops, so $\frac{8}{10}$.

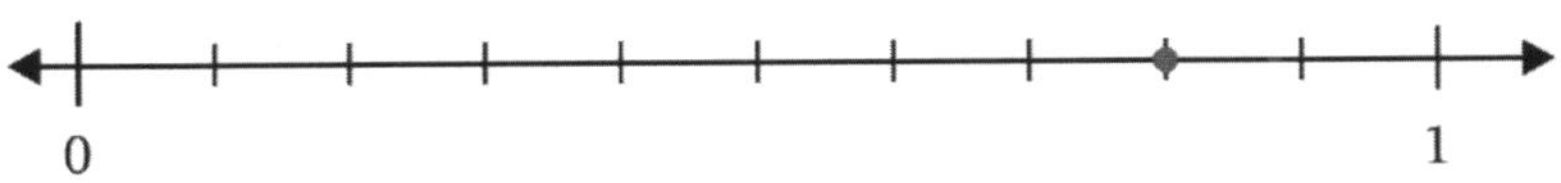

Unit Fractions

A **unit fraction** represents **one part** out of the whole. For example, $\frac{1}{2}, \frac{1}{4}, \frac{1}{6}$ and $\frac{1}{10}$ are all considered unit fractions. If the **numerator** is **1**, then the fraction is considered a unit fraction. Unit fractions can be shown in a model. For example, if a pan of brownies is cut into 8 equal pieces and 1 brownie is eaten, the consumed brownie represents the unit fraction $\frac{1}{8}$. The numerator is 1, and the denominator represents the total number of parts.

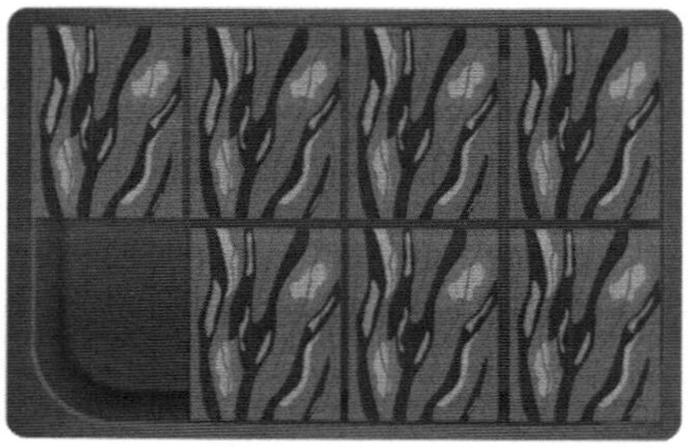

Composing and Decomposing Fractions

Fractions can be thought of as a **collection** of unit fractions. For example, the fraction $\frac{4}{5}$ is composed of $\frac{1}{5}+\frac{1}{5}+\frac{1}{5}+\frac{1}{5}$. The opposite of **composing** a fraction is **decomposing** a fraction. When a fraction is **broken up** into the sum of its unit fractions, it has been decomposed. For example, $\frac{6}{8}$ can be decomposed into $\frac{1}{8}+\frac{1}{8}+\frac{1}{8}+\frac{1}{8}+\frac{1}{8}+\frac{1}{8}$.

Using Models to Solve Problems Involving Fractions

Fractions represent part of a whole. One helpful way to see this is to draw a model. For example, if a cake is sliced into 8 equal slices, we can model the scenario by drawing lines to divide the cake into 8 slices. If 4 slices are eaten, then $\frac{4}{8}$ remain.

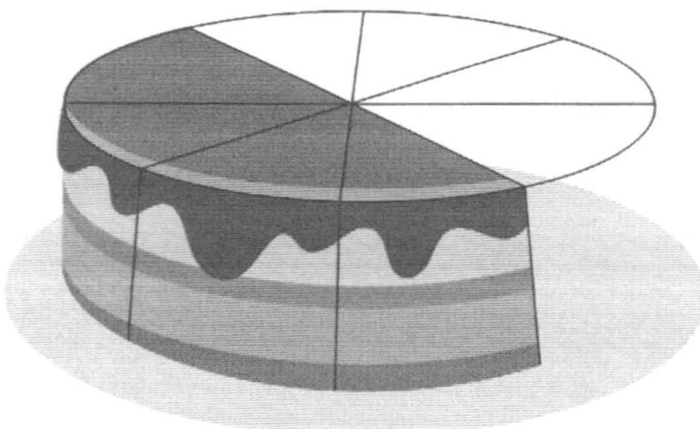

What if a cake had 10 slices, and each person wanted 2 slices? How many people could this cake feed?

Draw a quick picture of a cake sliced into 10 pieces. How many groups of 2 slices are there? A cake with 10 slices has 5 groups of 2. This cake would feed 5 people.

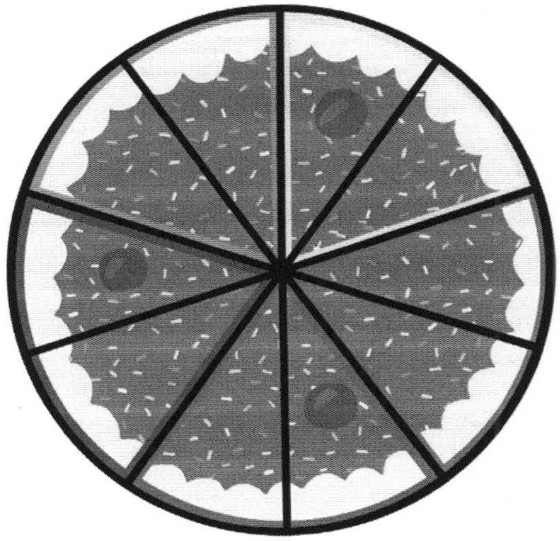

Drawing a quick sketch is often a helpful strategy for problems involving equal pieces.

EXAMPLE

Use the fraction strips to identify an equivalent fraction to $\frac{2}{3}$.

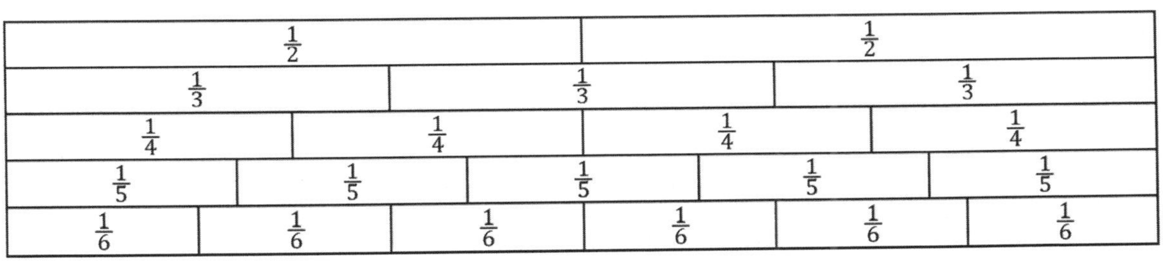

Locate the fraction strips for $\frac{1}{3}$. Move to the right to locate $\frac{2}{3}$. Notice how $\frac{2}{3}$ is the same length as $\frac{4}{6}$. The fractions $\frac{2}{3}$ and $\frac{4}{6}$ are considered equivalent fractions. $\frac{4}{6}$ is the correct answer.

EXAMPLE

Use the fraction number lines to identify three fractions that are equivalent to $\frac{4}{8}$.

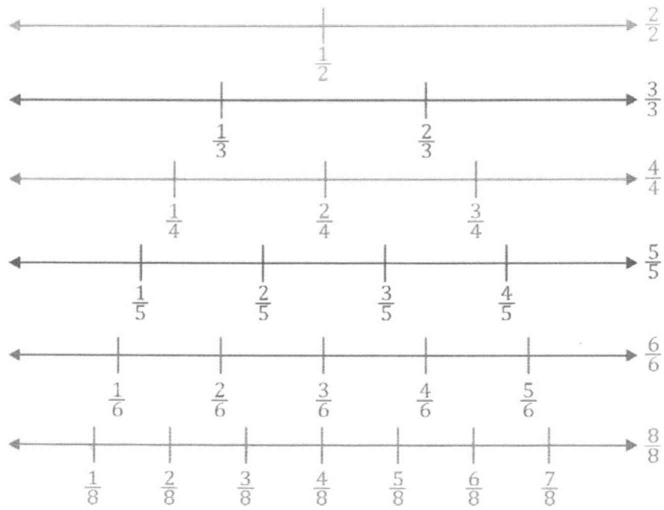

Equivalent fractions represent the same distance from 0 on a number line. Locate the fraction $\frac{4}{8}$. Compare this distance with the other number lines. Notice how the red, blue, and orange number lines have values at the same distance. The fractions $\frac{1}{2}$, $\frac{2}{4}$, and $\frac{3}{6}$ are the same distance from 0 as $\frac{4}{8}$. This means $\frac{1}{2}$, $\frac{2}{4}$, $\frac{3}{6}$, and $\frac{4}{8}$ are all equivalent fractions. The answer is $\frac{1}{2}$, $\frac{2}{4}$, $\frac{3}{6}$.

EQUIVALENT FRACTIONS

Equivalent fractions are fractions that represent the **same amount**. For example, $\frac{1}{2}$ of a pizza is the same amount as $\frac{2}{4}$ of a pizza. It can be helpful to show equivalent fractions on a number line.

Consider the number lines below. Each number line extends from 0 to 1, and all of the number lines are the same length.

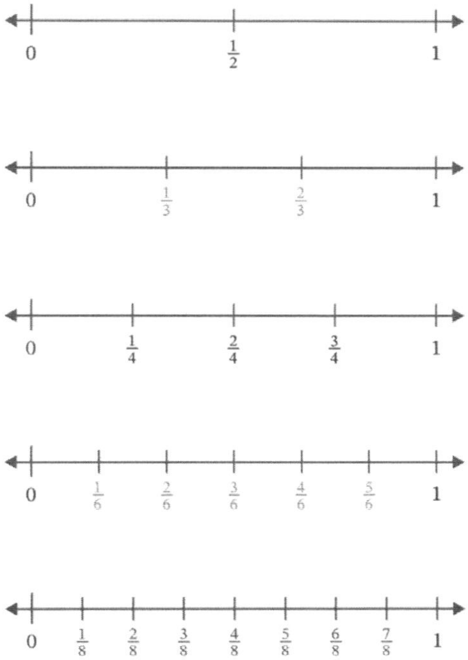

Notice how the distance at $\frac{1}{2}$ is the same distance as $\frac{2}{4}$, $\frac{3}{6}$, and $\frac{4}{8}$. These are all considered equivalent fractions because they all represent the same amount. $\frac{1}{2}$, $\frac{2}{4}$, $\frac{3}{6}$, and $\frac{4}{8}$ are all the same distance from 0 on the number line.

The same concept can be seen using a model. The circle below is made up of 3 equal parts. One part is shaded. This shaded part represents $\frac{1}{3}$. What is another fraction equivalent to $\frac{1}{3}$?

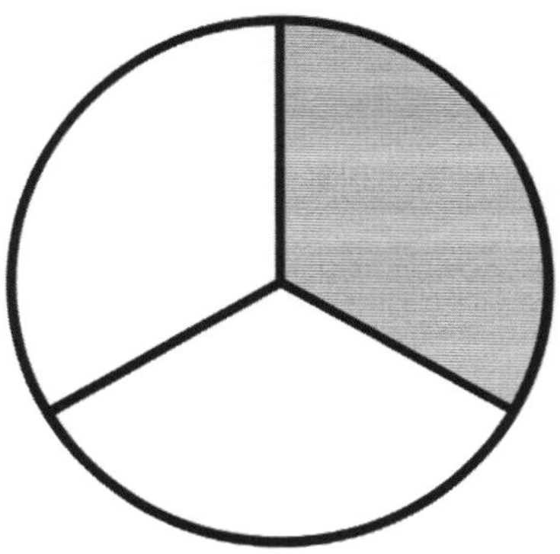

Instead of dividing the circle into 3 equal parts, divide it into 6 equal parts. Notice how 1 out of 3 becomes 2 out of 6. The fraction $\frac{2}{6}$ is equivalent to $\frac{1}{3}$.

Remember, the term **equivalent** means the same amount. It can be helpful to find equivalent fractions using a number line. Fractions that are the same distance from 0 on a number line are considered equivalent fractions. Notice how the two red points on the number lines below are the same distance from 0. The fractions $\frac{1}{3}$ and $\frac{2}{6}$ represent the same distance, therefore they are equivalent. Are there any other pairs of equivalent fractions visible on the number lines below?

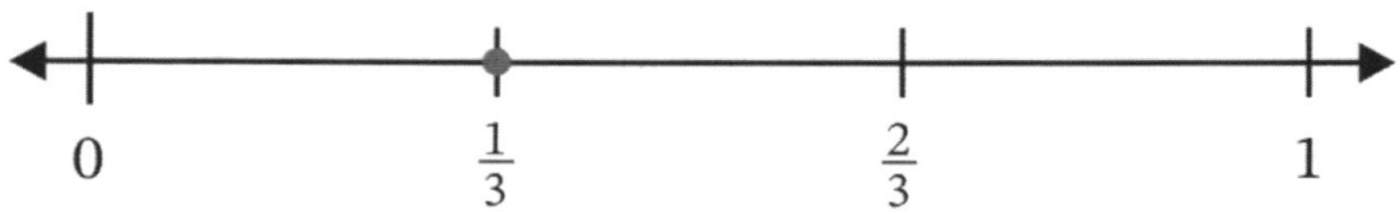

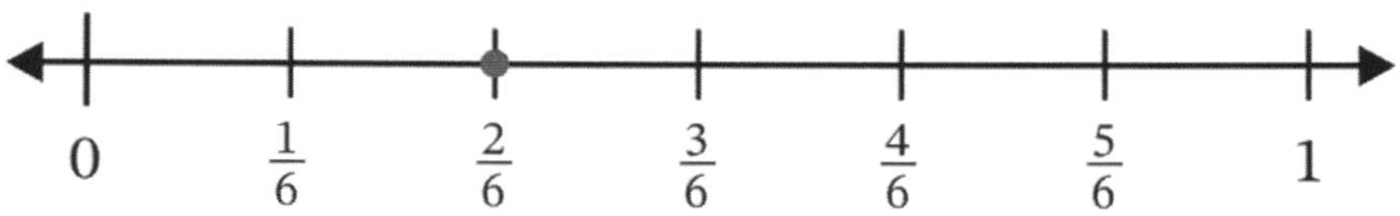

Yes! $\frac{2}{3}$ and $\frac{4}{6}$ are the same distance from 0. $\frac{2}{3}$ and $\frac{4}{6}$ are equivalent fractions.

Equivalent fractions can also be determined using an area model. Consider the fraction $\frac{1}{2}$. The area model shows a rectangle with 2 equal pieces, and 1 part shaded. This represents $\frac{1}{2}$. What is another way to express $\frac{1}{2}$? In other words, what is an equivalent fraction?

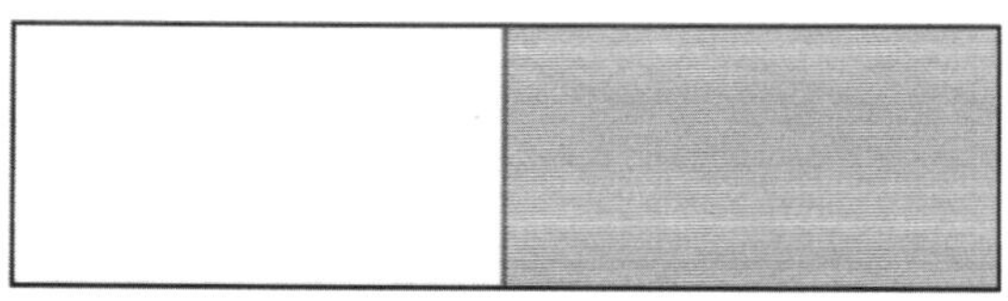

What if the same rectangle was sliced into 8 equal pieces? How many pieces would be shaded?

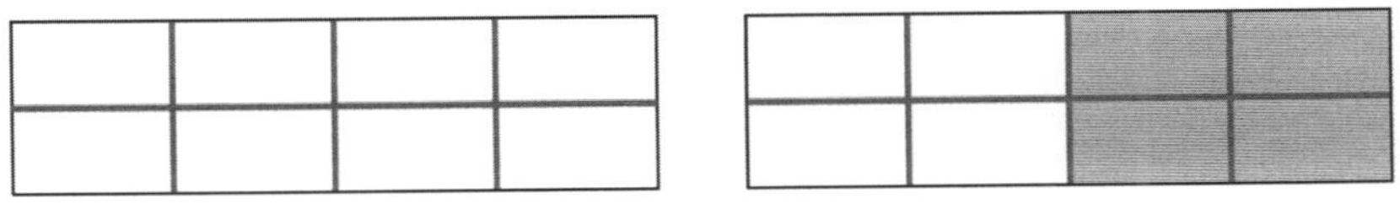

When the model is sliced into 8 equal pieces, 4 parts are shaded. $\frac{1}{2}$ and $\frac{4}{8}$ are considered equivalent fractions.

Comparing Fractions

Many fractions can be compared using logic. For example, consider the unit fractions $\frac{1}{4}$ and $\frac{1}{3}$. These fractions could be compared using a number line or by drawing a picture. However, these tools are not always necessary.

Both fractions are unit fractions, so they represent one part out of the total. $\frac{1}{4}$ represents one of the fourths. $\frac{1}{3}$ represents one of the thirds. Thirds are larger than fourths, so $\frac{1}{3}$ is larger than $\frac{1}{4}$.

The numerators are the same, and thirds are larger than fourths: $\frac{1}{3} > \frac{1}{4}$.

Now consider two fractions that have the same denominator. Compare the two fractions $\frac{2}{4}$ and $\frac{3}{4}$. Again, a picture or number line is not always necessary.

Both fractions have 4 in the denominator. This means both fractions have a whole of 4. However, 2 parts out of 4 is less than 3 parts out of 4. Think: 2 pieces are less than 3 pieces, so $\frac{2}{4}$ is less than $\frac{3}{4}$: $\frac{2}{4} < \frac{3}{4}$.

Example

Use an inequality symbol to compare the two fractions $\frac{4}{5}$ and $\frac{4}{6}$.

The numerator of a fraction represents the "parts". The denominator of a fraction represents the "whole". The fractions $\frac{4}{5}$ and $\frac{4}{6}$ have the same number of parts but a different number of total parts. Fifths are larger than sixths. Therefore, 4 out of 5 is more than 4 out of 6. Think about it this way: 4 large pieces is more than 4 small pieces.

Notice how 4 pieces out of 5 is more than 4 pieces out of 6.

$$\frac{4}{5} > \frac{4}{6}$$

Example

Use an inequality symbol to compare the two fractions: $\frac{3}{8}$ and $\frac{2}{8}$.

Both fractions have the same denominator. $\frac{3}{8}$ and $\frac{2}{8}$ both have 8 total parts. 3 out of 8 parts is more than 2 out of 8 parts. This means that $\frac{3}{8}$ is greater than $\frac{2}{8}$.

Notice how 3 pieces out of 8 is more than 2 pieces out of 8.

$$\frac{3}{8} > \frac{2}{8}$$

Solving Problems

Place Value Strategy

One- and two-step **addition and subtraction problems** can be solved using place value. For example, $432 + 826$ can be thought of as a group of 4 hundreds, 3 tens, and 2 ones, plus 8 hundreds, 2 tens, and 6 ones. Combine the place values to solve:

$$4 \text{ hundreds} + 8 \text{ hundreds} = 12 \text{ hundreds}$$

$$3 \text{ tens} + 2 \text{ tens} = 5 \text{ tens}$$

$$2 \text{ ones} + 6 \text{ ones} = 8 \text{ ones}$$

$$1{,}200 + 50 + 8 = 1{,}258$$

Two-Step Problems

Consider the scenario: A shopper starts with $456 in their wallet and then spends $128 on shoes. Later that day, the shopper finds a 20-dollar bill in their pocket. Altogether, how much money does the shopper have left after shoe shopping?

The scenario can be solved in two steps. The shopper starts with $456 and then spends $128. This means that $128 have been subtracted from $456. $456 consists of 4 hundreds, 5 tens, and 6 ones. $128 consists of 1 hundred, 2 tens, and 8 ones. 8 ones cannot be subtracted from 6 ones, which means **regrouping** needs to occur.

4 hundreds, 5 tens, and 6 ones becomes 4 hundreds, 4 tens, and 16 ones. Now subtraction can continue: $456 - 128 = 328$.

$$\begin{array}{r} 4\,5\,6 \\ -\,1\,2\,8 \\ \hline \end{array} \quad \rightarrow \quad \begin{array}{r} {\scriptstyle 4\ 16} \\ 4\,\not{5}\,\not{6} \\ -\,1\,2\,8 \\ \hline 3\,2\,8 \end{array}$$

The shopper then finds \$20 in their pocket. This indicates adding 20: $328 + 20 = 348$.

The shopper has \$348 after shoe shopping.

EXAMPLE

Find the value of the expression below:

$$(648 + 250) - 30$$

648 consists of 6 hundreds, 4 tens, and 8 ones. 250 consists of 2 hundreds, 5 tens, and 0 ones. Combine each place value to find the sum.

$$600 + 200 + 40 + 50 + 8 + 0 = 898$$

Now, subtract 30, which consists of 3 tens, from 898. 898 consists of 9 tens. Subtract 3 tens from this: $898 - 30 = 868$.

$$(648 + 250) - 30 = 868$$

The answer is 868.

EXAMPLE

Find the value of the expression below:

$$640 - 180$$

Think about 640 and 180 in terms of place value.

$$640 = 6 \text{ hundreds} + 4 \text{ tens} + 0 \text{ ones}$$

$$180 = 1 \text{ hundred} + 8 \text{ tens} + 0 \text{ ones}$$

640 has 4 tens, which is not enough to subtract 8 tens from.

Regrouping is necessary. 1 of the hundreds becomes 10 tens. So, 6 hundreds + 4 tens + 0 ones becomes 5 hundreds + 14 tens + 0 ones.

Now subtraction can begin.

(5 hundreds + 14 tens + 0 ones) − (1 hundred + 8 tens + 0 ones) becomes

4 hundreds + 6 tens + 0 ones. In standard form, this is 460.

$$640 - 180 = 460$$

The answer is 460.

Estimating Solutions

Estimating sums and differences is a way to come up with an answer that is close to the exact answer. For example, if you run 9 miles each week for 7 weeks, how many total miles have you run? 9 rounded to the nearest 10 is 10. 7 groups of 10 is 70. You have run about 70 miles. This is close to the actual answer, which is 63 miles.

Compatible numbers make addition and subtraction easier. **Compatible numbers** are numbers that make addition or subtraction easier to do, and often they end in a 0 or 5. Instead of calculating $257 - 49$, consider using compatible numbers. 257 is close to 250, and 49 is close to 50, and $250 - 50$ are compatible because they can be quickly subtracted: $250 - 50 = 200$. This is close to the actual answer of $257 - 49 = 208$.

Rounding

Rounding is another strategy that saves time when adding and subtracting. If the digit to the right is 5 or greater, then the rounded number will **round** up. If the digit to the right is less than 5, then the rounded number stays the same.

Round 248 to the nearest 10.

2**4**8: 4 is in the tens place. The digit to the right of the 4 will indicate whether the 4 stays the same or rounds up to 5. To the right of 4 there is an 8. This means the 4 will round up to 5. 248 becomes 250 when rounded to the nearest 10.

Round 248 to the nearest 100.

248: 2 is in the hundreds place. The digit to the right of the 2 will indicate whether the 2 stays the same or rounds up to 3. To the right of 2 there is a 4. This means the 2 will stay the same. 248 becomes 200 when rounded to the nearest hundred.

Rounding to the nearest ten or hundred can sometimes make addition or subtraction problems easier.

For example, use rounding to estimate the sum of 49 and 253. If 49 is rounded to the nearest ten, it becomes 50. If 253 is rounded to the nearest ten, it becomes 250. Now, add 50 and 250: $50 + 250 = 300$. In this case, rounding made the addition much simpler and is still close to the actual answer of 302.

Coins and Bills

The value of a collection of coins and bills can be found by adding the values according to place value.

<u>Place Value</u>

Penny: 1 cent or $0.01

Nickel: 5 cents or $0.05

Dime: 10 cents or $0.10

Quarter: 25 cents or $0.25

1-dollar bill: $1.00

5-dollar bill: $5.00

10-dollar bill: $10.00

50-dollar bill: $50.00

100-dollar bill: $100.00

Adding Coins and Bills

When adding coins and bills, make sure to line up the decimals. For example, consider the bills and coins below.

Start by combining the bills.

$5 + 1 + 1 + 1 = 8$. So far, there are $8.

Now add the coins. There are 2 quarters, 1 nickel, and 2 dimes.

Be sure to line up the decimals when adding.

$0.25 + 0.25 + 0.1 + 0.1 + 0.05 = 0.75$, or 75 cents.

$$\begin{array}{r} 0.25 \\ 0.25 \\ 0.10 \\ 0.10 \\ +\,0.05 \\ \hline 0.75 \end{array}$$

Combine the bills and the coins: $8 + 0.75 = 8.75$, or $8.75.

$$\begin{array}{r} 8.00 \\ +\,0.75 \\ \hline 8.75 \end{array}$$

Remember, when the sum of a collection of coins exceeds 99 cents, the amount can be expressed using bills. For example, 99 pennies is 99 cents, or $0.99, but 100 pennies is 100 cents, or 1 dollar bill.

Arrays

An array is a collection of **rows** and **columns** that can represent a multiplication scenario.

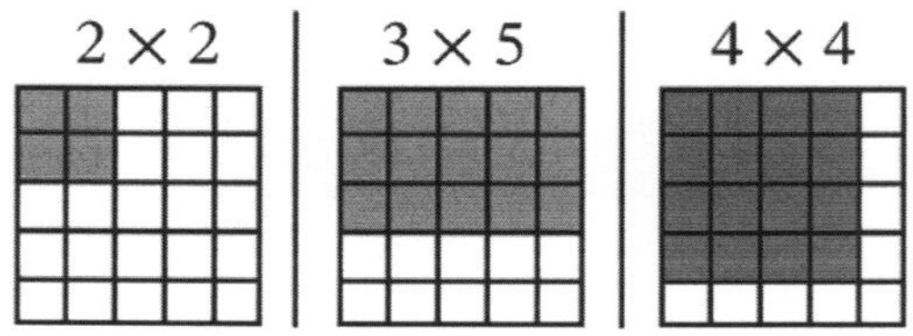

2 rows of 2 columns: $2 \times 2 = 4$

3 rows of 5 columns: $3 \times 5 = 15$

4 rows of 4 columns: $4 \times 4 = 16$

An **array** can be useful when solving real-world multiplication problems. For example, if a total of 7 blue fish are swimming in 3 separate groups, how many fish are there total?

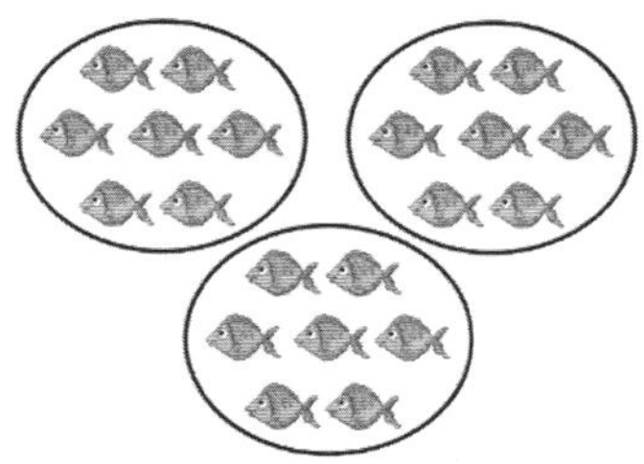

Drawing 3 groups of 7 is similar to creating an array of 3×7. Instead of creating 3 rows of 7 columns, the fish can be arranged into groups with 7 fish in each group. The total number of fish can be added up to find that $3 \times 7 = 21$.

Representing Multiplication

Repeated Addition

Multiplication is the process of counting equally sized groups. 5 groups of 7 means $7 + 7 + 7 + 7 + 7$. 5 groups of 7 is 35. The process of using addition to solve multiplication problems is known as **repeated addition**. This strategy is a great choice in many scenarios.

Number Lines

A number line can be used to show repeated addition. The **number line** below shows 4 equal hops of 3. 4 hops of 3 represents 4×3, which is 12: $3 + 3 + 3 + 3 = 12$.

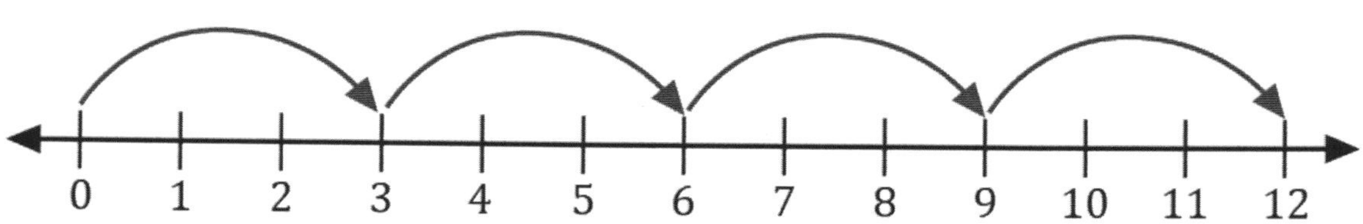

Arrays

An array is a collection and rows and columns representing a multiplication problem. This **array** has 10 columns and 4 rows. This array represents $10 \times 4 = 40$.

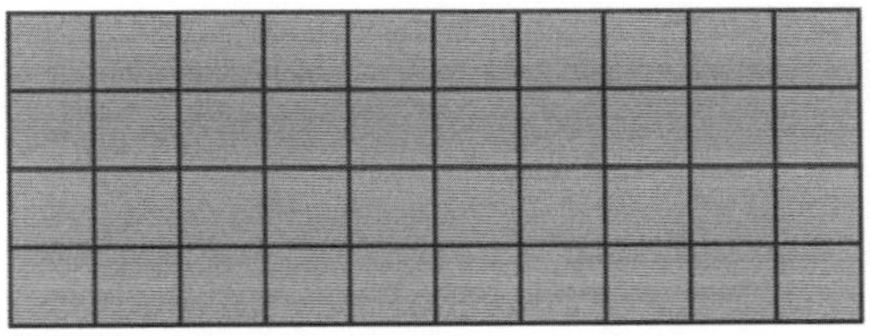

Recalling Multiplication Facts

It is a great accomplishment to memorize the multiplication and division facts from 0 to 10. This is a goal that can take some time, so keep practicing!

Some strategies that can help:

1. **Skip count by the larger number.** For example, for the problem 8×3 skip count by 8s not 3s. This can save some time. $8 + 8 + 8$ is quicker than $3 + 3 + 3 + 3 + 3 + 3 + 3 + 3$.
2. **Use facts that you do know to help you.** For example, if you are stuck on 7×4 but you know 5×7 is 35, use logic to help you. 5 groups of 7 is 7 more than 4 groups of 7, so subtract 7 from 35 to solve 4×7.
3. **Use multiplication to help with division.** Multiplication and division are inverse operations. This means they undo each other. For example, $9 \times 4 = 36$ and $4 \times 9 = 36$ represent the inverse of $36 \div 4 = 9$ and $36 \div 9 = 4$. Your multiplication facts and division facts go hand-in-hand! Remember, multiplication and division fact families use the same three numbers. For example, $8 \times 7 = 56$, $7 \times 8 = 56$, $56 \div 7 = 8$, and $56 \div 8 = 7$ all use the same three numbers.

Strategies for Multiplication

Strategies such as mental math, skip counting, and drawing a model are great for single digit multiplication problems. However, for larger numbers, these strategies are less ideal. For example, solving 7×82 by skip counting would take quite a long time. 7, 14, 21, 28... all the way up to 574! Luckily, there are faster strategies for multiplying by two-digit numbers.

Standard Algorithm

Place the two-digit number over the one-digit number. Start by multiplying the numbers in the ones place: $2 \times 7 = 14$. Regroup the 14 into 1 and 4, as shown.

Now multiply 7 by the number in the tens place: $7 \times 8 = 56$. Add the 1 from up above: $56 + 1 = 57$. Write 57 down below: $82 \times 7 = 574$.

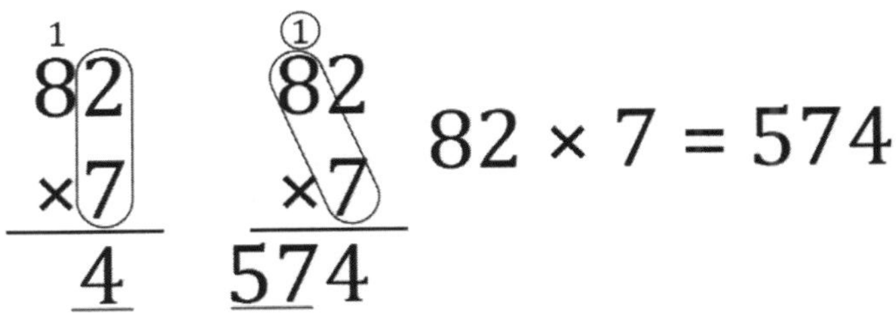

Partial Products

Think about the two-digit number in terms of its place value.

82 consists of 8 tens and 2 ones: $82 = 80 + 2$.

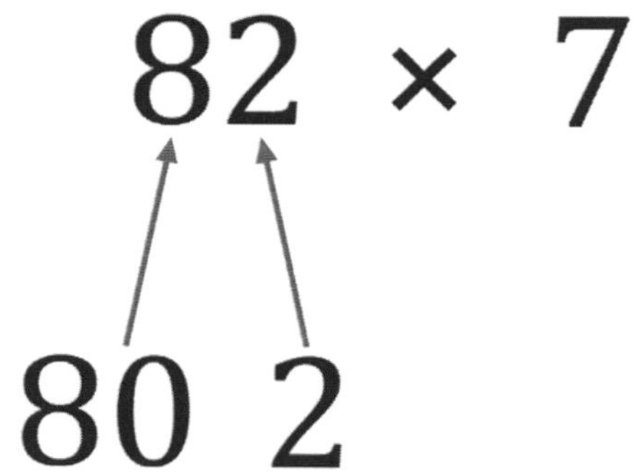

Now multiply each part by 7.

$$80 \times 7 = 560$$

$$2 \times 7 = 14$$

Now add the products.

$$\begin{array}{r} 560 \\ +\quad 14 \\ \hline 574 \end{array}$$

$$560 + 14 = 574$$

Distributive Property

Using the **distribute property** is very similar to using **partial products**.

Distribute the 7 to each part of 82. 7×80 and 7×2.

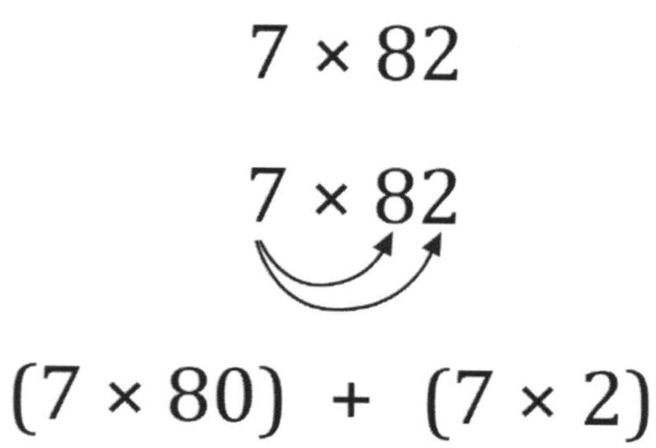

$$(7 \times 80) + (7 \times 2) = 560 + 14 = 574$$

Commutative Property

The **order** of the **factors** does not matter in multiplication.

$$3 \times 9 \times 4 = 4 \times 9 \times 3$$

Associative Property

In multiplication, the **arrangement** of **grouping symbols** does not affect the outcome.

$$(4 \times 9) \times 3 = 4 \times (9 \times 3)$$

Equal Groups

When a set of numbers are partitioned, or divided, into equal pieces, multiplication and division will be involved. For example, consider the following scenario:

There are 28 kids at a bowling party, and there are 7 lanes available. How many bowlers will be in each lane?

This kind of problem can be solved using a variety of strategies.

Solve Using a Picture or Model

Draw a quick sketch of 7 bowling lanes. There are 28 bowlers, so fill each lane one by one. Each lane holds 4 bowlers.

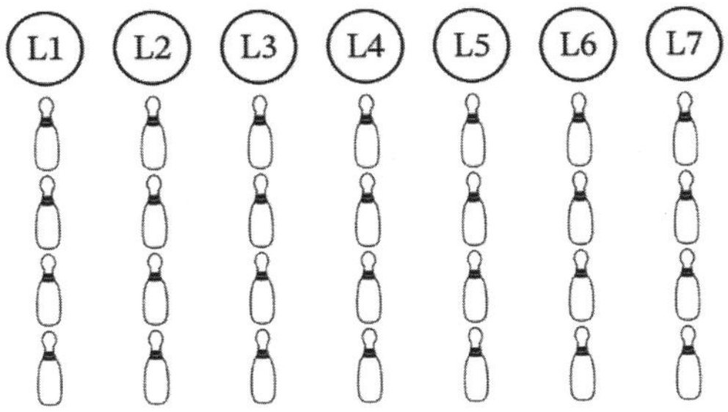

Solve Using Multiplication

7 groups of what equals 28? In other words, $7 \times ? = 28$.

$$7 \times 1 = 7$$

$$7 \times 2 = 14$$

$$7 \times 3 = 21$$

$$7 \times 4 = 28$$

Each lane will hold 4 bowlers.

Solve Using Division

$$28 \div 7 = ?$$

28 separated into 7 equal groups leaves 4 in each group.

$$28 \div 7 = 4$$

Even and Odd Numbers

You can determine if a number is even or odd by looking at the **ones** digit. Remember, the ones digit is the farthest digit to the right. If the ones digit can be divided, or is divisible, by 2, then the entire number is **even**. If the ones digit is not divisible by 2, then the entire number is **odd**. A number is divisible by 2 if it can be split into two groups without any remainders. For example, consider the number 3,916. The number 6 is in the ones place, and 6 is divisible by 2. Since the ones digit is divisible by 2, the number 3,916 is even. However, a number such as 83,097 is odd because the ones digit is 7, and 7 is not divisible by 2.

Numbers Divisible by 2

One way to determine if a number is divisible by 2 is to create a quick sketch or model. For example, consider the number 845,029. In this case, the ones digit is 9. Create a sketch with two groups and see if 9 can be divided into two groups with no remainders.

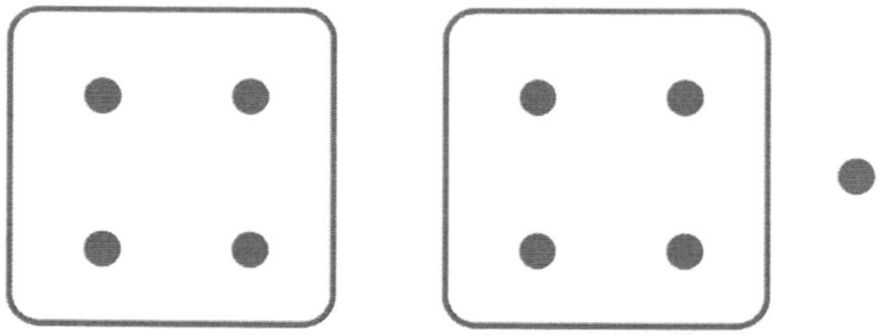

Notice that 9 cannot be split into two equal groups. It is close, but there is a remainder of 1. This means the number 845,029 is odd.

Now, consider the number 79,208. The ones digit is 8. The number 8 can be split into two equal groups, so 8 is divisible by 2. Therefore, 79,208 is even.

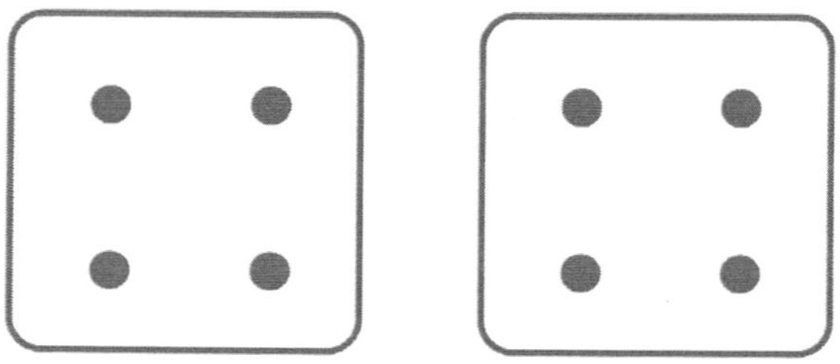

Quotients

Multiplication can be used to determine a **quotient**. Similar to addition and subtraction, multiplication and division are **inverse operations**. For example, $72 \div 9$ can be solved using the multiplication facts for 9. $72 \div 9 = ?$ Ask the question, "9 groups of what equals 72?"

$9 \times 6 = 54$ ... $9 \times 7 = 63$ ... $9 \times 8 = 72$. The missing number is 8. This means $72 \div 9 = 8$. This strategy is quite helpful because once the multiplication facts are automatic, division facts become automatic as well.

Consider the following examples:

$42 \div 7 = ?$ "7 groups of what equals 42?" $6 \times 7 = 42$. The product of 6 and 7 is 42. The quotient of 42 and 7 is 6.

$$42 \div 7 = 6$$

$48 \div 8 = ?$ "8 groups of what equals 48?" $6 \times 8 = 48$. The product of 6 and 8 is 48. The quotient of 48 and 8 is 6.

$$48 \div 8 = 6$$

Solving Multiplication and Division Problems

Multiplication and division can be **modeled** in many ways. Consider the problem 6×3. This can be solved using strategies such as **repeated addition**, **fact families**, **equal groups**, an **array**, **skip counting**, or a **tape diagram**. There are many options to choose from!

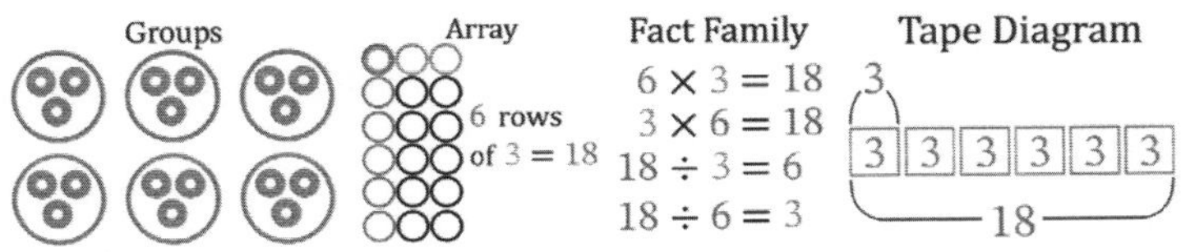

Skip Counting

3, 6, 9, 12, 15, 18

Repeated Addition

$$3 + 3 + 3 + 3 + 3 + 3 = 18$$

Two-step problems can be solved using the same strategies. Over time, these strategies will be replaced by memory.

Example

Write a multiplication sentence that matches the tape diagram below.

4	4	4

The model shows 3 groups of 4. This can be expressed as the multiplication sentence $3 \times 4 = 12$.

Example

Draw a model to represent $(15 \times 3) \div 5$.

The model shows 3 groups of 15, which equals 45.

45 is then divided into 5 equal groups. Each group contains 9 units.

$$(15 \times 3) \div 5 = 9$$

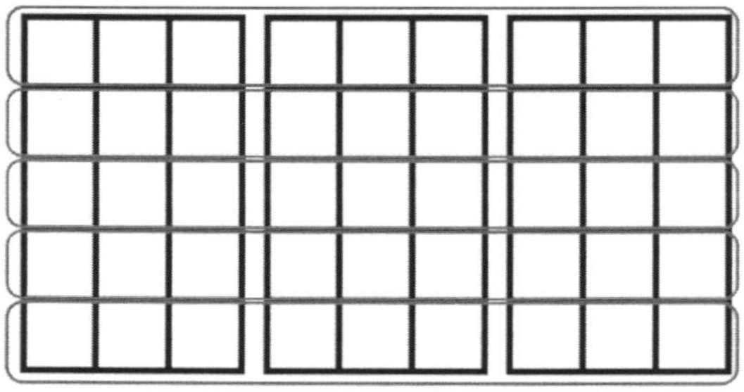

Algebraic Reasoning

Representing Problems

Addition and Subtraction Problems

Some word problems can be solved in one step. For example, suppose a baker makes 35 cakes and 150 cookies each day. Altogether, how many treats are baked each day? This can be solved in one step, using one operation. $35 + 150 = 185$. 185 treats are baked each day.

More advanced word problems will require two steps. For example, suppose a painter earns $450 for every room that they paint. After 2 rooms are completed, the painter spends $185 on more paint supplies. How much money remains? Many two-step problems can be solved using strategies such as drawing a picture or model, using a number line, or solving an equation.

Pictures and Models

Use base ten blocks to represent 185 taken from 2 groups of 450 to get 715.

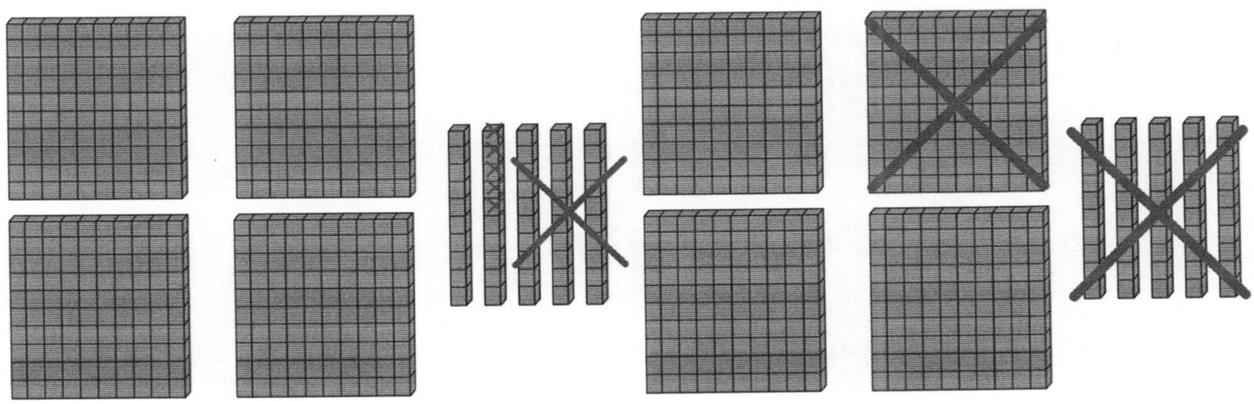

Number Lines

Make two jumps of 450, then back 185.

$$(450 + 450) - 185 = 715$$

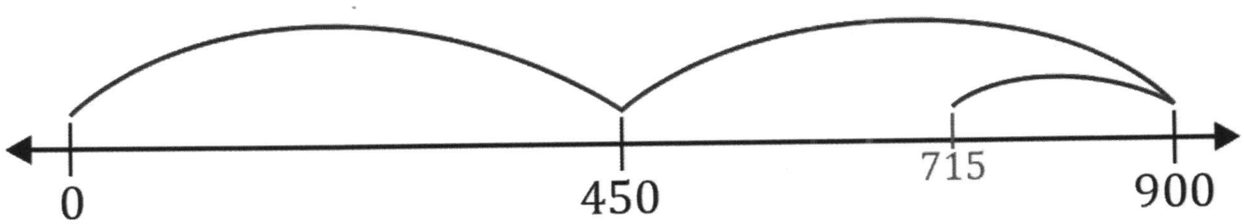

Equations

$$m = (450 + 450) - 185$$

The equation simplifies to $m = 715$, or $715.

Example

Use the number line to represent $200 + 50 - 125$.

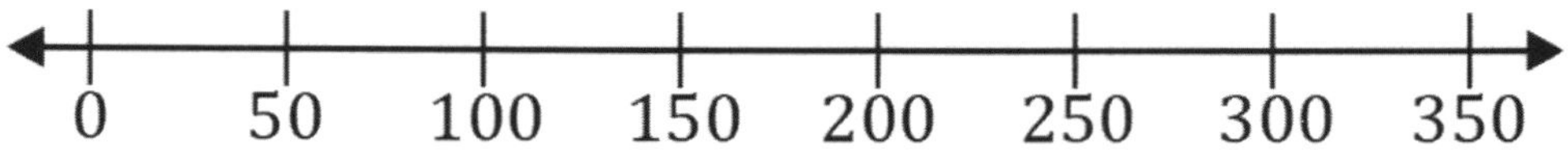

Start by adding 50 to 200. Make one jump forward from 200 to 250.

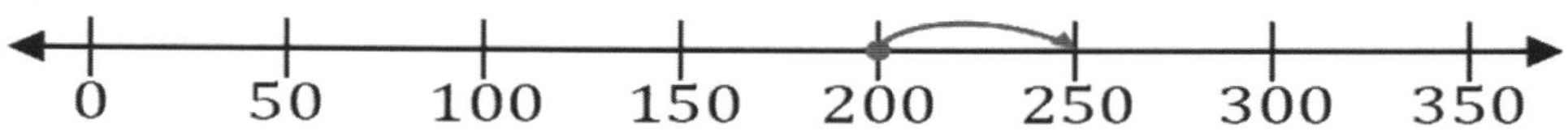

Now subtract 125. Jump back 100 and then back 25 more. 250 becomes 150 and then 125.

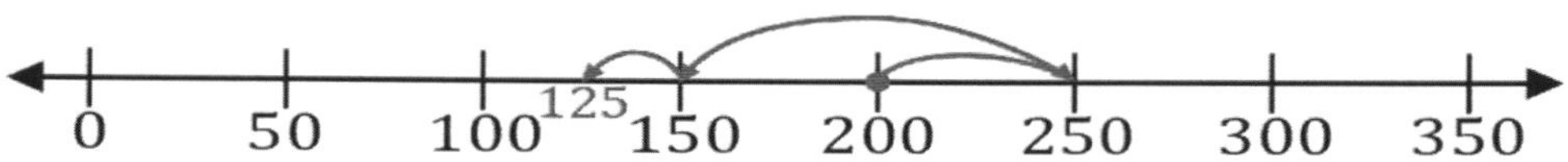

$$200 + 50 - 125 = 125.$$

Example

Write and solve a subtraction equation that matches the model below.

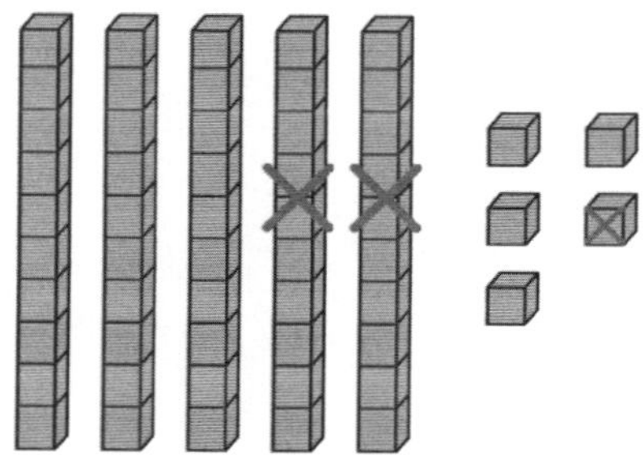

The model shows 5 groups of ten plus 5 groups of one, which represents 55. Then 2 groups of ten and 1 group of one are crossed out. This represents subtraction of 21. This leaves 3 groups of ten and 4 groups of one. So, $55 - 21$ leaves 34 remaining. The answer is $55 - 21 = 34$.

Multiplication and Division Problems

One- and two-step problems can also include multiplication and division. For example, consider the following one-step problem.

One-Step Problems

A rancher has 12 acres of farmland, and 8 sheep live on each acre. How many sheep does the rancher have in all?

This problem can be solved in one step. Think about it as a picture or a model. There are 12 acres, and each acre contains 8 sheep. 12 groups of 8 means 12×8. To find 12×8, break it down into $(10 \times 8) + (2 \times 8)$ and then $(80) + (16) = 96$. The rancher has 96 sheep.

Now, try a two-step problem. This time, consider using a picture or a model to solve.

Two-Step Problems

A florist is creating flower arrangements for an event. 72 bouquets can be arranged in 3 hours. How many bouquets can be arranged in 15 minutes?

72 bouquets divided into 3 hours means 24 bouquets in each hour.

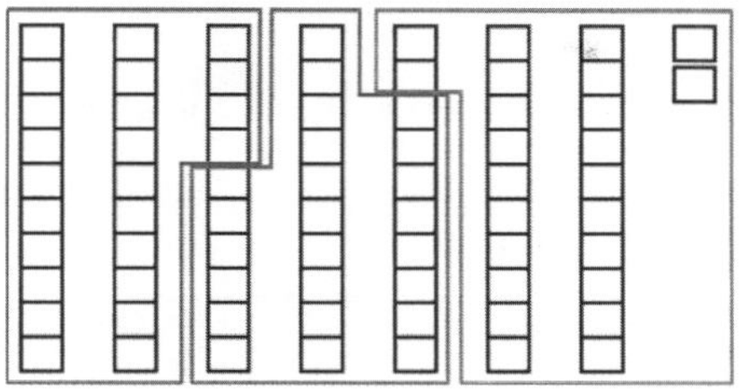

15 minutes is $\frac{1}{4}$ of an hour. We can see this by looking at a clock. The minute hand of a clock at 12:15 is $\frac{1}{4}$ through the circle.

So, divide 24 by 4.

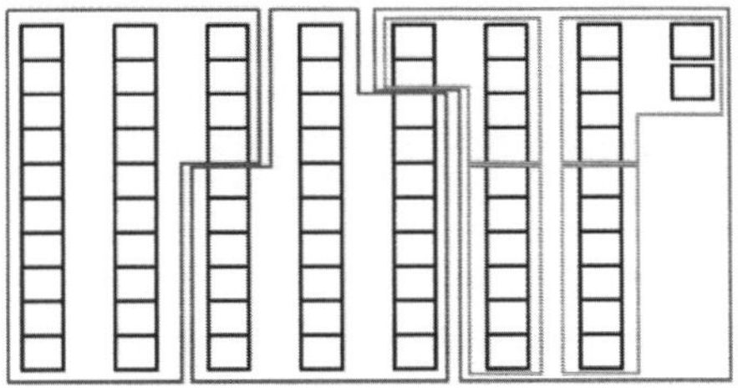

$$24 \div 4 = 6$$

So, 6 bouquets can be made every 15 minutes.

EXAMPLE

Write two multiplication equations the array below can represent.

The array shows rows and columns of stars. This can be described as 5 rows of 6, or 6 rows of 5. Both scenarios have a product of 30.

The answers are $5 \times 6 = 30$ and $6 \times 5 = 30$.

EXAMPLE

Use the numbers 3, 6, and 18 to write four equations using multiplication and division.

The numbers 3, 6, and 18 form a fact family.

3 groups of 6 equals 18: $3 \times 6 = 18$.

6 groups of 3 equals 18: $6 \times 3 = 18$.

18 divided into 3 equal groups results in 6 per group: $18 \div 3 = 6$.

18 divided into 6 equal groups results in 3 per group: $18 \div 6 = 3$.

The answers are $3 \times 6 = 18$, $6 \times 3 = 18$, $18 \div 3 = 6$, $18 \div 6 = 3$.

Multiplication Expressions

REPEATED ADDITION

Multiplication is often referred to as **repeated addition**. For example, 4×3 represents $4 + 4 + 4$ or $3 + 3 + 3 + 3$. Multiplication problems can be solved using repeated addition or skip counting, but it is important to eventually memorize the basic multiplication facts from 0–12.

COMPARISONS

Consider the multiplication problem 5×40. This represents 5 groups of 40, or 40 groups of 5, but it also represents a **comparison**. 5×40 is describing a scenario where the total amount is 5 times as much as 40. 5 times as much as 40 is 200.

Consider another example: 28×2. This represents a comparison where the total amount is 28 times as much as 2. 28 times as much as 2 is 56.

4×6 means "4 times as much as 6".

6×4 means "6 times as much as 4".

Finding Unknown Numbers

INVERSE OPERATIONS

Multiplication and division go hand in hand. Division and multiplication are considered **inverse operations**, which means they are the reverse, or opposite, of each other. This can be helpful when there is an **unknown number** in an equation. For example, $4 \times ? = 24$ is a multiplication equation that can be solved using division. $24 \div 4 = 6$, therefore $4 \times 6 = 24$. The missing number is 6.

Let's try another example: $72 \div ? = 9$. This is a division equation that can be solved using multiplication. What number times 9 equals 72? The missing number is 8.

FACT FAMILIES

Don't forget to use **fact families** when solving equations with **missing numbers**.

For example, the equations $5 \times 8 = 40$, $8 \times 5 = 40$, $40 \div 5 = 8$, $40 \div 8 = 5$ represent a fact family. The same three numbers are used in all the equations. This can be helpful when one of the numbers is missing. For example, $8 \times ? = 40$. Remember the fact families. 8 groups of 5 equals 40, so the missing number is 5.

$$\text{Factor} \times \text{Factor} = \text{Product}$$

$$8 \times 5 = 40$$

8 and 5 are considered factors, and 40 is the product.

Representing Real-World Relationships

Input-output tables are used to show the relationship between two variables. For example, consider the muffin pan below.

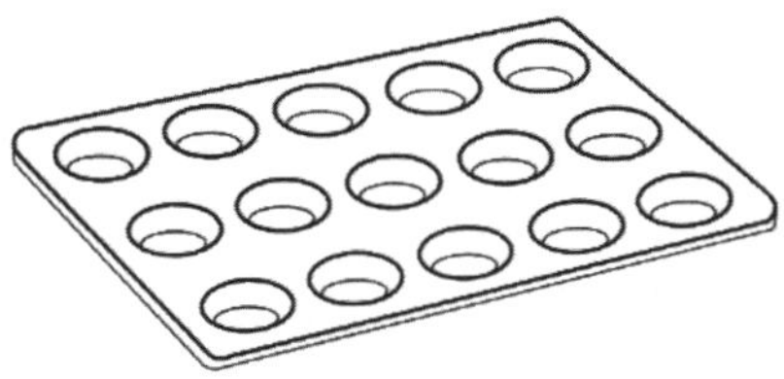

Each pan can hold 15 muffins. This means that 15 muffins can be baked in 1 pan, 30 muffins can be baked in 2 pans, 45 muffins can be baked in 3 pans, and so on. These values can be placed in an input-output table to show the relationship between the number of pans and the total number of muffins.

Pans	1	2	3	4
Muffins	15	30	45	60

The rule for this input-output table is number of muffins = number of pans × 15.

Here are some more examples:

Rule: Find y by adding 2 to x.

x	y
8	10
4	6
2	4
6	8
3	5

Rule: Find y by multiplying x by 4.

x	9	4	5	2
y	36	16	20	8

EXAMPLE

Complete the table so that the rule applies. Rule: James earns $42 per hour

Hours	1	2	3	4	5	6	7
Dollars		84				252	

The rule states that $42 is earned each hour. The number of dollars can be determined by multiplying the number of hours by 42, or by adding 42 to the previous dollar amount.

$$1 \times 42 = 42$$

$$2 \times 42 = 84$$

$$3 \times 42 = 126$$

$$4 \times 42 = 168$$

$$5 \times 42 = 210$$

$$6 \times 42 = 252$$

$$7 \times 42 = 294$$

Hours	1	2	3	4	5	6	7
Dollars	42	84	126	168	210	252	294

EXAMPLE

Write a rule that describes the relationship in the table.

x	4	5	6	7
y	32	40	48	56

Each value of y is 8 times as large as the corresponding x-value: $y = 8 \times x$. This can be expressed as "y is 8 times the value of x" or "multiply x by 8 to determine the value of y."

Geometry and Measurement

Classifying and Sorting Figures

Three-Dimensional Figures

The most common three-dimensional figures include cones, cylinders, spheres, triangular and rectangular prisms, and cubes. When identifying and classifying three-dimensional figures it is important to be aware of the number of faces, edges, and vertices. **Faces** are the flat surfaces, **edges** are where two faces come together, and **vertices** are like corners, where more than two faces come together. For example, a rectangular prism has 6 faces, 12 edges, and 8 vertices.

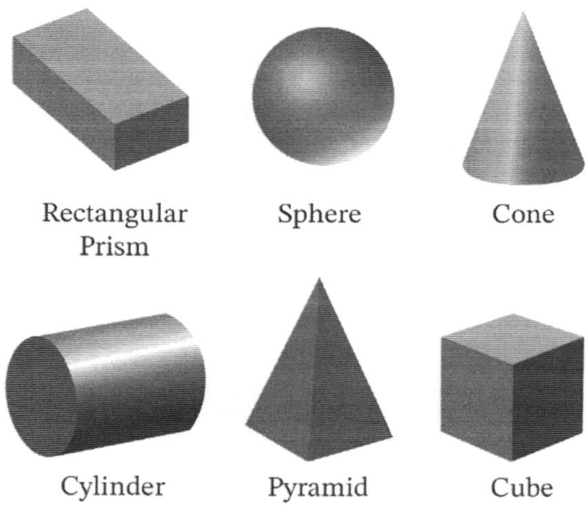

Three-dimensional figures can be identified based on their faces, edges, and vertices. For example, a **sphere** is a round shape where every point on the surface is an equal distance from the center. A sphere is shaped like a ball, and has no faces, no edges, and no vertices. **Cylinders** have two circular faces, and one curved surface. Cylinders have no edges and no vertices. **Cones** have one circular face and one curved surface. Cones consist of one face, one vertex, and no edges. Triangular prisms and rectangular prisms are in a similar family of shapes to each other. Remember, **prisms** have two ends that are the exact same shape and size, and the sides are rectangular. **Triangular prisms** have two triangular base shapes and rectangular sides. **Rectangular prisms** have two rectangular base shapes and rectangular sides. **Cubes** are similar to rectangular prisms, but with cubes, each of the six faces on a cube are identical. Cubes have six identical faces, twelve edges, and eight vertices. **Pyramids** have one base shape, and triangular sides that all come together at the *vertex*.

Another way to sort three-dimensional shapes is to identify whether the shape can roll, slide, or both. For example, a cube can slide, but a cylinder can roll and slide.

Review Video: 3D Geometric Shapes Visit mometrix.com/academy and enter code: 738045

EXAMPLE

List the shapes from least to greatest based on the number of vertices.

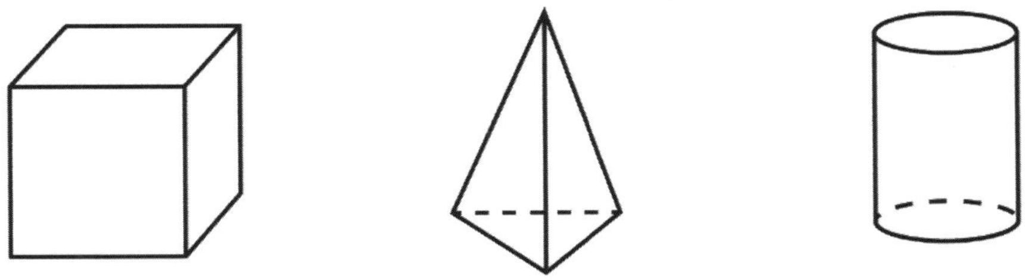

Vertices are like corners, where more than 2 faces meet.
A cylinder has 0 vertices.
A triangular pyramid has 4 vertices.
A cube has 8 vertices.

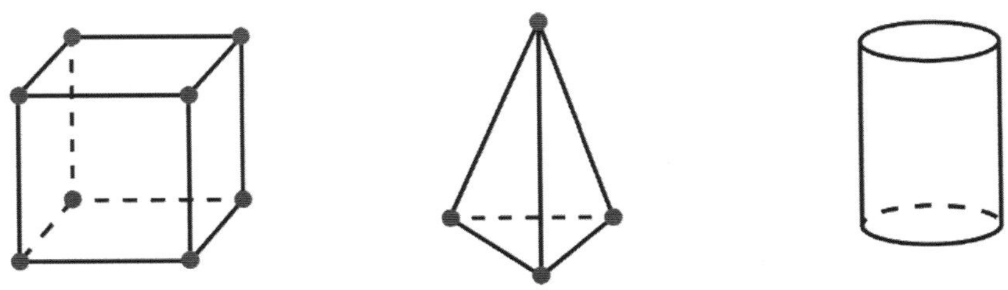

From least to greatest: Cylinder, Triangular Pyramid, Cube.

TWO-DIMENSIONAL FIGURES

Two-dimensional shapes can be classified by the number of sides they have. Polygons are considered **regular polygons** if all the sides are the same length. For example, a regular pentagon has 5 sides, and all of the sides are the same length. Side lengths that are the same are considered **congruent**. For example, a square has 4 congruent side lengths.

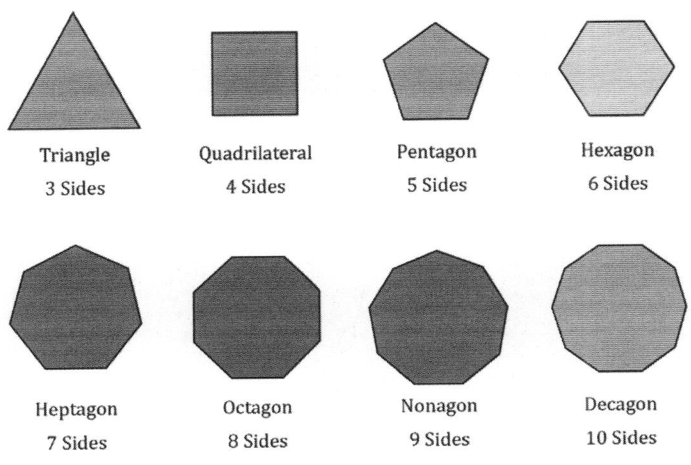

QUADRILATERALS

A **quadrilateral** is a 4-sided shape. There are many subcategories of quadrilaterals. The most common are parallelogram, rhombus, rectangle, square, and trapezoid.

Parallelogram: A parallelogram has two pairs of parallel sides. It sometimes looks like a leaning rectangle.

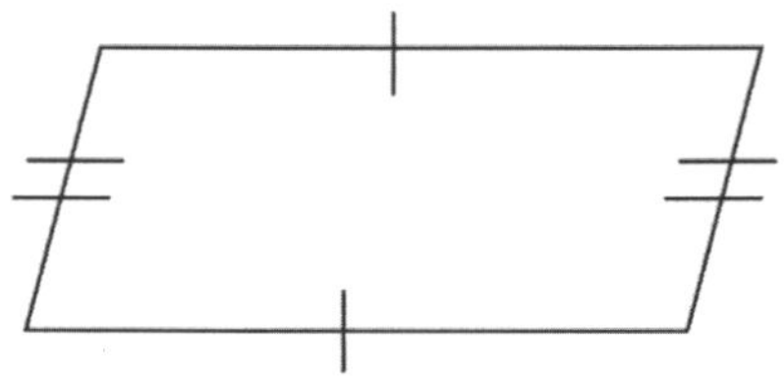

Rhombus: A rhombus is a parallelogram with four equal sides. It has no 90° angles.

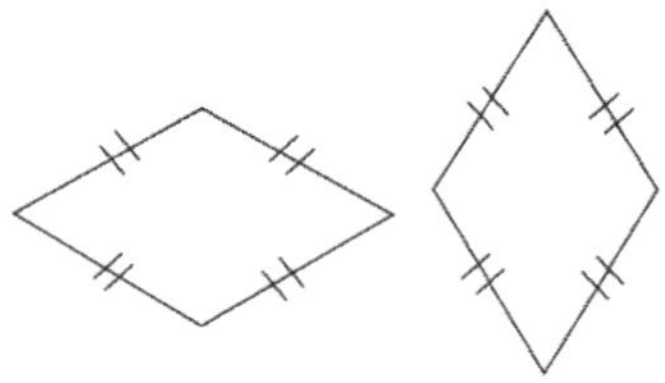

Rectangle: A rectangle has two equal parallel long sides, two equal parallel short sides, and four 90° angles.

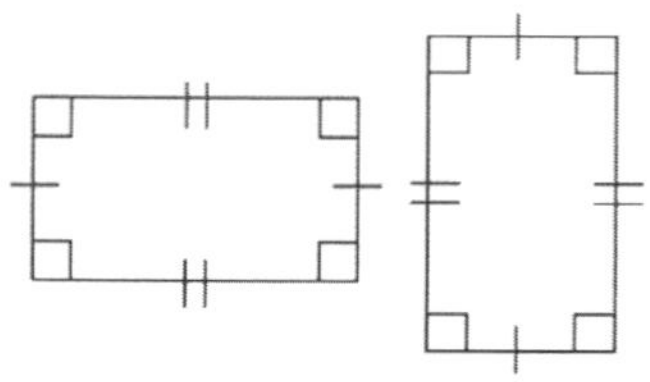

Square: A square has four equal sides. Its opposite sides are parallel, and it has four 90° angles.

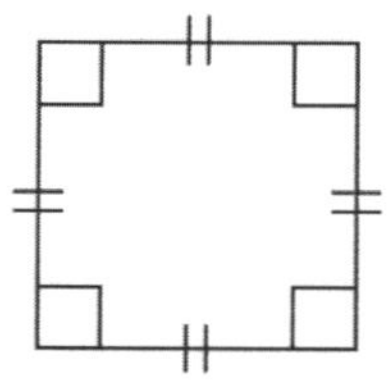

Trapezoid: A trapezoid has one pair of parallel sides and one pair of non-parallel sides.

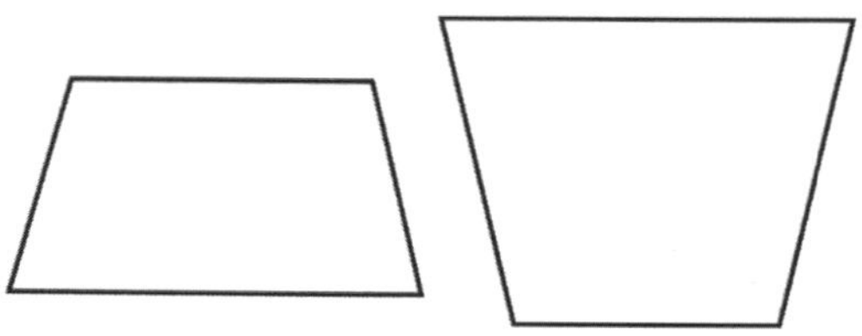

Not all 4-sided shapes fall into these categories. For example, the shapes below are quadrilaterals, but they do not fall into any of the subcategories mentioned above. They are simply referred to as quadrilaterals.

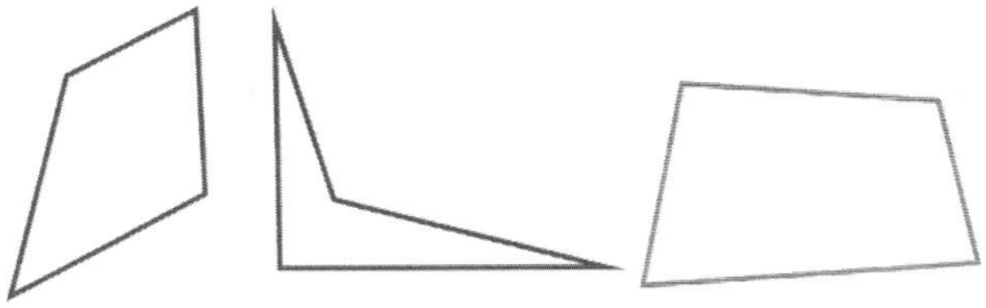

EXAMPLE

All the shapes below can be classified as ________. The top two shapes can also be classified as ________ or as ________.

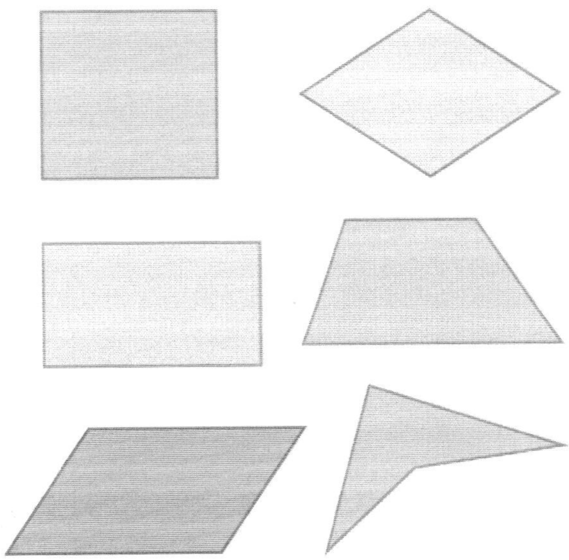

Quadrilateral: 4-sided polygon
Parallelogram: A quadrilateral that has 2 pairs of parallel sides
Rhombus: A parallelogram with 4 congruent side lengths

All the shapes below can be classified as quadrilaterals. The green and yellow shapes can also be classified as rhombi or as parallelograms.

Area

AREA OF A RECTANGLE

The **area formula** for a **rectangle** is Area = Length × Width. This means the area can be determined by multiplying the number of **rows** by the number of **columns**. Think about the area of a rectangle as an array. For example, a rectangle that is 6 ft by 4 ft is essentially 6 columns and 4 rows. 6 groups of 4 is the same thing as 4 groups of 6, so the area can be calculated as 6×4 or 4×6. $6 \times 4 = 24$ and $4 \times 6 = 24$. The area is 24 square units.

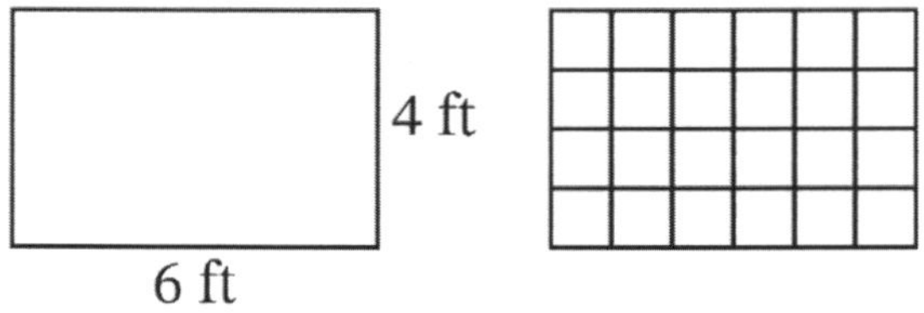

EXAMPLE

A pan of fudge needs to be cut into equally sized pieces. One row is already divided. How many pieces of fudge will there be in the entire pan?

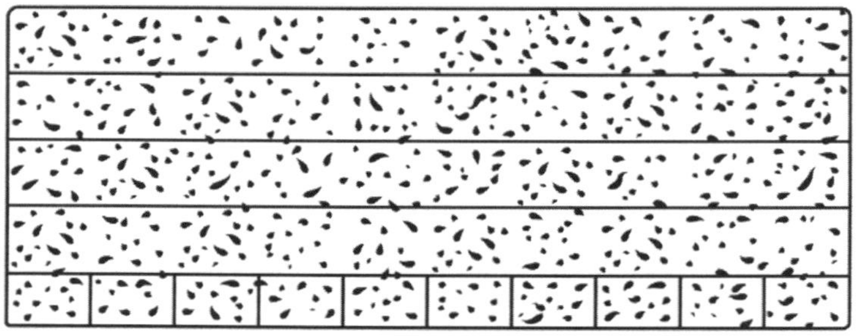

The total number of pieces can be calculated by multiplying the number of pieces in one row, by the total number of rows. This can be thought of as an array of 5 rows with 10 columns. 5 groups of 10 equals 50. The entire pan holds 50 pieces of fudge.

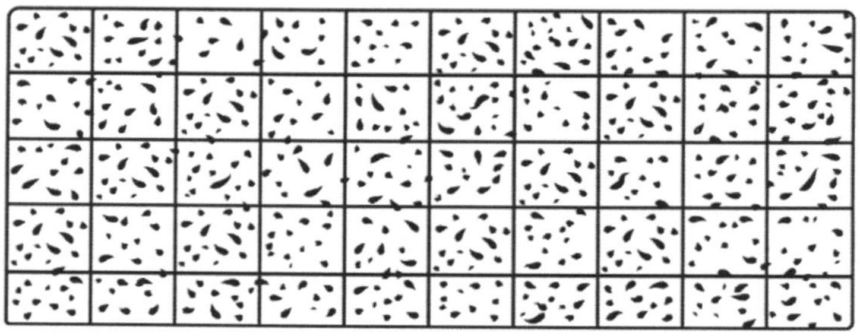

EXAMPLE

A rectangle has an area of 16 unit squares. The rectangle has two columns. How many rows does the rectangle have?

The area of the rectangle is 16 unit squares. The rectangle has 2 columns, so it must have 8 rows: $2 \times 8 = 16$. The rectangle forms an array of 2 columns and 8 rows.

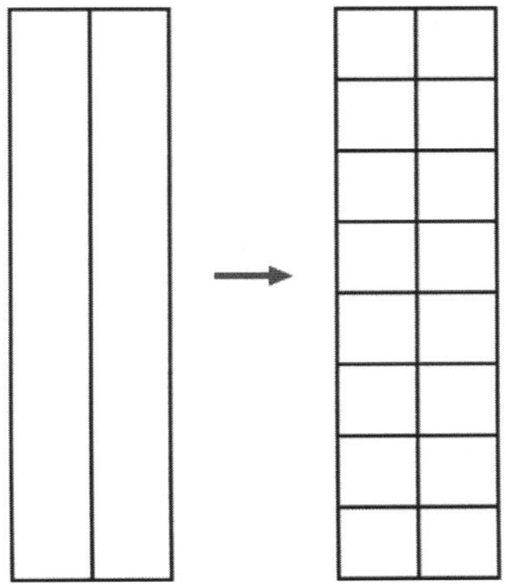

AREA OF A COMPOSITE FIGURE

A **composite figure** is made up of **multiple shapes**. When calculating the area of composite figures, consider dividing the shape into multiple smaller shapes. Consider the composite figure below. This shape can be decomposed into two separate rectangles. The area of each rectangle can be calculated using the formula $A = l \times w$, and then the area of both rectangles can be added together to determine the total area of the **entire figure**.

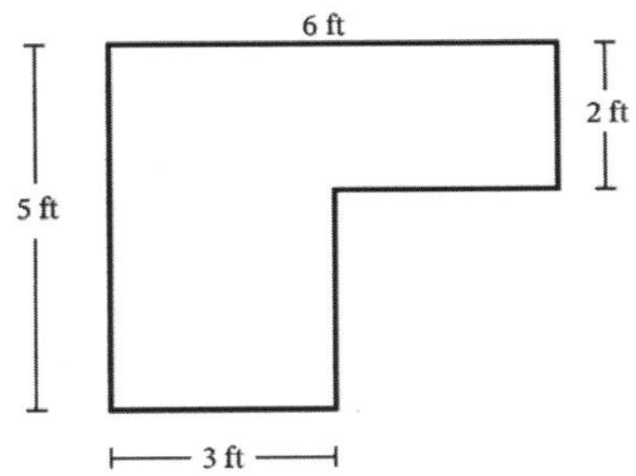

The figure can be decomposed into two rectangles. A 6 by 2 rectangle, and a 3 by 3 rectangle. $6 \times 2 = 12$ and $3 \times 3 = 9$. $12 + 9 = 21$, so the area of the entire figure is 21 square feet.

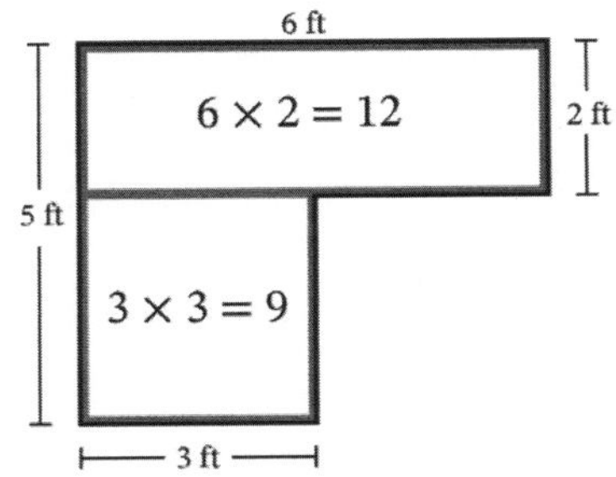

Equal Parts and Area

There is more than one correct way to decompose, or divide, a two-dimensional figure. For example, if a pan of brownies needs to be sliced into 8 equal pieces, there are a few ways to achieve this. Consider the rectangular brownie pans below. Notice how both pans have 8 **equally sized** brownies, even though the identical pieces are not the same shape for both pans. Each brownie can be represented as the unit fraction $\frac{1}{8}$. Remember, a unit fraction has a numerator of 1.

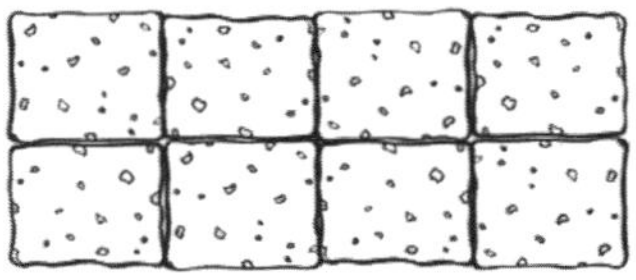

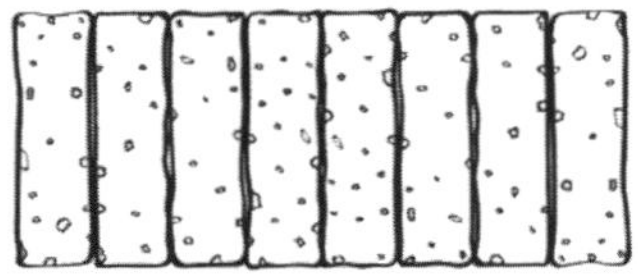

Representing Fractions

Number Lines

A fraction number line generally starts at 0 and ends at 1. This represents **one whole unit**. One whole can be **divided** into **equal pieces**, forming fractions. For example, if the number line is divided into 2 equal pieces, each piece represents $\frac{1}{2}$. If the number line is divided into 4 equal pieces, each piece represents $\frac{1}{4}$. If the number line is divided into 8 equal pieces, each piece represents $\frac{1}{8}$, and the pattern continues.

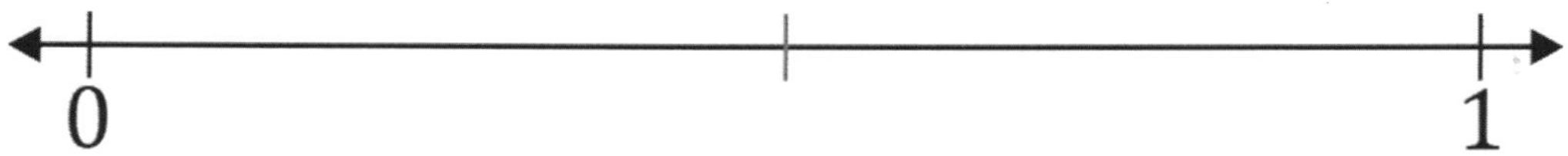

$\frac{1}{2}$ or 2 equal pieces

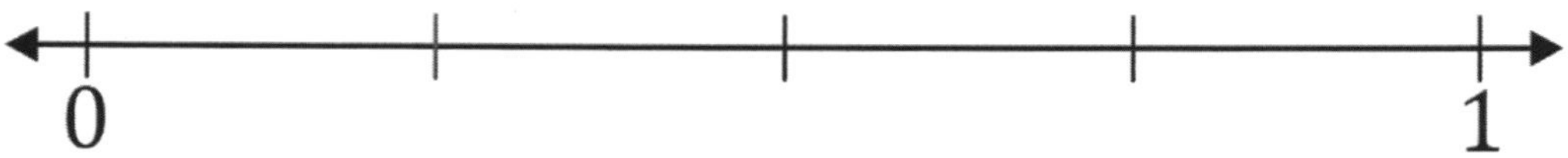

$\frac{1}{4}$ or 4 equal pieces

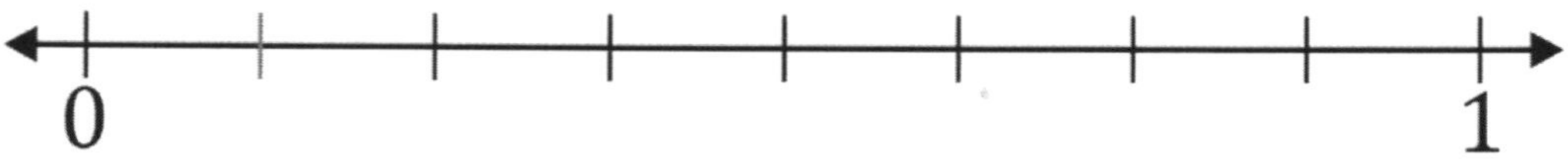

$\frac{1}{8}$ or 8 equal pieces

Remember, these fraction values represent a **distance from 0** on the number line. On a number line, the distance from 0 to 1 represents one whole unit. A fraction like $\frac{1}{2}$ means that the distance from 0 is one-half of a whole unit. $\frac{1}{4}$ indicates one-fourth of a whole unit. $\frac{1}{8}$ indicates one-eighth of a whole unit, and so on. As the denominator of a unit fraction gets larger, the distance from zero gets smaller.

Perimeter

Perimeter is the distance around the outside of a two-dimensional shape. Perimeter can be calculated by finding the **sum** of a shape's **side lengths**. When a shape has **congruent** side lengths, all the sides are the same length. These shapes are called **regular polygons**.

The shape below has 6 congruent side lengths. Find the sum of the side lengths to calculate the perimeter of the regular hexagon. One side length is labeled 3 inches, therefore all of the side lengths are 3 inches. Perimeter $= 3 + 3 + 3 + 3 + 3 + 3$, which simplifies to $P = 18$. The perimeter of the regular hexagon is 18 inches.

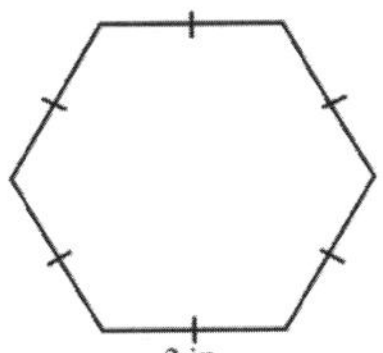

The same rules apply for polygons with missing side lengths. The triangle below has 3 congruent side lengths, and the perimeter is 18 cm. Ask the question, "$\_ + \_ + \_ = 18$?" Since $6 + 6 + 6 = 18$, the side lengths are all 6 cm.

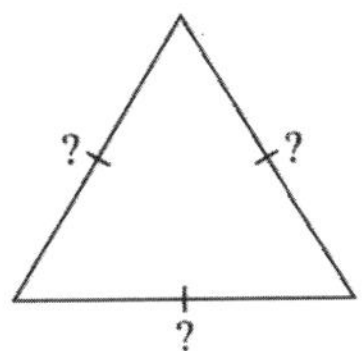

EXAMPLE

A carpenter is building an octagonal window for a boat. The outer octagon has side lengths of 8 inches, and the inner octagon has side lengths of 7 inches. What is the difference in the perimeters of the two octagons?

Perimeter of the outer octagon: $8 + 8 + 8 + 8 + 8 + 8 + 8 + 8 = 64$. Therefore, the perimeter is 64 inches.

Perimeter of the inner octagon: $7 + 7 + 7 + 7 + 7 + 7 + 7 + 7 = 56$. Therefore, the perimeter is 56 inches.

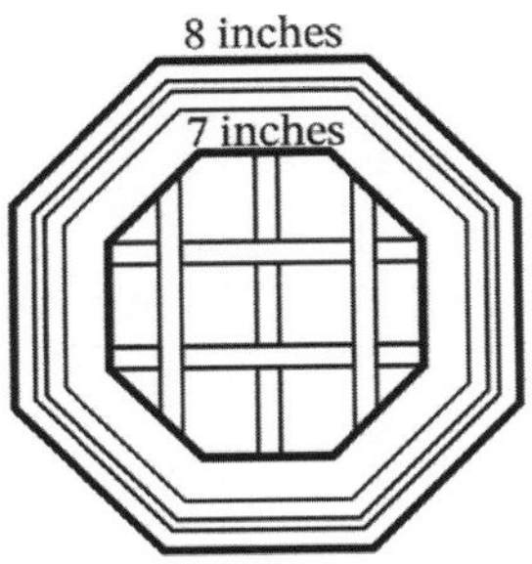

$64 - 56 = 8$, so the difference between the two perimeters is 8 inches.

EXAMPLE

An artist creates a grey picture frame around a painting. The width of the frame is 22 centimeters. The length of the frame is 7 inches longer than the width. What is the perimeter of the frame?

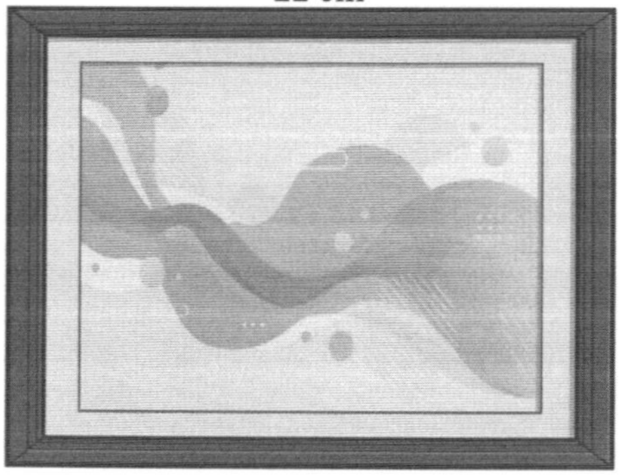

The perimeter can be calculated by finding the sum of all the side lengths:

Width: 22 cm
Length: 22 cm + 7 cm = 29 cm
Perimeter: 22 cm + 22 cm + 29 cm + 29 cm = 102 cm
The frame around the paining has a perimeter of 102 cm.

Time Intervals

Remember:

There are 60 seconds in 1 minute.

There are 60 minutes in 1 hour.

There are 24 hours in 1 day.

There are 365 days in 1 year.

ADDING AND SUBTRACTING TIME

When adding or subtracting time in minutes, an hour can be visualized as 4 sections of 15 minutes.

$\frac{1}{4}$ of an hour: 15 minutes

$\frac{2}{4}$ of an hour: 30 minutes

$\frac{3}{4}$ of an hour: 45 minutes

$\frac{4}{4}$ of an hour: 60 minutes

Strategies for Adding and Subtracting Time

For example, if a student practices the piano for 15 minutes a day, for 4 days, how long have they practiced in all?

Use a model. Each 15-minute session represents $\frac{1}{4}$ of an hour. $15 + 15 + 15 + 15 = 60$. So, the student has practiced for 60 minutes, which is 1 hour.

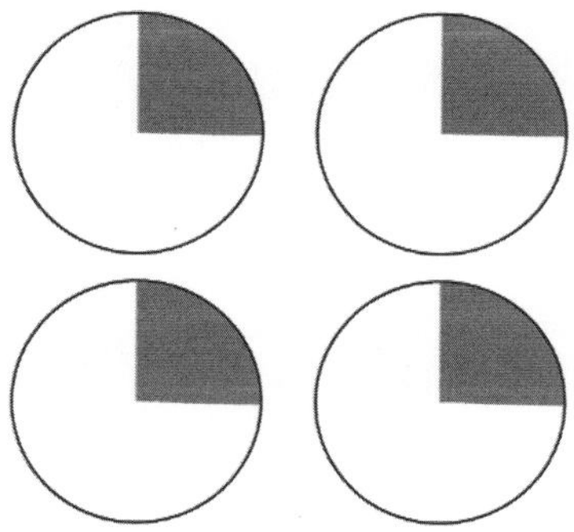

Using sections of the clock to add or subtract is a great way to solve problems mentally. Remember, one quarter of an hour is 15 minutes, and one half of an hour is 30 minutes. Skip counting by 15 or 30 is an efficient way to solve problems involving elapsed time. This also works for subtraction problems.

Consider the following scenario: A student studied 45 minutes for a math test, and 15 minutes for a science test. How much longer did the student study for the math test than the science test?

Math: 45 minutes

Science: 15 minutes

Subtract the time between studying for math and studying for science: $45 - 15 = 30$. This represents half an hour. The student spent 30 minutes more studying for the math test than the science test.

Volume and Weight

Volume is the amount of space something fills. **Weight** is the heaviness of an object. The terms are similar, but not interchangeable. Volume is not the same as weight.

For example, consider the image below. The two spheres have the same volume because they take up the same amount of space. However, their weights are very different. One sphere weighs 12 pounds and the other weighs 1 pound. Remember, volume and weight do not describe the same thing. They are similar, but one describes how much space is filled by an object, and one describes the heaviness of an object.

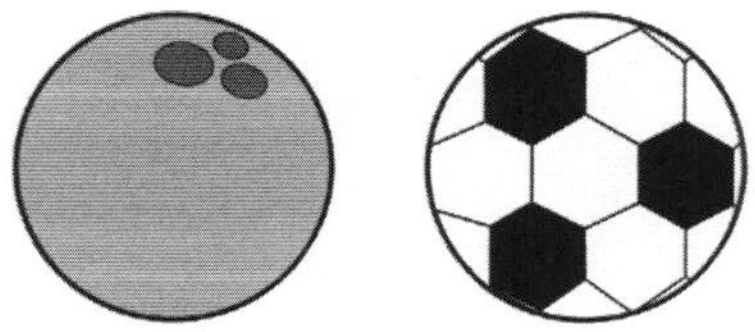

12 lb 1 lb

When determining how much space is filled, use volume. When determining the heaviness of an object, use weight.

Measuring Volume and Weight

Volume and weight are similar measurements but are not interchangeable. Volume measures capacity, or how much space is filled. Weight measures how heavy an object is.

Volume describes **capacity**. Capacity can be determined using tools such as a **beaker**. The amount of liquid in the beaker is 125 mL. This represents the volume.

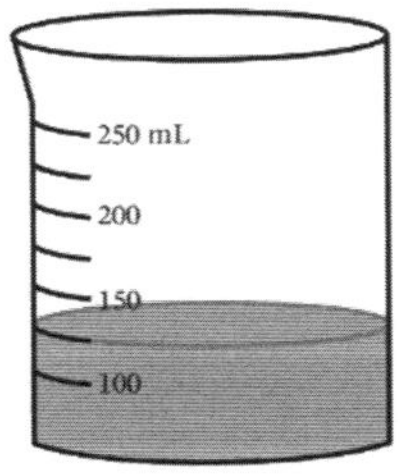

Weight describes how **heavy** an object is. A **scale** can be used to determine weight. Weight is measured in ounces, pounds, or tons.

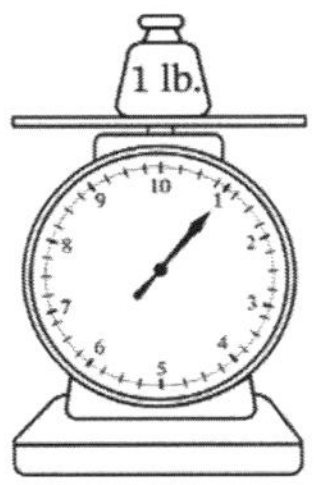

Data Analysis

Summarizing Data

Data refers to a collection of information. For example, when a survey is conducted, data points are collected. It is helpful to organize these data points before displaying the information in a table or graph. Typical data displays include bar graphs, frequency tables, pictographs, and dot plots.

Bar Graphs

Bar graphs use horizontal or vertical bars to represent the total amount for each category. For example, this bar graph shows the number of votes for a variety of snacks. The length of the bar represents the number of votes. Notice how the red popcorn bar represents 5 votes, the green crackers bar represents 2 votes, and so on. The interval should always be scaled and consistent when displaying data graphically. For example, the number of votes on this bar graph increases by 2 consistently.

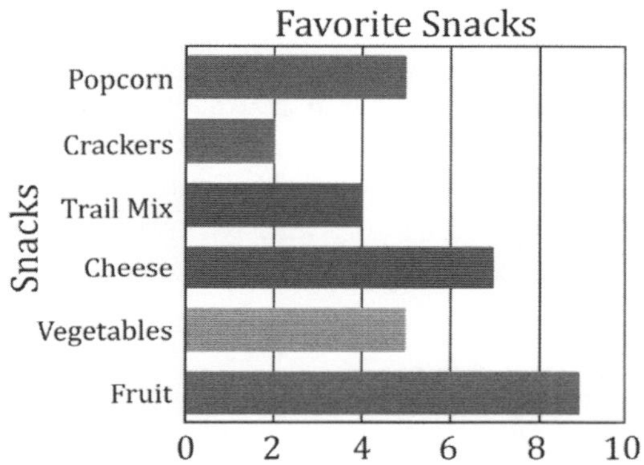

Frequency Tables

Frequency tables are used to show how often, or frequently, an event or value occurs. Frequency tables often use tally marks to show the total frequency for each category.

Favorite Club

Club	Tally	Frequency
Hockey	𝍸 |||	8
Badminton	𝍸 ||	7
Football	𝍸	5

Pictographs

Data can be summarized by studying graphical displays such as these. Consider the pictograph below. The **pictograph** uses pictures to represent the value for each category. In this pictograph, each picture represents 1 student. The pictograph shows the variety of ways students in a 3rd grade class commute to school each day. The graph can be used to summarize the data that was collected. For example, since each picture represents 1 student, we know there are 20 students in the class. We also know the most common mode of transportation is taking the bus, and the least common mode of transportation is walking on foot.

Ways to Get to School

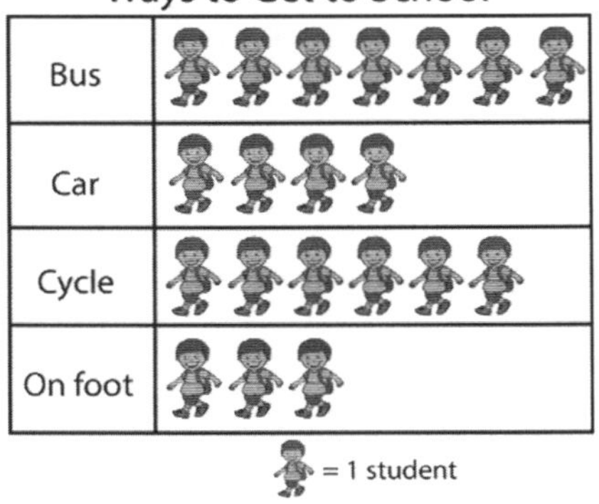

Review Video: Pictographs
Visit mometrix.com/academy and enter code: 147860

Dot Plots

Dot plots are another form of graphical display. **Dot plots** are used to show the distribution of data points. This kind of display is helpful for seeing patterns within data, and the overall shape of a large collection of values. For example, this dot plot shows the relationship between the height and weight of dogs. Dot plots can be used to solve one- and two-step problems. For example, what is the height difference between the lightest and heaviest dog?

Height and Weight of Dogs

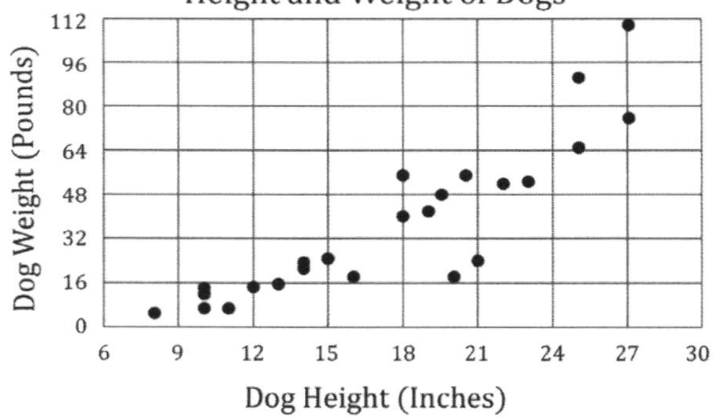

Use the dot plot to determine the height of the lightest dog: 8 inches.

Use the dot plot to determine the height of the heaviest dog: 27 inches.

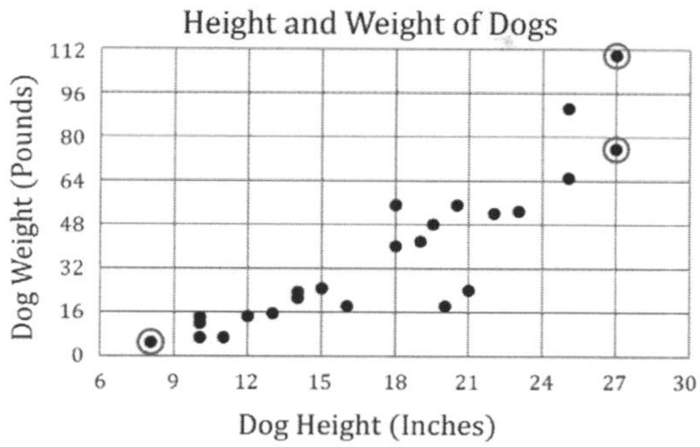

The difference in heights: $27 - 8 = 19$.

The height difference is 19 inches.

Example

Based on the information in the bar graph, how many more students prefer math or science than social studies or ELA?

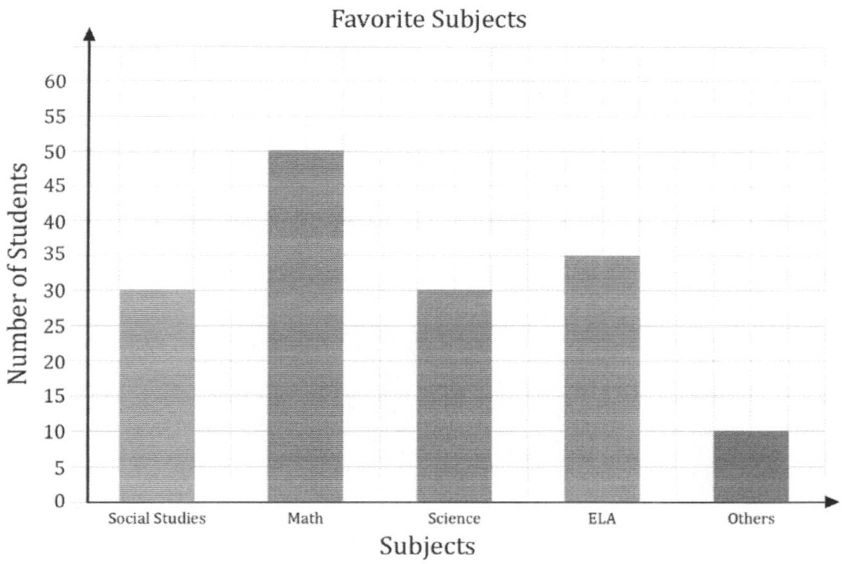

Students that prefer math or science: $50 + 30 = 80$.
Students that prefer social studies or ELA: $30 + 35 = 65$.
The difference: $80 - 65 = 15$.
There are 15 more students who prefer math or science than social studies or ELA.

Example

Which day of the week has a value of 30 cars?

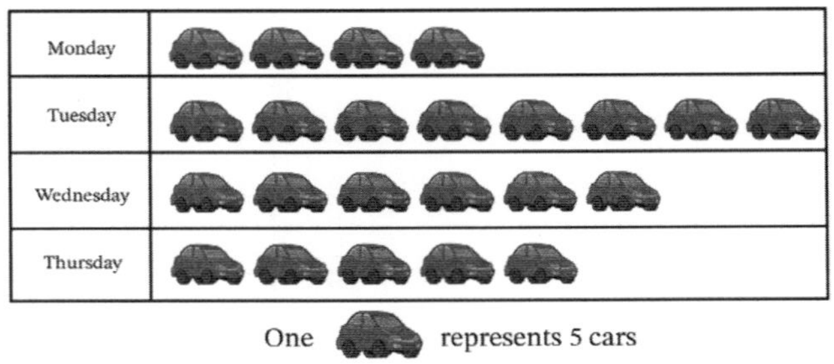

Each car in the pictograph represents 5 cars.
Monday shows 4 cars: $4 \times 5 = 20$ total cars.
Tuesday shows 8 cars: $8 \times 5 = 40$ total cars.
Wednesday shows 6 cars: $6 \times 5 = 30$ total cars.
Thursday shows 5 cars: $5 \times 5 = 25$ total cars.
Wednesday has a value of 30 total cars.

Personal Financial Literacy

Human Capital, Labor, and Income

Human capital is a person's abilities, skills, knowledge, experience, and education, which can help them do **labor**, or complete their work. Many careers require special skills or education. For example, a scientist needs to have a college degree, and a musician needs to have musical skills and abilities. Many career paths require a college education but not all. In general, a person's **income** will gradually increase as their level of education increases. When a person has specialized skills and a strong educational background, they are desirable for employers. Employers look for workers that have skills, experience, and knowledge that is relevant to the job.

Scarcity and Cost

When a product or service is considered **scarce**, it means that it is rare. The opposite of scarce is **available**. In general, the **cost** of a product will increase if it becomes more scarce. For example, consider a town that usually has 25 homes for sale each month. The home prices will be fairly consistent as long as there are about 25 homes for sale each month. However, what would happen if people in this town stopped selling their homes? Let's say this month the town only has 3 homes for sale. If the availability of homes for sale drops from 25 to 3, homes for sale are very scarce. Home buyers now need to compete with each other to get the product they want (a home). This scarcity can lead to competition and will inevitably raise the price of the homes in this town. The inventory has become limited so the prices will increase. People become willing to pay more for a home when they know there is a limited supply.

Credit and Interest

When large purchases need to be made, like buying a house, a car, or college tuition, a person can go to a bank and borrow money. When you borrow money from a lender such as a bank, you are eventually expected to pay back the money you borrowed, plus interest. Remember, **interest** is the amount that you owe on top of the original amount. For example, if you borrow $10,000 with an interest rate of 2.5%, you will owe the original $10,000 plus an additional $250 in interest. Taking out a loan is a very common practice when making large purchases. However, it is important to have a plan for how you will eventually pay back the loan plus interest. When a person has a great track record of paying the bank back the loaned money and interest, the borrower builds up what is called **credit**. Having good credit is similar to having a good reputation. Banks want to know that you will pay them back the money they loan you. A borrower can also build good credit by paying their bills on time. In general, a person with "good credit" has an easier time borrowing money from a bank.

Saving Money

Setting up a **savings account** is a great way to earn and save money over time. It is important to plan for large expenses, such as college tuition, buying a house, buying a car, health emergencies, or big vacations. These things can be quite expensive, so it is wise to start saving at an early age so that by the time these purchases need to be made, a savings account has had time to grow. Many banks will offer interest rates to encourage you to bank with them. For example, a bank might offer a 1.4% interest rate on its savings accounts. This might not seem like a lot, but over time it can really add up. Financial advisors provide people with many ways to save their money. The important thing is start saving early on.

Practice Test #1

1. In the number 60,701 the digit 7 represents ______. Write your answer in the blank.

2. A chocolate shop sells boxes of chocolate with a variety of styles and flavors. If a customer purchases 3 boxes of chocolate, how many total pieces will they have?

a. 72
b. 70
c. 68
d. 66

3. All of the choices below are reasons to set up a savings plan, except for two. Which choices do NOT belong? Select all that apply.

a. A savings plan is only necessary if you plan to go to college for more than 4 years.
b. With a savings plan, your money will grow slowly and consistently over time.
c. If you start saving early on in life, your savings will cover some or most of the cost of college.
d. College is expensive. Having a savings account is one way to put aside money for this large expense.

4. Decompose 564,771 into expanded form. Choose the correct answer to go in each blank.

500,000 + __________ +4,000 + 700 + __________ +1

600,000	77
60	70
60,000	7

5. Mrs. Martin was awarded $850 to spend on classroom materials. She decided to purchase tablets and headphones for her students. Mrs. Martin spent $450 on tablets and $225 on pairs of headphones. After these purchases, how much money did Mrs. Martin have left?

6. Add pumpkins to the graph to show that Logan picked 5 pumpkins and Marlene picked 25 more pumpkins than Logan.

Pumpkin Picking	
Elizabeth	
Marlene	
John	
Logan	
Ning	

Each  = 10 pumpkins

7. The dot plot represents a student's scores on math tests. Each dot represents one test. How many tests did the student score a 93?

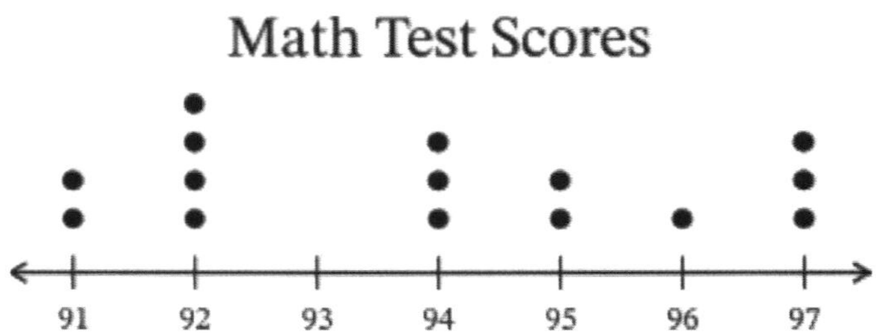

a. 0
b. 1
c. 2
d. 3
e. Having a savings account can help you pay for expenses within a few weeks.

8. Which fractions can the shaded region be expressed as? Select all that apply.

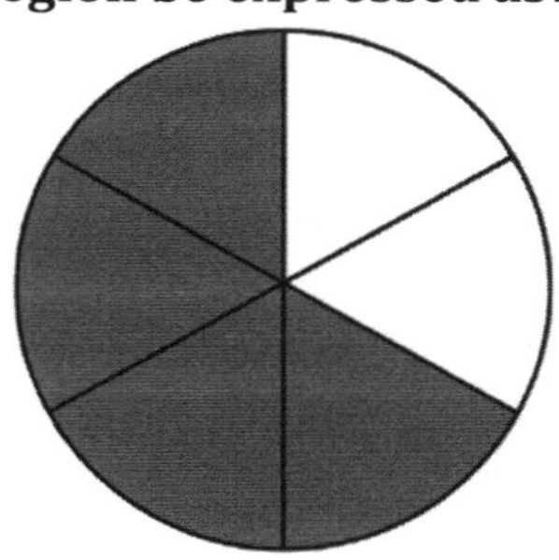

a. $\frac{4}{6}$
b. $\frac{2}{3}$
c. $\frac{8}{10}$
d. $\frac{3}{4}$
e. $\frac{3}{2}$

9. What fraction corresponds to the dot on the number line below?

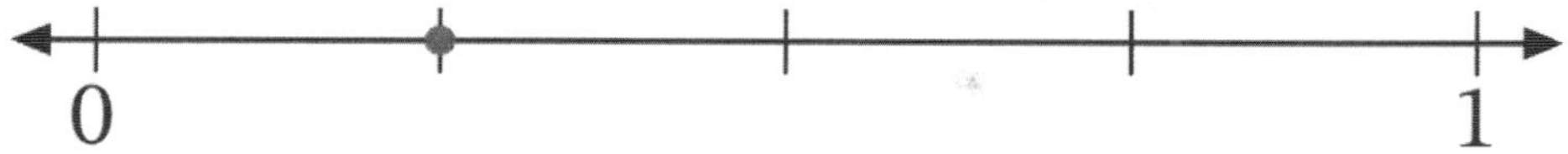

Create a fraction that represents the dot on the graph. Choose a number from 1 through 10 for both the numerator and denominator and write your answers in the blank below:

Numerator: ___
Denominator: ___

10. ___ is 346 rounded to the nearest hundred. Write your answer in the blank below.

11. How many times larger is 1,500 than 15?

a. 10 times larger
b. 100 times larger
c. 1,000 times larger
d. 10,000 times larger

12. Which repeated addition equation represents a product of 42?

a. $6 + 6 + 6 + 6 + 6$
b. $7 + 7 + 7 + 7$
c. $7 + 7 + 7 + 7 + 7$
d. $6 + 6 + 6 + 6 + 6 + 6 + 6$

13. Calculate the sum of 5 hundreds, 6 tens, 2 thousands, and 9 ones.

a. 2,569
b. 2,345
c. 2,624
d. 2,983

14. The expression 9×15 can be represented as a comparison. Which description matches the expression 9×15? Choose the correct answer to go in each blank.

___ times as much as	___
3	9
9	20
15	8

15. Determine the location of $\frac{1}{3}$ on the number line below. $\frac{1}{3}$ and __ are the same distance from 0.

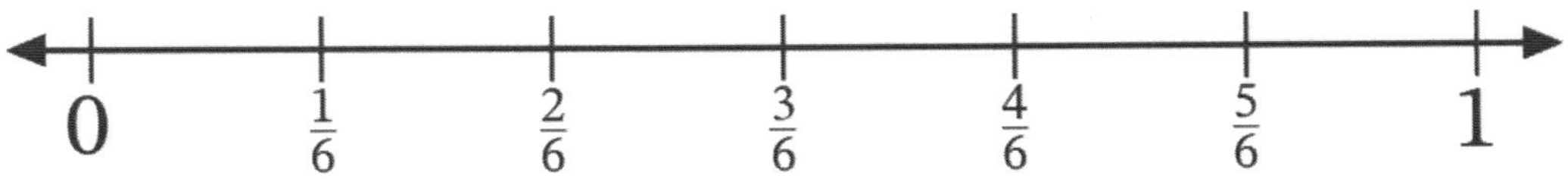

a. $\frac{1}{6}$
b. $\frac{2}{6}$
c. $\frac{3}{6}$
d. $\frac{4}{6}$

16. Find the missing number: $72 = \_ \times 9$

a. 6
b. 7
c. 8
d. 9

17. Is it possible to draw a quadrilateral with exactly 2 right angles? Explain.

a. No, a quadrilateral needs to have 4 right angles.
b. Yes, a rhombus can have exactly 2 right angles.
c. Yes, a trapezoid can have exactly 2 right angles.
d. No, a quadrilateral cannot be drawn with exactly 2 right angles.

18. A music director is setting up chairs in an auditorium before a performance. 42 chairs need to be placed in 7 equal rows. How can multiplication be used to determine the number of chairs to be placed in each row?

Choose which numbers in the list below should go in each blank. Each number may be used more than once.

42	7	6	2	21

__ × __ = 42, so ___ chairs should be in each row.

19. A large rectangular pan of fudge is 12 inches long and 8 inches wide. The fudge is sliced into small pieces, each piece being 1 inch by 1 inch. How many small pieces of fudge can be cut from 2 pans?

a. 96
b. 192
c. 40
d. 240

20. A stone pathway is built from regular hexagonal stones. Each stone has a perimeter of 24 cm. What is the length of each side of the stone in centimeters?

a. 3
b. 4
c. 6
d. 8

21. Which equation describes the total number of windows in the tallest city building?

a. $8 \times 4 = 32$
b. $8 \times 3 = 24$
c. $8 \times 2 = 16$
d. $7 \times 3 = 21$

22. An art student creates a three-dimensional figure using paper. What is the most accurate name for the shape that was created?

a. Triangular prism
b. Pyramid
c. Triangular pyramid
d. Prism

23. The equation $5 + 4 + 6 =$ ___ represents the addition scenario on the number line below. Write your answer in the blank below.

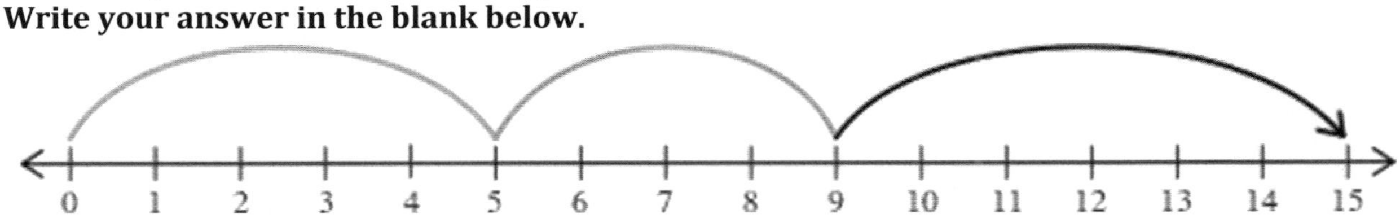

24. Mary works at a coffee shop and earns tips based on great service. Her tip jar has $120 in 10-dollar bills, $45 in 5-dollar bills, and $60 in 20-dollar bills. How much money is in the tip jar altogether?

a. $220

b. $285

c. $245

d. $225

25. The table below shows the relationship between the number of juice boxes and the number of juice packs. Write a number from the list below in each blank.

3	5	6	10	16	18

Number of Packs	1	2	___	4	5	6
Number of Juice Boxes	3	6	9	12	15	___

26. A truck driver records his mileage each year. Order the years from greatest to least based on mileage.

2019: 102,445 miles
2020: 98,220 miles
2021: 98,234 miles
2022: 97,882 miles

a. 2022, 2021, 2020, 2019

b. 2019, 2021, 2020, 2022

c. 2019, 2020, 2021, 2022

d. 2022, 2021, 2022, 2019

27. Grace has 12 photos of family members and 12 photos of pets. She wants to place all the photos in a scrapbook. Each page of the scrapbook holds 4 photos. How many pages does she need if she places the same number of photos on each page?

a. 6 pages

b. 7 pages

c. 8 pages

d. 9 pages

28. When one whole is divided into six equal shares, what unit fraction is represented by each share? Write your answer in the blank.

29. Compare the fractions $\frac{3}{6}$ and $\frac{3}{8}$ without calculating a common denominator.

a. $\frac{3}{6} < \frac{3}{8}$
b. $\frac{3}{6} > \frac{3}{8}$
c. $\frac{3}{6} = \frac{3}{8}$
d. These two fractions cannot be compared.

30. The beaker below measures capacity in milligrams. A scientist needs to fill the beaker up to the line with water. How many milliliters of water will be in the beaker?

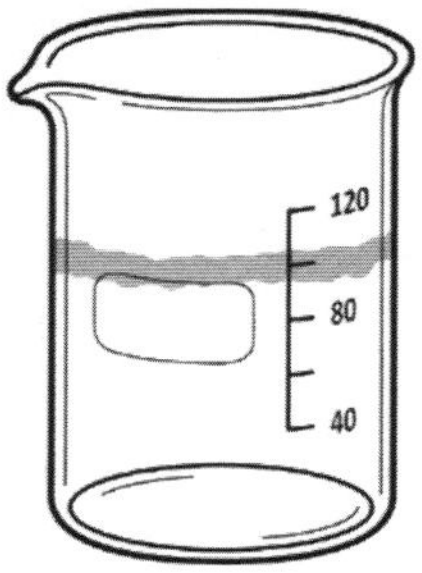

a. 115 mL
b. 110 mL
c. 90 mL
d. 100 mL

Answer Key and Explanations for Test #1

1. 700: TEKS Standard (3.2)(A)

In the value 60,701, there is 1 group of 1, 0 groups of 10, 7 groups of 100, 0 groups of 1,000, and 6 groups of 10,000. The 7 is in the hundreds place, so it represents 700.

2. A: TEKS Standard (3.5)(B)

Each box of chocolates is made up of 6 columns and 4 rows. This forms an array of $6 \times 4 = 24$. Each box contains 24 pieces of chocolate. 3 boxes contain $24 + 24 + 24$, which simplifies to 72. There are 72 pieces of chocolate in 3 boxes.

3. A, E: TEKS Standard (3.9)(E)

Setting up a savings plan is an easy way to make money over time. College is a large expense. Following a savings plan early on in life is an effective way to pay for part or all of college tuition. However, even if you do not plan on going to college, having a savings plan is still very important. There are a wide variety of savings plans to choose from. Talking to your local bank is one way to learn more about the best options to achieve your savings goals.

4. 60,000, 70: TEKS Standard (3.2)(A)

564,771 is in standard from. In order to express the value in expanded form, break apart each digit based on its place value.

564,771 can be expressed as the sum of its parts. 564,771 in expanded form is $500{,}000 + 60{,}000 + 4{,}000 + 700 + 70 + 1$.

5. 175: TEKS Standard (3.5)(A)

First, figure out how much money Mrs. Martin spent by adding the two amounts.

$$\$450 + \$225 = \$675$$

Mrs. Martin spent $675. Subtract this amount from the amount she was awarded to calculate the amount of money remaining.

$$\$850 - \$675 = \$175$$

She has $175 left.

6. TEKS Standard (3.8)(A)

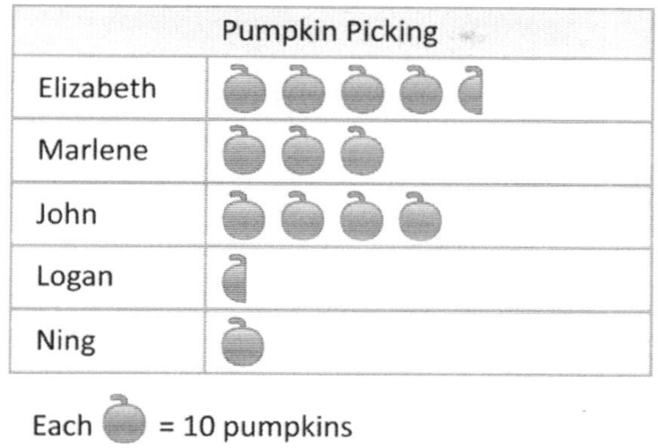

Each pumpkin picture represents 10 pumpkins. Logan picked 5 pumpkins. Half of 10 is 5. There should be half of a pumpkin picture next to Logan's name. Since Marlene picked 25 more pumpkins than Logan did, and $5 + 25 = 30$, the pumpkins next to Marlene's name should show 30 pumpkins.

$$30 \div 10 = 3$$

30 pumpkins can be represented by 3 whole pumpkins. By adding half of a pumpkin next to Logan's name and 3 pumpkins next to Marlene's name, the graph shows the Marlene picked 25 more pumpkins than Logan.

7. A: TEKS Standard (3.8)(B)

Each dot represents one test. A score of 93 displays no dots; therefore, the student did not score 93 on a test.

8. A, B: TEKS Standard (3.3)(F)

There are 4 shaded sections and 6 sections total. 4 out of 6 simplifies to 2 out of 3. $\frac{4}{6}$ is equivalent to $\frac{2}{3}$ because $\frac{4}{6}$ becomes $\frac{2}{3}$ when the numerator and denominator are divided by 2.

9. 1, 4: TEKS Standard (3.3)(B)

There are 4 equal parts between 0 and 1 on the number line. The dot represents 1 part out of 4 parts, or the fraction $\frac{1}{4}$. The dot is one-quarter of the distance between 0 to 1.

10. 300: TEKS Standard (3.4)(B)

346 is between 300 and 400. On a number line, 346 is closer to 300 than 400. This means that 346 rounded to the nearest hundred is 300.

Another way to determine this is to locate the number in the hundreds place, 3, and then look at the number to right, 4. If the number to the right is 5 or more, the original number rounds up and every number to the right becomes a 0. If this number to the right is 4 or less, the original number stays the same and every number to the right becomes a 0. In this case, the number to the right is 4, so the hundreds value stays the same. When 346 is rounded to the nearest hundred it becomes 300.

11. D: TEKS Standard (3.2)(B)

1,500 is 15 with two 0s after it, which is the same as 15×100.

$$15 \times 100 = 1{,}500$$

Therefore, 1,500 is 100 times larger than 15.

12. D: TEKS Standard (3.4)(E)

Multiplication can be expressed as repeated addition. 42 can be expressed as 6 groups of 7 or 7 groups of 6: $6 + 6 + 6 + 6 + 6 + 6 + 6 = 42$ or $7 + 7 + 7 + 7 + 7 + 7 = 42$.

13. A: TEKS Standard (3.4)(A)

Place value can be used to find the sum.

5 hundreds is 500.

6 tens is 60.

2 thousands is 2,000.

9 ones is 9.

Add the values based on place value.

$$2{,}000 + 500 + 60 + 9 = 2{,}569$$

14. 15, 9: TEKS Standard (3.5)(C)

9×15 represents 9 groups of 15, or 15 groups of 9. This means that the product will be 9 times as much as 15, or 15 times as much as 9.

15. B: TEKS Standard (3.3)(G)

Fractions are considered equivalent if they represent the same distance from 0 on a number line. $\frac{2}{6}$ can be simplified to $\frac{1}{3}$ by dividing the top and bottom of the fraction by 3. The location of $\frac{1}{3}$ will be at the same location as $\frac{2}{6}$.

16. C: TEKS Standard (3.5)(D)

What number times 9 equals 72? Or how many groups of 9 are needed to reach 72? The missing number is 8. So, $8 \times 9 = 72$. 8 groups of 9 are needed to reach 72.

17. C: TEKS Standard (3.6)(B)

A trapezoid has exactly 1 pair of parallel sides. Trapezoids can be drawn with exactly 2 right angles, as shown.

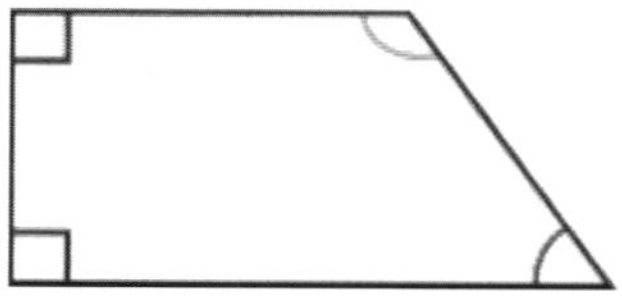

18. 6, 7, 6 or 7, 6, 6: TEKS Standard (3.4)(J)

There needs to be 42 chairs total, and there will be 7 equal rows. This describes the division scenario $42 \div 7$. This division scenario can be changed into the multiplication scenario $7 \times \_ = 42$. Since $7 \times 6 = 42$, the number of chairs in each row is 6.

19. B: TEKS Standard (3.6)(C)

The area of one pan of fudge can be determined by multiplying the length by the width. $12 \times 8 = 96$, which means 96 pieces of fudge can be cut from one pan. Two pans will have twice as many slices, add $96 + 96 = 192$. 192 pieces of fudge can be cut from 2 pans.

20. B: TEKS Standard (3.7)(B)

A regular hexagon has 6 congruent side lengths. The perimeter of the stone is 24 cm, so divide to find $24 \div 6 = 4$. This means that each side length is 4 cm.

21. B: TEKS Standard (3.4)(K)

The tallest city building has 3 columns and 8 rows. The columns and rows form an array. The total number of windows can be determined by multiplying the number of rows by the number of columns: $8 \times 3 = 24$. There are 24 windows in the tallest building.

22. A: TEKS Standard (3.6)(A)

The figure has two faces, the triangles, that are in parallel planes. All the other faces are parallelograms. This means the figure is defined as a triangular prism.

23. 15: TEKS Standard (3.5)(A)

The left arc represents an increase of 5 (+5). The middle arc represents an increase of 4 (+4). The right arc represents an increase of 6 (+6). The sum of all arcs is 15. So, $5 + 4 + 6 = 15$.

24. D: TEKS Standard (3.4)(A)

To find the total amount of money in the tip jar, add the 3 values together: $\$120 + \$45 + \$60 = \$225$. There is \$225 in the tip jar.

25. 3, 18: TEKS Standard (3.5)(E)

The table shows the relationship between packs of juice and boxes of juice. 1 box of juice contains 3 packs of juice. The number of boxes is 3 times the number of packs. This rule is true throughout the table. The number of boxes is determined by multiplying the number of packs by 3.

$$6 \times 3 = 18 \text{ boxes}$$

Division and fact families can be used to find the other blank. $3 \times 3 = 9$, so $9 \div 3 = 3$, and the missing value in the top row is 3.

26. B: TEKS Standard (3.2)(D)

Move from left to right when comparing the place value of multiple numbers. Start by comparing the hundred-thousands place, then the ten-thousands place, then the thousands place, hundreds place, tens place, and ones place. 102,445 in 2019 is the greatest value because it is the only number in the hundred-thousands. 98,234 in 2021 is the next largest because its ten-thousands place is larger than 97,220 and its tens place is larger than 98,234. The next largest is 98,220 in 2020, followed by 97,882 in 2022.

27. A: TEKS Standard (3.4)(K)

Grace has $12 + 12 = 24$ photos. These 24 photos need to be divided into groups of 4. Divide to find the number of pages required: $24 \div 4 = 6$. This means that 6 pages are required.

28. $\frac{1}{6}$: TEKS Standard (3.3)(C)

Unit fractions have 1 in the numerator. For example, $\frac{1}{2}, \frac{1}{3}, \frac{1}{4}, \frac{1}{5}$, and $\frac{1}{6}$ are unit fractions. When one whole is divided into 6 equal shares, each share represents 1 out of 6, or the unit fraction $\frac{1}{6}$.

29. B: TEKS Standard (3.3)(H)

$\frac{3}{6}$ has a denominator of 6. $\frac{3}{8}$ has a denominator of 8. A whole that is divided into 8 parts will produce smaller parts than a whole that is only divided into 6 parts. Using this logic, 3 large parts will be more than 3 small parts. $\frac{3}{6}$ is more than $\frac{3}{8}$, so $\frac{3}{6} > \frac{3}{8}$.

30. D: TEKS Standard (3.7)(E)

The provided measurement lines on the beaker show 40 mL, 80 mL, and 120 mL. Each value increases by an increment of 40 mL. The line between 80 mL and 120 mL has to be 100 mL because it is half the distance from 80 to 120. The scientist needs 100 mL of water.

Practice Test #2

1. A unit fraction is a fraction with a numerator of ___. Write your answer in the blank below.

2. The bar graph below shows the number of trees planted by the Green Lake Middle School after school club. Choose the answers that make the statement below correct.

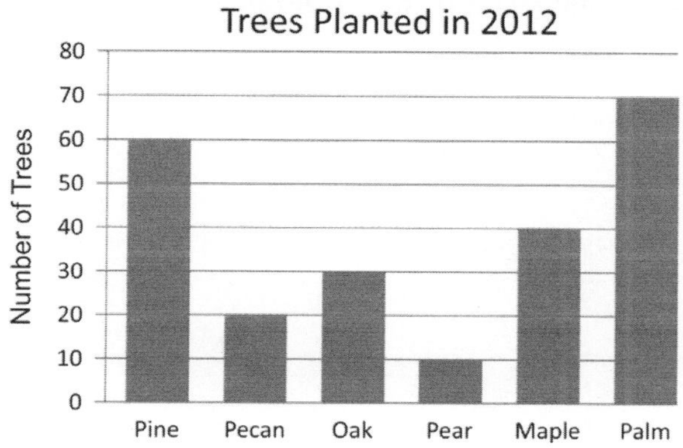

The club planted three _____________ _______ trees ________ trees.

more	pine	as pecan
times as many	pear	as maple
fewer	maple	than oak

3. All of the choices below have the same missing number except for one. Which choice does not belong with the rest?

a. $7 \times \_ = 56$
b. $\_ \times 1 = 8$
c. $3 \times \_ = 24$
d. $4 \times \_ = 40$

4. Use logic to compare $\frac{2}{10}$ and $\frac{6}{10}$.

a. $\frac{2}{10} > \frac{6}{10}$
b. $\frac{2}{10} < \frac{6}{10}$
c. $\frac{2}{10} = \frac{6}{10}$
d. These two fractions cannot be compared.

5. $400,000 + 2,000 + 400 + 90 + 3$ is in expanded form. Express the amount in standard form.

a. 409,493
b. 401,455
c. 402,493
d. 409,432

6. A biologist is studying butterfly migration. On the first day of observation, the biologist counts 766 butterflies. On the second day, the biologist observes 615 butterflies. The biologist observed __ more butterflies on day one than on day two. Write your answer in the blank below.

7. On the number line below, the box represents __. Write your answer in the blank below.

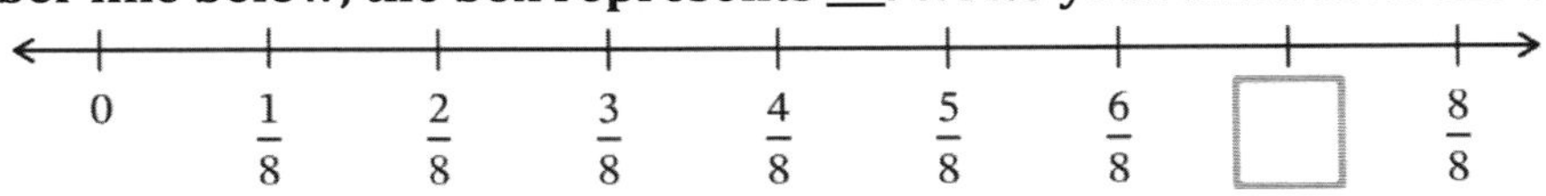

8. Circle three choices that show a true statement.

$309,300 > 309,281$ $444,290 > 444,920$ $104,300 > 300,401$

$92,344 < 92,433$ $638,544 > 628,844$

9. The value of z is 8 feet. The perimeter of the figure below is _ feet.

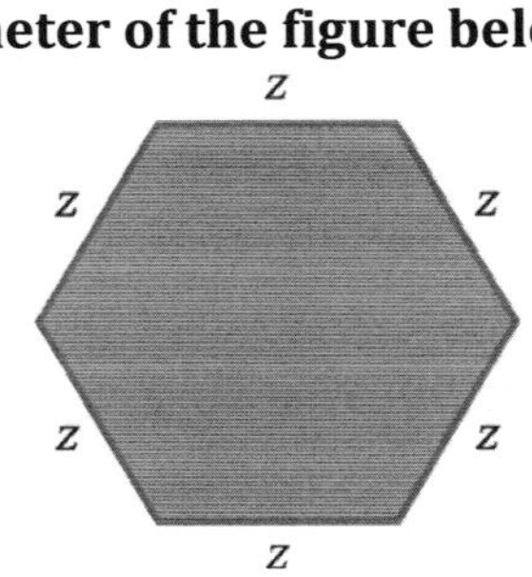

a. 6
b. 14
c. 36
d. 48

10. A baker is measuring ingredients for bread. The baker needs to measure the correct amount of flour. To be precise, the baker measures the flour by its weight instead of its volume. Which unit of measure should the baker use to measure the flour?

a. Ounces
b. Liquid ounces
c. Either ounces or liquid ounces
d. Gallons

11. The Larson family is packing up cars for a family vacation. They have 12 suitcases and 3 vehicles. They want to load the same number of suitcases into each vehicle. How many suitcases should the Larsons into each vehicle? Write your answer in the blank.

12. $1,000 - 360 = 240 + \_\_\_$

a. 120
b. 400
c. 640
d. 760

13. Jeremy has read $\frac{3}{10}$ of his book. He wants to finish his book in 7 days. If he reads the same amount each day, what fraction of the total book does he need to read each day?

a. $\frac{1}{10}$ each day: $\frac{1}{10}+\frac{1}{10}+\frac{1}{10}+\frac{1}{10}+\frac{1}{10}+\frac{1}{10}+\frac{1}{10}=\frac{7}{10}$
b. $\frac{1}{4}$ each day: $\frac{1}{4}+\frac{1}{4}+\frac{1}{4}=\frac{3}{4}$
c. $\frac{1}{6}$ each day: $\frac{1}{6}+\frac{1}{6}+\frac{1}{6}+\frac{1}{6}+\frac{1}{6}+\frac{1}{6}+\frac{1}{6}=\frac{7}{6}$
d. $\frac{1}{3}$ each day: $\frac{1}{3}+\frac{1}{3}=\frac{2}{3}$

14. Which of the following multiplication sentences is modeled on the number line?

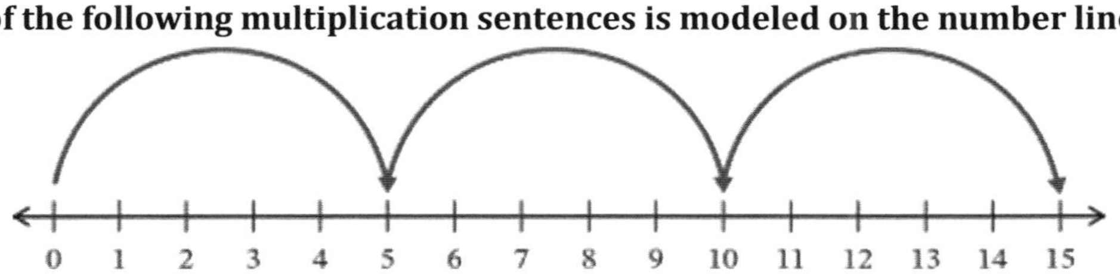

a. $3 \times 15 = 45$
b. $5 \times 3 = 15$
c. $3 \times 6 = 18$
d. $5 \times 3 = 20$

15. Which division equation matches the tape diagram below?

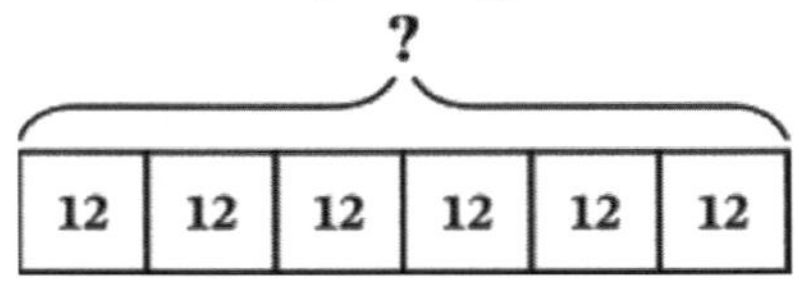

a. $? \div 6 = 12$

b. $6 \div ? = 12$

c. $12 \div 6 = ?$

d. $? \div 12 = 5$

16. Which two choices are NOT examples of the relationship between scarcity and cost? Select all that apply.

a. A limited-edition video game is expensive because it is rare.

b. A diamond ring is expensive in part because of the scarcity of diamonds.

c. A gold bracelet is inexpensive because of the scarcity of gold.

d. During a water shortage or drought, water prices increase due to the lack of supply.

e. A piece of furniture is expensive because it is large and requires many different materials.

17. The government building known as the Pentagon has __ sides.

a. 6

b. 4

c. 3

d. 5

18. The librarian has set up a new book display. There are 8 book shelves with 35 books displayed on each shelf. How many books are there altogether?

a. 250

b. 260

c. 270

d. 280

19. The dark shaded region represents 4 out of 8. As a fraction in simplest form this is ___.

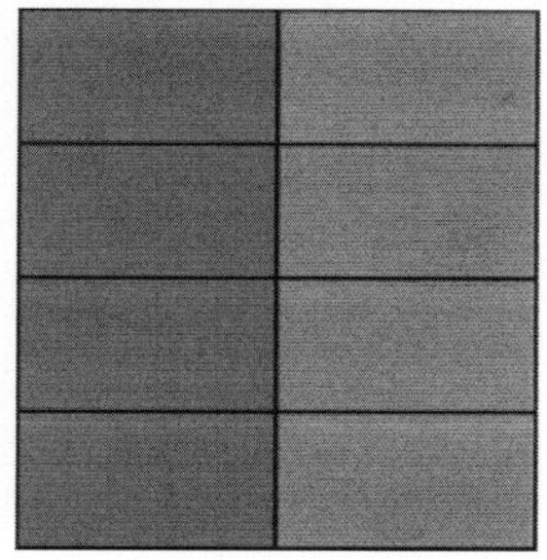

a. $\frac{4}{2}$
b. $\frac{2}{1}$
c. $\frac{2}{4}$
d. $\frac{1}{2}$

20. The area of the rectangle can be calculated by multiplying 8 by __. Write your answer in the blank below.

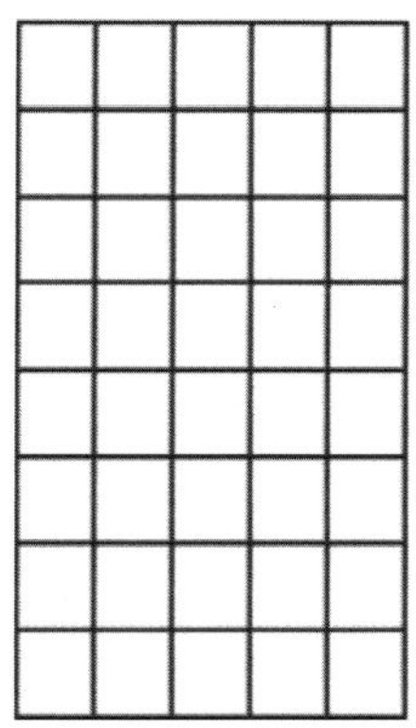

21. Which scenario represents the following division equation: $45 \div 9 = 5$?

a. You pay 9 employees $45 for one hour of work. If each employee works for 5 hours, how much do you owe your employees?
b. You earn $45 per hour, and you work for 9 hours per day. How much do you earn after 5 days?
c. You walk 9 miles each day, for 45 days. How many miles do you walk altogether?
d. You purchase 9 bagels, and your total bill is $45 before tax. How much did each bagel cost?

22. The depth of Green Frog Lake is 977 feet. The depth of Black Rock Lake is 779 feet. How much deeper is Green Frog Lake than Black Rock Lake?

a. 167 feet
b. 199 feet
c. 198 feet
d. 189 feet

23. Which two comparisons do NOT have a product of 56? Select all that apply.

a. 14 times as much as 4
b. 2 times as much as 28
c. 6 times as much as 8
d. 7 times as much as 6
e. 8 times as much as 7

24. Choose the correct answer for each blank:

The value 3,209 lies between ______ and ______ on the number line.

3,400	3,500
3,100	3,200
3,200	3,300
3,000	3,100

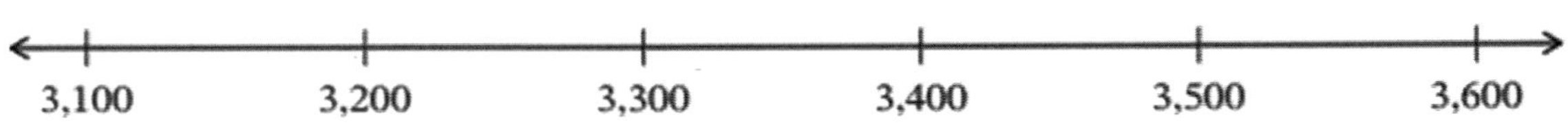

25. The value of Matt's car was $1,000 in 2018. What will his car be worth in 2022 if it loses $800 in value in those 4 years?

a. $200
b. $250
c. $300
d. $350

26. Write the correct answers in the blanks below.

Pacific Crest Trail: 2,651 miles
Great Divide Trail: 702 miles
Appalachian Trail: 2,193 miles

Great Divide Trail, ________________, ________________,

Pacific Crest Trail	Appalachian Trail

The trails are ordered from ________ length to ________ length.

greatest	least

27. Color in the fraction model to represent the unit fraction $\frac{1}{8}$.

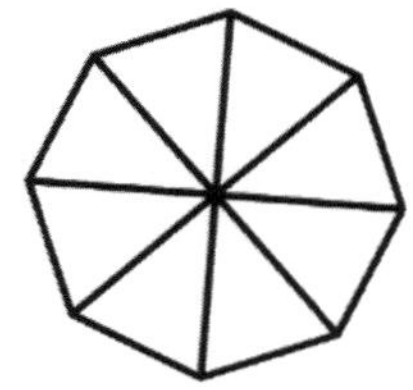

28. All of the choices except one show ways that workers can achieve a higher income. Which choice does not belong?

a. Gaining specialized skills
b. Strong abilities related to the specific job
c. Completing an advanced education
d. Avoiding parts of the job that are challenging

29. Complete the table using the relationship expressed in the first two rows of the table. Write the correct numbers from the list below in the blanks in the table.

6	8	11	12	14	15

Input	Output
3	8
12	17
1	
7	

30. Use multiplication to solve the division problem.

$$48 \div 8 = \_\_\_$$

a. $6 \times 6 = 48$, which means the missing value is 6.
b. $8 \times 8 = 64$, which means the missing value is 8.
c. $6 \times 8 = 48$, which means the missing value is 6.
d. $6 \times 8 = 40$, which means the missing value is 8.

Answer Key and Explanations for Test #2

1. 1: TEKS Standard (3.3)(C)

A unit fraction has a numerator of 1. When a whole is divided into equal parts, the total number of parts is represented as the denominator. For example, if one whole is divided into 4 equal parts, the unit fraction $\frac{1}{4}$ represents 1 part out of 4.

2. times as many, pine, as pecan: TEKS Standard (3.8)(A)

The club planted 60 pine trees and 20 pecan trees. Since $20 \times 3 = 60$, it is correct to say that 60 is three times as many as 20. The options "more" and "fewer" would show that this is an addition or subtraction problem. Since none of the amounts are 3 more or less than another amount, neither of these are correct. The club picked 10 pear trees. Since this is the smallest group of trees, it cannot include three times as many trees as another group of trees. The club picked 40 maple trees. 40 is about 3 times as many as 13.33. None of the other groups of trees include this number of trees. This shows that *pear* and *maple* are not correct choices for the second blank. Additionally, only the group of pecan trees contains 20 trees, so the other options for the last blank are incorrect.

3. D: TEKS Standard (3.5)(D)

Choices A, B, and C, have a missing value of 8. Choice D has a missing value of 10, so it does not belong with the rest.

$$7 \times \mathbf{8} = 56$$

$$\mathbf{8} \times 1 = 8$$

$$3 \times \mathbf{8} = 24$$

$$4 \times \mathbf{10} = 40$$

4. B: TEKS Standard (3.3)(H)

Both fractions have the same denominator, so they both have the same number of total parts. Logic can be used to understand that 2 of these parts is less than 6 of these parts, because the parts are the same size. So, $\frac{2}{10} < \frac{6}{10}$.

5. C: TEKS Standard (3.2)(A)

$400{,}000 + 2{,}000 + 400 + 90 + 3$ is split apart based on its place value. The sum of $400{,}000 + 2{,}000 + 400 + 90 + 3$ is 402,493. 402,493 is in standard form.

6. 151: TEKS Standard (3.5)(A)

To answer the question, find the difference between day 1 and day 2, $766 - 615 = 151$. The biologist observed 151 more butterflies on day 1 than on day 2.

7. $\frac{7}{8}$**: TEKS Standard (3.7)(A)**

The number line is divided into 8 equal sections. Each section represents $\frac{1}{8}$. Each fraction represents a distance from 0 on the number line. The box is $\frac{7}{8}$ of the distance from 0 to 1.

8. 309, 300 > 309, 281; 92, 344 < 92, 433; 638, 544 > 628, 844: TEKS Standard (3.2)(D)

When comparing numbers, compare the largest place values first. Compare the digits in the hundred-thousands place, then the ten-thousands place, then the thousands place, hundreds place, tens place, and ones place. 309,300 > 309,281 is a true statement because they have different values in the hundreds place. 3 > 2, so 309,300 > 309,281. 92,344 < 92,433 is a true statement. Both values have a 9 in the ten-thousands place and a 2 in the thousands place, but the hundreds digits are different. 3 < 4 so 92,344 < 92,433. 638,544 > 628,844 is true because these values have different values in the ten-thousands place. Since 3 > 2, 638,544 > 628,844.

9. D: TEKS Standard (3.7)(B)

The figure is a hexagon. Each side has a length of 8 feet. Since perimeter is the sum of all the side lengths, and in this figure the sides are all the same length, you can use multiplication to find the perimeter. There are 6 sides, so the perimeter can be calculated as $6 \times 8 = 48$. The perimeter of the hexagon is 48 feet.

10. A: TEKS Standard (3.7)(D)

Weight is measured in ounces and pounds. Capacity, or volume, is measured in fluid ounces, cups, pints, quarts, liters and gallons. A fluid ounce is not the same thing as an ounce. Ounces measure weight, and fluid ounces measure volume. In this case, ounces measure dry ingredients such as flour, and fluid ounces measure liquid ingredients such as water. The baker needs to measure the flour in ounces, not in fluid ounces.

11. 4: TEKS Standard (3.4)(H)

The Larsons have 12 suitcases that need to be divided equally into 3 vehicles. Use division: $12 \div 3 = 4$. The family should load 4 suitcases into each car.

12. B: TEKS Standard (3.5)(A)

Both sides of the equation need to have the same value. The left side of the equation simplifies to 640, that is $1{,}000 - 360 = 640$. The right side of the equation needs to also simplify to 640. If 400 is added to 240, the sum is 640. This means the missing value is 400.

13. A: TEKS Standard (3.3)(D)

Jeremy has read $\frac{3}{10}$ of his book, which means $\frac{7}{10}$ are unread. If he reads $\frac{1}{10}$ of the total book each day for 7 days, the book will be finished as $\frac{3}{7} + \frac{7}{10} = \frac{10}{10} = 1$. The fraction $\frac{7}{10}$ can be decomposed into $\frac{1}{10} + \frac{1}{10} + \frac{1}{10} + \frac{1}{10} + \frac{1}{10} + \frac{1}{10} + \frac{1}{10}$. So, he needs to read $\frac{1}{10}$ each day.

14. B: TEKS Standard (3.4)(E)

The number line models the equation $3 \times 5 = 15$. Since 5 is being multiplied by 3, there are 3 groups of 5. This means that the graph should show 3 jumps of 5, which will go from 0 to 5, from 5 to 10, and from 10 to 15.

15. A: TEKS Standard (3.5)(B)

The strip diagram shows 6 groups of 12 with an unknown total. This describes the multiplication scenario $6 \times 12 = 72$. This also describes a division scenario $72 \div 6 = 12$. Since 72 is unknown in the model, the division equation can be expressed as $? \div 6 = 12$.

16. C, E: TEKS Standard (3.9)(B)

"Scarcity mindset" refers to the concept that when a product or resource is scarce, or limited, people are willing to pay more for the product. This inevitably increases the price. Suppliers know that people are willing to pay more, so they can increase the price and feel confident that they will still make sales. In general, as products or resources become limited or less available, the cost increases. All of the choices describe this phenomenon except choices C and E. Gold is not a renewable resource. It is considered scarce, which contributes to its high price. The pieces and materials that makeup a piece of furniture are not usually rare or scarce. The size of the object affects its price, not the rarity of it.

17. D: TEKS Standard (3.6)(A)

The Pentagon is a government building located near Washington D.C. which is the shape of a pentagon. A pentagon has 5 sides, which is why the building is referred to as the Pentagon.

18. D: TEKS Standard (3.4)(G)

There are 8 shelves with 35 books on each shelf. This represents a multiplication scenario. Consider using the standard algorithm.

$$\begin{array}{r} \scriptstyle 4 \\ 35 \\ \times\ 8 \\ \hline 280 \end{array}$$

8 times 5 is 40. Write 4 above the 3 and 0 on the answer line. Now multiply 8 times 3, and add 4. This is 28. Write 28 on the answer line. The product is 280, so there is a total of 280 books.

19. D: TEKS Standard (3.3)(F)

The dark region shows 4 out of 8 pieces. $\frac{4}{8}$ can be simplified to $\frac{1}{2}$. 4 is the greatest common multiple of 4 and 8, so divide the numerator and denominator of $\frac{4}{8}$ by 4. $\frac{4}{8}$ becomes $\frac{1}{2}$, which is in simplest form.

20. 5: TEKS Standard (3.6)(C)

There are 8 rows in the rectangle, and there are 5 units in each row. 8 rows of 5 is calculated by multiplying 8 by 5. The area of the rectangle is $8 \times 5 = 40$ square units.

21. D: TEKS Standard (3.4)(K)

The total cost can be represented as \$45, and the number of bagels purchased is 9. Divide 45 by 9 to determine the cost per bagel, $45 \div 9 = 5$. So, each bagel cost \$5.

22. C: TEKS Standard (3.4)(A)

The difference between the two depths can be determined using subtraction based on place value.

$$\begin{array}{r} {\scriptstyle 16} \\ {\scriptstyle 8\ \cancel{6}/16} \\ \cancel{9}\cancel{7}\cancel{7} \\ -779 \\ \hline 198 \end{array}$$

23. C, D: TEKS Standard (3.5)(C)

The comparison "6 times as much as 8" has a product of $6 \times 8 = 48$. The comparison "7 times as much as 6" has a product of $7 \times 6 = 42$.

All of the other comparisons have a product of 56.

$$14 \times 4 = 56$$

$$2 \times 28 = 56$$

$$8 \times 7 = 56$$

24. 3,200, 3,300: TEKS Standard (3.2)(C)

3,209 is greater than 3,200 and less than 3,300.

$$3{,}200 < 3{,}209 < 3{,}300$$

25. A: TEKS Standard (3.4)(A)

The car starts with a value of \$1,000 and reduces by \$800 over four years. To find the new value, subtract \$800 from \$1,000. \$1,000 − \$800 = \$200. The car is worth \$200 in the year 2022.

26. Appalachian Trail, Pacific Crest Trail, least, greatest: TEKS Standard (3.2)(D)

The three distances are 2,651 miles, 702 miles, and 2,193 miles. In order to arrange these from least to greatest, each place value needs to be compared. 702 has no digit in the thousands place, so it is the smallest distance. Now, compare 2,651 and 2,193. Both have a 2 in the thousands place, but 2,651 has a 6 in the hundreds place and 2,193 has a 1 in the hundreds place. This means 2,193 is smaller than 2,651. The distances from least to greatest are 702 miles, Great Divide Trail; 2,193 miles, Appalachian Trail; and then 2,651 miles, Pacific Crest Trail.

27. TEKS Standard (3.6)(E)

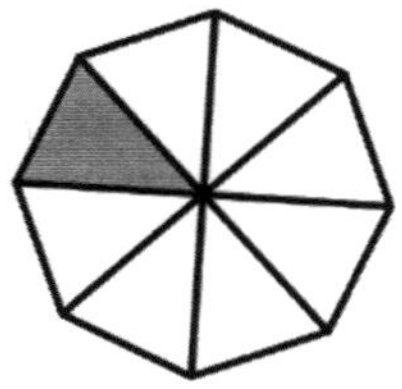

A unit fraction always has a numerator of 1. Unit fractions represent one share of the total. In this case, one piece out of 8 total pieces. The model shows the unit fraction $\frac{1}{8}$.

28. D: TEKS Standard (3.9)(A)

Human capital is skills or knowledge relevant to a specific job. When a person has specialized skills or a solid education related to the job, they are desirable to employers because they can add value to the company or business. Striving for a specialized education, gaining specialized skills, and having abilities related to a position can help workers earn more income. Companies want to reward highly skilled workers with incomes that will ensure that they stay with the company or business.

29. 6, 12: TEKS Standard (3.5)(E)

The rule that is expressed in the first two rows of the table is "add 5". Each output is 5 more than the corresponding input. The missing outputs are 6 and 12.

$$1 + 5 = 6$$

$$7 + 5 = 12$$

Input	Output
3	8
12	17
1	6
7	12

30. C: TEKS Standard (3.4)(K)

Fact families relate multiplication and division. A fact family consist of the same 3 numbers, and creates 2 multiplication equations and 2 division equations. For example, $48 \div 8 = 6$,

$48 \div 6 = 8$, $6 \times 8 = 48$, and $8 \times 6 = 48$ create a fact family. Multiplication can be used to solve division problems using fact families. $6 \times 8 = 48$, which means the missing number in $48 \div 8 =$ ___ is 6.

Practice Test #3

1. Which equation represents one way to calculate the area of the composite figure?

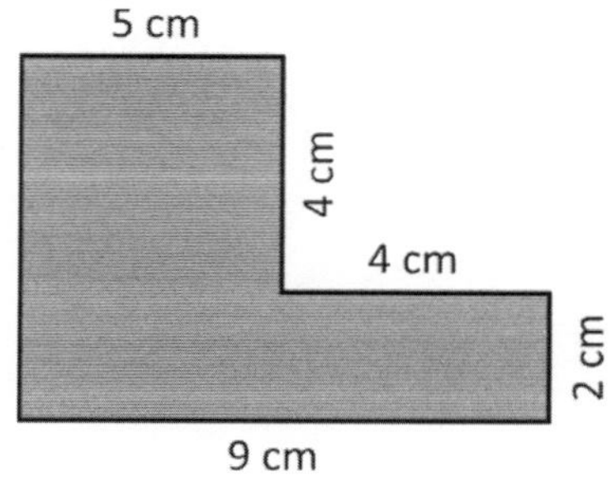

a. $(9 \times 4) + (4 \times 2) = 44$
b. $(5 \times 9) + (4 \times 2) = 53$
c. $(6 \times 5) + (9 \times 3) = 57$
d. $(4 \times 5) + (9 \times 2) = 38$

2. The amount of money below is $_____. Write your answer in the blank below.

3. A group of friends have calculated their combined total height. One friend is 60 inches, one friend is 58 inches, and one friend is 46 inches. What is the total height of the friends? Write your answer in the blank below.

inches

4. Write a division equation to match the model below.

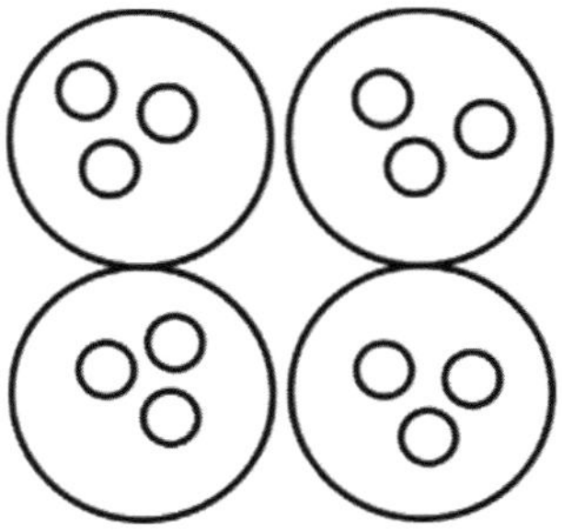

a. $12 \div 4 = 3$
b. $3 \times 4 \times 2 = 24$
c. $12 \div 3 = 5$
d. $4 \div 3 = 12$

5. Describe the rule expressed in the table below.

Input	Output
30	3
100	10
50	5
90	9
80	8

a. Divide the input by 2 to determine the output.
b. Divide the input by 3 to determine the output.
c. Divide the input by 9 to determine the output.
d. Divide the input by 10 to determine the output.

6. Ryan calculates the product of 12 and 4 by setting up the following equation: $12 \times 4 = (10 \times 4) + (2 \times 4)$. What strategy is Ryan using?

a. Repeated addition
b. The distributive property
c. The standard algorithm
d. Using an array

7. Which two choices show an incorrect way to express the number 24? Select all that apply.

a. 4 groups of 5
b. 4 groups of 6
c. $6 + 6 + 6 + 6$
d. $4 + 4 + 4 + 4 + 4$
e. 6 groups of 4

8. A jug of juice holds $\frac{6}{8}$ of a liter. The juice needs to be shared equally by two people. What fraction shows what portion of a liter of juice each person should get?

Create the correct fraction by choosing a number from 1 through 10 for both the numerator and denominator. Write your answers in the blank below:

Numerator: ___
Denominator: ___

9. Choose the correct answer to go in each blank.

Mrs. Yang has a jar of candy that gets refilled each month. Today the jar is $\frac{6}{8}$ full. The amount of candy that is missing can be represented as a fraction in simplest form.

This fraction has a numerator of _____ and a denominator of _____.

Numerator	Denominator
1	4
4	2
3	6

10. A soccer league allows 90 total players to participate. So far, there are 63 players with 9 players on each team. If each team needs to have 9 players, how many more full teams can the league add?

a. 2 more teams
b. 3 more teams
c. 4 more teams
d. 1 more team

11. $(346 - 199) + \_\_ = 1,000$

a. 853
b. 1,147
c. 455
d. 654

12. Write the model as an expression in expanded form.

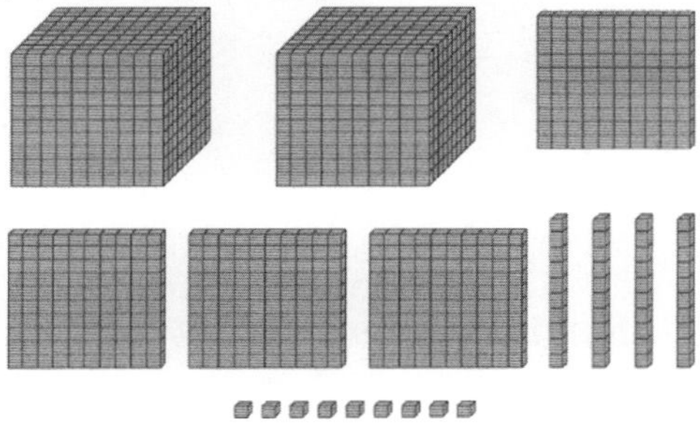

a. 2,000 + 400 + 50 + 9
b. 2,000 + 400 + 50
c. 1,000 + 400 + 50 + 9
d. 2,000 + 300 + 50 + 9

13. The model represents the fraction ____, which simplifies to the fraction ___.

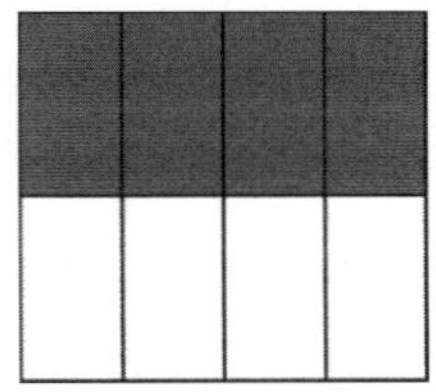

a. $\frac{8}{4}, \frac{2}{1}$
b. $\frac{8}{4}, \frac{1}{2}$
c. $\frac{4}{8}, \frac{2}{3}$
d. $\frac{4}{8}, \frac{1}{2}$

14. Circle the fraction on the number lines below that is equivalent fraction to $\frac{2}{8}$.

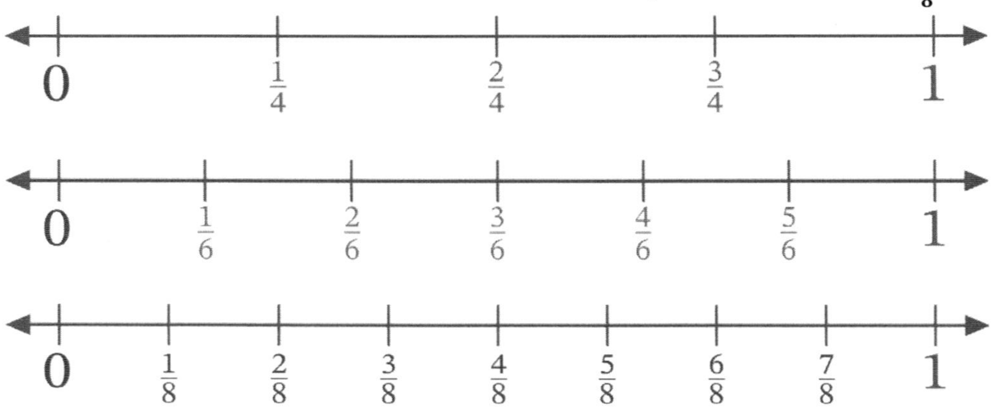

15. When you borrow money from a bank to make a large purchase, the bank will assess your _____ in order to determine if it is a good idea to loan you money. Banks do this to see how well you have paid your bills or previous loans in the past.

a. rates
b. credit
c. deductions
d. profit

16. A typical stop sign has 8 side lengths that are each 12 inches. What is the perimeter of a typical stop sign?

a. 20 inches
b. 48 inches
c. 88 inches
d. 96 inches

17. What is the missing equation in the following fact family?

$6 \times 8 = 48;\ 8 \times 6 = 48;\ 48 \div 6 = 8;$ _____

a. $48 \times 8 = 6$
b. $48 \div 2 = 24$
c. $48 \div 8 = 6$
d. $6 \times 8 = 48$

18. Is the number 138 odd or even? Explain how you know.

a. 138 is odd. 138 is 3 digits, and 3 is an odd number. Therefore, 138 is odd.
b. 138 is even. If the number in the ones place is even, then the entire number is even. 8 is in the ones place, and 8 is even. Therefore, 138 is even.
c. 138 is odd. Not all the digits are even, which means the entire number cannot be even.
d. 138 is even. If a number contains at least one digit that is even, the entire number is even.

19. Choose the correct answer to go in each blank.

Student A and B are collecting seashells at the beach. Student A collects 24 shells. Student B collects 4 shells.

__________ collected ____ times as many shells as __________.

Student A	7	Student A
Student B	6	Student B
	4	

20. 460 + _____ = 893

a. 433
b. 455
c. 403
d. 430

21. Student A states that 99,887 is greater than 101,022 because 99,887 has higher digits than 101,022. Student B states that 101,022 is greater than 99,887 due to place value. Choose the answers that make each statement correct.

Student A is ______________________________.

correct
incorrect
not clearly correct or incorrect

Student B is ______________________________.

correct
incorrect
not clearly correct or incorrect

22. Find the missing value: $4 = x \div 8$

a. $x = 32$
b. $x = 40$
c. $x = 16$
d. $x = 36$

23. Given the equation $\frac{1}{5} + \frac{1}{5} + \frac{1}{5} + \frac{1}{5} + \frac{1}{5} = 1$, what is the unit fraction in this scenario? Write your answer in the blank below.

24. The dot plot shows scores for a History Exam. Which two summaries accurately describe the data? Select all that apply.

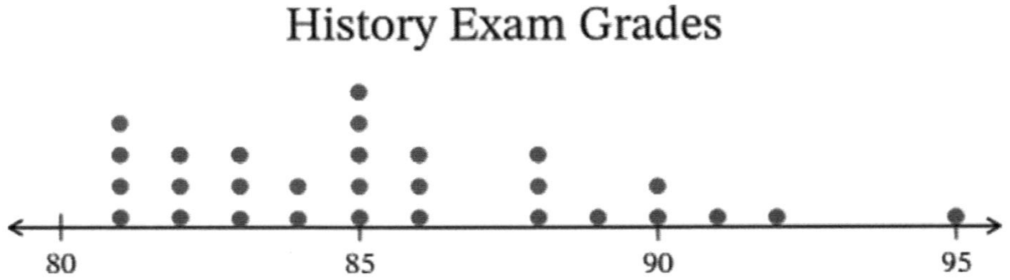

a. Two students scored higher than 95.
b. Almost all the students scored above 90.
c. Most of the students scored between, and including, 80 and 85.
d. The most common score was 85.
e. Most of the students scored between, and including, 90 and 95.

25. A cube has __ more vertices than a cylinder.

a. 5
b. 6
c. 7
d. 8

26. A rectangle with side lengths of 9 meters and _ meters will have an area of 54 square meters. Write your answer in the blank below.

27. 32 is the result of an array built from 4 columns and _ rows. Write your answer in the blank below.

28. Choose from the choices below and write the correct answers in the blanks.

$\frac{1}{6}$, ___, ___, ___

$\frac{4}{6}$ $\frac{6}{6}$ $\frac{3}{6}$

These fractions are listed from __________ to __________.

greatest	least

29. Which choice correctly describe the relationship between scarcity of resources and price?

a. A product that is scarce generally costs more than a product that is not scarce.

b. A resource that is widely available generally costs more than a scarce resource.

c. Scarcity and cost are not at all related.

d. When a resource is easily available, it is always expensive.

30. Student A practices piano 5 days a week for 15 minutes each day. Student B practices piano 4 days a week for 20 minutes each day. Which student practices piano longer each week? How much longer? Choose the answers that correctly fill each blank.

__________ practices ___ more minutes than __________.

Student A	10	Student A
Student B	5	Student B
	15	

Answer Key and Explanations for Test #3

1. D: TEKS Standard (3.6)(D)

Composite figures can be split into separate pieces to determine the total area. The composite figure in this scenario can be separated into two rectangles. The top rectangle has dimensions of 5 cm and 4 cm. The bottom rectangle has dimensions of 9 cm and 2 cm.

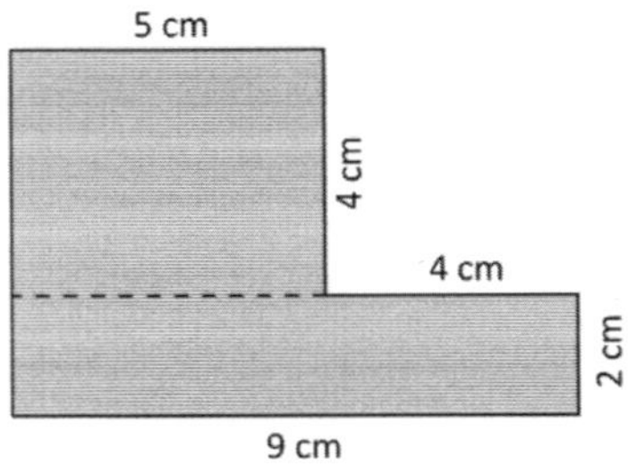

Area is calculated as length times width, so the area of each rectangle can be calculated separately. $5 \times 4 = 20$ and $9 \times 2 = 18$. The total area is $20 + 18$ which simplifies to 38 square centimeters. This is expressed as $(4 \times 5) + (9 \times 2) = 38$.

2. 13.68: TEKS Standard (3.4)(C)

There are two 5-dollar bills, three 1-dollar bills, 2 quarters, 1 dime, 1 nickel, and 3 pennies.

$$5 + 5 + 1 + 1 + 1 + 0.25 + 0.25 + 0.1 + 0.05 + 0.01 + 0.01 + 0.01 = 13.68$$

$13.68 is shown.

3. 164: TEKS Standard (3.5)(A)

Calculate the total height of the friends by adding all three heights together: $60 + 58 + 46 = 164$. Therefore, the total height of the friends is 164 inches.

4. A: TEKS Standard (3.4)(K)

There are 12 small circles. The circles are separated into 4 groups. Each group contains 3 small circles. 12 divided into 4 groups creates groups of 3. So, $12 \div 4 = 3$.

5. D: TEKS Standard (3.5)(E)

Each output value is 10 times less than the corresponding input value. This means that if an input value is divided by 10, the result will be the corresponding output value.

6. B: TEKS Standard (3.4)(G)

The distributive property breaks numbers down into their place value before multiplying. 12 becomes 10 and 2. Each of these parts is then multiplied by 4. Then, (10×4) is added to (2×4). $(10 \times 4) + (2 \times 4)$ becomes $(40) + (8)$, which simplifies to 48. So, $12 \times 4 = 48$.

7. A, D: TEKS Standard (3.4)(K)

4 groups of 5, or 5×4, is equal to 20. $4 + 4 + 4 + 4 + 4$ is also equal to 20. All the other choices are equal to 24. The choice $6 + 6 + 6 + 6$ shows the correct repeated addition for 24. The choices 4 groups of 6 and 6 groups of 4 also show correct ways to describe 24.

8. 3, 8: TEKS Standard (3.3)(E)

$\frac{6}{8}$ liter of juice is available. Since $\frac{3}{8} + \frac{3}{8} = \frac{6}{8}$, the fraction $\frac{6}{8}$ can be shared equally if each person receives $\frac{3}{8}$ liter

9. 3, 4: TEKS Standard (3.3)(F)

$\frac{6}{8}$ can be simplified by dividing the numerator and denominator by 2. Since $6 \div 2 = 3$, the numerator will be 3. Since $8 \div 2 = 4$, the denominator will be 4. $\frac{6}{8}$ simplifies to $\frac{3}{4}$.

10. B: TEKS Standard (3.5)(B)

There are currently 63 players in the league, and the maximum number of players 90. Subtract to find the difference: $90 - 63 = 27$. Since $27 \div 3 = 9$, 27 players can be divided into 3 teams with 9 players on each team. 3 more teams can be added to the league.

11. A: TEKS Standard (3.5)(A)

Simplify the parentheses first. $(346 - 199)$ simplifies to 147. Both sides of the equation need to be balanced. The right side of the equation shows 1,000. Subtract to determine what needs to be added to 147 for the sum to be 1,000. Since $1{,}000 - 147 = 853$, the missing number is 853.

12. A: TEKS Standard (3.2)(A)

Each block represents 1,000. There are two blocks so this represents 2,000. Each flat square represents 100. There are 4 flat squares so this represents 400. Each rod represents 10. There are 5 rods so this represents 50. Each small cube represents 1. There are 9 small cubes so this represents 9. When all of these values are combined, they form the expression $2{,}000 + 400 + 50 + 9$, which is in expanded form.

13. D: TEKS Standard (3.3)(A)

The model shows 4 shaded parts and 8 parts total. 4 out of 8 represents the fraction $\frac{4}{8}$. The fraction $\frac{4}{8}$ is equivalent to $\frac{1}{2}$ because $\frac{4}{8}$ becomes $\frac{1}{2}$ when both the numerator and denominator are divided by 4.

14. TEKS Standard (3.3)(F)

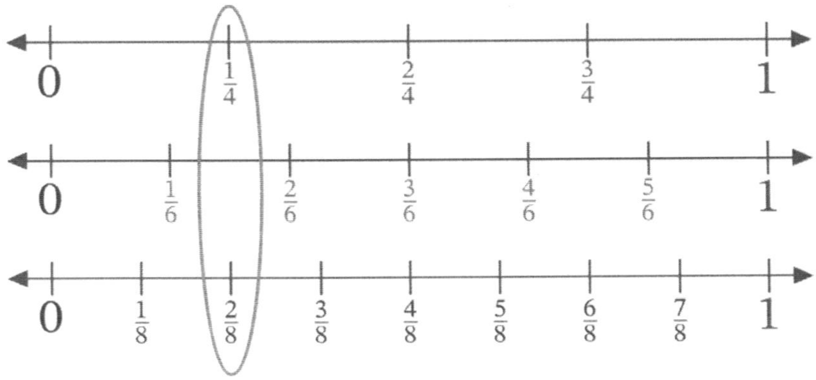

The number line shows that $\frac{2}{8}$ and $\frac{1}{4}$ are equivalent fractions because both fractions are the same distance from 0.

15. B: TEKS Standard (3.9)(D)

Good credit indicates that a person pays his or her bills on time and pays back the money he or she was loaned on time. Poor credit indicates that a person does not pay back his or her loans on time. Banks want to loan money only if they feel certain they will get their money back, plus interest.

16. D: TEKS Standard (3.7)(B)

The perimeter of the stop sign is calculated by multiplying the length of one side length by the total number of sides. In this case, one side length is 12 inches, and there are 8 sides, $12 \times 8 = 96$. The perimeter is 96 inches.

17. C: TEKS Standard (3.4)(F)

Every fact family has three numbers. Fact families can be built into two multiplication scenarios and two division scenarios. The same three numbers are used in all three scenarios. $48 \div 8 = 6$ is the missing division equation.

18. B: TEKS Standard (3.4)(I)

If the number in the ones place is even, then the entire number is even. 8 is in the ones place, and 8 is even. Therefore, 138 is even.

According to the rules of divisibility, any number with an even digit in the ones place is an even number. 138 has an 8 in the ones place, and 8 is even because it can be split into 2 equal groups, so 138 is even.

19. Student A, 6, Student B: TEKS Standard (3.5)(C)

Student A collects 24 shells, and Student B collects 4 shells. 24 is 6 times as much as 24 because $24 = 6 \times 4$. This means Student A collects 6 times as many shells as Student B.

20. A: TEKS Standard (3.4)(A)

The addition equation can be solved using subtraction.

The subtraction can be done using mental math using place value.

$$893 - 460 = \_\_\_\_\_$$

3 ones minus 0 ones equals 3 ones.

9 tens minus 6 tens equals 3 tens.

8 hundreds minus 4 hundreds equals 4 hundreds.

3 ones, 3 tens, and 4 hundreds forms the number 433.

$$893 - 460 = 433$$

21. incorrect, correct: TEKS Standard (3.2)(D)

Place value is significant when comparing and ordering numbers. Compare digits from left to right when ordering numbers. In this case, 99,887 has 0 groups of hundred-thousands, and 101,022 has 1 group of hundred-thousands. This means 99,887 is less than 101,022 even though the digits in 101,022 appear smaller.

22. A: TEKS Standard (3.5)(D)

32 divided into 8 equal groups is 4. This means that the value of x is 32.

23. $\frac{1}{5}$: TEKS Standard (3.3)(C)

Unit fractions can combine to form a whole. For example, 5 groups of $\frac{1}{5}$ is equivalent to 1 whole. So, $\frac{1}{5}+\frac{1}{5}+\frac{1}{5}+\frac{1}{5}+\frac{1}{5}=1$. In this scenario, $\frac{1}{5}$ is the unit fraction.

24. C, D: TEKS Standard (3.8)(A)

Choice C correctly summarizes the data since, "Most of the students scored between 80 and 85". There are 17 dots on the dot plot between 80 and 85. There are 29 dots altogether, so 17 represents "most of the students" because 17 is more than half of 29. Choice D is also true since the most points are placed above 85 on the graph.

25. D: TEKS Standard (3.6)(A)

A vertex is formed when the edges of a shape come together forming a corner. A cylinder has no vertices. A cube has 8 vertices. A cube has 8 more vertices than a cylinder.

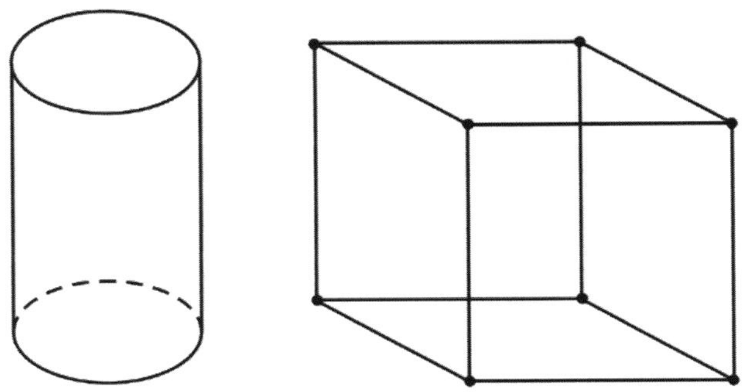

26. 6: TEKS Standard (3.6)(C)

The area of a rectangle is determined using the formula $A = l \times w$. In this case, the area A is provided. Plug in 54 for A, and 9 for l. The width w can be solved for using multiplication or division. $A = l \times w$ becomes $54 = 9 \times w$. To find w, think, "9 groups of what equals 54?" 9 groups of 6 equals 54, because $9 \times 6 = 54$. Or, $54 \div 9 = 6$. The missing width is 6 meters.

27. 8: TEKS Standard (3.4)(D)

An array is a visual model for multiplication. Arrays are built from rows and columns. 4 columns and 8 rows create 32 total units: $4 \times 8 = 32$.

28.$\frac{3}{6}, \frac{4}{6}, \frac{6}{6}$, least, greatest: TEKS Standard (3.3)(H)

If fractions have the same denominator, it means they have an equal number of total parts. If the denominators are the same, then the fraction with the larger numerator will be the larger fraction. $\frac{1}{6}, \frac{3}{6}, \frac{4}{6}, \frac{6}{6}$ shows fractions with the same denominator and numerators ordered from least to greatest.

29. A: TEKS Standard (3.9)(B)

In general, as a product or resource becomes scarce, the price increases. Similarly, products that are abundant and easily available are generally less expensive.

30. Student B, 5, Student A: TEKS Standard (3.7)(C)

Student A practices 15 minutes, for 5 days. 5 groups of 15 minutes is 75 minutes.

Student B practices 20 minutes, for 4 days. 4 groups of 20 minutes is 80 minutes.

$$75 \text{ minutes} < 80 \text{ minutes}$$

Student B practices more. Subtract to find how much more.

$$1 \text{ hour and } 20 \text{ minutes} - 1 \text{ hour and } 15 \text{ minutes}$$

$$80 \text{ minutes} - 75 \text{ minutes} = 5 \text{ minutes}$$

Student B practices piano 5 more minutes each week than Student A.

How to Overcome Test Anxiety

Just the thought of taking a test is enough to make most people a little nervous. A test is an important event that can have a long-term impact on your future, so it's important to take it seriously and it's natural to feel anxious about performing well. But just because anxiety is normal, that doesn't mean that it's helpful in test taking, or that you should simply accept it as part of your life. Anxiety can have a variety of effects. These effects can be mild, like making you feel slightly nervous, or severe, like blocking your ability to focus or remember even a simple detail.

If you experience test anxiety—whether severe or mild—it's important to know how to beat it. To discover this, first you need to understand what causes test anxiety.

Causes of Test Anxiety

While we often think of anxiety as an uncontrollable emotional state, it can actually be caused by simple, practical things. One of the most common causes of test anxiety is that a person does not feel adequately prepared for their test. This feeling can be the result of many different issues such as poor study habits or lack of organization, but the most common culprit is time management. Starting to study too late, failing to organize your study time to cover all of the material, or being distracted while you study will mean that you're not well prepared for the test. This may lead to cramming the night before, which will cause you to be physically and mentally exhausted for the test. Poor time management also contributes to feelings of stress, fear, and hopelessness as you realize you are not well prepared but don't know what to do about it.

Other times, test anxiety is not related to your preparation for the test but comes from unresolved fear. This may be a past failure on a test, or poor performance on tests in general. It may come from comparing yourself to others who seem to be performing better or from the stress of living up to expectations. Anxiety may be driven by fears of the future—how failure on this test would affect your educational and career goals. These fears are often completely irrational, but they can still negatively impact your test performance.

Elements of Test Anxiety

As mentioned earlier, test anxiety is considered to be an emotional state, but it has physical and mental components as well. Sometimes you may not even realize that you are suffering from test anxiety until you notice the physical symptoms. These can include trembling hands, rapid heartbeat, sweating, nausea, and tense muscles. Extreme anxiety may lead to fainting or vomiting. Obviously, any of these symptoms can have a negative impact on testing. It is important to recognize them as soon as they begin to occur so that you can address the problem before it damages your performance.

The mental components of test anxiety include trouble focusing and inability to remember learned information. During a test, your mind is on high alert, which can help you recall information and stay focused for an extended period of time. However, anxiety interferes with your mind's natural processes, causing you to blank out, even on the questions you know well. The strain of testing during anxiety makes it difficult to stay focused, especially on a test that may take several hours. Extreme anxiety can take a huge mental toll, making it difficult not only to recall test information but even to understand the test questions or pull your thoughts together.

Effects of Test Anxiety

Test anxiety is like a disease—if left untreated, it will get progressively worse. Anxiety leads to poor performance, and this reinforces the feelings of fear and failure, which in turn lead to poor performances on subsequent tests. It can grow from a mild nervousness to a crippling condition. If allowed to progress, test anxiety can have a big impact on your schooling, and consequently on your future.

Test anxiety can spread to other parts of your life. Anxiety on tests can become anxiety in any stressful situation, and blanking on a test can turn into panicking in a job situation. But fortunately, you don't have to let anxiety rule your testing and determine your grades. There are a number of relatively simple steps you can take to move past anxiety and function normally on a test and in the rest of life.

Physical Steps for Beating Test Anxiety

While test anxiety is a serious problem, the good news is that it can be overcome. It doesn't have to control your ability to think and remember information. While it may take time, you can begin taking steps today to beat anxiety.

Just as your first hint that you may be struggling with anxiety comes from the physical symptoms, the first step to treating it is also physical. Rest is crucial for having a clear, strong mind. If you are tired, it is much easier to give in to anxiety. But if you establish good sleep habits, your body and mind will be ready to perform optimally, without the strain of exhaustion. Additionally, sleeping well helps you to retain information better, so you're more likely to recall the answers when you see the test questions.

Getting good sleep means more than going to bed on time. It's important to allow your brain time to relax. Take study breaks from time to time so it doesn't get overworked, and don't study right before bed. Take time to rest your mind before trying to rest your body, or you may find it difficult to fall asleep.

Along with sleep, other aspects of physical health are important in preparing for a test. Good nutrition is vital for good brain function. Sugary foods and drinks may give a burst of energy but this burst is followed by a crash, both physically and emotionally. Instead, fuel your body with protein and vitamin-rich foods.

Also, drink plenty of water. Dehydration can lead to headaches and exhaustion, especially if your brain is already under stress from the rigors of the test. Particularly if your test is a long one, drink water during the breaks. And if possible, take an energy-boosting snack to eat between sections.

Along with sleep and diet, a third important part of physical health is exercise. Maintaining a steady workout schedule is helpful, but even taking 5-minute study breaks to walk can help get your blood pumping faster and clear your head. Exercise also releases endorphins, which contribute to a positive feeling and can help combat test anxiety.

When you nurture your physical health, you are also contributing to your mental health. If your body is healthy, your mind is much more likely to be healthy as well. So take time to rest, nourish your body with healthy food and water, and get moving as much as possible. Taking these physical steps will make you stronger and more able to take the mental steps necessary to overcome test anxiety.

Mental Steps for Beating Test Anxiety

Working on the mental side of test anxiety can be more challenging, but as with the physical side, there are clear steps you can take to overcome it. As mentioned earlier, test anxiety often stems from lack of preparation, so the obvious solution is to prepare for the test. Effective studying may be the most important weapon you have for beating test anxiety, but you can and should employ several other mental tools to combat fear.

First, boost your confidence by reminding yourself of past success—tests or projects that you aced. If you're putting as much effort into preparing for this test as you did for those, there's no reason you should expect to fail here. Work hard to prepare; then trust your preparation.

Second, surround yourself with encouraging people. It can be helpful to find a study group, but be sure that the people you're around will encourage a positive attitude. If you spend time with others who are anxious or cynical, this will only contribute to your own anxiety. Look for others who are motivated to study hard from a desire to succeed, not from a fear of failure.

Third, reward yourself. A test is physically and mentally tiring, even without anxiety, and it can be helpful to have something to look forward to. Plan an activity following the test, regardless of the outcome, such as going to a movie or getting ice cream.

When you are taking the test, if you find yourself beginning to feel anxious, remind yourself that you know the material. Visualize successfully completing the test. Then take a few deep, relaxing breaths and return to it. Work through the questions carefully but with confidence, knowing that you are capable of succeeding.

Developing a healthy mental approach to test taking will also aid in other areas of life. Test anxiety affects more than just the actual test—it can be damaging to your mental health and even contribute to depression. It's important to beat test anxiety before it becomes a problem for more than testing.

Study Strategy

Being prepared for the test is necessary to combat anxiety, but what does being prepared look like? You may study for hours on end and still not feel prepared. What you need is a strategy for test prep. The next few pages outline our recommended steps to help you plan out and conquer the challenge of preparation.

Step 1: Scope Out the Test

Learn everything you can about the format (multiple choice, essay, etc.) and what will be on the test. Gather any study materials, course outlines, or sample exams that may be available. Not only will this help you to prepare, but knowing what to expect can help to alleviate test anxiety.

Step 2: Map Out the Material

Look through the textbook or study guide and make note of how many chapters or sections it has. Then divide these over the time you have. For example, if a book has 15 chapters and you have five days to study, you need to cover three chapters each day. Even better, if you have the time, leave an extra day at the end for overall review after you have gone through the material in depth.

If time is limited, you may need to prioritize the material. Look through it and make note of which sections you think you already have a good grasp on, and which need review. While you are studying, skim quickly through the familiar sections and take more time on the challenging parts.

Write out your plan so you don't get lost as you go. Having a written plan also helps you feel more in control of the study, so anxiety is less likely to arise from feeling overwhelmed at the amount to cover.

Step 3: Gather Your Tools

Decide what study method works best for you. Do you prefer to highlight in the book as you study and then go back over the highlighted portions? Or do you type out notes of the important information? Or is it helpful to make flashcards that you can carry with you? Assemble the pens, index cards, highlighters, post-it notes, and any other materials you may need so you won't be distracted by getting up to find things while you study.

If you're having a hard time retaining the information or organizing your notes, experiment with different methods. For example, try color-coding by subject with colored pens, highlighters, or post-it notes. If you learn better by hearing, try recording yourself reading your notes so you can listen while in the car, working out, or simply sitting at your desk. Ask a friend to quiz you from your flashcards, or try teaching someone the material to solidify it in your mind.

Step 4: Create Your Environment

It's important to avoid distractions while you study. This includes both the obvious distractions like visitors and the subtle distractions like an uncomfortable chair (or a too-comfortable couch that makes you want to fall asleep). Set up the best study environment possible: good lighting and a comfortable work area. If background music helps you focus, you may want to turn it on, but otherwise keep the room quiet. If you are using a computer to take notes, be sure you don't have any other windows open, especially applications like social media, games, or anything else that could distract you. Silence your phone and turn off notifications. Be sure to keep water close by so you stay hydrated while you study (but avoid unhealthy drinks and snacks).

Also, take into account the best time of day to study. Are you freshest first thing in the morning? Try to set aside some time then to work through the material. Is your mind clearer in the afternoon or evening? Schedule your study session then. Another method is to study at the same time of day that you will take the test, so that your brain gets used to working on the material at that time and will be ready to focus at test time.

Step 5: Study!

Once you have done all the study preparation, it's time to settle into the actual studying. Sit down, take a few moments to settle your mind so you can focus, and begin to follow your study plan. Don't give in to distractions or let yourself procrastinate. This is your time to prepare so you'll be ready to fearlessly approach the test. Make the most of the time and stay focused.

Of course, you don't want to burn out. If you study too long you may find that you're not retaining the information very well. Take regular study breaks. For example, taking five minutes out of every hour to walk briskly, breathing deeply and swinging your arms, can help your mind stay fresh.

As you get to the end of each chapter or section, it's a good idea to do a quick review. Remind yourself of what you learned and work on any difficult parts. When you feel that you've mastered the material, move on to the next part. At the end of your study session, briefly skim through your notes again.

But while review is helpful, cramming last minute is NOT. If at all possible, work ahead so that you won't need to fit all your study into the last day. Cramming overloads your brain with more information than it can process and retain, and your tired mind may struggle to recall even previously learned information when it is overwhelmed with last-minute study. Also, the urgent nature of cramming and the stress placed on your brain contribute to anxiety. You'll be more likely to go to the test feeling unprepared and having trouble thinking clearly.

So don't cram, and don't stay up late before the test, even just to review your notes at a leisurely pace. Your brain needs rest more than it needs to go over the information again. In fact, plan to finish your studies by noon or early afternoon the day before the test. Give your brain the rest of the day to relax or focus on other things, and get a good night's sleep. Then you will be fresh for the test and better able to recall what you've studied.

Step 6: Take a Practice Test

Many courses offer sample tests, either online or in the study materials. This is an excellent resource to check whether you have mastered the material, as well as to prepare for the test format and environment.

Check the test format ahead of time: the number of questions, the type (multiple choice, free response, etc.), and the time limit. Then create a plan for working through them. For example, if you have 30 minutes to take a 60-question test, your limit is 30 seconds per question. Spend less time on the questions you know well so that you can take more time on the difficult ones.

If you have time to take several practice tests, take the first one open book, with no time limit. Work through the questions at your own pace and make sure you fully understand them. Gradually work up to taking a test under test conditions: sit at a desk with all study materials put away and set a timer. Pace yourself to make sure you finish the test with time to spare and go back to check your answers if you have time.

After each test, check your answers. On the questions you missed, be sure you understand why you missed them. Did you misread the question (tests can use tricky wording)? Did you forget the information? Or was it something you hadn't learned? Go back and study any shaky areas that the practice tests reveal.

Taking these tests not only helps with your grade, but also aids in combating test anxiety. If you're already used to the test conditions, you're less likely to worry about it, and working through tests until you're scoring well gives you a confidence boost. Go through the practice tests until you feel comfortable, and then you can go into the test knowing that you're ready for it.

Test Tips

On test day, you should be confident, knowing that you've prepared well and are ready to answer the questions. But aside from preparation, there are several test day strategies you can employ to maximize your performance.

First, as stated before, get a good night's sleep the night before the test (and for several nights before that, if possible). Go into the test with a fresh, alert mind rather than staying up late to study.

Try not to change too much about your normal routine on the day of the test. It's important to eat a nutritious breakfast, but if you normally don't eat breakfast at all, consider eating just a protein bar. If you're a coffee drinker, go ahead and have your normal coffee. Just make sure you time it so that the caffeine doesn't wear off right in the middle of your test. Avoid sugary beverages, and drink enough water to stay hydrated but not so much that you need a restroom break 10 minutes into the test. If your test isn't first thing in the morning, consider going for a walk or doing a light workout before the test to get your blood flowing.

Allow yourself enough time to get ready, and leave for the test with plenty of time to spare so you won't have the anxiety of scrambling to arrive in time. Another reason to be early is to select a good seat. It's helpful to sit away from doors and windows, which can be distracting. Find a good seat, get out your supplies, and settle your mind before the test begins.

When the test begins, start by going over the instructions carefully, even if you already know what to expect. Make sure you avoid any careless mistakes by following the directions.

Then begin working through the questions, pacing yourself as you've practiced. If you're not sure on an answer, don't spend too much time on it, and don't let it shake your confidence. Either skip it and come back later, or eliminate as many wrong answers as possible and guess among the remaining ones. Don't dwell on these questions as you continue—put them out of your mind and focus on what lies ahead.

Be sure to read all of the answer choices, even if you're sure the first one is the right answer. Sometimes you'll find a better one if you keep reading. But don't second-guess yourself if you do immediately know the answer. Your gut instinct is usually right. Don't let test anxiety rob you of the information you know.

If you have time at the end of the test (and if the test format allows), go back and review your answers. Be cautious about changing any, since your first instinct tends to be correct, but make sure you didn't misread any of the questions or accidentally mark the wrong answer choice. Look over any you skipped and make an educated guess.

At the end, leave the test feeling confident. You've done your best, so don't waste time worrying about your performance or wishing you could change anything. Instead, celebrate the successful completion of this test. And finally, use this test to learn how to deal with anxiety even better next time.

Review Video: Test Anxiety
Visit mometrix.com/academy and enter code: 100340

Important Qualification

Not all anxiety is created equal. If your test anxiety is causing major issues in your life beyond the classroom or testing center, or if you are experiencing troubling physical symptoms related to your anxiety, it may be a sign of a serious physiological or psychological condition. If this sounds like your situation, we strongly encourage you to seek professional help.

Online Resources

Due to our efforts to try to keep this book to a manageable length, we've created a link that will give you access to all of your online resources:

mometrix.com/resources719/staarg3math

It's Your Moment, Let's Celebrate It!

Share your story @mometrixtestpreparation

Mometrix
TEST PREPARATION

MTEL®

Reading Specialist (62) Secrets Study Guide

DEAR FUTURE EXAM SUCCESS STORY

First of all, **THANK YOU** for purchasing Mometrix study materials!

Second, congratulations! You are one of the few determined test-takers who are committed to doing whatever it takes to excel on your exam. **You have come to the right place.** We developed these study materials with one goal in mind: to deliver you the information you need in a format that's concise and easy to use.

In addition to optimizing your guide for the content of the test, we've outlined our recommended steps for breaking down the preparation process into small, attainable goals so you can make sure you stay on track.

We've also analyzed the entire test-taking process, identifying the most common pitfalls and showing how you can overcome them and be ready for any curveball the test throws you.

Standardized testing is one of the biggest obstacles on your road to success, which only increases the importance of doing well in the high-pressure, high-stakes environment of test day. Your results on this test could have a significant impact on your future, and this guide provides the information and practical advice to help you achieve your full potential on test day.

Your success is our success

We would love to hear from you! If you would like to share the story of your exam success or if you have any questions or comments in regard to our products, please contact us at **800-673-8175** or **support@mometrix.com**.

Thanks again for your business and we wish you continued success!

Sincerely,
The Mometrix Test Preparation Team

Need more help? Check out our flashcards at:
http://MometrixFlashcards.com/MTEL

Written and edited by the Mometrix Exam Secrets Test Prep Team
Printed in the United States of America

TABLE OF CONTENTS

Introduction

Thank you for purchasing this resource! You have made the choice to prepare yourself for a test that could have a huge impact on your future, and this guide is designed to help you be fully ready for test day. Obviously, it's important to have a solid understanding of the test material, but you also need to be prepared for the unique environment and stressors of the test, so that you can perform to the best of your abilities.

For this purpose, the first section that appears in this guide is the **Secret Keys**. We've devoted countless hours to meticulously researching what works and what doesn't, and we've boiled down our findings to the five most impactful steps you can take to improve your performance on the test. We start at the beginning with study planning and move through the preparation process, all the way to the testing strategies that will help you get the most out of what you know when you're finally sitting in front of the test.

We recommend that you start preparing for your test as far in advance as possible. However, if you've bought this guide as a last-minute study resource and only have a few days before your test, we recommend that you skip over the first two Secret Keys since they address a long-term study plan.

If you struggle with **test anxiety**, we strongly encourage you to check out our recommendations for how you can overcome it. Test anxiety is a formidable foe, but it can be beaten, and we want to make sure you have the tools you need to defeat it.

Secret Key #1 – Plan Big, Study Small

There's a lot riding on your performance. If you want to ace this test, you're going to need to keep your skills sharp and the material fresh in your mind. You need a plan that lets you review everything you need to know while still fitting in your schedule. We'll break this strategy down into three categories.

Information Organization

Start with the information you already have: the official test outline. From this, you can make a complete list of all the concepts you need to cover before the test. Organize these concepts into groups that can be studied together, and create a list of any related vocabulary you need to learn so you can brush up on any difficult terms. You'll want to keep this vocabulary list handy once you actually start studying since you may need to add to it along the way.

Time Management

Once you have your set of study concepts, decide how to spread them out over the time you have left before the test. Break your study plan into small, clear goals so you have a manageable task for each day and know exactly what you're doing. Then just focus on one small step at a time. When you manage your time this way, you don't need to spend hours at a time studying. Studying a small block of content for a short period each day helps you retain information better and avoid stressing over how much you have left to do. You can relax knowing that you have a plan to cover everything in time. In order for this strategy to be effective though, you have to start studying early and stick to your schedule. Avoid the exhaustion and futility that comes from last-minute cramming!

Study Environment

The environment you study in has a big impact on your learning. Studying in a coffee shop, while probably more enjoyable, is not likely to be as fruitful as studying in a quiet room. It's important to keep distractions to a minimum. You're only planning to study for a short block of time, so make the most of it. Don't pause to check your phone or get up to find a snack. It's also important to **avoid multitasking**. Research has consistently shown that multitasking will make your studying dramatically less effective. Your study area should also be comfortable and well-lit so you don't have the distraction of straining your eyes or sitting on an uncomfortable chair.

The time of day you study is also important. You want to be rested and alert. Don't wait until just before bedtime. Study when you'll be most likely to comprehend and remember. Even better, if you know what time of day your test will be, set that time aside for study. That way your brain will be used to working on that subject at that specific time and you'll have a better chance of recalling information.

Finally, it can be helpful to team up with others who are studying for the same test. Your actual studying should be done in as isolated an environment as possible, but the work of organizing the information and setting up the study plan can be divided up. In between study sessions, you can discuss with your teammates the concepts that you're all studying and quiz each other on the details. Just be sure that your teammates are as serious about the test as you are. If you find that your study time is being replaced with social time, you might need to find a new team.

Secret Key #2 – Make Your Studying Count

You're devoting a lot of time and effort to preparing for this test, so you want to be absolutely certain it will pay off. This means doing more than just reading the content and hoping you can remember it on test day. It's important to make every minute of study count. There are two main areas you can focus on to make your studying count.

Retention

It doesn't matter how much time you study if you can't remember the material. You need to make sure you are retaining the concepts. To check your retention of the information you're learning, try recalling it at later times with minimal prompting. Try carrying around flashcards and glance at one or two from time to time or ask a friend who's also studying for the test to quiz you.

To enhance your retention, look for ways to put the information into practice so that you can apply it rather than simply recalling it. If you're using the information in practical ways, it will be much easier to remember. Similarly, it helps to solidify a concept in your mind if you're not only reading it to yourself but also explaining it to someone else. Ask a friend to let you teach them about a concept you're a little shaky on (or speak aloud to an imaginary audience if necessary). As you try to summarize, define, give examples, and answer your friend's questions, you'll understand the concepts better and they will stay with you longer. Finally, step back for a big picture view and ask yourself how each piece of information fits with the whole subject. When you link the different concepts together and see them working together as a whole, it's easier to remember the individual components.

Finally, practice showing your work on any multi-step problems, even if you're just studying. Writing out each step you take to solve a problem will help solidify the process in your mind, and you'll be more likely to remember it during the test.

Modality

Modality simply refers to the means or method by which you study. Choosing a study modality that fits your own individual learning style is crucial. No two people learn best in exactly the same way, so it's important to know your strengths and use them to your advantage.

For example, if you learn best by visualization, focus on visualizing a concept in your mind and draw an image or a diagram. Try color-coding your notes, illustrating them, or creating symbols that will trigger your mind to recall a learned concept. If you learn best by hearing or discussing information, find a study partner who learns the same way or read aloud to yourself. Think about how to put the information in your own words. Imagine that you are giving a lecture on the topic and record yourself so you can listen to it later.

For any learning style, flashcards can be helpful. Organize the information so you can take advantage of spare moments to review. Underline key words or phrases. Use different colors for different categories. Mnemonic devices (such as creating a short list in which every item starts with the same letter) can also help with retention. Find what works best for you and use it to store the information in your mind most effectively and easily.

Secret Key #3 – Practice the Right Way

Your success on test day depends not only on how many hours you put into preparing, but also on whether you prepared the right way. It's good to check along the way to see if your studying is paying off. One of the most effective ways to do this is by taking practice tests to evaluate your progress. Practice tests are useful because they show exactly where you need to improve. Every time you take a practice test, pay special attention to these three groups of questions:

- The questions you got wrong
- The questions you had to guess on, even if you guessed right
- The questions you found difficult or slow to work through

This will show you exactly what your weak areas are, and where you need to devote more study time. Ask yourself why each of these questions gave you trouble. Was it because you didn't understand the material? Was it because you didn't remember the vocabulary? Do you need more repetitions on this type of question to build speed and confidence? Dig into those questions and figure out how you can strengthen your weak areas as you go back to review the material.

Additionally, many practice tests have a section explaining the answer choices. It can be tempting to read the explanation and think that you now have a good understanding of the concept. However, an explanation likely only covers part of the question's broader context. Even if the explanation makes perfect sense, **go back and investigate** every concept related to the question until you're positive you have a thorough understanding.

As you go along, keep in mind that the practice test is just that: practice. Memorizing these questions and answers will not be very helpful on the actual test because it is unlikely to have any of the same exact questions. If you only know the right answers to the sample questions, you won't be prepared for the real thing. **Study the concepts** until you understand them fully, and then you'll be able to answer any question that shows up on the test.

It's important to wait on the practice tests until you're ready. If you take a test on your first day of study, you may be overwhelmed by the amount of material covered and how much you need to learn. Work up to it gradually.

On test day, you'll need to be prepared for answering questions, managing your time, and using the test-taking strategies you've learned. It's a lot to balance, like a mental marathon that will have a big impact on your future. Like training for a marathon, you'll need to start slowly and work your way up. When test day arrives, you'll be ready.

Start with the strategies you've read in the first two Secret Keys—plan your course and study in the way that works best for you. If you have time, consider using multiple study resources to get different approaches to the same concepts. It can be helpful to see difficult concepts from more than one angle. Then find a good source for practice tests. Many times, the test website will suggest potential study resources or provide sample tests.

Practice Test Strategy

If you're able to find at least three practice tests, we recommend this strategy:

Untimed and Open-Book Practice

Take the first test with no time constraints and with your notes and study guide handy. Take your time and focus on applying the strategies you've learned.

Timed and Open-Book Practice

Take the second practice test open-book as well, but set a timer and practice pacing yourself to finish in time.

Timed and Closed-Book Practice

Take any other practice tests as if it were test day. Set a timer and put away your study materials. Sit at a table or desk in a quiet room, imagine yourself at the testing center, and answer questions as quickly and accurately as possible.

Keep repeating timed and closed-book tests on a regular basis until you run out of practice tests or it's time for the actual test. Your mind will be ready for the schedule and stress of test day, and you'll be able to focus on recalling the material you've learned.

Secret Key #4 – Pace Yourself

Once you're fully prepared for the material on the test, your biggest challenge on test day will be managing your time. Just knowing that the clock is ticking can make you panic even if you have plenty of time left. Work on pacing yourself so you can build confidence against the time constraints of the exam. Pacing is a difficult skill to master, especially in a high-pressure environment, so **practice is vital**.

Set time expectations for your pace based on how much time is available. For example, if a section has 60 questions and the time limit is 30 minutes, you know you have to average 30 seconds or less per question in order to answer them all. Although 30 seconds is the hard limit, set 25 seconds per question as your goal, so you reserve extra time to spend on harder questions. When you budget extra time for the harder questions, you no longer have any reason to stress when those questions take longer to answer.

Don't let this time expectation distract you from working through the test at a calm, steady pace, but keep it in mind so you don't spend too much time on any one question. Recognize that taking extra time on one question you don't understand may keep you from answering two that you do understand later in the test. If your time limit for a question is up and you're still not sure of the answer, mark it and move on, and come back to it later if the time and the test format allow. If the testing format doesn't allow you to return to earlier questions, just make an educated guess; then put it out of your mind and move on.

On the easier questions, be careful not to rush. It may seem wise to hurry through them so you have more time for the challenging ones, but it's not worth missing one if you know the concept and just didn't take the time to read the question fully. Work efficiently but make sure you understand the question and have looked at all of the answer choices, since more than one may seem right at first.

Even if you're paying attention to the time, you may find yourself a little behind at some point. You should speed up to get back on track, but do so wisely. Don't panic; just take a few seconds less on each question until you're caught up. Don't guess without thinking, but do look through the answer choices and eliminate any you know are wrong. If you can get down to two choices, it is often worthwhile to guess from those. Once you've chosen an answer, move on and don't dwell on any that you skipped or had to hurry through. If a question was taking too long, chances are it was one of the harder ones, so you weren't as likely to get it right anyway.

On the other hand, if you find yourself getting ahead of schedule, it may be beneficial to slow down a little. The more quickly you work, the more likely you are to make a careless mistake that will affect your score. You've budgeted time for each question, so don't be afraid to spend that time. Practice an efficient but careful pace to get the most out of the time you have.

Secret Key #5 – Have a Plan for Guessing

When you're taking the test, you may find yourself stuck on a question. Some of the answer choices seem better than others, but you don't see the one answer choice that is obviously correct. What do you do?

The scenario described above is very common, yet most test takers have not effectively prepared for it. Developing and practicing a plan for guessing may be one of the single most effective uses of your time as you get ready for the exam.

In developing your plan for guessing, there are three questions to address:

- When should you start the guessing process?
- How should you narrow down the choices?
- Which answer should you choose?

When to Start the Guessing Process

Unless your plan for guessing is to select C every time (which, despite its merits, is not what we recommend), you need to leave yourself enough time to apply your answer elimination strategies. Since you have a limited amount of time for each question, that means that if you're going to give yourself the best shot at guessing correctly, you have to decide quickly whether or not you will guess.

Of course, the best-case scenario is that you don't have to guess at all, so first, see if you can answer the question based on your knowledge of the subject and basic reasoning skills. Focus on the key words in the question and try to jog your memory of related topics. Give yourself a chance to bring the knowledge to mind, but once you realize that you don't have (or you can't access) the knowledge you need to answer the question, it's time to start the guessing process.

It's almost always better to start the guessing process too early than too late. It only takes a few seconds to remember something and answer the question from knowledge. Carefully eliminating wrong answer choices takes longer. Plus, going through the process of eliminating answer choices can actually help jog your memory.

Summary: Start the guessing process as soon as you decide that you can't answer the question based on your knowledge.

How to Narrow Down the Choices

The next chapter in this book (**Test-Taking Strategies**) includes a wide range of strategies for how to approach questions and how to look for answer choices to eliminate. You will definitely want to read those carefully, practice them, and figure out which ones work best for you. Here though, we're going to address a mindset rather than a particular strategy.

Your odds of guessing an answer correctly depend on how many options you are choosing from.

Number of options left	5	4	3	2	1
Odds of guessing correctly	20%	25%	33%	50%	100%

You can see from this chart just how valuable it is to be able to eliminate incorrect answers and make an educated guess, but there are two things that many test takers do that cause them to miss out on the benefits of guessing:

- Accidentally eliminating the correct answer
- Selecting an answer based on an impression

We'll look at the first one here, and the second one in the next section.

To avoid accidentally eliminating the correct answer, we recommend a thought exercise called **the $5 challenge**. In this challenge, you only eliminate an answer choice from contention if you are willing to bet $5 on it being wrong. Why $5? Five dollars is a small but not insignificant amount of money. It's an amount you could afford to lose but wouldn't want to throw away. And while losing $5 once might not hurt too much, doing it twenty times will set you back $100. In the same way, each small decision you make—eliminating a choice here, guessing on a question there—won't by itself impact your score very much, but when you put them all together, they can make a big difference. By holding each answer choice elimination decision to a higher standard, you can reduce the risk of accidentally eliminating the correct answer.

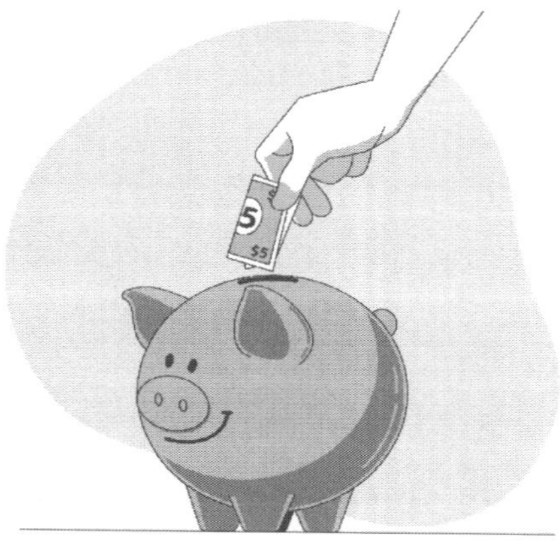

The $5 challenge can also be applied in a positive sense: If you are willing to bet $5 that an answer choice *is* correct, go ahead and mark it as correct.

Summary: Only eliminate an answer choice if you are willing to bet $5 that it is wrong.

Which Answer to Choose

You're taking the test. You've run into a hard question and decided you'll have to guess. You've eliminated all the answer choices you're willing to bet $5 on. Now you have to pick an answer. Why do we even need to talk about this? Why can't you just pick whichever one you feel like when the time comes?

The answer to these questions is that if you don't come into the test with a plan, you'll rely on your impression to select an answer choice, and if you do that, you risk falling into a trap. The test writers know that everyone who takes their test will be guessing on some of the questions, so they intentionally write wrong answer choices to seem plausible. You still have to pick an answer though, and if the wrong answer choices are designed to look right, how can you ever be sure that you're not falling for their trap? The best solution we've found to this dilemma is to take the decision out of your hands entirely. Here is the process we recommend:

Once you've eliminated any choices that you are confident (willing to bet $5) are wrong, select the first remaining choice as your answer.

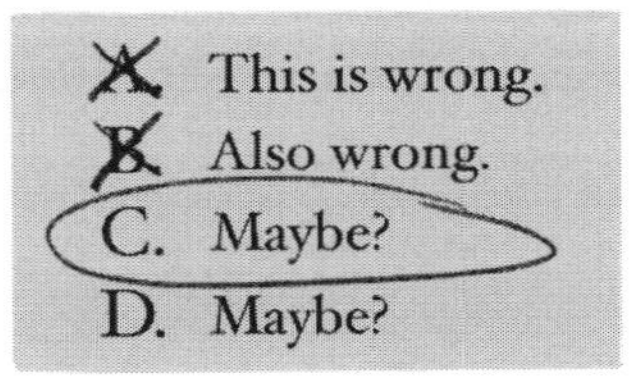

Whether you choose to select the first remaining choice, the second, or the last, the important thing is that you use some preselected standard. Using this approach guarantees that you will not be enticed into selecting an answer choice that looks right, because you are not basing your decision on how the answer choices look.

This is not meant to make you question your knowledge. Instead, it is to help you recognize the difference between your knowledge and your impressions. There's a huge difference between thinking an answer is right because of what you know, and thinking an answer is right because it looks or sounds like it should be right.

Summary: To ensure that your selection is appropriately random, make a predetermined selection from among all answer choices you have not eliminated.

Test-Taking Strategies

This section contains a list of test-taking strategies that you may find helpful as you work through the test. By taking what you know and applying logical thought, you can maximize your chances of answering any question correctly!

It is very important to realize that every question is different and every person is different: no single strategy will work on every question, and no single strategy will work for every person. That's why we've included all of them here, so you can try them out and determine which ones work best for different types of questions and which ones work best for you.

Question Strategies

✓ Read Carefully

Read the question and the answer choices carefully. Don't miss the question because you misread the terms. You have plenty of time to read each question thoroughly and make sure you understand what is being asked. Yet a happy medium must be attained, so don't waste too much time. You must read carefully and efficiently.

✓ Contextual Clues

Look for contextual clues. If the question includes a word you are not familiar with, look at the immediate context for some indication of what the word might mean. Contextual clues can often give you all the information you need to decipher the meaning of an unfamiliar word. Even if you can't determine the meaning, you may be able to narrow down the possibilities enough to make a solid guess at the answer to the question.

✓ Prefixes

If you're having trouble with a word in the question or answer choices, try dissecting it. Take advantage of every clue that the word might include. Prefixes can be a huge help. Usually, they allow you to determine a basic meaning. *Pre-* means before, *post-* means after, *pro-* is positive, *de-* is negative. From prefixes, you can get an idea of the general meaning of the word and try to put it into context.

✓ Hedge Words

Watch out for critical hedge words, such as *likely, may, can, often, almost, mostly, usually, generally, rarely,* and *sometimes.* Question writers insert these hedge phrases to cover every possibility. Often an answer choice will be wrong simply because it leaves no room for exception. Be on guard for answer choices that have definitive words such as *exactly* and *always.*

✓ Switchback Words

Stay alert for *switchbacks.* These are the words and phrases frequently used to alert you to shifts in thought. The most common switchback words are *but, although,* and *however.* Others include *nevertheless, on the other hand, even though, while, in spite of, despite,* and *regardless of.* Switchback words are important to catch because they can change the direction of the question or an answer choice.

✓ Face Value

When in doubt, use common sense. Accept the situation in the problem at face value. Don't read too much into it. These problems will not require you to make wild assumptions. If you have to go beyond creativity and warp time or space in order to have an answer choice fit the question, then you should move on and consider the other answer choices. These are normal problems rooted in reality. The applicable relationship or explanation may not be readily apparent, but it is there for you to figure out. Use your common sense to interpret anything that isn't clear.

Answer Choice Strategies

✓ Answer Selection

The most thorough way to pick an answer choice is to identify and eliminate wrong answers until only one is left, then confirm it is the correct answer. Sometimes an answer choice may immediately seem right, but be careful. The test writers will usually put more than one reasonable answer choice on each question, so take a second to read all of them and make sure that the other choices are not equally obvious. As long as you have time left, it is better to read every answer choice than to pick the first one that looks right without checking the others.

✓ Answer Choice Families

An answer choice family consists of two (in rare cases, three) answer choices that are very similar in construction and cannot all be true at the same time. If you see two answer choices that are direct opposites or parallels, one of them is usually the correct answer. For instance, if one answer choice says that quantity x increases and another either says that quantity x decreases (opposite) or says that quantity y increases (parallel), then those answer choices would fall into the same family. An answer choice that doesn't match the construction of the answer choice family is more likely to be incorrect. Most questions will not have answer choice families, but when they do appear, you should be prepared to recognize them.

✓ Eliminate Answers

Eliminate answer choices as soon as you realize they are wrong, but make sure you consider all possibilities. If you are eliminating answer choices and realize that the last one you are left with is also wrong, don't panic. Start over and consider each choice again. There may be something you missed the first time that you will realize on the second pass.

✓ Avoid Fact Traps

Don't be distracted by an answer choice that is factually true but doesn't answer the question. You are looking for the choice that answers the question. Stay focused on what the question is asking for so you don't accidentally pick an answer that is true but incorrect. Always go back to the question and make sure the answer choice you've selected actually answers the question and is not merely a true statement.

✓ Extreme Statements

In general, you should avoid answers that put forth extreme actions as standard practice or proclaim controversial ideas as established fact. An answer choice that states the "process should be used in certain situations, if…" is much more likely to be correct than one that states the "process should be discontinued completely." The first is a calm rational statement and doesn't even make a definitive, uncompromising stance, using a hedge word *if* to provide wiggle room, whereas the second choice is far more extreme.

⊘ Benchmark

As you read through the answer choices and you come across one that seems to answer the question well, mentally select that answer choice. This is not your final answer, but it's the one that will help you evaluate the other answer choices. The one that you selected is your benchmark or standard for judging each of the other answer choices. Every other answer choice must be compared to your benchmark. That choice is correct until proven otherwise by another answer choice beating it. If you find a better answer, then that one becomes your new benchmark. Once you've decided that no other choice answers the question as well as your benchmark, you have your final answer.

⊘ Predict the Answer

Before you even start looking at the answer choices, it is often best to try to predict the answer. When you come up with the answer on your own, it is easier to avoid distractions and traps because you will know exactly what to look for. The right answer choice is unlikely to be word-for-word what you came up with, but it should be a close match. Even if you are confident that you have the right answer, you should still take the time to read each option before moving on.

General Strategies

⊘ Tough Questions

If you are stumped on a problem or it appears too hard or too difficult, don't waste time. Move on! Remember though, if you can quickly check for obviously incorrect answer choices, your chances of guessing correctly are greatly improved. Before you completely give up, at least try to knock out a couple of possible answers. Eliminate what you can and then guess at the remaining answer choices before moving on.

⊘ Check Your Work

Since you will probably not know every term listed and the answer to every question, it is important that you get credit for the ones that you do know. Don't miss any questions through careless mistakes. If at all possible, try to take a second to look back over your answer selection and make sure you've selected the correct answer choice and haven't made a costly careless mistake (such as marking an answer choice that you didn't mean to mark). This quick double check should more than pay for itself in caught mistakes for the time it costs.

⊘ Pace Yourself

It's easy to be overwhelmed when you're looking at a page full of questions; your mind is confused and full of random thoughts, and the clock is ticking down faster than you would like. Calm down and maintain the pace that you have set for yourself. Especially as you get down to the last few minutes of the test, don't let the small numbers on the clock make you panic. As long as you are on track by monitoring your pace, you are guaranteed to have time for each question.

⊘ Don't Rush

It is very easy to make errors when you are in a hurry. Maintaining a fast pace in answering questions is pointless if it makes you miss questions that you would have gotten right otherwise. Test writers like to include distracting information and wrong answers that seem right. Taking a little extra time to avoid careless mistakes can make all the difference in your test score. Find a pace that allows you to be confident in the answers that you select.

⊘ Keep Moving

Panicking will not help you pass the test, so do your best to stay calm and keep moving. Taking deep breaths and going through the answer elimination steps you practiced can help to break through a stress barrier and keep your pace.

Final Notes

The combination of a solid foundation of content knowledge and the confidence that comes from practicing your plan for applying that knowledge is the key to maximizing your performance on test day. As your foundation of content knowledge is built up and strengthened, you'll find that the strategies included in this chapter become more and more effective in helping you quickly sift through the distractions and traps of the test to isolate the correct answer.

Now that you're preparing to move forward into the test content chapters of this book, be sure to keep your goal in mind. As you read, think about how you will be able to apply this information on the test. If you've already seen sample questions for the test and you have an idea of the question format and style, try to come up with questions of your own that you can answer based on what you're reading. This will give you valuable practice applying your knowledge in the same ways you can expect to on test day.

Good luck and good studying!

Foundational Literacy Development

Phonetics, Phonics, and Print Concepts

Building Rapid Word Identification and Automaticity

Rapid word identification and **automaticity** refer to the quick, effortless, and accurate recognition of individual words when reading. Speed and accuracy are strong predictors of comprehension, so the ability to identify words automatically plays an important role in reading development.

When readers come to unfamiliar words in texts, they pause to use reading strategies. This includes applying phonics skills and using semantic and syntactic clues. Using these strategies takes time, which may cause the reader to slow down. Applying strategies to decode words also requires significant processing in working memory, which is limited. This diverts attention away from comprehending the text, and comprehension may be negatively affected. When readers develop the ability to accurately and automatically identify words, they free up space in working memory to use for comprehension. This shift often occurs around second and third grade.

It is also important to remember that rapid word identification and automaticity are necessary for fluency but not sufficient on their own. Fluency also involves reading with appropriate phrasing and intonation.

Strategies to Build Automatic Recognition of High-Frequency Sight Words

Readers need several opportunities to see words before they can automatically recognize them. Therefore, providing opportunities for repeated exposure to high-frequency sight words is an important goal of reading instruction and should be included along with explicit phonics instruction.

Sight words are commonly introduced to students a few at a time. The most frequently used words, such as *a*, *you*, and *the*, are typically introduced first. Some reading programs coordinate sight word lists with weekly texts, ensuring that students will have frequent exposure to each set of words as they are introduced.

There are several types of activities that can be done to build sight word recognition. Having students go on "word hunts" to locate and circle sight words in texts is one activity. Sight words can be built using magnetic letters or spelled in the air with fingers or wands. Activities that require students to read, build, and write each word are also commonly used. Additionally, flash card drills can be incorporated into the school day.

Typical Progression of Phonological Awareness Skills

One of the earliest phonological awareness skills children develop is the ability to recognize rhyming words. After recognizing rhyming words heard in stories, songs, and poems, children begin to produce their own sets of rhyming words. Alliteration, or identifying and producing words with the same initial sounds, is another early phonological awareness skill.

Later, children develop awareness of syllables. This involves both the ability to blend syllables to form whole words and the ability to break whole words into syllables. They also develop the ability to blend and segment onsets and rimes. **Onsets** are composed of the initial consonants or consonant blends in syllables, whereas **rimes** consist of the vowels and remaining consonants that follow. For example, in the word *star*, /st/ is the onset, and /ar/ is the rime. Phonemic awareness is the most advanced phonological awareness skill, and it is usually developed after the others.

Relationship Between Phonological Awareness and Phonemic Awareness

Although they are often used interchangeably, phonological awareness and phonemic awareness are distinct terms. **Phonological awareness** is a broader term that refers to the ability to identify and manipulate sounds in spoken language. This can refer to identifying and manipulating sounds at the word, syllable, or phoneme level. Example activities include rhyming, alliteration, breaking words into syllables, dividing syllables into onsets and rimes, and blending and segmenting phonemes.

Phonemic awareness is one specific component of phonological awareness. It focuses on the ability to identify and manipulate sounds at the phoneme level only. Phonemes are the smallest units of speech, and phonemic awareness is therefore the most advanced component of phonological awareness. It usually develops after other phonological awareness skills.

Review Video: Phonological and Phonemic Awareness, and Phonics
Visit mometrix.com/academy and enter code: 197017

Phonemic Awareness Skills

One early phonemic awareness skill is **phoneme isolation**, which is the ability to identify specific phonemes in spoken words. This includes identifying beginning (initial), middle (medial), and ending (final) sounds. Another skill is **phoneme identification**, which involves identifying the common sound in a list of words that have either the same beginning, middle, or ending sound. In phoneme categorization, students are given a set of words in which all but one have the same beginning, middle, or ending phoneme, and they must identify the word that doesn't belong.

In **blending**, a more complex skill, students are given the phonemes that make up a word in isolation. They must then identify the whole word formed by putting the phonemes together. In **segmentation**, students are given a whole word and must identify the individual phonemes that make up that word. **Phoneme deletion** involves removing one phoneme from a word and identifying what new word was formed. **Phoneme substitution** involves changing one phoneme in a word and identifying what new word was formed.

Activities Used to Teach Phoneme Blending and Segmentation

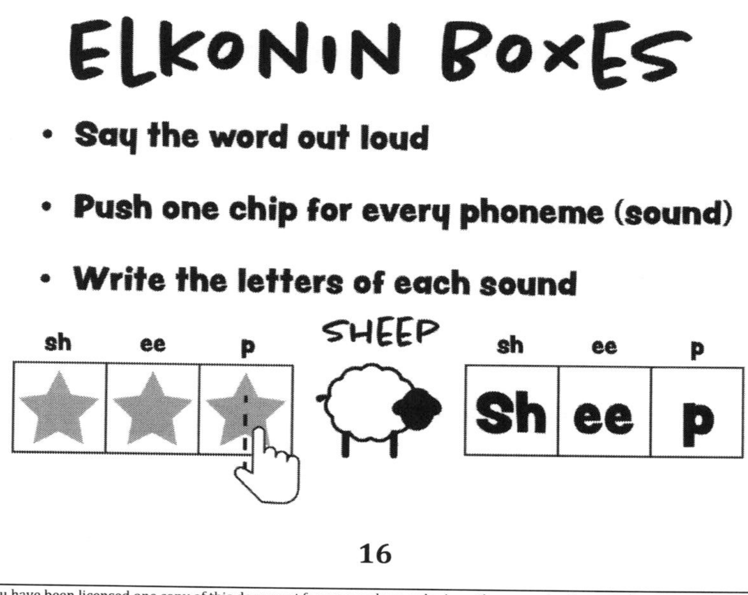

Children often benefit from a multisensory approach to phonemic blending and segmentation. **Elkonin boxes** are one tool that can be used. Elkonin boxes consist of a series of connected boxes on paper. Students listen to a word and slide a penny or other token into a box each time they hear a new sound. For example, while listening to the word *cat*, students would slide three pennies into the boxes.

Students can also be given strings of beads, and they can move one bead for every sound, or phoneme, they hear. They can slide the beads back together as they blend the sounds to form the whole words again. Rubber bands can be used in a similar manner. Students can say whole words with the rubber bands un-stretched and then slowly stretch the bands as they segment the sounds. They can then push the rubber bands back together again as they blend the sounds to form the whole words.

Phonics

Phonics refers to the relationship between letters and the sounds they make. After children learn to identify letter names, they learn that each letter makes a predictable sound. They later learn that groups of letters, such as consonant blends and digraphs, make predictable sounds as well. This understanding of letter-sound relationships is known as phonics.

Understanding the predictable relationship between letters and the sounds they make is important for the development of both decoding and encoding skills. When early readers come across unfamiliar words, they use knowledge of letter-sound relationships to decode the words as one common reading strategy. For early readers, this is especially helpful for unknown words that follow predictable spelling patterns, such as CVC words. When children are engaging in early writing activities, they use knowledge of letter-sound relationships to write words, which is known as **encoding**.

Phonemic Awareness Vs. Phonics

Phonemic awareness and phonics are commonly confused terms, but they are not the same. **Phonemic awareness** refers to identifying and manipulating phonemes in spoken language. **Phonics** refers to the relationship between letters and the sounds they make. A key question to ask when deciding if an activity is related to phonemic awareness or phonics is whether or not any letters are involved. If letters and their sounds are involved, the activity is related to phonics rather than phonemic awareness.

For example, asking students what sounds they hear in the word *cat* is a phonemic awareness activity because they are identifying sounds in a spoken word. However, asking students to decode the word *cat* when it is written in a text is a phonics activity because students must use their understanding of letter-sound relationships to successfully decode the word. Students are also using phonics skills if they write the word *cat* by identifying the sounds that they hear and writing the letters that make those sounds.

Fluency

Fluency is defined as reading accurately with the appropriate speed and intonation. Beginning readers typically have to stop and decode unknown words frequently, which affects both speed and intonation. Over time, as readers develop rapid word recognition, their reading speed increases. Appropriate intonation is also developed through frequent shared and guided reading experiences.

Relationship Between Fluency and Comprehension

Research has shown that reading fluency is one major predictor of reading comprehension. Non-fluent readers burden their working memories with decoding. Sentences are read in a fragmented way, making it difficult for the brain to organize and make sense of what was read. After expending the energy to decode difficult words, they may forget what they have previously read. Fluent readers are free to use working memory for comprehending the text. They read using smooth, continuous phrasing, making it easier for the brain to make sense of what has been read.

Using Syntactic and Semantic Cues to Figure out Unknown Words

Readers can use multiple cueing systems to figure out unknown words and make meaning from texts. When readers use **syntactic cues**, they use knowledge about correct oral language structures and the ways sentences are put together to decode and make meaning. For example, readers may use knowledge about subject-verb agreement and word order to decode new words and make meaning from sentences. When readers use **semantic cues**, they use prior knowledge from personal experiences along with meaning contained in the text and pictures to make sense of what they are reading. When they are stuck on unknown words, they consider what they already know about the topic or look to context clues or pictures for hints. While many readers still will use cueing systems to help them read unknown words, the best practice is to teach students to decode words using systematic and explicit phonics instruction rather than cueing systems.

Decoding Vs. Encoding

Decoding refers to the process of translating print to speech, which is done by translating graphemes into phonemes. **Graphemes** are letters or groups of letters that represent a single sound, and phonemes are the smallest units of sound in language. When a reader uses strategies to read the printed word *chair*, he or she is decoding the word.

Encoding refers to the process of translating sounds to print using knowledge of letter-sound relationships. This is done by translating phonemes to graphemes. When a writer uses knowledge of the sounds letters make to write the word *hop*, he or she is encoding the word.

Review Video: Phonics (Encoding and Decoding)
Visit mometrix.com/academy and enter code: 821361

Observing how a developing writer spells can be used to assess phonics knowledge. It can provide information about the writer's understanding of when to apply certain spelling patterns. By observing the writer's work over time, a teacher can determine which phonics strategies the writer has mastered and which are still developing. This information can be used to plan individualized phonics instruction. For example, if a writer frequently spells CVCe words without the e at the end, the teacher may focus on this spelling pattern during guided reading lessons with the student.

Review Video: Print Awareness and Alphabet Knowledge
Visit mometrix.com/academy and enter code: 541069

Instructional Strategies Used to Teach Decoding of Common Spelling Patterns

Blending is a common strategy to teach decoding of CVC words. Students say the sound represented by each letter in the word and then state the whole word they made. To increase fluency, students can be encouraged to increase the speed of blending over time. Once CVC words have been mastered and students have been introduced to consonant blends and digraphs, they can use the same blending process with CVCC words.

For CVVC and CVCe words that cannot be decoded using blending, students can be introduced to the sounds made by each spelling pattern. They can then build and explore word families that contain the same spelling pattern, changing the initial sounds to build new, related words. For example, after identifying the sound that /ake/ makes, students can build *rake*, *cake*, and *lake* using letter tiles or magnetic letters.

INSTRUCTIONAL STRATEGIES USED TO TEACH DECODING OF MULTISYLLABIC WORDS

Although decoding instruction typically tapers off around second grade, it is at this point that students begin reading texts with more complex, multisyllabic words. Therefore, it is important to teach specific strategies that readers can use to decode these types of words.

One strategy is to teach students to identify the different syllables present in a word. This can be done by clapping each syllable or saying the word while looking in a mirror and observing how many times the mouth opens. Students can then be taught to recognize common syllable spelling patterns and the sounds that they make. These common syllable spelling patterns include the following:

- closed syllables, which end in a consonant and usually have a short vowel sound (e.g., rabbit)
- open syllables, which end in a vowel and usually have a long vowel sound (e.g., bagel)
- r-controlled vowels (e.g., carpet)
- vowel digraph pairs (e.g., detain)
- vowel-consonant-silent-e syllables, which usually have a long vowel sound (e.g., athlete)
- consonant-le words, which are usually found at the end of a word (e.g., maple)

Readers can also be taught to look for known parts of words, such as known prefixes and suffixes.

CONSONANT BLENDS AND CONSONANT DIGRAPHS

A **consonant blend** is a group of two or three consonants that blend together to make a sound, but each individual letter sound is still heard. Examples include *bl*, *fr*, and *sw*. Blends are typically introduced after readers have learned to decode basic CVC words, and they are introduced in groups according to the second consonant they contain. Blends containing two consonants are usually introduced before blends containing three consonants. When introducing each blend, the teacher shows students how the sounds of each consonant are blended together to form the new sound. Common words containing the blend can be listed, and students can go on word hunts to find additional examples of words containing the blend. Students can also sort cards containing pictures of objects whose names are spelled with consonant blends.

A **consonant digraph** is a group of two consonants that form a new consonant sound when combined. Examples include *th*, *sh*, and *ch*. Digraphs are also typically introduced a few at a time, with beginning digraphs introduced before ending digraphs. Creating lists of example words, going on word hunts, and completing matching and sorting activities can also be used to teach digraphs.

R-CONTROLLED VOWELS

R-controlled vowels are vowels that appear before the letter r in a word. Words containing this spelling pattern are sometimes referred to as bossy-r words, because the letter r changes the sound of the vowel. The r-controlled vowel pairs are *ar*, *ir*, *or*, and *er*.

To teach decoding of words containing r-controlled vowels, teachers can model blending of simple words containing these spelling patterns by sliding their fingers along the words as they blend them. For each word, they can point out that the vowel and r together make one sound, and they can generate a list of other words containing the same letter pair and sound. Students can also be given word or picture cards to sort according to which r-controlled vowel sound they contain. Another strategy is to provide a picture of an object that contains an r-controlled vowel in its name. The word can be written below the picture, with the r-controlled vowel omitted. Students can be asked to provide the missing letters to complete the word.

Benefits of Explicit Phonics Instruction

Research has shown that early readers benefit from an explicit and systematic approach to phonics instruction. Developing readers who receive explicit and systematic phonics instruction at an early age often show increased ability to decode and spell, along with increased reading comprehension skills when older.

Explicit instruction means that phonics lessons are purposely planned to address specific skills rather than waiting until problems arise with decoding words while reading. For example, a teacher may plan to focus on a set of consonant blends during one week of reading instruction. Systematic instruction means that the lessons follow a carefully planned scope and sequence, with phonics lessons progressing from basic to advanced. Early phonics lessons for kindergarteners may focus on letter-sound relationships, whereas first grade students may focus on decoding different spelling patterns.

Role of Phonological Awareness and Phonics Skills in Reading Development

English Language Learners

For English language learners (ELLs), research has shown that **phonological awareness** in a reader's first language is a **strong predictor** of his or her ability to learn to read in a second language. This is especially true when the native language is closely related to English. Despite the fact that phonological awareness in the native language can be beneficial when learning English, it may lead to **overgeneralization** of rules of the native language. Continued language experiences in the native language along with language scaffolding can be beneficial to ELLs as they learn English.

Some ELLs may also speak native languages in which there is not a **one-to-one correspondence** between letters and phonemes. They may also speak languages that use the same alphabet as English but where the letters represent different sounds. It is important for teachers to understand their ELLs' prior knowledge and consider this when planning appropriate phonics instruction.

Additionally, some English phonemes may not be used in other languages. Introducing English vocabulary words that contain these phonemes helps give these sounds a meaningful context. Using poems and songs with repetition and rhyme can also be helpful.

Review Video: ESL/ESOL/Second Language Learning
Visit mometrix.com/academy and enter code: 795047

Struggling and Proficient Students

Research has shown that phonological awareness and phonics skills are important predictors of reading success. For struggling readers, daily phonological awareness and phonics practice are important. Explicit and systematic instruction should be tailored to the individual needs of each student and based upon observation and assessment data. Once a teacher has determined which skills the student needs to improve, instruction should be regularly included to target these skills until mastered. Ongoing reading assessments and flexible groupings can help make sure that struggling readers' individual needs are consistently met.

Phonological awareness and phonics assessments are important for proficient readers as well. Some proficient readers have developed strong rapid word identification skills without mastering the underlying phonological awareness and phonics skills. When they get into older grade levels and more frequently encounter unfamiliar vocabulary, they will have difficulty decoding the text. Assessment data can be used to identify specific skills to practice in small-group instruction with these proficient readers.

Role of Natural Exposure to Phonics in Early Reading Development

Like explicit phonics instruction, natural exposure to phonics also plays a role in early reading development. This exposure occurs when children are involved in natural reading experiences, and they come across words they are unable to decode. Phonics instruction is provided in the moment to address the unknown words.

This type of phonics instruction is known as **implicit** instruction. It differs from explicit instruction, which progresses from part (letter sounds) to whole (whole words). Implicit instruction progresses from whole (unknown words encountered in text) to part (breaking down the words in order to decode them).

Implicit phonics instruction has some benefits. Because it occurs during natural reading experiences, the phonics skills are taught **in context** rather than in isolation. Readers are motivated to learn the skills needed to decode the unknown words and continue reading. Teachers can allow time to address unknown words while reading aloud or listening to students reading independently. However, research has shown that it is still important to schedule time for explicit and systematic phonics instruction as well.

Strategies to Teach Letter Identification

Most reading programs introduce letters gradually. Some suggest introducing letters that have high value to learners first, such as the first letters of their names. Others focus on letters that play prominent roles in the books they are reading for the week, whereas others sequence letters by physical characteristics. In general, it is best to avoid teaching commonly confused letter pairs simultaneously, such as b and d.

To develop **letter recognition**, students can be given texts and instructed to circle certain letters. They can play alphabet bingo and cover specific letters when they are called. They can sing the alphabet song while pointing to each letter. Additionally, they can go on letter hunts, where they search the classroom or building to find examples of specific letters in environmental print. To practice recognizing capital and lowercase forms of letters, students can play memory and find matches consisting of both letter forms.

Strategies to Teach Letter Formation

To teach letter formation, students can be given letter stencils to trace with pencils. They can also be provided cutout letters made from different materials, such as felt and sandpaper, to trace with their fingers. Later, they can attempt to write letters independently on writing paper following the school's selected handwriting program guidelines.

To practice letter formation using a **multisensory approach**, students can write letters with shaving cream or fingerpaint. They can also write letters in containers filled with salt or sand. Wax craft sticks, modeling dough, and pipe cleaners can be used to construct letter models. Large-sized letters can also be drawn using sidewalk chalk, and students can hop along the letter shapes to trace them. They can also trace letter shapes in the air with their fingers or toy wands. Additionally, students can be given outlines of letters, which they can fill in with buttons, dried beans, or other common objects.

STRATEGIES TO TEACH LETTER-SOUND RELATIONSHIPS

Once students understand that letters are combined to form words that convey meaning in print, they begin learning that each letter makes a predictable sound. This is known as the **alphabetic principle**. Although different reading programs introduce the letters and sounds in different orders, most introduce the letter-sound relationships gradually.

In some reading programs, each letter has a song, poem, or chant that incorporates repetition of the letter name and sound. In others, a letter character or visual is produced, which includes a hint about the sound it makes. The visual often includes a picture of a common object that starts with the letter. Students can also be encouraged to find objects beginning with the letter sound they are learning. Tactile activities, such as building letters out of wax craft sticks or writing them in shaving cream while repeating the names and sounds, are also commonly used. Bingo and other similar games that require matching letters to their sounds can also be used.

CONCEPTS OF PRINT THAT COLLECTIVELY FORM A FOUNDATION FOR EARLY READING INSTRUCTION

Concepts of print are the conventions used to convey meaning in printed text. Children begin developing an understanding of these concepts from an early age through shared reading experiences with others and interactions with printed materials.

Understanding concepts of print includes recognizing the front cover, back cover, and title of a book. It also includes recognizing that the print, rather than the pictures, carries the message. Additionally, it includes directionality concepts, such as knowing that you read from left to right and from the top of the page to the bottom, with a return sweep at the end of each line of text. One-to-one correspondence between written and spoken words is another concept of print. Letter concepts are also important, such as knowing that words are made up of individual letters, identifying letter names, and identifying both capital and lowercase letters. Identifying the names and purposes of common punctuation marks used to end sentences is also a key concept of print.

STRATEGIES TO TEACH PRINT AWARENESS

Starting at an early age, caregivers and teachers can begin introducing children to concepts of print. While reading storybooks and big books aloud, they can model how to hold the books, where the front and back covers and titles are located, and where to begin reading. They can also model directionality by following the text with their fingers as they read, showing the left-to-right movement and return sweep. They can point out different text features, such as capital letters and punctuation marks, and discuss their purposes.

When students are interacting with texts independently, teachers can ask them questions regarding concepts of print. For example, they can instruct students to follow the text with their fingers and pause after encountering punctuation marks at the ends of sentences. Teachers can also point out text features in environmental print, such as hallway signs.

Writing Development

Relationship Between Reading and Writing Development

Reading and writing are **interrelated** and should be taught together. Students who read a lot tend to have stronger writing skills, and students who write a lot tend to have stronger reading comprehension skills.

When students read varied types of texts, they learn how authors convey meaning differently through tone, language use, and sentence structure. They learn about different types of genres. They often use the texts as models and experiment with these elements in their own writing. Students also increase their vocabularies through reading, and they develop automatic recognition of high-frequency words. Students may then integrate the new vocabulary words into their own writing and remember how to spell words they have seen repeatedly in texts.

When students learn to write, they learn about and use different sentence and text structures. Awareness of these structures can help students recognize and make sense of them when encountered in other texts. Additionally, when students write about texts they have read, it facilitates additional analysis and comprehension. For example, writing about whether or not they would recommend books to others requires students to evaluate the texts and provide support for their reasoning.

Characteristics of Writers in the Preliterate Stage of Writing Development

The earliest stage of children's writing development is **scribbling**. Children begin scribbling at random places on the pages and do not proceed in any consistent direction. They typically hold writing utensils, such as pencils or crayons, with their fists. Scribbling helps children improve their fine motor skills and sets the stage for the understanding that writing carries meaning.

Over time, scribbling begins to follow a left-to-right directionality across the pages. Drawings may be included to help convey meaning.

Eventually, strings of pretend, letter-like symbols are used. They are sometimes mixed with numbers. Students are able to explain the meanings they are trying to convey through their writing. This phase demonstrates a beginning awareness of concepts of print. Spacing between words is not initially included but develops over time. There is no evidence of letter-sound relationships in the writing at this stage.

Characteristics of Writers in the Emergent Stage of Writing Development

In the **emergent stage,** writers begin to form letters correctly. Initially, they often write using all capital letters. They also begin to use their understandings of letter-sound relationships to write words. Some sounds are correctly represented in words, typically starting with the initial sounds.

In this stage, writers also begin spelling some words correctly. The first written words typically hold high personal meaning to students, such as their names and words like *mom* and *dad*. They may also write words found in environmental print, such as the names of popular restaurants frequently seen on signs. Some high-frequency sight words begin to be spelled correctly.

Students in the emergent stage write with left-to-right directionality and begin using spacing to separate words. They also begin to use common punctuation marks to split their writing into sentences, although this skill is still developing. Because it requires a lot of energy to encode words at this stage, writing pieces are typically short.

Characteristics of Writers in the Transitional Stage of Writing Development

In the **transitional stage** of writing development, students begin using a mixture of capital and lowercase letters appropriately. They also correctly use several different punctuation marks. Their writing includes a broader vocabulary than when they were in the emergent stage.

Transitional writers know how to automatically spell many high-frequency words, and they use multiple strategies to encode words they do not know how to spell. These strategies include considering letter-sound relationships to record the sounds they hear, considering known spelling patterns, and thinking of related, known words. Writing includes a mixture of conventionally spelled words and phonetically spelled words that are readable.

Because transitional writers are able to encode many words quickly, they have more available energy to focus on writing development. They focus more attention on developing story elements and including descriptive details. They write longer texts than they wrote in the emergent stage, and their writing includes a mixture of text structures and genres. Transitional writers also have the ability to reread and edit their work.

Characteristics of Writers in the Fluent Stage of Writing Development

Fluent writers spell most words correctly and use capitalization and punctuation marks conventionally throughout their writing. They are able to edit and evaluate their own writing and provide constructive feedback to others.

With the ability to spell most words quickly and automatically, fluent writers are able to focus more on writing craft, such as using descriptive language and developing story elements. Author's voice begins to develop. Writing may span several pages. Fluent writers consider their audiences and purposes for writing and consider them during the planning process. They use multiple strategies to plan their writing, such as brainstorming and using graphic organizers. They are able to write texts in a wide range of genres and select appropriate text structures to fit their purposes. Additionally, fluent writers are able to independently use tools like dictionaries and thesauri to improve their writing pieces.

Review Video: Sensory Language
Visit mometrix.com/academy and enter code: 177314

Oral Language and Nonverbal Language Development

Stages of First Language Acquisition

- Until about four to six months of age, babies are in the **cooing stage**. Babies in this stage commonly make vowel sounds, which represent their first attempts at oral language.
- From about four to six months until one year of age, babies are in the **babbling stage**. At first, they commonly make repeated consonant-vowel sounds, such as *ma-ma*. Over time, their babbling begins to show the expressive patterns they hear in the language around them. They repeat sounds that others respond to and reinforce.
- From about 12 to 24 months of age, children are in the **one-word stage**. In this stage, children begin referring to objects by consistent, one-word names. These words may be real or invented, and children begin to use language to convey meaning to others.

- From ages two to three, most children enter the **telegraphic stage**, when they string together words to convey meaning. The words that convey the most meaning in sentences are often included, whereas articles, conjunctions, and other words are omitted.
- After age three, most children enter the beginning **oral fluency stage**. They now use more complex sentences and begin using sentence structure and syntax appropriately. They use language for a variety of purposes.

Early milestones in language

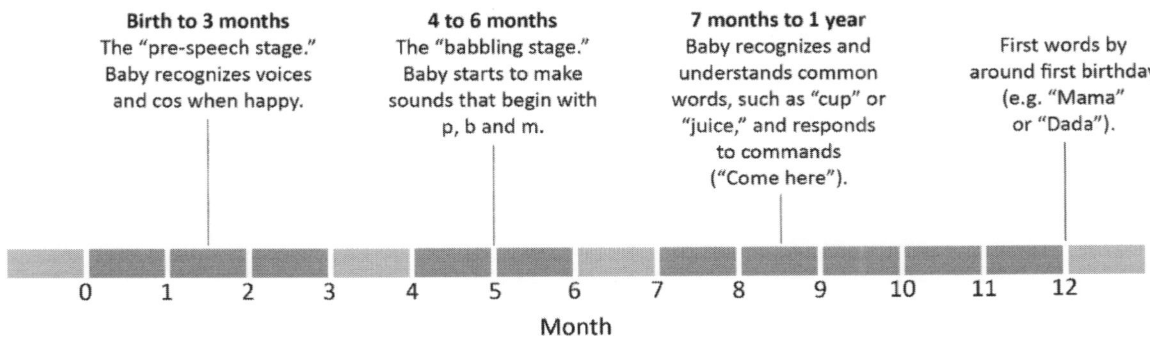

Stages of Second Language Acquisition

- In the **preproduction stage**, English language learners (ELLs) are listening and taking in the second language. Comprehension is minimal at this point. ELLs may not yet speak to others in the second language, and this stage is therefore sometimes referred to as the silent period. ELLs may communicate with gestures or single words.
- In the **early production stage**, comprehension is still limited. ELLs begin responding using one- or two-word answers. Vocabulary in the second language begins to grow.
- The **speech emergence stage** is marked by increased comprehension. ELLs begin speaking in longer sentences, but grammatical errors may be present. Vocabulary in the second language greatly increases.
- In the **intermediate proficiency stage**, ELLs are able to comprehend much of what they hear. They begin speaking in more complex sentences that contain fewer grammatical errors. They are able to fluently communicate with others in the second language for a variety of purposes.
- In the **advanced fluency stage**, ELLs understand academic vocabulary and need little support to participate actively in the classroom. Students in this stage speak with near-native English fluency.

Components of Oral Language Development

- **Phonological skills** are one component of oral language development. These skills include the ability to recognize and manipulate sounds in spoken words. Rhyming and identifying syllables are examples of phonological skills.
- **Syntactic skills** are another component. Syntactic skills (syntax) include understanding grammatical rules and how to correctly arrange words in sentences. Children begin by using simple syntax, such as combining two words to express needs and wants. Over time, their sentence structure becomes more complex.
- **Oral language** also includes a semantic component, which refers to the ability to understand the meanings of words, phrases, sentences, and longer texts. The semantic component is vital for comprehension.

- **Morphological skills** are another component of oral language development. Morphological skills include understanding the meanings of word parts.
- Finally, **pragmatics** refers to understanding the social rules of language. Examples of pragmatics include knowing how to adjust the formality of language depending on the audience and knowing how to respond in certain social situations.

Review Video: Components of Oral Language Development
Visit mometrix.com/academy and enter code: 480589

Relationship Between Oral Language Development and Literacy Development

Most children learn to speak through immersion in language-rich environments, with no formal speech instruction necessary. Starting at birth, these early language interactions help set the stage for later literacy development. Early language play, such as sharing songs, nursery rhymes, and poems, assists young children with the development of phonological awareness skills. Strong phonological awareness skills are a solid predictor of future reading success. Hearing spoken language also helps children understand syntax and how sounds and words are combined to form meaning.

- As children engage in frequent and varied oral language opportunities, they also increase their **vocabularies**. Opportunities to use both social and academic vocabulary during listening and speaking activities assists students with comprehending vocabulary words encountered in texts.
- **Oral language experiences** also help readers understand that language can be used for a variety of purposes, such as meeting needs, social interaction, and persuading others. This assists with recognizing an author's purpose. An understanding of cultural norms and nuances is also developed through oral language experiences.
- Additionally, comprehension requires the ability to combine literal meanings of words with prior knowledge and world experiences. Oral language activities, such as following directions, can assist with this.

Role That Oral Language Plays in the Development of Critical Thinking Skills

Oral language leads to the development of other communication skills. Babies first listen to their caregivers and later say their first words before they learn to read and write. Through listening, children learn to evaluate the messages of others and make sense of newly learned information. Through speaking, they learn to organize and communicate their thoughts to others. All of these skills assist with the development of critical thinking skills.

Teachers can ask students to explain their thinking to others. They can also teach students to defend their answers using support and evidence. Students can also be explicitly taught to use strategic questioning when interacting with classmates. Strategic questions require higher-level thinking to answer, and questions with yes-or-no answers should be limited. For example, students explaining the results of science experiments might be asked to evaluate their processes and explain what they might do differently in the future. Additionally, students can respond to high-level questions about texts during class discussions and literature circles. For example, they can be asked to evaluate the ways that authors use persuasive techniques.

Promoting Oral Language Skills

When engaging in listening and speaking activities with students, it is recommended to use vocabulary words in context to promote comprehension later. Research has shown that identifying vocabulary words on flash cards and other similar types activities has **little effect** on later reading comprehension, whereas the ability to recognize and use words **in context** does.

Students should also have many opportunities to listen and speak for a **variety of purposes** to both peers and adults. Friendly conversations, academic discussions, formal presentations, and social interactions are all examples of different types of oral language activities. Varied activities will help students learn to change their language structures to fit the purposes of the interactions. Teachers can change their language structures throughout the school day. For example, they might chat informally with students about their interests during a morning meeting and switch to academic language when discussing a novel.

Additionally, students of all ages can benefit from reading and listening to a large variety of texts containing different types of sentence structure, language, and vocabulary. Young children can also benefit from word play and phonological awareness activities.

Developing Listening and Speaking Skills

Like reading and writing, listening and speaking activities should be incorporated throughout all content areas rather than taught in isolation. Students should be given multiple opportunities each day to listen and speak for a variety of purposes.

Students can listen to texts in audio form, listen to teachers read aloud, or participate in paired reading activities in all content areas. Before beginning, they can be given specific purposes for listening to focus their attention. They can participate in role-playing scenarios to model common social situations and conflict resolution. They can be given frequent opportunities to present their learning to others using a variety of formats. Audience members can be instructed to ask specific and relevant questions, and presenters can be instructed to provide well-supported and evidence-based answers. Additionally, collaborative, problem-based learning activities can be planned, requiring all students to have roles within their groups.

For ELLs and students who struggle with speaking, partially completed scripts and/or sentence stems can be provided. These tools can assist students with outlining thoughts and organizing sentence structure before speaking.

Teaching Students Nonverbal Communication Skills

Nonverbal communication, sometimes known as body language, includes gestures, facial expressions, and posture. Verbal and nonverbal communication work together to convey desired messages. If nonverbal communication is inappropriate for the audiences or purposes used, the meaning of the verbal communication may be lost or misconstrued. For example, a child may thank a grandparent for a gift. However, if the child has a disappointed look on his or her face while speaking, the grandparent may believe the child does not like the gift.

Additionally, certain types of nonverbal communication can be interpreted differently depending on culture. What is socially acceptable in one culture may be considered rude in another. Students should be aware of the messages their nonverbal communication sends to different audiences.

Teachers can engage students in discussions about what messages are sent by different types of nonverbal communication. They can role-play common scenarios and have other students evaluate the messages conveyed through both verbal and nonverbal communication. Students can also watch video clips of realistic situations, such as job interviews, and evaluate the nonverbal language of the participants. When giving presentations, teachers also provide checklists outlining expected nonverbal communication, such as eye contact with others and strong posture.

Supporting the Development of Writing Skills

Stages of the Writing Process

- In the **prewriting stage**, writers brainstorm ideas, decide on topics, and plan the structure of their writing. This may include brainstorming, using webs or other graphic organizers to map out main ideas and details, and creating outlines. Writers consider who their audiences will be and what their purposes are for writing.
- In the **drafting stage**, writers create their rough drafts. The focus of this stage is recording thoughts. Students are encouraged not to worry about spelling, grammar, and punctuation errors, which will be corrected later.
- In the **revising stage**, writers consider if any portions of their writing lack clarity or if any parts should be added or removed. They examine word choice and consider if there are ways to make the writing more descriptive. They also seek feedback from others about ways their writing could be improved.
- In the **editing stage**, writers carefully check their writing for spelling, capitalization, punctuation, and grammatical errors. They also ask others to edit their writing to ensure no errors are overlooked.
- In the **publishing stage**, writers share their writing with others. This may involve creating illustrated books, reading aloud in authors' circles, putting on plays, or presenting in other ways.

Review Video: The Recursive Writing Process
Visit mometrix.com/academy and enter code: 951611

Teaching Students the Writing Process

Modeling is an important strategy to help students become familiar with the writing process. Teachers can lead their classes in creating shared pieces of writing, going through each step as a group. Teachers can also share examples of their personal writing as they introduce each step of the process. Multiple examples that represent writing from various genres should be included to show students how the process can be applied to different types of writing.

Teachers can post charts outlining the **steps of the writing process** in their classrooms. Regular time should be set aside to work on writing so that, at the beginning of each session, students can identify which steps of the writing process they will focus on that day. This will help them establish goals for each session and maintain focus.

Teachers should also schedule time for frequent conferring with students to provide feedback and ensure they are staying focused on the process. Additionally, teachers can provide opportunities for students to reflect on the process and the changes they have made to improve their writing.

Benefits of Conferring with Students During the Writing Process

There are several benefits of conferring with students during the writing process. When writers know they will be frequently meeting with teachers, it increases accountability for following the writing process. It also gives teachers opportunities to provide timely feedback to students and personalize instruction based on their individual needs.

It is important for teachers to model the conference process for students before beginning. Students should be aware of the purposes of the conferences and the expectations for their roles. Additionally, students should practice routines for what to do while their teachers are conferring with others. This modeling and practice will increase the likelihood that conferences can be conducted without interruptions.

There are multiple ways that conferences can be conducted, but they typically include students sharing the progress they have made since their last conference and discussing any questions or concerns they have. Teachers usually pick a few points to focus on with each student, showing specific ways that improvements can be made using examples or mentor texts. Teachers should use the academic language of writing in their conferences. Additionally, conferences should be positive and motivating in nature to help students develop positive feelings about writing.

Helping Students Write Effectively for Different Audiences

As part of the prewriting process, writers should be encouraged to identify their **intended audience**. Once they have identified their audience, they should consider several factors. One factor is how much **prior knowledge** their audience has about the topics. This will affect what level of background information and detail the writers should go into to meet the **audience members' needs**. For example, writers who are explaining how to use computer programs will focus on different program capabilities depending on whether the audience members are beginners or advanced users. Another factor to consider is what type of relationship the writers have to their audience. This will affect the level of **formality** used in the writing. For example, a friendly letter to a classmate will be less formal than a letter written to a government representative.

Teachers should give students frequent opportunities to complete **authentic writing activities** for varied audiences rather than only submitting assignments for teacher evaluation. They can also provide opportunities for students to compare and contrast texts that are written about the same topics but written for different audiences.

Helping Students Effectively Write in Various Forms and Genres

Genre studies are one way to help students learn to effectively write in different genres. In **genre studies**, classes study one genre at a time, in detail, over the course of a few weeks. They read many different mentor texts in the genre and discuss common characteristics. Students can then be encouraged to complete their own writing activities within the genre, using the mentor texts as models.

A similar approach can be used to teach students to effectively write in different forms. For example, when learning to write friendly letters, students can explore many different examples. They can discuss common characteristics and use the examples as models when writing their own friendly letters.

Another strategy is to provide a mixture of **strong and weak examples** of a genre or writing form and ask students to evaluate their effectiveness. They can discuss which examples they think are the most effective and what characteristics these examples display that make them more successful. Similarly, they can discuss which features the weak examples contain or lack that make them less successful. They can then be encouraged to consider these findings during their own writing activities.

Developing Writing Skills

Developing effective writing skills requires a multifaceted approach. Like reading, writing should be interwoven through the school day and all content areas rather than taught in isolation. It requires a combination of explicit skills instruction and opportunities to freely explore and experiment with writing. Skills instruction should include a wide range of topics, including spelling, grammar, language use, text structures, and more.

It is important to help students develop **positive attitudes** about writing. Building a community of writers where students can freely collaborate, share, and solicit feedback can help students feel safe and supported in the writing process. Students need to be explicitly taught how to solicit feedback from classmates and how to provide constructive and respectful feedback to others.

Because reading and writing are interrelated, students also need frequent opportunities to both read and write texts of different genres and purposes. They need to compare and contrast different texts and evaluate both their own writing and the writing of others. They should be explicitly taught how to participate in the five steps of the writing process, and they should receive frequent feedback on their writing. Feedback should provide specific suggestions for improvement in a positive and encouraging manner.

Helping Students Effectively Compose Written Texts

While teaching the writing process, teachers should help students understand that quality writing takes time. They can model their own writing processes and share stories about the writing processes of favorite authors. Writing stamina can be developed gradually in younger students, with writing workshop time increasing as the year goes on.

- Although students need models of **quality writing**, they also benefit from seeing **weak examples**. Students can evaluate a range of writing samples and contrast their effectiveness. Comparing both strong and weak examples will help writers identify the characteristics of quality texts and consider them in their own writing.
- Students should also be encouraged to engage in **multiple rounds of revision**. Revisions should be based on feedback from both peers and teachers as well as personal reflection. Students should also be explicitly taught how to consider feedback critically and decide which suggestions to implement and which to disregard.
- Additionally, teachers should monitor students' writing through observation and conferences and plan mini-lessons based on the issues they notice. For writing that will be evaluated, **rubrics** should be given in advance. Students should be encouraged to consult the rubrics and **self-evaluate** their own writing at multiple stages throughout the process.

Assisting Students with the Revision Process

Revising is often a difficult part of the writing process as students may struggle to see how they can improve their own writing pieces. First, it is important that students understand that the **focus of revision** is on improving clarity, detail, word choice, and other features rather than on the spelling and mechanical issues they will address during editing.

Modeling is often an effective way to help students understand the revision process. Teachers can share their own writing pieces and ask students to identify areas that do not make sense or could be explained in better detail. For example, teachers may ask students to close their eyes and visualize while they read one portion of their written pieces aloud. After asking students to share their visualizations, teachers may revise the writing to include more sensory details. Students can repeat the **visualization process** and note the differences. Teachers can also model writing sentences in multiple ways and ask which ways sound best. They may also help students identify descriptive words that can be used to replace commonly used words, such as replacing the word *nice* with *amiable*. These lists can be posted in classrooms for students to refer to when writing.

Helping Students Produce Quality Writing in the Content Areas

In preparation for the workforce and independent living, students must be able to successfully write for a variety of purposes and audiences. This is essential because effective writing is required in many professions. For example, scientists publish research studies, sales professionals write sales reports, and marketing specialists create advertisements.

Going through the steps of the writing process helps students organize, synthesize, analyze, and evaluate complex information. They must make judgments about what information is relevant and which text structures should be used to best convey meaning. Putting content into their own words helps students comprehend difficult information and vocabulary. Therefore, writing in the content areas supports comprehension in these areas as well.

Teachers can provide varied types of texts to support learning in the content areas. This may include fiction books, journal articles, diaries, field guides, research studies, maps, interview transcripts, and more. Students should interact with various quality texts and discuss the roles they play in different professions.

Helping Students Recognize and Use Abbreviations and Acronyms

Because there are numerous abbreviations and acronyms, teachers need to selectively choose which ones to focus on for instructional purposes. Therefore, teachers often address abbreviations and acronyms as they come up in students' reading and writing. For example, when writing letters, teachers can explain the abbreviations Dr., Mr., and Mrs. Teachers can also observe issues with abbreviations and acronyms as they occur in students' writing and address them through mini-lessons. Examples of abbreviations and acronyms can be pointed out in texts. Charts displaying common abbreviations and their long-form versions can also be displayed in classrooms to provide scaffolding before they are memorized.

In the age of digital communication and social media, it is also important to teach students when it is appropriate to use abbreviations and acronyms. Students need to consider their purpose for communication and their relationship with their audience. For example, informal acronyms may be appropriate for texts between friends but not for use in business letters.

Principles of Effective Writing

- **Clarity** and **brevity** are two related principles of effective writing. They require writers to include sufficient detail to convey their intended meanings while simultaneously omitting any extraneous or repetitive information. Students should be encouraged to consider the value that each word and sentence adds to their writing to determine whether or not it should be included. They should also consider the background knowledge of their intended audiences to ensure they go into the appropriate amount of detail to meet their needs.
- **Author's craft** and **voice** are also important principles of effective writing that draw readers in and compel them to read more. In fictional texts, they help readers identify with characters and make the stories seem realistic. These principles help maintain reader engagement with the texts.
- Additionally, careful **editing** is important for effective writing. If numerous errors are present, the meanings of the texts may be affected.

Helping Students Edit Their Writing to Correct Errors with Mechanics

Frequent modeling is helpful when teaching students to edit. Teachers can model using editing checklists or rubrics to check for errors in their own work. The class can edit writing pieces they have composed together during shared writing experiences or edit texts containing errors written by other authors.

Teachers can also instruct students to **follow routines** when editing. This may include completing editing checklists or recalling mnemonic devices to ensure that all areas have been checked. CUPS is one mnemonic device that can be used to remind young writers to check for capitalization, usage, punctuation, and spelling. Because it can be difficult for students to recognize errors in their own writing, teachers can also encourage students to edit their own work first and then ask other students to edit it as well.

Additionally, students benefit from frequent, shared reading experiences using large print books, projected digital texts, or other means that allow them to follow along as teachers read. Teachers can stop to point out how authors use capital letters, punctuation marks, and other conventions. Frequently seeing these conventions in use will help students understand their purposes and notice when they are used incorrectly in other texts.

Helping Students Use Correct Punctuation in Their Writing

Teachers can explicitly teach students about each punctuation mark by introducing it, discussing its purpose, and demonstrating how to use it correctly in writing.

Students should also have frequent opportunities to explore how punctuation is used in context. They can be asked to find examples of certain punctuation marks in texts and examine the roles they play in the sentences. They can try reading the sentences with the given punctuation marks. They can then reread them with the punctuation marks omitted or substituted and discuss the differences in meaning and tone. For example, students could read a sentence in a book ending with a period, using appropriate intonation and pausing. They could then substitute the period for an exclamation point, adjusting their intonation. They could discuss how the meaning and tone of the sentence changed. Students can also edit their own writing by reading it aloud, using the intonation and phrasing suggested by the punctuation marks they included. They can ask themselves if any areas sound unclear, such as if sentences seem to blend together. They can also use punctuation checklists and ask other classmates to edit their work to double-check for errors.

Review Video: Consistency in Punctuation
Visit mometrix.com/academy and enter code: 169489

Helping Students Use Correct Capitalization in Their Writing

One strategy to teach proper capitalization is to give students texts and ask them to circle all capital letters. Students can then be asked to identify what the words with capital letters have in common, leading to a discussion of capitalization rules. These rules can also be explicitly taught with examples provided.

- Posters can be displayed in classrooms as reminders of when to capitalize letters, such as at the beginnings of sentences, when using proper nouns, or when writing the word *I*.
- Additionally, students can be asked to edit texts, including their own writing pieces, to locate capitalization errors. Students should be reminded that errors may include both randomly capitalized letters and lowercase letters that should be capitalized.
- The ability to differentiate between common and proper nouns is needed to apply capitalization rules correctly. To assist with this skill, students can complete word sorts with common and proper nouns. They can also locate and circle examples of each type in texts.

Review Video: Capitalization in Grammar
Visit mometrix.com/academy and enter code: 369678

Motivating Students to Read

Creating School Environments That Promote a Love of Reading

Helping students develop a lifelong love of reading is an important goal of literacy instruction. Teachers can model their own love of reading by talking about their favorite books and authors and modeling their own use of reading strategies. They can share stories of how reading has positively affected their own lives and opened up new opportunities.

- Teachers can also help develop **communities of readers** within their classrooms, making reading a social experience. Fun and interactive read-alouds and shared reading experiences can help create communities of readers, along with organizing literature circles and reader's theater activities. Favorite books can be reread multiple times, with students participating in the reading.
- Teachers can give students frequent opportunities to read **books of choice**. They can create classroom libraries containing multiple types of texts that students can access easily. Comfortable reading spaces, such as reading chairs and pillows, are also beneficial. Students should also have opportunities to visit their school libraries regularly.
- Additionally, teachers can guide students in completing **author studies**. Students may form connections to favorite authors and seek additional books they have written.

Review Video: Literacy-Rich Content-Area Classrooms
Visit mometrix.com/academy and enter code: 571455

Promoting Successful Independent Reading Experiences at School

Independent reading is beneficial for students' reading development and is sometimes necessary when teachers are working with other students. Therefore, some strategies can be used to make independent reading experiences successful.

It is important to teach students to select appropriate texts that will not lead to boredom or frustration. Some teachers instruct students to apply the five-finger rule. In this approach, students randomly select a single page of text to read. If they struggle to decode five or more words, the book is too difficult. Other teachers inform students of their reading levels and keep labeled boxes of leveled texts available. Students can also be encouraged to maintain personal book boxes that contain several appropriate books so that they are ready for independent reading time.

To remind students of decoding and comprehension strategies they can use during independent reading time, teachers can display posters in their classrooms. Students can also be given small, personalized copies of these strategies to use.

Additionally, students can be encouraged to analyze and discuss what they have read to build interest and engagement. They can maintain reader-response logs or join literature circles with others who have read the same texts.

Motivating Students to Read

One technique to motivate students to read is to make reading an enjoyable part of the daily routine. This includes designating daily time for reading, providing a comfortable, relaxed atmosphere, helping students select texts of interest, and showing genuine interest in discussing the texts together. This technique is easy to implement, and students who look forward to this reading time as children may continue reading for enjoyment in adulthood. A disadvantage is that some students may not respond to this approach.

Another technique is to use rewards and incentives for reading. Some programs reward students after they have read a certain number of books or for a certain number of minutes. Sometimes students are tested on the books they have read to assess comprehension. Read-athons are one example of this approach. Peer participation, competition, and opportunities to earn rewards may increase short-term motivation to read. Disadvantages include the costs of the incentives and the possibility that motivation will decrease once the rewards are removed.

Teachers frequently use a combination of these techniques by providing daily reading time while also incorporating some incentives for reading.

Print-Rich Learning Environments

Characteristics of Literacy-Rich, Content-Area Classrooms

Literacy-rich, content-area classrooms include frequent teacher modeling of academic behaviors. This includes teacher modeling of thinking aloud, use of reading and writing strategies, and incorporation of academic vocabulary into regular activities.

These classrooms also include daily reading, writing, listening, and speaking activities. Students are engaged in reading, writing, and discussing a range of different texts and media in both print in digital form. Depending on the content area, this may include lab reports, journal articles, maps, historical fiction, diaries, graphic organizers, narratives, and more.

Students in literacy-rich classrooms are encouraged to make connections between different sources and content areas. For example, readers may make connections between a historical fiction text about the Dust Bowl and what they have learned in science about weather patterns.

Additionally, teachers in literacy-rich classrooms encourage the respectful sharing of information and ideas among classmates.

Creating Environments Supportive of Cultural and Linguistic Differences

Classrooms should incorporate **culturally** and **linguistically diverse materials**, including those that represent the cultures of students. Reading materials, artwork, classroom labels, and posters are all examples of diverse materials that can be included. Students should also have opportunities to share items that are meaningful to them with other classmates.

Additionally, ELLs should not be punished for reluctance to participate in discussions. Instead, they should be offered **support** and **scaffolding** when needed. When ELLs are in the early stages of English language acquisition, teachers can also use simple sentence structures and provide visual clues to support students' comprehension.

Teachers should also work to create nonthreatening and supportive classroom environments by modeling accepting attitudes. They can model and explicitly teach how to compare and contrast different cultures respectfully. When studying historical and current events, teachers can help students explore the events from different perspectives and discuss how culture can affect people's experiences.

Review Video: Importance of Promoting Literacy in the Home
Visit mometrix.com/academy and enter code: 862347

Using Word Walls to Support Reading and Writing Development

Word walls are collections of words that are prominently displayed in classrooms. Words selected for display on word walls should be meaningful for students. They might include high-frequency words that students need to read and write often or academic vocabulary words related to units of study. Word walls are flexible, and words may be added or removed throughout the year based on students' needs.

Teachers should model how to use word walls to locate and spell high-frequency words. Words may be attached using Velcro, magnets, or other methods that allow them to be removed. This allows students to take the words down while using them and return them to the wall when finished.

There are many ways to organize word walls. Words can be listed alphabetically under letter headings, helping young writers quickly locate them for spelling assistance. If focused on academic vocabulary, the words can be grouped by topic. Visuals can be included with vocabulary words to assist students with remembering meanings.

Leveled Book Rooms

Leveled book rooms are consolidated collections of leveled readers that can be checked out by all teachers within a school. Reading specialists often help organize and maintain leveled book rooms as part of their responsibilities. Because teachers frequently have students who read both well above and well below grade level, these types of book rooms ensure that all students have access to books within their instructional reading levels.

To implement successful leveled book rooms, books should be clearly organized and labeled according to level. The same leveling system used by classroom teachers should be used in the leveled book rooms for consistency. Books may also be organized in additional ways, such as by genre, topic, or author. Teachers should be taught the procedures for checking out and returning books. Records should be maintained in order to keep track of where all books are located.

Instructional Technologies Supporting Literacy Development

There are many ways that instructional technologies can be used to create classroom environments that support literacy development. Computer programs and apps can be used to practice and assess literacy skills, and there are many options that differentiate instruction based on students' existing skills. Many of these programs and apps also save and track students' progress, helping both students and teachers track progress toward goals.

- Projectors, document cameras, and interactive whiteboards can also be used to **magnify texts** so students can follow along during instruction. Interactive whiteboards also allow students to actively participate in literacy activities with classmates.
- **Digital texts** can be used to support listening development and assist students with reading texts that are too difficult for them to read independently. Interactive storybooks that display and track text for emergent and beginning readers can also be used.
- There are many **digital tools** and **software options** that can be used to create forms of media such as slideshow presentations, infographics, digital storybooks, and newsletters. Modern tools can also be used to help students collaborate on projects, even if they are working remotely.

Print-Rich Environments for Early Childhood

Print-Rich Classrooms

In early childhood classrooms, print-rich environments contain books and texts of different genres and topics, including both audio and digital texts. Walls and shelves have signs and labels to help with classroom procedures and organization. Posters display information related to content students have been studying. Reading, writing, and listening centers are available for students to explore during center time. Puppet theaters and flannel boards are present to encourage oral language and storytelling. There are also many literacy-related materials, such as letter tiles and sight word cards. Word walls are posted.

In **print-rich environments**, students are encouraged to share and display texts they have created. They may add their own stories to the classroom libraries or hang up signs they have made. Materials created during shared and interactive reading and writing experiences may also be displayed.

In classrooms for older students, signs and posters are displayed containing academic vocabulary, content students have been studying, and classroom procedures. Written and digital texts from a range of genres are present. There are also ample resources available for students to use to locate and share information, such as computers, tablets, dictionaries, and thesauri.

Promoting Literacy Development with Dramatic Play Centers

Dramatic play centers are common in early childhood classrooms. These centers allow children to act out realistic situations through play. Examples include pretend restaurants, homes, veterinary clinics, and grocery stores. While engaging in dramatic play, children read, write, listen, and speak for authentic purposes.

As children role-play and interact with other children in dramatic play centers, they develop oral language skills. They engage in conversations and practice using language to accomplish tasks, such as ordering in restaurants. They also listen to peers and follow directions, such as when they are pretending to be restaurant servers.

Children also engage in reading activities in dramatic play centers. Labels and realistic print materials can be included. For example, pretend restaurants may include labeled cabinets and menus. Children can practice writing through dramatic play. For example, children who are pretending to be servers may write down orders on notepads.

Building Literacy Activities into Daily Routines and Activities

Teachers can plan reading, writing, listening, and speaking activities across all subject areas. This can include a mixture of independent literacy activities and shared and interactive reading and writing experiences. Texts focusing on topics that are being studied in all content areas can be accessible in the classroom. Students can also write in all subject areas. For example, they can write the processes used to solve problems in math and create travel brochures in social studies.

Teachers of early childhood and elementary students can plan morning meetings in which daily written messages are read and discussed. Students can share current events and topics of interest with their classmates during these meetings, while other students listen and ask questions.

Early childhood and elementary teachers can also incorporate oral language and listening into daily routines. For example, they may recite specific chants or songs during transitions.

Print-Rich Home and Community Environments

Print-Rich Homes

An important component of print-rich homes is easy access to developmentally appropriate texts in a range of genres. Although favorite texts can be kept and reread repeatedly, children should also have access to new and changing texts over time as their interests and skills develop. Both digital and print-based texts are commonly found in print-rich homes. This may include books, magazines, newspapers, online literacy games, and digital stories.

In addition to books, print-rich homes also contain a lot of environmental print that children can read. This may include cereal boxes, board game directions, recipes, mail, and more. Exploring this environmental print helps children understand different purposes for reading and writing.

Children in print-rich homes have easy access to a variety of writing materials, such as paper, pencils, and crayons. Computers can also be available to type texts. Children should be encouraged to write for a variety of purposes and audiences.

Family Members' Promoting Reading

Family members can help children make reading a part of everyday activities both at home and while out in the community. Helping children explore environmental print and its purposes is one important step family members can take. They can point out business and road signs while driving, for example. At home, they can help children explore environmental print like food labels, posters, and mail.

Family members can also help children understand how reading is used to accomplish daily tasks. They can ask children to help create and read lists at the grocery store and select meal choices from restaurant menus. While driving, they can ask children to help read road signs to determine which routes they will take. At home, they can read directions together to assemble new toys and follow recipes to prepare shared meals.

There are many benefits to reading with children for authentic purposes; it helps children understand that reading is part of daily life and learn that it can be used for many practical purposes. This approach also blends learning with daily life and real-world tasks, helping engage children in the learning process.

Family Members' Encouraging Oral Language Development

Parents and family members should talk to children frequently from the moment they are born. Children learn how to use language by listening to those around them. Family members can respond to their children's initial sounds and beginning attempts at speech by making eye contact and replying. When children begin speaking words and sentences, family members can respond by repeating what they have said and adding additional information. They can encourage children to imitate their words and actions, using games like peekaboo. Family members can talk about what they are doing and ask their children open-ended questions. They can use varied vocabulary and sentence structure in their speech.

Family members can also engage in wordplay with children. They can read rhyming and repetitive texts, songs, and poems together, encouraging their children to participate. Additionally, they can retell favorite stories orally and make up stories of their own.

Family Members' Promoting a Love of Reading at Home

Family members can incorporate reading time into their children's daily routines to promote a love of reading at home. This can include a variety of types of reading experiences. Sometimes family members can read aloud to their children, sometimes children can read aloud to their family members, and sometimes they can take turns reading. Each of these experiences has its own benefits. Children benefit from hearing their family members reading fluently and using reading strategies, and they also benefit from practicing their own reading skills in safe environments.

While reading together at home, families can read a mixture of new and favorite texts. The experiences should be fun and relaxing, with opportunities to talk about the stories and characters. They can also listen to audio texts together at various times, such as when they are in the car.

Children can benefit from seeing family members reading frequently and for a variety of purposes. Family members can talk about their favorite books and authors. They can also take children to the library regularly to find new books to read together.

Promoting Community Involvement in Literacy Activities

Teachers can share information with parents about free public story time events to promote parent involvement in community literacy activities. These events are commonly held at public libraries and bookstores. Teachers can also forge partnerships with their local public libraries. They can inquire about programs that issue library cards to students. Local librarians can be invited to visit classrooms to read aloud to students and share information about upcoming events.

Teachers can set up **community volunteer programs**. Community members can be invited to visit classrooms to read with students. Students can also potentially visit senior centers or other locations to read to adults. Local authors and business people who use reading and writing in their jobs can also be invited to visit classrooms to discuss the role that literacy plays in their lives.

Additionally, teachers can encourage students to communicate with community members for **authentic purposes**. For example, students can send thank-you letters to businesses that hosted field trips or sponsored school events. With parents' permission, student work can also be displayed during community events.

Using Instructional Technologies to Promote Literacy Development at Home

There are many free and inexpensive online games and apps that students of all ages can use to practice literacy skills. These include letter recognition activities, phonics skills practice, digital texts with comprehension questions, and more. School districts that subscribe to certain online programs may provide parents with links and passwords so students can practice at home.

Students can also listen to digital storybooks. Online versions are available that track the text for students and show pictures. Audio versions can be downloaded or checked out from public libraries. Family members can listen to and discuss these stories with their children to practice comprehension strategies.

With guidance and supervision, students can communicate with others using digital tools. They can create presentations and written texts using word processing and presentation tools. They can communicate with family members using emails, texts, and videoconferencing tools. They can also use free online tools to create and publish their own digital stories.

Review Video: Collaborating with Families
Visit mometrix.com/academy and enter code: 679996

Increasing Family Involvement in Reading Development

Teachers should communicate with caregivers frequently to increase family involvement in reading development. They should convey to caregivers that they are viewed as partners and assure them that they welcome questions and concerns. Teachers should frequently communicate positive information to caregivers in addition to sharing reading concerns. Teachers should also recognize that different families have different resources available, so they should try communicating through multiple channels. This may include phone calls, texts, classroom websites, paper newsletters, emails, and more. Teachers should also be aware of scheduling, cultural, and linguistic differences. Information can be sent home in multiple languages, if possible.

Teachers can share links to reading activities and strategies using classroom websites and newsletters. They can also send home reproducible books and texts from classroom libraries, that students can read with their families. Consumable supplies can also be sent home, such as cardstock letter tiles that can be used to practice spelling and building words.

Parent and family nights can also be scheduled to share strategies and display student work. These events can be recorded and shared with parents who are unable to attend.

Types of Language Disorders

Language delays and disorders can fall into three categories. **Receptive disorders** make it difficult for people to understand the messages communicated by others. **Expressive disorders** make it difficult for people to communicate their thoughts and ideas to others. **Mixed receptive-expressive language disorders** involve difficulties in both areas. These disorders can either be developmental or acquired. Acquired disorders are caused by injury or illness.

Within each of these categories, there are many different types of disorders. Apraxia, stuttering, and articulation disorders are some examples of expressive disorders. Students with expressive disorders may find it difficult to produce certain sounds, organize their thoughts into sentences, or use language appropriately in social situations. Therefore, classroom activities that require speaking and/or writing may be difficult. Students with receptive disorders may find it difficult to remember details or follow spoken directions. For example, they may not remember multistep directions that are given verbally for assignments.

Meeting the Needs of Students with Language Delays and Disorders

Although students with **language delays** and disorders often receive professional speech therapy, there are many strategies teachers can use to support these students within the classroom.

Teachers should model treating students with language disorders respectfully. They should not interrupt students with expressive disorders or attempt to finish their sentences. Instead, adequate response time should be provided. Students can also be given advance notice of the questions they will be asked, allowing them time to formulate responses.

Students with **receptive disorders** who have difficulties processing or remembering speech may benefit from receiving information in multiple forms. When giving project directions, for example, teachers can provide written directions and explain them verbally. Multistep directions can be broken down into simple steps. Visuals can be used to help students comprehend vocabulary used in speech. Additionally, teachers can ensure that they have obtained students' attention before speaking, and they can monitor students for understanding.

For students who struggle with language pragmatics, role-playing activities can be used to practice appropriate responses for a variety of common social situations, such as asking for help or greeting people.

Review Video: Least Restrictive Environment
Visit mometrix.com/academy and enter code: 100354

Chapter Quiz

Ready to see how well you retained what you just read? Scan the QR code to go directly to the chapter quiz interface for this study guide. If you're using a computer, simply visit the online resources page at **mometrix.com/resources719/mtelreadsp62** and click the Chapter Quizzes link.

Literacy Components and Instructional Resources

Morphology and Word Analysis Skills

Homographs

Homographs are words that are spelled the same but may be pronounced differently and have different meanings. An example of a homograph pair is *bat* (baseball bat) and *bat* (the flying mammal).

After explaining the meaning of homographs, teachers can assist students with generating lists of homograph pairs. Teachers can provide sentences using homographs, and students can identify them and their meanings. Students can also look for homographs in texts and play matching games to find cards with two different definitions for the same word.

Homographs have different meanings, so it is important for readers to be able to identify which meanings are being used when they encounter homographs in texts. Readers can be encouraged to use context clues to assist with determining the meanings. Readers can also be encouraged to self-monitor their understanding of each homograph's meaning by asking themselves if what they have read makes sense. Because homograph pairs can also be pronounced differently, readers can be encouraged to try reading the sentences with each possible pronunciation and ask themselves which one sounds right.

Compound Words

A **compound word** is formed by combining two or more words to form one word with a new, unique meaning. Examples of compound words include *houseboat, moonlight,* and *basketball.*

Identifying compound words rapidly can assist readers with decoding multisyllabic words. Identifying the smaller, known words contained in the compound words will help students decode the words quickly and maintain fluency.

To teach students to identify compound words, they can practice breaking them into parts. Compound words can be provided using letter tiles, magnetic letters, or in writing, and students can be asked to split them into the two smaller word parts. Puzzle cards can be created with which two smaller words join together to create a compound word. Readers can also be asked to find and mark compound words in texts. When students struggle to decode compound words while reading independently, teachers can ask what smaller, known words they see in the unknown words.

Types of Context Clues

- There are several different types of context clues that are often provided in sentences. One common type is a **definition clue**. In this type of clue, a definition for the unfamiliar word is provided somewhere within the same sentence; for example, *the precocious toddler surprised her parents by learning to read at a much earlier age than her peers.*
- Another type of context clue is an **antonym clue**. In this type of clue, an antonym or contrasting definition of the unfamiliar word is provided somewhere within the same sentence; for example, *unlike his amiable coworker, Mark was quite unfriendly when interacting with customers.*

- **Synonym clues** are a third type of context clue. In this type, a synonym for the unfamiliar word is provided somewhere within the same sentence; for example, *the altruistic donor was so selfless that she donated all of her lottery winnings to her favorite charity*.
- **Inference clues** are another type of context clue. With this type of clue, the unknown word's meaning is not explicitly given, and the reader must infer it from the context of the sentence; for example, *Sam was thirsty after hiking the three-mile trail, so he ordered a cold beverage at the café*.

AFFIXES

Affixes are letters or groups of letters that are added to root words. **Prefixes** and **suffixes** are two common types of **affixes**. Root words may have one or multiple affixes attached to them.

Learning to identify affixes and understand their meanings is important for both fluency and comprehension. Because the same affixes are used repeatedly in English, immediately recognizing them and knowing how they are pronounced can assist readers with decoding multisyllabic words. Decoding the words quickly will help the readers maintain fluency. Because affixes also have predictable meanings, understanding these meanings can help readers comprehend new words in texts and build vocabulary. For example, if readers encounter the word *declutter*, they may know that *de* means the opposite of something, and *clutter* means a messy collection of things. Using this knowledge, they can put the parts together and determine the meaning of *declutter*.

Review Video: Affixes
Visit mometrix.com/academy and enter code: 782422

PREFIXES

A **prefix** is a letter or group of letters added to the beginning of a root word. The prefix modifies the existing word's meaning, and a new word is formed. For example, the prefix *dis-* can be added to the word *respect* to form the new word *disrespect*.

Students need to understand the difference between a prefix and base word. It should be emphasized that the base is a whole word, whereas the prefix is a letter or group of letters that cannot stand alone. Examples of words containing prefixes can be provided, and students can practice identifying both the prefixes and root words. Non-examples can also be provided, such as the word *decal*. *De-* is not a prefix in this example because *cal* is not a word on its own.

The meanings of different prefixes can then be introduced. Root words can be presented, and their meanings discussed. Prefixes can then be added, and students can discuss how the meanings of the words change. They can list other words containing the same prefixes, along with their meanings.

Students can also be encouraged to find examples of words containing prefixes in texts independently and use clues to determine their meanings.

SUFFIXES

A **suffix** is a letter or group of letters added to the end of a root word. When added, it sometimes changes the meaning of the root word and forms a new word. It may also change the part of speech of the root word. An example of a suffix is *-ful*. When added to the end of the root word *thank*, it forms the word *thankful*, which means full of thanks.

To introduce the topic, students can be given lists of words containing suffixes and asked to identify what the words have in common. The suffixes can then be identified, and teachers can explain how the suffixes change the root words. Three-column charts can be created, with columns dedicated to suffixes, their meanings, and example words. Students can be given cards containing root words and suffixes, and they can experiment with pairing them. They can explain whether the combinations form real or nonsense words and define any real words they create. Students can be encouraged to find examples of words containing suffixes and identify their meanings based on context clues in the texts.

Derivational vs. Inflectional Affixes

- **Derivational affixes** are letters or groups of letters added to root words to change the meanings of the words or the parts of speech.For example, if the affix *un-* is added to the root *kind*, the new word *unkind* is formed. Both the original and newly formed words are adjectives, but the meanings of the two words are different. However, if the affix *-ment* is added to the root word *fulfill*, the new word *fulfillment* is formed. The original word is a verb, and the newly formed word is a noun. Both of these examples demonstrate derivational affixes.
- **Inflectional affixes** do not change the part of speech of a word, but they do serve a grammatical function. Inflectional affixes include the suffixes *-s*, *-ed*, *-ing*, *-en*, *-'s*, *-er*, and *-est*. For example, adding an inflectional affix can change the word *walk* to *walked*. The part of speech does not change as both words are verbs. The affix only changes the tense of the verb. Inflectional affixes can indicate whether a noun is singular or plural, the verb tense, superlatives, or possessives.

Relationship Between Knowledge of Roots and Affixes

Knowledge of roots and affixes and the use of **context clues** are closely related. Proficient readers use a combination of these strategies to determine the meanings of unknown words, check their initial guesses, and revise their guesses if necessary.

- When encountering an unknown multisyllabic word, a reader may first look for kno**wn parts** of the word. This may lead the reader to break the word down into the root and affixes. Using knowledge of what each of these components means, the reader may then guess the word's meaning.
- However, both roots and affixes can have multiple meanings. The reader's initial guess may not make sense in this particular context. Therefore, it is important for the reader to also consider **context clues** to check the conjectured meaning. If it does not fit the context, the reader may consider other meanings of the root and affixes that better fit the context clues.
- The reader may also begin by guessing the word's meaning using context clues and then use knowledge of the root and affixes to check the initial conjecture. Teachers should encourage readers to use both of these strategies to **check** and **self-correct** their deductions.

Spelling Development

Stages of Spelling Development

Students typically progress through a series of stages of spelling development. Researchers name the stages differently, but they contain common characteristics.

In the **pre-phonetic stage**, students spell using random letter and number strings. There are no letter-sound relationships evident in words. In the **semi-phonetic stage**, some letter-sound relationships are used to spell words. Students typically learn to correctly spell the beginning and ending sounds in words first, followed later by the medial sounds. In the **phonetic stage**, some simple words begin to be spelled correctly, such as CVC words. In addition to initial, medial, and final sounds, some more complex sounds are accurately represented. This includes some consonant blends and digraphs. In the transitional, or **word extension stage**, students learn to use syllable patterns to spell more complex words. Most words are spelled correctly in this stage. In the **derivational constancy stage**, students use knowledge of roots and affixes to spell related words. Most or all words in students' writing pieces are spelled correctly in this stage.

Orthography

Orthography refers to the conventional spelling of words in a language. Because many words are spelled using the same patterns, studying orthography helps students increase the number of words they can spell correctly. Learning to apply orthographic patterns is an important part of any literacy program.

Word studies, or word work, should be regularly included in the school day. Word work should be sequential and built upon the knowledge of orthographic patterns that students already possess.

There are three layers of orthography that students can explore during word work. The **alphabet layer** refers to letter-sound relationships. Activities in which students combine letters or letter groups to form words will help them explore the alphabet layer. When students explore the **pattern layer**, they look for larger patterns that guide the spellings of words. Activities in which students build words within word families, such as CVCe words, help them explore the pattern layer. The **meaning layer** explores the relationships between word meanings and spellings. Sorting and writing words that contain the same Latin roots will help students explore the meaning layer of orthography.

Layers of English Orthography

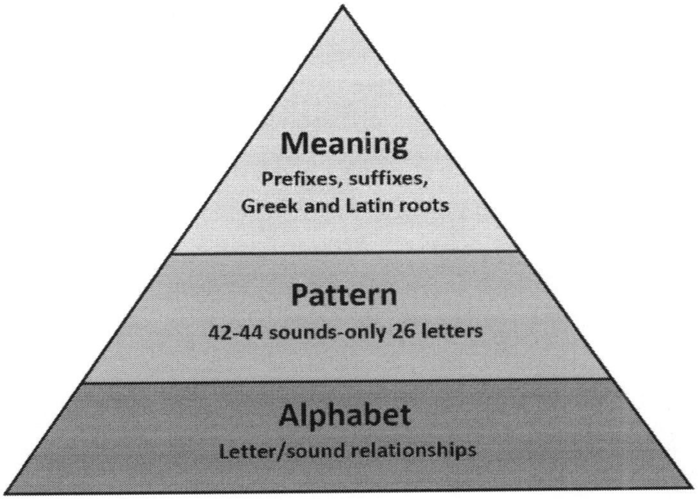

Phonetic Spelling

Phonetic spelling is common in the early stages of writing development. When writing words, students consider what sounds they hear. They use knowledge of phonics rules to select letters or groups of letters to represent those sounds. For example, a student who is familiar with CVC words might write *love* as *luv*.

Parents are sometimes concerned with the amount of misspelled words in their children's writing. However, phonetic spelling plays a role in reading and writing development and is a stepping stone to conventional spelling.

At this stage, students know how to automatically spell a limited number of words. Using known phonics rules helps them efficiently encode words they do not know how to spell. If students are worried about spelling every word conventionally, they must continuously ask others for help. This slows the writing process and puts more emphasis on spelling than on recording ideas. Therefore, teachers typically tell students in this stage to write the sounds they hear and move on. This process also allows students to apply the phonics skills they use while reading.

Over time, students learn more complex spelling patterns and automatically remember how to spell more words. At this point, spelling becomes more conventional.

Role of Memorization in Spelling Development and Instruction

There are some words that students cannot learn to spell by learning spelling patterns. These include many high-frequency words with irregular spelling patterns, such as the word *the*. Students should have frequent and repeated exposure to these words to memorize their spellings. Practice activities are helpful, such as building these words with letter tiles.

Some academic vocabulary words are also difficult for students to spell using knowledge of spelling patterns. For example, second graders may learn about camouflage as part of a science unit on animal adaptations. However, it would be difficult for students of this age to spell the word *camouflage* using knowledge of spelling patterns. Frequent exposure to these academic words in print will help students learn to spell them over time. Adding these words to word walls or classroom charts can serve as tools to assist with spelling initially. Being given numerous opportunities to write these words with scaffolding will assist with memorization.

Although memorization plays a role in spelling some words, its use as an instructional strategy should be balanced with explicit instruction in spelling patterns. When choosing weekly spelling lists, teachers should focus on patterns that can be applied to multiple words.

Different Approaches to Teaching Students to Spell

There are many methods and commercial programs available to teach spelling. Although they vary in approach, the methods that are most effective share some common characteristics.

Effective spelling instruction should be explicit. Although students naturally learn to spell many words through frequent reading experiences, some explicit spelling instruction is still helpful to teach common spelling patterns and relationships among words. The instruction should be both incremental and sequential.

Teachers can introduce weekly spelling patterns, and students can complete activities to familiarize themselves with the patterns. Depending on the ages of the students, this may include word sorts, word hunts, and tracing. Multisensory activities are also helpful, such as building words with letter tiles and writing words in sand. Teachers may assess students' applications of the spelling patterns at the end of each week. Some teachers give students lists of words to study ahead of time. Other teachers assess students by asking them to spell new words that follow the patterns they have been studying.

Components of Reading Comprehension

Reading Comprehension

A basic definition of **reading comprehension** is understanding what has been read. However, reading comprehension is quite complex. It involves both taking meaning from the text and creating meaning by integrating the text with prior knowledge. It is an active process that requires the use of multiple skills and strategies, such as decoding, fluency, understanding word meanings, predicting, inferring, and more. It involves different levels of understanding, including comprehending both the literal meanings of the words and the unstated themes and implications of the text. Comprehension is one of the main goals of reading instruction.

Comprehension is essential to developing proficient readers. If readers are able to decode the words but cannot comprehend the messages, they won't make any meaning from the texts and will become easily frustrated. Because comprehension is an **active process**, it is also important for developing engaged readers who enjoy reading for a variety of purposes.

Literal Comprehension

Literal comprehension refers to understanding the written meaning of a text. It involves a basic understanding of the text's vocabulary, events, main ideas, and other features. Literal comprehension is important because it is the foundation upon which deeper levels of comprehension are formed.

Promoting Literal Comprehension

Answering **literal comprehension questions** using text evidence is one strategy to support development of this skill. This can be done through class discussions or written activities. Readers can be asked to identify the setting of the story, main characters, sequence of events, or other topics where the answers can be found directly in the text. Readers should be asked to provide text evidence for their answers, which might involve marking the sentences where the answers are found. Graphic organizers, such as story maps and problem/solution charts, can also help students develop literal comprehension skills.

To **scaffold** the development of literal comprehension, the teacher can begin by asking questions about a portion of the text immediately after it is read, using the same wording as the text. Over time, the wording can be varied and the teacher can wait for longer intervals before asking the questions.

Inferential Comprehension

Inferential comprehension is a deeper level of understanding than literal comprehension. It requires inferring what the author meant. The answers to inferential comprehension questions are not found directly in the text. Readers must instead make inferences, draw conclusions, determine points of view, and make other informed decisions based upon the evidence provided in the text.

Promoting Inferential Comprehension

To develop **inferential comprehension skills**, readers can be asked to make **predictions** or **inferences** and **draw conclusions**. This can be done using class discussions, written activities, or graphic organizers. For predictions, inferences, and conclusions, readers should be asked to provide text evidence to support their choices. This may involve marking parts of the text or recording relevant sentences. They should then be encouraged to evaluate their predictions, inferences, and conclusions as they continue reading. If new evidence conflicts with their initial predictions, inferences, or conclusions, readers should be encouraged to revise them as needed. Proficient readers self-monitor their comprehension and continually revise their understanding as additional evidence is gathered.

Evaluative Comprehension

Evaluative comprehension is a deeper level of understanding than literal comprehension and goes further than inferential comprehension. It requires readers to make judgments and share opinions about what they have read based upon evidence found in the text and prior knowledge. For example, evaluative comprehension questions might ask readers to consider if they would have handled an event in the text differently or explain whether they agree or disagree with the author's point of view.

Promoting Evaluative Comprehension

Because evaluative comprehension requires deeper thinking than literal comprehension, it is helpful for teachers to frequently model their thinking when responding to these types of questions. They can model how to identify relevant information within the text and draw upon prior experiences to form judgments about topics.

It is also helpful to provide readers with evaluative question stems they can reference when reading independently. These question stems can also be displayed on charts in the classroom.

Summarization

Summarization refers to providing a concise description of the main idea and key details of a text. Summarization assists with comprehension by helping readers separate important information and vocabulary from unimportant information. It also helps readers remember what they have read.

Summarization is often a difficult skill for students to learn. Their initial summaries may provide too few or too many details from the text. Modeling and explicit instruction can help students learn to provide **effective summaries**. Students can be taught to reread a text and cross off unimportant or repetitive information. They can then be encouraged to locate and mark the main idea and key details that are essential to understanding the meaning of the text. Additionally, they can be encouraged to substitute general words for lists of related words in a category. For example, rather than listing all of the animals belonging to a character's family, students could use the word *pets* instead.

Readers can also complete **graphic organizers** to develop their summaries. One common type of graphic organizer asks students to complete the following sentence stems to form summaries: Someone, Wanted, But, So, Then.

Review Video: Summarizing Text
Visit mometrix.com/academy and enter code: 172903

Role of Prior Knowledge in Reading Comprehension

Research has shown that students learn best when they can relate new information to existing knowledge already stored in long-term memory. This helps them organize and make sense of the new information and apply it in future situations. When reading, prior knowledge can help students determine the meaning of unfamiliar vocabulary words, form predictions about what might happen next, make inferences, and make sense of story events. All of these skills are important for comprehension.

To activate students' prior knowledge, the teacher can ask what students already know about a topic when it is introduced. Students' contributions can be listed on a chart or graphic organizer. Know, want, and learned (KWL) charts can be completed, listing what students already know, want to know, and learned about the topic. The teacher can also ask students to make comparisons by asking how the new topic is similar to and different from something they have already learned.

Denotative vs. Connotative Meanings

Words often have multiple meanings. **Denotative** meanings are the literal meanings of words. **Connotative** meanings are the secondary meanings of words and refer to the positive and negative associations that arise from them. For example, the denotative meaning of the word *heart* is a muscular organ in the circulatory system that pumps blood. A connotative meaning of the word *heart* is love.

There are several reference tools that can be used to locate the meanings of words. Dictionaries can be used to find the denotative and connotative meanings of words, along with other information like word origin and pronunciation. Thesauri can be used to find lists of synonyms for words, and antonyms are sometimes included as well. Glossaries list the definitions of important vocabulary words and are often found at the end of texts. All of these reference tools can be found in both print and digital forms.

Review Video: Denotation and Connotation
Visit mometrix.com/academy and enter code: 310092

Helping Learners Retell Fictional Stories

There are specific steps teachers can take to focus readers' attention on key parts of stories to assist with retelling. Teachers can preview the stories with students and point out the key events they should listen for before they begin reading. During reading, they can pause and ask students to summarize the key events they have heard in the stories so far. After reading, teachers can lead students in shared retellings or ask students to retell the stories independently.

Students can fill out graphic organizers or create flip books that describe what happened in the beginning, middle, and end. They can also draw or act out the main story events. Additionally, students can be given sentence strips containing the main story events in a mixed-up order and asked to sequence them. Story ropes can also be used, where students tell story events in order as they move their hands along sets of beads or knots on ropes.

Retelling is important for story comprehension because it requires readers to identify and sequence the main story events. Readers must also consider other story elements, such as characters, setting, and plot, during retellings.

Purposes for Reading

One purpose of reading is for entertainment, which is known as **aesthetic reading**. Sometimes readers select texts because they look interesting to read, and they read them just for fun. Selecting a fairy tale from the library for silent reading time and choosing a bedtime story are examples of times students read for entertainment.

Additionally, sometimes people read for information. This is known as **efferent reading**. It occurs when readers select nonfiction texts to learn something new. This might include learning new facts about a topic or learning the steps needed to accomplish a task. Selecting a book about whales while studying ocean life is an example of reading for information. Reading a recipe to prepare dinner is also an example of reading for information.

Reading to learn opinions is another purpose for reading. This type of reading occurs when people are trying to make decisions about things and look to others for advice. Reading online reviews before purchasing a product is an example of reading for opinions.

Assisting with Comprehension by Recognizing the Author's Purpose

Recognizing the author's purpose can assist with comprehension in multiple ways. First, it can offer the readers clues about the text structures and features they are likely to encounter. If readers recognize that the author is writing to inform, they will know to look for features of informational texts, such as headings and content-specific vocabulary words. If readers recognize that the author is writing to entertain, they will know to pay attention to character traits, plot development, and other features of entertaining texts.

Additionally, knowing the **author's purpose** can help the reader evaluate the text more effectively. If readers recognize that the author is trying to persuade them, they will know to think critically about any claims that the author makes rather than accepting them at face value.

Knowing the author's purpose can also assist readers with determining if texts will meet their needs. For example, students may need to gather factual background information for a science experiment they are completing. They may preview a text and recognize that it is written for entertainment. They may then decide that the text is not suited to meet their needs in this circumstance.

Review Video: Understanding the Author's Intent
Visit mometrix.com/academy and enter code: 511819

Teaching Readers to Recognize an Author's Purpose

The author's purpose may be stated either explicitly or implicitly in a text. Readers can be taught to recognize text structures and features that help identify the author's purpose. Texts that are written to entertain often contain interesting characters and engaging plots. They may contain entertaining phrases and humor, and illustrations may be present.

Texts written to persuade usually contain evidence to support the author's points of view. This may include statistics, facts, and/or personal opinions. Readers can be asked if the authors appear to be for or against something to determine if texts are written to persuade.

Texts written to inform often include facts, which may be stated using text, charts, graphs, or other features. These texts may contain captioned photographs to provide additional information about the topics. Content-specific vocabulary words are often present. Readers can be asked if the authors appear to be trying to teach them about something to determine if texts are written for this purpose.

It is also important for readers to recognize that authors may have multiple purposes for writing. Readers may recognize text structures and features characteristic of two or more purposes within one text.

Making Predictions

When making predictions, readers gather evidence from the text and pictures to make inferences. They sequence story events and make connections between the text and prior experiences to predict what might happen next. Continually making and revising predictions also helps keep readers engaged. All of these activities support reading comprehension.

To help learners make predictions before shared reading experiences, teachers can conduct picture walks of texts. While showing the pictures, teachers can provide brief overviews of the stories, asking students to contribute their predictions about what each section might be about. During reading, teachers can pause to ask students to summarize what has happened so far and predict what might happen next. Teachers can model using prior experiences, picture and context clues, and memories of similar texts when making predictions.

Readers should be taught to evaluate their predictions to determine if they were correct. They should also be taught to look for additional information that might cause them to revise their original predictions. Readers can fill out charts listing their predictions, the evidence used to support these predictions, and what actually happened in the texts.

Review Video: Predictive Reading
Visit mometrix.com/academy and enter code: 437248

Inferring

Authors sometimes provide clues in their writing rather than stating things explicitly. When this occurs, readers must make **inferences** or draw conclusions based on facts, prior knowledge, or text evidence rather than explicit statements. For example, an author might state that a character marched off and slammed the door. Although the author did not state it directly, readers may infer that the character is angry based on his actions.

- Making **inferences** is important for comprehension because much of the meaning in a text can be stated indirectly. If readers comprehend only direct statements, they may miss out on major themes or events in the story.

- Because **prior knowledge** can be used to make inferences, it is helpful for teachers to activate students' prior knowledge before reading through previewing and discussing what is known about the topic. Providing students with frequent opportunities to read varied texts can also build prior knowledge that will assist with inferring.
- Teachers can also show **pictures** to students and ask what inferences they can make based upon picture clues. Additionally, teachers can model **thinking aloud** while reading, discussing what inferences they are making and what prior knowledge, facts, or text clues they are using as evidence.

Review Video: Inference
Visit mometrix.com/academy and enter code: 379203

Drawing Conclusions

Drawing conclusions is important for reading comprehension because it helps readers understand important events or concepts in a text that are not directly stated. Drawing conclusions about an author's purpose for writing can also help readers better evaluate the text because they will be aware of potential bias.

To help readers learn to draw conclusions, teachers can provide students with several supporting details about common topics and ask what conclusions they can draw. For example, they could describe a house with balloons, streamers, presents, and a cake in the kitchen, leading to a conclusion that it is somebody's birthday. A graphic organizer can be used to organize this information, with the conclusion in the middle and the supporting details branching off from this conclusion. This process can then be repeated using details found in texts. This will show readers how they can use prior knowledge and text evidence to form conclusions when they read independently.

Metacognition

Metacognition is when readers think about their own thinking. Proficient readers continuously self-monitor their own reading. They ensure that they are making meaning from the text. If things do not make sense, they use strategies to self-correct the issues. Metacognitive strategies are important for reading comprehension because they ensure that readers are actively engaged while reading and that they understand what they have read. Modeling these strategies by thinking aloud is an important way to help students learn and apply these strategies in their independent reading.

Metacognitive strategies before reading include previewing the text, making predictions, and setting a purpose for reading. Metacognitive strategies during reading include visualizing, making connections, rereading to clarify confusion, and asking self-monitoring questions. Readers also utilize text features to locate and make sense of key information. Metacognitive strategies after reading include summarizing, drawing conclusions, and determining if any unanswered questions remain that need additional clarification.

Comparing and Contrasting

Readers can **compare and contrast** many things when reading, such as characters, settings, story events, multiple texts, and more. This supports comprehension because readers must recall details and find text evidence to compare and contrast. Comparing and contrasting also requires higher-level thinking skills, can help readers organize information, and can clarify confusion between two things.

Venn diagrams are a common way to help readers **compare and contrast** information. Text evidence and prior knowledge can be used to identify features that are the same and different between two things, and they can then be listed in the appropriate sections of the diagram.

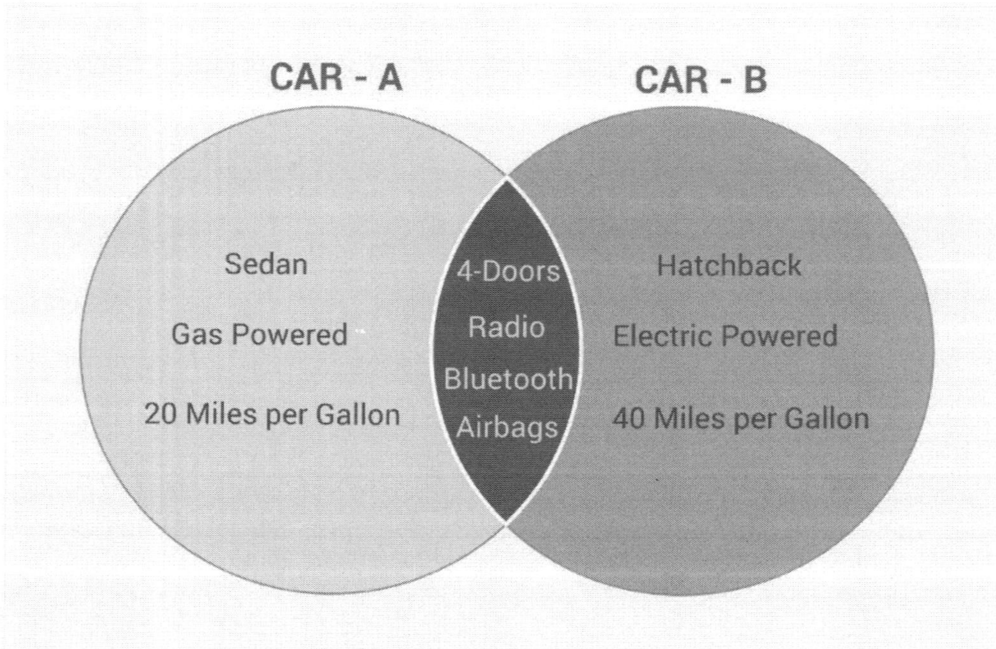

Students can also be taught to identify key words that signal whether two things in a text are the same or different. Word such as *similarly* and *like* signal that two things are the same, whereas words and phrases such as *although* and *on the other hand* signal that two things are different. A chart that lists these key words and phrases can be displayed in the classroom as a reminder for students to use when reading.

Review Video: Compare and Contrast
Visit mometrix.com/academy and enter code: 798319

Recognizing Main Ideas and Details

The ability to recognize the main ideas and supporting details of texts assists with comprehension. Main ideas and supporting details help readers identify what the texts are covering and determine what message an author is trying to send.

Understanding paragraph structure can help readers locate the main idea and supporting details. Readers can be taught that the main idea is typically located in either the first or last sentence of the paragraph.

Readers can be encouraged to locate the main idea and mark it and then locate all supporting details and mark them in a different way. Main ideas and details can also be written on webs or other graphic organizers to help readers comprehend what they have read. Scaffolding can be provided when readers are first learning to complete these graphic organizers and then gradually withdrawn.

Prereading activities, such as discussing the title and previewing the pictures, can also help readers form initial thoughts about the main idea of a text. They can revise their initial thoughts as they read.

Distinguishing Between Facts and Opinions

Facts are statements that can be proven to be true. For example, stating that George Washington was the first president of the United States is a fact. **Opinions** are statements that cannot be proven true or false. They represent people's judgements or views of something. Stating that cats are easier to take care of than dogs is an opinion.

It is important for readers to distinguish between facts and opinions. Recognizing when statements are opinions can help readers identify any biases the authors may have and recognize that the authors may be trying to persuade them. Distinguishing between facts and opinions is important when reading any text, but it necessitates special consideration when using digital sources. Anyone can post information online, and readers must be able to evaluate the sources effectively to determine if they are based on fact or opinion.

To teach students to identify facts and opinions, teachers can introduce the terms and provide examples of each. Students can be asked to mark examples of facts and opinions in texts using different colors. They can also be encouraged to look for key words that signal opinions, such as *think*, *believe*, *feel*, *best*, and *favorite*.

Review Video: Distinguishing Fact and Opinion
Visit mometrix.com/academy and enter code: 870899

Analyzing and Interpreting an Author's Craft and Structure

An **author's craft** refers to an author's style of writing. It includes all of the choices an author makes when writing a text, such as word choice, text structure, point of view, use of literary elements, message, tone, and more. When focusing on an author's craft, readers analyze all of these choices and consider the effects they have on readers.

Analyzing and interpreting an author's craft and structure helps readers reach a deeper level of comprehension than surface comprehension. It aids them in understanding how different elements of the text work together to convey a certain meaning and tone. It helps them recognize that authors make several deliberate choices throughout the writing process about how to convey their messages most effectively, which will assist readers with making choices in their own writing. Additionally, it encourages active engagement with the text because readers are continuously analyzing and interpreting while they read. Comparing and contrasting an author's craft using different texts and other authors can also help readers make connections.

Close Reading

Close reading refers to reading and analyzing a text in a thoughtful manner to develop a deep understanding of its meaning, theme, use of language, and other elements. When close reading, readers first read through the text to determine the general meaning. They then reread the text to analyze the use of language and theme. They also make connections between the text and themselves, other texts, or real-world events and form evaluations. The goal of close reading is to develop independent readers who are able to gather deep meaning from texts with little or no scaffolding. Therefore, close reading activities do not involve previewing, picture walks, or other prereading activities.

Not all texts are ideal for close reading activities. Teachers should choose texts with deep meaning and multiple elements to discuss and analyze. They should consider the **complexity** of vocabulary, syntax, and meaning when choosing appropriate texts for close reading. Teachers should also consider the complexity of text features and structures.

Teachers can model how to reread texts and analyze different elements each time. They can guide students in this process by asking questions that require increasingly higher-level thinking skills after each reading of the text.

Importance of Being Able to Synthesize

Synthesis is the ability to gather information from multiple sources and combine it to make meaning. It is important because it requires readers to think critically about which parts of texts hold key information. Synthesis also requires readers to summarize and put ideas into their own words rather than repeat the texts verbatim. All of these skills assist with comprehension. Synthesis is also important when readers need to gather information about topics from multiple sources. The sources may differ in format and viewpoint, and readers must be able to find and combine the important points from each.

To teach students to **synthesize**, teachers can model tracking their thinking throughout the reading of a text and explain how it changes as new information is gathered. They can use phrases such as, "I used to think ____, but now I think ____. My thinking changed because____." Text evidence can be cited to explain the changes.

Readers can also be given **graphic organizers** to fill out as they read, recording key points in their own words. After compiling the key points, students can explain the main ideas they learned from the texts and how their thinking changed as they read.

Reading Various Types of Texts

Genres of Fiction

Realistic fiction stories are about events that could happen in real life. The characters and settings are realistic. **Historical** fiction stories also contain realistic characters, settings, and events, but they take place in the past—often during important times in history. **Mysteries** contain crimes or puzzling events that the characters must solve. **Fantasies** contain story elements that are unrealistic, such as talking animals or magic. **Science-fiction** stories focus on imagining life with advanced science or technological capabilities and other theorized situations, such as the existence of extraterrestrial life.

Folktales are another type of fiction. They are popular stories that are passed down from generation to generation, often by word of mouth. Fairy tales are one type of folktale. They often contain magical events and creatures, take place in enchanted places, have happy endings, and have good characters battling evil characters. There are often multiple versions of fairy tales. Cinderella is one example. Tall tales are folktales that are portrayed as if they were realistic but include characters with superhuman traits and exaggerated events. Paul Bunyan is an example of a tall tale.

Review Video: Best Tips for Effectively Reading Fiction
Visit mometrix.com/academy and enter code: 391411

Review Video: Myths, Fables, Legends, and Fairy Tales
Visit mometrix.com/academy and enter code: 347199

Importance of Being Able to Recognize Different Genres of Fiction

Understanding the characteristics of different genres and being able to correctly classify texts by type is beneficial to readers for many reasons. Knowledge of the typical text structures of each genre assists readers with making predictions. For example, knowing that fairy tales typically end with good overcoming evil can help readers predict how stories will end. It also helps readers analyze texts deeply and incorporate characteristics of the genres in their own writing.

There are different approaches that can be used to teach about genres. One approach is to complete genre studies in which genres are explored in detail one at a time. Teachers may begin by providing explicit instruction on the characteristics of each genre and then give students opportunities to analyze examples. Teachers may also begin by sharing multiple texts of the same genre and asking students to identify common characteristics on their own. Another approach is to present multiple genres at once using a compare-and-contrast approach. No matter which approach is used, readers should have opportunities to explore many texts of each type of genre to develop an understanding of their common characteristics and text structures.

Fictional Story Elements

Fictional texts contain characters. There are both **primary characters**, who are central to the conflicts and resolutions of the stories, and **secondary characters**, who play smaller roles. The settings of the stories are another feature. The **settings** include both the times in history and the geographical locations where the stories occur. Fictional stories also contain problems or conflicts. The **conflicts** are usually introduced early in the stories to hook readers and encourage them to continue reading. The **plots** contain the main events of the stories, when the characters work to resolve the problems. The **solutions** contain the resolutions to the problems, which typically occur toward the ends of the stories. Fictional texts also typically contain **themes**, which are the underlying messages the authors are trying to convey to readers.

It is important for readers to understand that not all fictional texts contain every element. However, recognizing the common features will assist readers with making predictions and comprehending the texts.

Review Video: Determining Relationships in a Story
Visit mometrix.com/academy and enter code: 929925

Review Video: How to Make a Story Map
Visit mometrix.com/academy and enter code: 261719

Teaching Students to Identify Fictional Story Elements

A common way for teachers to introduce students to fictional story elements is modeling their thinking during shared reading experiences. For example, teachers may pause their reading when evidence is provided about the story's settings. The teachers may explain what they have gathered about the settings and show students which textual clues they used to make these determinations.

Graphic organizers, including story maps, are commonly used tools that help students locate and record story elements. These story maps typically ask students to locate the characters, settings, problems, events, and solutions in stories. Foldables or flip books can also be used to record these elements. These elements can be recorded using a combination of pictures and text depending on the ages and needs of the students. Students can also fill out these graphic organizers as prewriting activities when outlining their own stories.

Teachers should ask guiding questions to focus students' attention on story elements before reading. For example, they can ask students to listen for the problem in the story before they begin reading.

TYPES OF CHARACTERS FOUND IN FICTIONAL STORIES

There are several common types of characters found in fictional stories. However, not all fictional stories contain all types of characters.

- **Protagonists** are the main characters in fictional stories that readers can relate to and want to succeed. Protagonists can be complex characters with both positive and negative traits. Although readers empathize with protagonists, these characters do not always demonstrate admirable behavior.
- **Antagonists** are characters who stand in the way of protagonists accomplishing their goals. Antagonists are not necessarily bad characters and can also have both positive and negative traits.
- **Flat characters** do not change over time. Their actions and personalities are consistent throughout the stories. They are sometimes known as static characters.
- **Dynamic characters** change over time, usually as a result of experiencing the events in the narrative. Readers can identify changes in these characters as the story progresses. Dynamic characters change over time, usually as a result of experiencing the events in the stories. Readers can identify changes in these characters as the stories progress.

Review Video: Definition of a Character in a Story
Visit mometrix.com/academy and enter code: 429493

ANALYZING CHARACTER DEVELOPMENT

Authors of fictional texts present a variety of information about their characters. They describe the characters' physical characteristics, personality traits, hobbies, dreams and goals, and approaches to solving problems. After reading the stories, readers get to know the characters and develop the ability to predict how the characters might react to different types of situations. They also identify the roles that the characters play in the stories, such as being the protagonists or antagonists. Additionally, they determine whether or not any characters have changed as the stories progressed, and they identify reasons for these changes. All of these steps are part of analyzing **character development**.

Students can be asked to discuss character traits and complete character maps using text evidence from the stories. They can be asked to predict how characters would likely react in other situations, based upon their actions in the stories. Students can also be asked to describe how characters have changed from the beginnings of the stories to the ends, using text clues for support. They can compare and contrast characters from different texts or the same characters during different periods of time.

ROLE THAT THE SETTING PLAYS IN A STORY

Setting plays an important role in a story. It describes both the geographical location where the story takes place and the time in history when it occurs. A well-described setting also has the power to set the mood for the story. It can help readers visualize the story's events and imagine that they are present. This can assist readers with comprehension and increase engagement with the text.

To recognize setting, readers can be asked to identify both where and when the story takes place as well as to locate key words within the story that signal the answers to these questions. To explore setting more deeply, readers can be asked to identify how the story evokes their five senses. Using a graphic organizer, they can explore what the characters see, hear, taste, smell, and feel in the story. They can discuss how the use of these details helps readers visualize the setting, and they can be encouraged to use similar details in their own writing.

Teachers can also find examples of mentor texts with detailed settings. Students can explore the ways that the authors describe the settings and discuss how these details affect readers.

ELEMENTS OF POETRY

Discussing and analyzing poetry is a common part of literacy instruction. As part of this instruction, teachers can help students learn to recognize common elements in poetry and use the appropriate terminology to describe them.

There are several elements of poetry. A **verse** is a single line of poetry. Verses can be grouped together to form **stanzas**. The **rhythm** in a poem is developed from patterns of stressed and unstressed syllables. **Meter** refers to a poem's rhythmic structure. Some poems incorporate rhyme, which occurs when words end with the same sounds. **Rhymes** are often found at the ends of verses. Poetry can also use other literary elements, such as alliteration, similes, and metaphors.

Students can learn much about elements of poetry by exploring different types of poems. Students can be asked what they like or dislike about each poem, and these observations can be used to introduce the elements that are used. Students can also compare and contrast different types of poems to see how the elements can be used in different ways. While discussing these observations, teachers can also introduce the correct terminology and provide additional examples to explain how the elements are used by different poets.

Review Video: Structural Elements of Poetry
Visit mometrix.com/academy and enter code: 265216

HELPING STUDENTS DEVELOP AN APPRECIATION OF POETRY

There are many ways teachers can make learning about poetry fun and engaging for students. Early childhood and elementary students can be introduced to poetry during read-alouds and shared reading experiences. They can be encouraged to participate by clapping, making hand motions, and joining in the reading. As students get older, they can participate by highlighting and annotating poems and presenting them aloud to others.

Students can also be encouraged to explore different types of poetry to find styles that appeal to them. Free verse, sonnets, limericks, haikus, villanelles, and sestinas are just some examples of the many types of poetry. Students can also be encouraged to experiment with writing their own examples of different types of poetry.

Additionally, teachers can design poetry challenges for students. For example, students can be given magnetic words or print media that can be cut apart. Students can then explore rearranging the words into verses and stanzas to create different types of poems—seeing how the rhythm, meter, and other elements change. Students can also explore poetic elements in their favorite songs.

ENCOURAGING STUDENTS TO LOCATE AND USE EVIDENCE FROM NONFICTION TEXTS

Students can use T-charts while reading nonfiction texts. On the left side, they can record opinions, predictions, inferences, and similar thoughts made while reading. On the right side of the T-chart, students can record the **text evidence** used to support these thoughts.

Students can also complete scavenger hunts to find text evidence. Teachers can ask students **broad questions** that require higher-level thinking skills and instruct them to search nonfiction texts to find the answers. Information in the texts that are used to answer the questions can be highlighted or recorded on graphic organizers.

Teachers can also **model** this process for students. They can begin shared reading experiences by identifying what questions they want to answer by reading the texts. They can then model stopping when they reach evidence that answers the questions and making annotations as they go. Possible annotations include strong evidence presented by the author and additional questions that have arisen.

Promoting Close Reading of Nonfiction Texts

Close reading activities are designed to help students deeply analyze texts. In all close reading activities, students begin reading without first completing any pre-reading activities. They reread the text multiple times, analyzing different layers each time.

The first time that students read the text, they can be encouraged to determine the overall main idea and supporting details. The second time they read the text, they can be encouraged to analyze the author's craft and the text structure. This might include determining which text structure the author used, identifying the key vocabulary words and their meanings, locating nonfiction text features, and establishing the author's purpose for writing. The third time that students read, they can be encouraged to evaluate the text, draw conclusions, and make connections to other texts, personal experiences, or real-world events.

Teachers can model this process for students during shared reading experiences. They can also provide students with graphic organizers to help them record information during each reading. Additionally, they can encourage students to highlight or make notes in the text to label key information.

Role Reading Fluency Plays in the Comprehension of Nonfiction Texts

Fluency is important in comprehending any type of text. When readers are able to recognize words quickly and accurately, their working memories are available to focus on comprehension. Additionally, their thinking is not interrupted by stopping frequently to decode words.

Nonfiction texts present some special considerations for readers because they can utilize many types of structures. They also may contain several **content-specific vocabulary** words. Readers who are unfamiliar with these text structures and words may have difficulty locating key information and predicting what will come next, impeding comprehension.

Therefore, it is important to expose readers of all ages to a variety of text genres and structures. When practicing fluency passages, a combination of fiction and nonfiction texts should be included. Teachers should also model reading nonfiction texts so students will recognize what fluent reading sounds like.

Promoting Comprehension of Nonfiction Texts with Writing Activities

Writing can assist students with comprehension of nonfiction texts in many ways. Students often read nonfiction texts to learn new information or figure out how to accomplish tasks. They can create lists of questions they would like to have answered by the texts and record their answers as they read. They can also add additional questions that are generated by reading the texts.

Readers can **take notes** to record the main ideas and supporting details of nonfiction texts. There are many note-taking formats that can be used, such as outlining. Readers can also write text summaries or record the main concepts on semantic maps.

Additionally, there are many written response activities that can be used to encourage the use of **higher-level thinking skills**. Readers can write evaluations, compare and contrast essays, alternate endings, recommendations, and other similar responses.

Applying Comprehension Strategies to Digital Texts

Digital literacy includes the ability to make meaning from **digital texts**. Because the use of digital texts is now commonplace, teachers should give students opportunities to interact with both digital and print-based texts frequently.

Readers need to develop the ability to search **efficiently**. This includes generating lists of questions they want to have answered before they begin searching. It also includes selecting relevant search key words. Once search results are displayed, readers need to be able to scan the options and identify the links most likely to be relevant to their needs.

Digital texts are often nonlinear and contain multiple hyperlinks, so readers need the ability to break down the texts and **locate key information**. They can be taught to use note-taking strategies. This may involve using digital tools, like highlighting and annotation tools, or using graphic organizers.

Readers also need to develop the ability to identify author **bias** in digital sources. They should be encouraged to verify the sources and the validity of authors' claims.

Digital communications vary in **formality**. Readers should develop the ability to identify the **main points** in formal texts, like research articles, and informal texts, like blog posts.

Promoting Comprehension by Building Students' Academic Language

Academic language is language used in textbooks, class discussions, tests, and other school-related situations. It includes both vocabulary and syntax that differs from social language, which is less formal and structured.

Understanding the **vocabulary** of academic language is vital to understanding the authors' messages. If readers do not know the meanings of several key words, they will not understand the meanings of the texts and will be unable to analyze them deeply. Understanding academic syntax is also important because it helps students break down complex sentence structure to locate key information.

Students need **frequent exposure** to academic language and opportunities to use it across all content areas. For example, rather than asking students how texts are arranged, teachers can ask them to describe the *text structures*. Using these terms builds familiarity over time. Additionally, teachers can provide partial scripts that students can use to incorporate academic language when making presentations. To help students see the differences between social and academic language, teachers can also help students translate texts from one type to the other.

Types of Informational Texts

- **Literary nonfiction** texts contain true information about topics but are presented using structures similar to fictional texts.They often include clear beginnings and endings and contain literary elements such as figurative language and imagery. Biographies, memoirs, and travel writing are examples of literary nonfiction.
- **Expository** texts are written to explain things using facts. They are structured differently than literary nonfiction texts.They often contain headings, tables of contents, glossaries, charts, graphs, and similar features. These text structures help readers navigate expository texts and locate specific information quickly. A science book explaining the water cycle is an example of an expository text.
- **Persuasive** texts are written to influence readers. They contain evidence to support the authors' claims. An advertisement urging readers to vote for a specific candidate is an example of a persuasive text.
- **Procedural** texts provide step-by-step directions for how to complete tasks. A manual describing how to complete office tasks using specific software is an example of a procedural text.

Review Video: Informational Text
Visit mometrix.com/academy and enter code: 924964

Teaching Readers to Identify Different Types of Informational Texts

Readers can look for specific features to identify types of informational texts. These features can be explicitly taught using example texts, and charts outlining each type of informational text and its features can be displayed in the classrooms.

- To identify **literary nonfiction** texts, readers can look for accurate and factual texts that are written using text structures commonly used in fiction. Although true, these texts read more like stories, with clear beginnings and endings. Literary elements such as figurative language and symbolism may also be included.
- To identify **expository texts**, readers can look for common expository text structures, including tables of contents, headings, sidebars, glossaries, charts, and other similar features. Readers should also be encouraged to check that the texts are factual because some fictional texts may contain these text features as well.
- To identify **persuasive texts**, readers can look for key phrases that signal opinions. These phrases include *I believe*, *you should*, and *in my opinion*. Readers can also look for details provided by the authors to support their viewpoints.
- To identify **procedural texts**, readers can look for clues that indicate sequence. This might include numbered steps or key words like *first*, *next*, and *finally*.

Purposes of Nonfiction Texts

- One purpose of nonfiction texts is to **persuade**. In this type of text, authors try to convince readers to adopt their points of view using supporting statements. An article written by a doctor urging parents to limit their children's soda consumption is an example of a persuasive text.
- Another purpose is to **compare and contrast** two things. An essay comparing and contrasting the forms of government in two different countries is an example of this type.
- Other nonfiction texts are written to **inform**. These texts describe and explain topics using facts. A nonfiction book about characteristics of reptiles is an example of a text written to inform.

- Some nonfiction texts are written to **instruct**. These texts explain how to do something. A text about how to change a tire is an example of this type.
- Other nonfiction texts are written to **narrate** real-world events. These texts convey real information in entertaining and/or engaging ways. A personal narrative describing a funny event that occurred on a family vacation is an example of a text written for this purpose.

Adjusting Reading Strategies When Reading Different Types of Texts

It is important for students to self-monitor their reading and adjust their use of strategies depending upon the situation. This will help them focus their attention on key information. It will also ensure that they are comprehending the text and meeting their expected purposes for reading.

When students are reading fiction, they typically read from beginning to end rather than skipping around. This helps them understand the plot and correctly sequence story events. When reading nonfiction texts to answer specific questions, readers may utilize text features like the table of contents to jump to specific sections. This helps readers locate the desired information quickly.

When students are reading for entertainment, they may read the text at a faster rate than when they are reading to analyze specific literary elements or answer comprehension questions. Slowing the reading rate or rereading passages may allow for deeper interaction with the text.

Features of Expository Texts

Expository texts often contain some common features. These features help readers locate and organize key information, and they also provide additional information about the content of the text.

The **table of contents** and **index** help readers know what information is presented in the text and on which pages to find certain topics. **Titles** and **headings** are used to separate content into sections of related information. Enlarged and/or **bolded print** is often used to draw attention to these titles and headings. Important vocabulary words are often highlighted or written in bold print to catch readers' attention. A **glossary** or set of sidebars is often included to provide definitions for these vocabulary words. Photographs or **illustrations** are used to convey information visually, and captions are used to explain their content. Charts, graphs, and tables are frequently used to present relevant data. Maps are also included to provide additional information about places discussed in the text.

Helping Readers Locate and Identify Features of Expository Texts

There are many instructional strategies that can be used to help readers locate and identify features of expository texts. Leading students in feature walks is one common strategy. Using this strategy, teachers share informational and expository texts with students, previewing each section of the texts together. They point out each of the text's features, such as the titles, headings, table of contents, captions, and charts, and discuss the purposes of each. When reading the texts out loud, they model how to use the features to locate and make sense of key information.

To help readers locate and use these text features independently, charts listing the features and their functions can be posted in classrooms. Students can also be given blank charts they can use to record text features found while reading independently. Additionally, students can be given comprehension questions that require the use of text features to answer.

Nonfiction Text Structures

Some nonfiction texts use a **compare-and-contrast** structure. In this type of structure, both similarities and differences between two or more topics are explained. Sometimes the author presents each topic separately and then includes a discussion of similarities and differences. Other times, the author weaves back and forth between the two topics, comparing and contrasting different features along the way.

- **Cause and effect** is another nonfiction text structure. In this structure, the author describes an event and provides reasons why it happened.
- Another nonfiction text structure is **chronological order**. An author who retells the details of an event or period of time in the order that they happened is using this text structure.
- In the **problem/solution** text structure, a problem is introduced by the author. Possible solutions to the problem are then discussed.
- A **description** or **list** structure can also be used. In this type of structure, a topic is introduced. Descriptive details about the topic are then listed.

Review Video: Organizations of Texts: Chronological and Cause and Effect
Visit mometrix.com/academy and enter code: 804598

Faulty Reasoning in Nonfiction Texts

Faulty reasoning occurs when conclusions are not supported by facts and evidence. The ability to recognize faulty reasoning is important because it helps readers evaluate the claims made in texts to determine if they are factual or not. It also helps readers identify potential author bias.

To assist readers with recognizing faulty reasoning, teachers can explicitly teach several different types and provide examples of how they are used in real texts. **Overgeneralizations** occur when authors draw conclusions based upon insufficient data. An example is stating that all fourth graders must like pizza because one fourth grader likes pizza. **Personal bias** occurs when authors base conclusions on personal opinions rather than factors or data. **Illogical conclusions** occur when authors draw conclusions about the relationships between things without data supporting the relationships. An example is stating that because someone was outside in the rain and later got a cold, the rain must have caused the cold.

Students can be encouraged to locate and share examples of faulty reasoning found during their independent reading experiences. They can also be encouraged to verify the sources used by authors to validate their claims and be wary of unsubstantiated online sources.

Figurative Language

Types of Figurative Language

- **Similes** are one common type of figurative language used to compare two things using the terms *like* or *as*; for example, the child grew as fast as a weed.
- **Metaphors** are another common type of figurative language used to compare two things. Unlike similes, metaphors do not use the terms *like* or *as*. They simply state that one thing is another; for example, the star was a glistening diamond.
- **Personification** is a type of figurative language that gives human characteristics to nonhuman things, such as animals, objects in nature, or ideas; for example, the creek danced across the prairie.
- **Hyperbole** is a type of figurative language that uses exaggeration for effect. The exaggeration is so excessive that it is not intended to be taken literally; for example, if I don't eat now, I will starve to death.
- **Symbolism** is another type of figurative language. In symbolism, a writer uses a physical object as a representation of something other than its literal meaning. The symbol often represents something abstract, such as a feeling or idea; for example, diverging physical paths in a text can represent two people making different life choices.

Review Video: Figurative Language
Visit mometrix.com/academy and enter code: 584902

Helping Students Recognize and Interpret Figurative Language

Some types of figurative language can be identified by recognizing **key words**. For example, students can be taught to recognize the words *like* and *as* in examples of similes. Students can be taught to recognize sound words, such as *buzz*, in examples of onomatopoeia. Charts displaying these key words can be displayed in the classroom.

Figurative language can also be explicitly taught, with teachers explaining each type and providing examples. Mentor texts can be used to provide examples of each type of figurative language, and students can be encouraged to locate additional examples on their own. When examples are identified, students can analyze the messages the authors are trying to convey through the use of figurative language.

Authors use figurative language to make their writing more descriptive and interesting. Because phrases containing figurative language cannot be literally translated, readers must have adequate background knowledge and/or use context clues to determine their meanings. The ability to recognize and interpret figurative language ensures that readers understand the authors' intended messages and are able to comprehend the depth of the story beyond the literal, surface meanings of the phrases.

Allusions

When authors use **allusions**, they refer to well-known people or events familiar to readers without describing them explicitly. For example, a character being warned to avoid opening Pandora's box is an example of an allusion. It refers to a commonly known story in Greek mythology, and readers are expected to know the meaning of the statement without any further explanation. Biblical, mythological, historical, and literary allusions are four common types. Allusions are commonly found in similes and metaphors.

To help readers recognize allusions, students can be asked to find examples of allusions in texts and discuss their types and meanings. Additionally, they can explore and evaluate the effects that allusions have on the meanings and tones of stories. Students can also be taught strategies for researching the meaning of unknown allusions they encounter while reading independently.

Review Video: Allusions
Visit mometrix.com/academy and enter code: 294065

IDIOMS

Idioms are a type of figurative language. They are expressions that have unique meanings that differ from the literal meanings of their component words. They are typically passed down within cultures. For example, "It's raining cats and dogs" is an idiom that means it is raining hard.

Idioms can be introduced to students a few at a time, with students contrasting the literal and figurative meanings. They can practice using context clues to determine the meanings of unknown idioms, and they can look for examples of idioms in texts. They can also explore the ways that idioms make writing interesting. For example, they can write a paragraph using the idiom, "It's raining cats and dogs." They can then rewrite the paragraph, substituting the words, "It's raining hard." They can compare the effects of each option on readers.

Special consideration should be given when using idioms with ELLs in the early stages of English language acquisition. Because vocabulary knowledge cannot be used to assist with comprehension of idioms, students may miss the meanings and become frustrated.

PROVERBS

Proverbs are short, well-known sayings that offer wisdom or advice. They are commonly passed down within cultures using oral language. An example of a proverb is: "Actions speak louder than words." Proverbs often use figurative language, and their literal meanings do not make sense. Therefore, students need to be taught to recognize proverbs and understand their figurative meanings to comprehend the overall messages of the texts containing them.

When introducing proverbs, teachers can help students understand the cultural and historical significance behind them. For example, the proverb "Don't look a gift horse in the mouth" refers to the historical practice of assessing a horse's teeth to determine its age. The proverb refers to being grateful for what you are given rather than assessing the worth of a gift. Teachers can help students research these proverbs to provide historical contexts for their meanings.

Students can write proverbs on graphic organizers and list both their literal and figurative meanings. They can analyze what the proverbs have in common, such as offering wisdom or advice about life. Additionally, when they are encountered in texts, readers can analyze how the meanings of the proverbs contribute to the meanings of the stories.

Role of Grammar in Reading Comprehension

Understanding English Grammar/Usage and Comprehension

There is evidence that having a strong understanding of English grammar and usage assists with reading comprehension. When readers are able to untangle complex sentences in texts and understand how the components work together to form meaning, they are better able to comprehend what was read. When answering comprehension questions, they are better able to locate key information within complex sentences. Readers are also better able to incorporate complex sentence structure in their own writing.

Understanding English grammar and usage includes knowledge of parts of speech, the roles that they play, and how they are arranged in English sentences. It also includes knowledge of how simple sentences can be combined to form complex sentences. Readers with strong syntactic knowledge are able to self-monitor their reading and recognize when something does not sound right due to decoding errors. The ability to self-monitor and make corrections when needed is important for comprehension.

Review Video: Grammar Skills and Reading Comprehension
Visit mometrix.com/academy and enter code: 411287

Teaching English Grammar and Usage to Aid Comprehension

One strategy to teach English grammar and usage to aid comprehension is to **break sentences apart** and analyze their components. Depending on the age and prior knowledge of the student, this may include **sentence diagramming**, dividing sentences into subjects and predicates, and splitting compound sentences into simple sentences. Students may also be asked to label sentence types—choosing from simple, compound, and complex sentences.

An alternative strategy is to combine words to form different types of sentences. Young readers may begin by combining only subjects and predicates to form the most basic types of sentences. As new parts of speech are learned, students can add additional words to form more complex sentences. Students can also be given word cards containing scrambled sentences. They can be asked to arrange the cards to form sentences, analyzing each attempt by asking if the sentences they have built sound right and make sense.

When given comprehension questions about texts, students can also highlight the parts of the sentences that contain the relevant information needed to respond.

Spoken vs. Written English

Although there are some occasions for formal, scripted speech, most spoken English is informal and conversational in nature. Speech often includes a mixture of fragments and complete sentences and may include interrupting and switching between speakers. Grammar in spoken English tends to be less strict, and there is more flexibility in word order. There may be differences in pronunciation, pacing, and intonation among speakers, and listeners must adjust to these differences to comprehend what was said. Speakers can gauge the understanding of listeners and rephrase or re-explain when necessary. Unlike written text, there is no formal record of what was said to review later unless notes were taken or the speech was recorded. If speaking is part of an instructional lesson, listeners may benefit from being given overviews of the topics and guiding questions in advance to help focus their attention on key information.

On the other hand, written English allows for careful and deliberate organization. It is typically more formal and features more complex structures than spoken English. Word order is more rigid. Writers cannot gauge readers' understanding or re-explain if necessary, so the meaning needs to be clear. Readers are able to review the text later to further clarify information.

Role of Frequent and Varied Reading Experiences

Frequent and varied reading experiences allow readers to see diverse examples of how authors write. They can compare and contrast different writing styles and analyze how the audience, topic, and purpose of writing may affect formality and structure. For example, expository science texts will likely differ from graphic novels in formality. The science texts may also include more content-specific vocabulary words and use sentence patterns designed to present facts rather than resemble conversations. Additionally, readers can see vocabulary words and different parts of speech in context and observe how they work together to build meaning. They can also see the effects of different writers' word choices on the moods of the texts. Overall, frequent and varied reading experiences help readers become more comfortable with language.

Being exposed to varied texts also provides students with models of sentence structure and writing styles to emulate in their own writing. Students often consider examples of familiar texts that fit certain genres or themes, called mentor texts, when they write their own. Being exposed to a variety of reading experiences gives students more examples to draw upon when they are writing.

Inductive vs. Deductive Methods of Teaching Grammar

- In **inductive** teaching, students read and analyze texts that contain similarities. They look for patterns and identify grammar rules by themselves. For example, a teacher might give students several compound sentences that contain semicolons to join the two component sentences. Students might be asked to determine what the sentences have in common, leading them to identify and discuss the use of semicolons to join two simple sentences. Benefits include active participation by students to determine the grammar rules and use of critical thinking skills.
- **Deductive** teaching is another method. In deductive teaching, students are explicitly told grammatical concepts and rules before being asked to apply them to their own reading and writing. For example, a teacher might present a lesson on using semicolons to create compound sentences and then ask students to look for examples of this rule during independent reading experiences. One benefit of this approach is that it can be quicker than inductive teaching. Some students may also be more accustomed to this teacher-centered type of approach.

Both methods of teaching grammar can be useful, and teachers often use a combination of both in their teaching.

Many teachers also use writing workshops to introduce grammar through mini-lessons and conferences with students. Using students' writing as informal assessment tools, teachers can determine which grammatical concepts and rules individual students need to practice.

Role of Grammar in Helping ELLs with Comprehension

Understanding grammar can assist English language learners (ELLs) with reading comprehension. It helps them comprehend different types of sentences. Understanding punctuation marks and word order of different types of sentences helps ELLs determine if something is a statement, a command, or a question.

Additionally, discerning the functions of different **parts of speech** helps ELLs identify the parts of sentences that carry the most meaning. This aids in focusing their attention on the most important words in each sentence. Recognizing words and affixes that signal verb tense also helps ELLs determine when the action takes place. For example, an ELL might recognize that the verbs in a text end in *-ed* and realize that the story takes place in past tense.

Using **syntactic clues** is one important strategy readers use to make meaning from texts. To use syntactic clues, readers must have an understanding of what sounds right in English. When ELLs develop an understanding of English grammar and word order, they are better able to self-monitor their reading and determine if something sounds right. They are also better able to use context clues if they have an understanding of correct word order in English sentences.

Teaching ELLs English Grammar and Usage

English language learners (ELLs) should be taught grammar and usage skills in realistic contexts rather than in isolation. It is also helpful to design grammar lessons around familiar topics and vocabulary so learners can focus on the grammar and usage concepts rather than trying to decipher the meaning.

Teachers should frequently **model** correct grammar and sentence structure through listening, reading, and speaking activities. One strategy is to read texts that model a specific grammar rule and ask ELLs to listen for examples of its use or apply it in their own writing. They can also be encouraged to look for patterns in grammar and usage, such as *-ed* and *-ing* endings.

Teachers need to carefully consider when and how to address grammatical and usage errors made by ELLs. Frequent and immediate corrections can cause **frustration**. However, if specific errors are not addressed over time, they may become **fossilized** and difficult to correct. One strategy is to note repeated errors and address them later in mini-lessons rather than at the time they are made. Teachers can also pick a small number of errors to focus on at any one time.

English Language Parts of Speech

The following are the eight parts of speech in the English language:

1. **Nouns** describe people, places, and things, for example, he ate a chocolate **cupcake**.
2. **Verbs** describe action or being; for example, the dog **chased** the squirrel around the yard.
3. **Pronouns** are words used in place of nouns, for example, **she** works in the office building downtown.
4. **Adjectives** describe nouns or pronouns. They usually describe which one, what kind, or how many of something, for example, the **yellow** house is located on the corner.
5. **Adverbs** describe verbs, adjectives, or other adverbs. They usually describe when, where, why, or how something happens, and they often end in *-ly*; for example, the fish swam **quickly** away from the shark.
6. **Prepositions** are words that relate nouns or pronouns to other words in the sentence; for example, the chef put the dough **in** the oven.
7. **Conjunctions** join words, phrases, or clauses; for example, the teacher **and** the principal attended the meeting.
8. **Interjections** show emotion in sentences; for example**, ouch**—I bumped my elbow.

When readers come across words whose meanings they do not know, knowing the parts of speech can help them determine the function of the words in the sentences. This will make it easier to guess the meanings using context clues.

Review Video: Parts of Speech
Visit mometrix.com/academy and enter code: 899611

Review Video: Nouns
Visit mometrix.com/academy and enter code: 344028

Teaching Students to Recognize Different Parts of Speech

Parts of speech are typically introduced one or a few at a time. **Nouns** and **verbs** are often introduced first because they can be used as the building blocks of basic sentences. If an inductive method is used, students may be given a group of sentences with the same parts of speech highlighted and asked to determine what the words have in common. If a deductive method is used, teachers might explicitly teach what each part of speech does and provide examples.

Mini-lessons can also be used. A **mini-lesson** on nouns, for example, might include listing nouns that fit into the categories of people, places, and things. It might also include finding examples of nouns in texts or sorting words according to whether or not they are nouns. Teachers can also use shared reading and writing activities as opportunities to discuss parts of speech in context.

Sentence diagrams are pictorial representations that show how parts of speech work together to form sentences. Although sentence diagramming can help some students visualize sentence structure, it can be frustrating and tedious for others. Therefore, it can be considered as one component of grammar instruction as long as it fits the needs of the learners.

Diagram format: Components of a sentence	**Diagram example:** Identify the components in the sentence
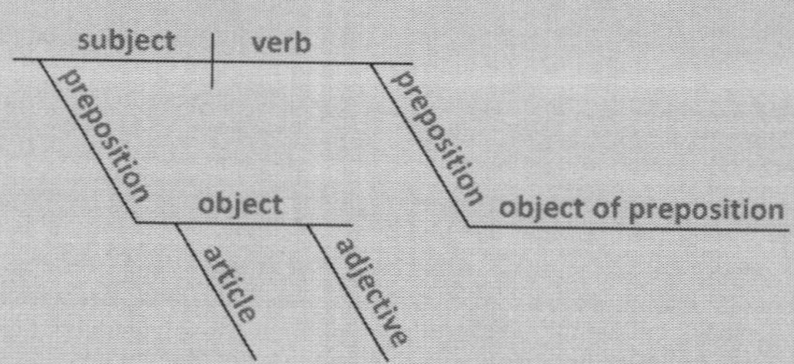	Sentence: Children in the preschool classroom nap after lunch. 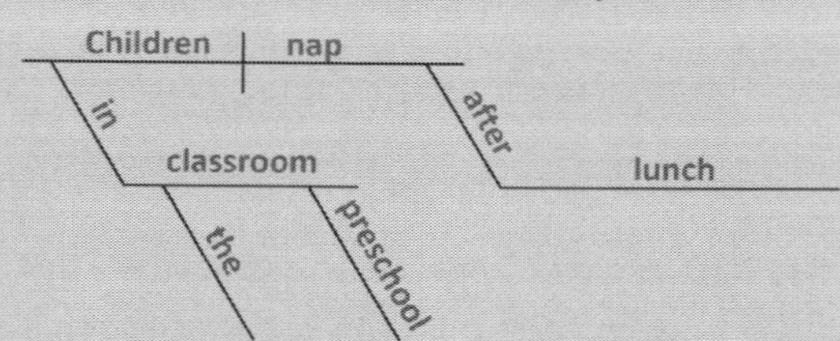

Reading Comprehension Tools and Strategies

Graphic Organizers That Promote Reading Comprehension and Analysis

Know, want, and learn (KWL) **charts** can be filled out before and after reading to identify what readers know, want to know, and learned about a topic. These charts help activate prior knowledge and give readers a purpose for reading.

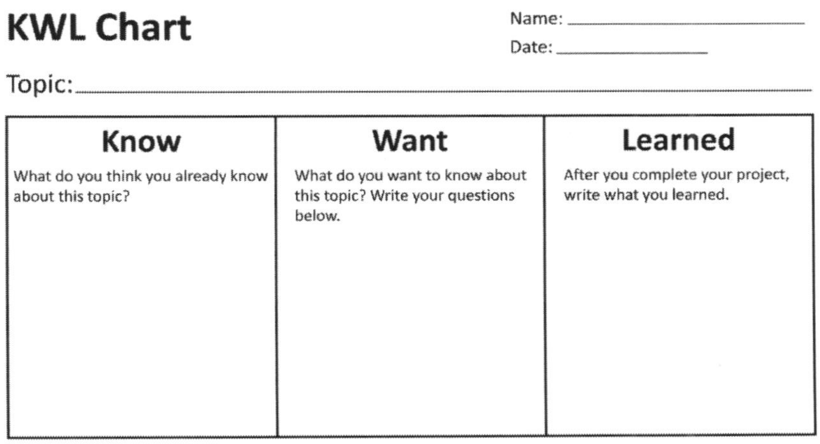

Story maps can be used to help readers identify the main elements of a story, such as characters, setting, problem, events, and solutions. **Character maps** can be used to describe traits of characters in the story.

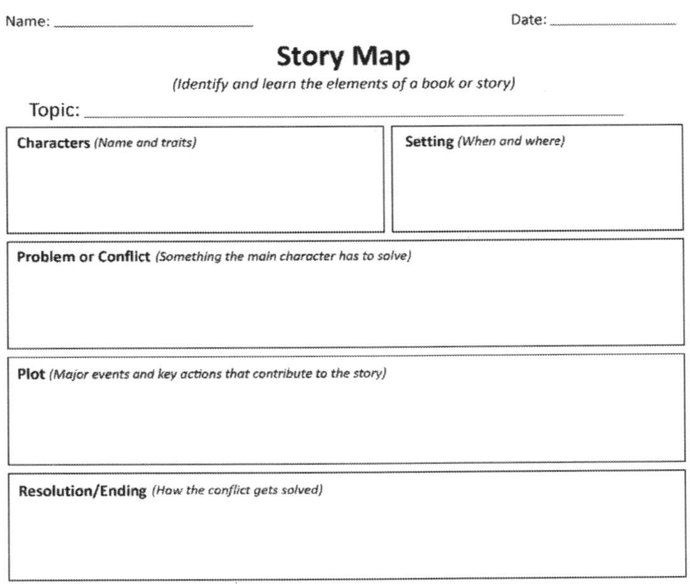

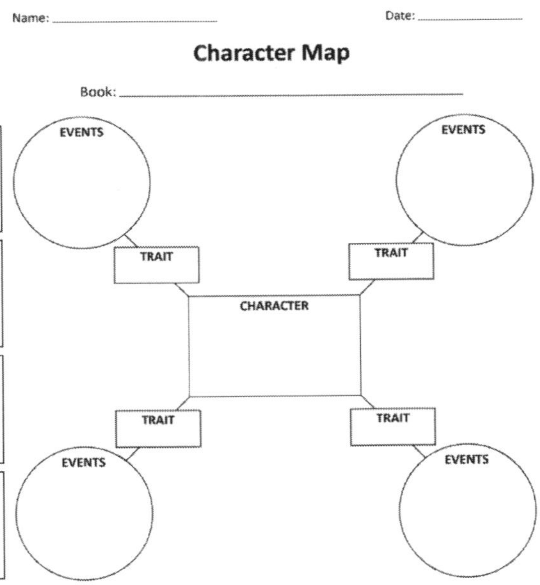

Other graphic organizers can be used to help readers explain the relationships among events or ideas in a story. **Graphic organizers** can be used to help readers identify the problem and solution in a story, along with the events that led to the solution. Other graphic organizers can be used to record inferences and the text evidence used to make them. Graphic organizers like webs can be used to record the main idea and supporting details of a story. Venn diagrams can also be used to compare and contrast two stories, characters, or other elements.

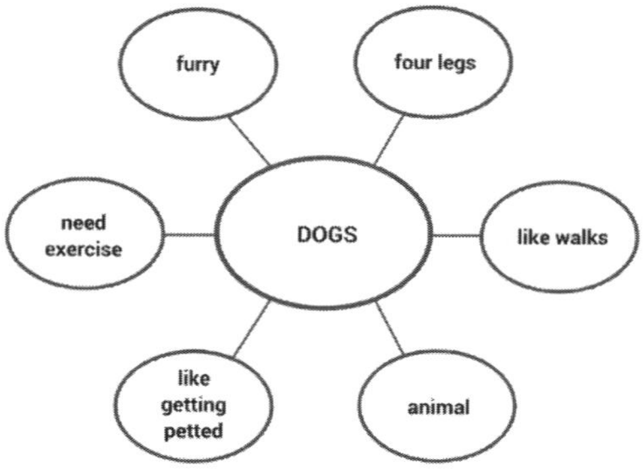

SQ3R Reading Strategy

SQ3R is a strategy used to help students comprehend textbooks. The S stands for **survey**. In this step, students preview the text and note features like headings, graphs, and charts. They use this information to predict what the text is about. In the Q or **question** step, students reread the headings and convert them into questions. They then predict the answers to these questions. The first R stands for **reading**. In this step, students read the text and attempt to answer the questions they listed. They may also make annotations to note important points or additional questions. The second R stands for **recite**, and this step involves summarizing each section of the text immediately after it is read. The last R stands for **review**. Students attempt to answer their original questions without using the text. If they are unable to answer any questions from memory, they review the text and their notes for assistance.

The SQ3R strategy has several benefits. By surveying the text, students activate prior knowledge and set purposes for reading. Listing questions helps focus students' attention during reading.

Annotating helps students analyze and make meaning from the text. Summarizing and reviewing help students remember key information.

Name: ____________________ Date: ____________

SQ3R Chart

Title of Work: ________________________________

Survey: Record important titles and subtitles from work.

____

____

Question: Write "Who, What, When, Where, and Why" questions from main topics.

____

____

Read: Write answers to questions from above.

____

____

Recite: Record key facts and phrases as needed for each question.

____

____

Review: Create a summary paragraph for each question.

____

____

Instructional Activities that Support Reading and Writing Skills

Activities That Support Reading, Writing, Listening, and Speaking Development

Reading, writing, listening, and speaking are the four main components of English language development. All of these components are important and interdependent. They all play roles in making and conveying meaning, which are goals of literacy instruction.

These skills are sometimes practiced in isolation, such as when students listen to audio texts without any follow-up activities. However, when solving real-world problems, these skills are often used together. For example, doctors must listen to their patients' symptoms, make notes on the patients' charts, and then explain their treatment plans. Therefore, it is important for teachers to plan activities that integrate these four skills.

Project-based learning activities and performance assessments are useful for integrating these four skills. As an example, students could read about the benefits of recycling. They could then speak to the school principal to recommend implementing a school-wide recycling plan, listening and responding to the principal's concerns. They could then create posters to advertise the new program to other students.

Cloze Reading Procedure

Cloze reading is an instructional strategy in which students read brief passages containing omitted words. They rely on background knowledge, semantic clues, and/or syntactic clues to determine the unknown words.

When designing cloze reading passages, teachers should consider a few key factors. The passages should be at the appropriate reading levels for the students. Students should be able to guess the omitted words by using reading strategies. If students need additional scaffolding to determine the missing words, word banks can be provided.

Cloze reading activities can be done independently or with partners. They can also be done as whole-class activities, with teachers reading the main passages and students supplying the missing words.

Cloze reading has several benefits. It requires students to use a variety of reading strategies, including using context clues, to determine the missing words. Students also cross-check their use of cueing systems to determine unknown words in cloze passages. If students read the passages multiple times to determine the missing words, it builds fluency as well.

LANGUAGE EXPERIENCE APPROACH TO READING INSTRUCTION

The **language experience approach** focuses on using students' own experiences as the topics of literacy experiences. Students think about experiences they would like to share. They dictate the experiences to teachers, who write the students' words down in front of them. The teachers then read the texts aloud while pointing to each word, modeling appropriate fluency. Students are then invited to join the teachers in rereading the texts.

The language experience approach can also be done as a whole-class activity, with classes writing about shared experiences together. For example, they could write about projects recently completed at school. Teachers help students generate ideas for what to include and list relevant vocabulary words that may be used. Students then dictate sentences to their teachers, who record them on chart paper. The classes then reread the texts multiple times.

A benefit of the language experience approach is that it involves reading, writing, listening, and speaking. It also builds upon students' prior knowledge and interests. If students are given multiple opportunities to reread the texts they have created, it also assists with fluency.

GUIDED READING AND SMALL GROUP READING INSTRUCTION

Guided reading is a term closely related to balanced literacy programs. Even though these programs are not considered to be best practice anymore, small groups should still be implemented in reading instruction. In guided reading, teachers arrange students in flexible groups and meet with each group separately. While meeting with each group, teachers provide leveled texts to each student, conduct picture walks, and focus on strategies that might be helpful when reading the texts. Instead of this, teachers should provide students with their own copies of decodable texts that are based off previously taught phonics skills. Before reading, teachers should review any irregular sight words that may appear and review previously taught phonics rules that will be helpful when reading the given texts. Teachers also should encourage the students to apply the rules they have learned to decode unknown words. Similarly to guided reading, students then read the texts independently in whisper voices while the teachers observe and make notes about students' reading. After students have read the texts independently, the teacher should conduct mini-lessons on skills that are targeted in the texts, such as specific phonics rules that are used a lot through the text. Students then take the texts to reread later, helping build fluency.

The flexible nature of reading groups ensures that students are always reading books within their instructional reading levels. Because the groups are small, teachers can target phonics skills that students within that specific group may still be struggling with. Teachers also have frequent opportunities to observe students' progress and determine which skills need additional practice.

Shared Reading Experiences

During **shared reading experiences**, teachers read aloud to students using materials like large print books, texts written on chart paper, and projected texts. Students follow along as teachers read and point to each word. Shared reading is an interactive experience, and teachers stop frequently to ask questions and model use of strategies. Depending on the ages and reading levels of the students, teachers focus on different teaching points. For example, kindergarten teachers may model and discuss concepts of print, whereas teachers of students in older grades may model and discuss comprehension strategies. Students may join the teachers in reading the texts as well.

Shared reading can be used across all subject areas and has several benefits. It allows students to see teachers modeling the use of reading strategies and practice using these strategies with scaffolding. It also allows students to participate in reading and discussing quality texts that they may not yet be able to read independently. Students learn about text features like punctuation marks and spelling patterns that they can incorporate into their own writing. They also have opportunities to hear examples of fluent reading.

Read-Alouds

During **read-alouds**, teachers read texts aloud to students. Depending on their purposes for reading, they may or may not pause to model the use of strategies or ask questions. Some read-alouds may be done strictly for entertainment purposes, whereas others may be done to provide background knowledge in content areas or allow for the modeling of reading strategies.

The key difference between read-alouds and shared reading experiences is that students do not have access to the texts during read-alouds. They listen as teachers read aloud, and they are sometimes shown the pictures. The focus is on listening to the texts and the teachers' use of strategies; students do not join in reading.

Benefits of Independent Daily Reading Time

Independent daily reading has several benefits. Reading self-selected books can boost engagement with reading and help students develop a love of reading. When given opportunities to reread favorite texts, fluency may also increase. Independent reading also gives students opportunities to apply reading strategies to new texts autonomously.

Books for independent reading are usually self-selected. Students in the early stages of reading development who cannot read texts independently can be encouraged to "read the pictures." Teachers can model how to use prior knowledge and picture clues to tell the stories in their own words. Students who are able to read the words can be encouraged to select appropriate texts for independent reading time. Depending on the ages of the students, teachers may need to help readers build reading stamina. They can schedule a few minutes of daily independent reading time early in the school year and gradually add additional minutes. Teachers may schedule whole-class independent reading time or establish it as one station for students to complete during literacy stations.

Students can also be encouraged to have book boxes that contain several texts at the appropriate reading levels for use during independent reading time.

Role of Flexible Groupings in Effective Reading Instruction

Flexible groupings are one way that teachers can differentiate instruction. When using **flexible grouping**, teachers strategically group students together to accomplish specific instructional goals. The groups may be large or small, and they vary depending on the activity. For example, a teacher may work with a small group of students who are all having difficulties with cause-and-effect relationships. The teacher is able to target instruction in this skill area to only the students who need extra practice. Guided reading groups are also flexible because students typically progress through instructional reading levels at different rates. Teachers can use both formal and informal assessment data to group students.

Flexible groupings have several benefits. They allow students to receive targeted instruction, often in small-group settings that allow for more teacher interaction. Students who have mastered these skills are able to work on other things, preventing them from becoming bored or frustrated. Additionally, students may feel more comfortable participating in small groups of their peers. Flexible groupings also mean that students will have opportunities to work with many other students throughout the year.

Review Video: Differentiated Instruction
Visit mometrix.com/academy and enter code: 100342

Considerations When Grouping Students for Instructional Purposes

When determining when and how to group students for instructional purposes, teachers should take many factors into consideration. They should consider what instructional goals they want to accomplish. These goals are often based upon specific learning objectives.

Once teachers know what goals they want to accomplish, they can consider what types of groupings to use. Possibilities include partner learning as well as small or large group instruction. Teachers also need to consider the characteristics of the students in each group. For example, teachers may group students who need to practice specific skills together to target instruction. Other times, they may group students who have differing perspectives on topics to facilitate active discussion and sharing of viewpoints. These decisions should support the learning objectives. Teachers also need to consider what types of learning activities to use within the groups. Additionally, they need to consider what roles students will be assigned within their groups, if any. It is common for classrooms to use a variety of grouping arrangements throughout the year to accomplish different instructional goals.

Classroom Management Strategies for Effective Reading Groups

Reading groups are important components of literacy instruction because they allow students to receive differentiated, small-group instruction on a routine basis. However, they may be ineffective if frequent interruptions or classroom management issues occur. Clearly established and practiced routines can prevent these issues from occurring.

Students who are not working with their teachers in reading groups should be engaged in activities that they are able to successfully complete either independently or with the help of their peers. If center rotations are being used, students should know in what order to proceed through the centers and what the expectations are for each rotation.

Additionally, routines should be in place for how to solve problems without interrupting the reading groups. There should be clear criteria in place for when the teachers can be interrupted, such as in the case of emergencies. Students should be taught how to independently access any materials they may need to complete their activities. Hand signals or sign-out sheets may be utilized to minimize interruptions when students need permission to leave the classroom. Students can also be taught to ask a set number of classmates for assistance with problems before asking their teachers.

Characteristics of Shared Writing Experiences

During **shared writing experiences**, teachers and students collaboratively plan the content of shared writing pieces. Teachers assist their students with choosing topics, deciding which details to include, selecting words, and organizing text structure. Students are asked to share their ideas, and teachers help students organize their thoughts and put them into writing. Teachers control the writing instruments and put the words down on paper. Along the way, they may ask students for assistance with spelling words, determining how to punctuate, and other issues. Teachers model their thinking and use of writing strategies throughout the process. Once the drafting is finished, students may assist with revising, editing, and reading the texts aloud.

Shared writing experiences give students opportunities to be active participants in scaffolded versions of the writing process and work collaboratively to develop quality writing pieces. Additionally, they benefit from observing their teachers as they model the use of writing strategies.

Characteristics of Interactive Writing Experiences

During **interactive writing experiences**, teachers and students work together to create shared writing pieces. With teacher guidance, students help plan writing topics, determine which details to include, and organize text structure. Students share the writing utensils with teachers and contribute to recording the words on paper. Teachers provide guidance along the way. For example, they may remind students of recently learned spelling patterns while students are spelling the words on paper. Classes may also work together to revise, edit, and read the writing pieces.

Giving students control over the writing utensils is what differentiates interactive writing from shared writing. In shared writing, teachers record the words on paper.

Interactive writing allows students to be active participants in the writing process while receiving scaffolding from teachers. It also allows students to collaboratively create quality writing pieces they are unable to produce independently at their current stages of writing development. Additionally, teachers can build targeted mini-lessons into the interactive writing process.

Instructional Strategies to Support Reading Skills

Supporting Reading Comprehension in ELLs and Struggling Readers

It is helpful to build background knowledge before introducing new texts to English language learners (ELLs) and struggling readers. Readers can then draw upon this background knowledge to make meaning from the new texts. After assessing what students already know about the topics, background knowledge can be developed using other texts, charts, graphs, photographs, videos, discussions, and additional methods.

- ELLs and struggling readers can benefit from **previewing** new texts before reading them independently. This may include picture walks or receiving text outlines that identify the **main ideas** covered in each section.
- **Pre-teaching vocabulary** can also help ELLs and struggling readers comprehend new texts. Teachers can introduce the vocabulary words and use photos or real objects to help explain their meanings. The vocabulary words can be frequently incorporated into class discussions to familiarize students with them.
- Additionally, **graphic organizers** can be used to help ELLs and struggling readers identify and organize key parts of texts that assist with comprehension. To offer scaffolding, partially completed graphic organizers and/or sentence stems can be provided initially, and support can be gradually withdrawn over time.

Supporting Reading Comprehension in Proficient Readers

Proficient readers can be encouraged to comprehend at the inferential and evaluative levels in addition to the literal level. They can analyze texts deeply and make inferences, draw conclusions, and form evaluations. They can also be encouraged to complete activities that require higher-level thinking skills. Rather than listing the main characters, for example, proficient readers can be asked to retell the stories from each character's point of view or evaluate the choices the characters made.

To **challenge proficient readers** and encourage them to be enthusiastic about reading, they can also be given choices about book selection. Teachers can guide students in expanding their text selections to include different topics and genres but allow them to make their own selections. Teachers can also encourage students to choose texts that are appropriately challenging. Proficient readers can benefit from ownership in reading-related activities. Teachers can create menus of challenging questions or projects that readers can choose from based on their interests.

Engaging in Collaborative Discussions About Print and Digital Texts

Engaging in **collaborative discussions** can have several benefits for readers. It allows them to learn from other people's experiences and perspectives, which may differ from their own. Readers may hear additional evidence that strengthens their own initial understandings and conclusions. Conversely, they may hear evidence that challenges their initial thoughts and requires them to make revisions. Readers also have to support their points with text evidence to explain their thoughts to classmates. Locating and analyzing text evidence can assist with comprehension.

Discussing texts with others also has broader social benefits. It gives students opportunities to be **active and social learners**. Sharing ideas and collaborating helps build a community of learners who are able to communicate and respect different points of view. It also allows students to experience different social roles within the group and develop conflict resolution skills.

Influence of Culture on Reading Comprehension

Culture affects the ways people view and interact with the world around them. As a result, readers of different cultural backgrounds may comprehend the same texts differently. Readers rely on prior knowledge and existing schemata to make sense of what was read. Texts that are culturally familiar and related to readers' existing cultural schemata are more easily comprehended than those that are unfamiliar. When reading culturally familiar topics, readers are better able to make predictions, inferences, and conclusions based on existing schemata.

Therefore, it is important for teachers to activate both students' content knowledge and cultural knowledge prior to reading. For example, students may read a text describing a birthday celebration. The teacher can activate students' knowledge about how birthdays are celebrated in different cultures.

Research has indicated that cultural differences in syntactic complexity are less likely to affect comprehension.

Structuring Collaborative Discussions About Print and Digital Texts

Literature circles are one way to structure collaborative discussions about print. **Literature circles** consist of small groups of students who lead discussions about shared texts, which may or may not have been self-selected. Students collaboratively analyze the texts, discussing topics such as character development and theme. In some classrooms, guiding questions are provided by the teachers, whereas discussion questions are student-generated in others. Sometimes students are assigned roles within the group, such as summarizer and discussion leader.

Other times, there may be whole-class collaborative discussions. These types of discussions may occur when the whole class is completing an author study, for example, and are comparing and contrasting the events of different texts. These discussions are typically teacher-led.

There may also be small-group, teacher-led, collaborative discussions about teacher-selected texts. For example, discussion time may be included during guided reading groups.

Reciprocal Teaching Strategy

Reciprocal teaching is a strategy designed to assist students with reading comprehension. In reciprocal teaching, students and teachers **share the responsibilities** of leading small-group discussions about texts. Teachers initially take the lead and model using four main comprehension strategies, including generating questions, summarizing, clarifying, and predicting. They gradually share more responsibility with students, who eventually take over leading the groups in applying these strategies to analyze texts.

Reciprocal teaching has several benefits. It requires students to be actively engaged in the reading process, as they must understand and apply the reading strategies to guide their classmates. It encourages the use of higher-level reading strategies that can then be applied to other texts. It also encourages discussion and collaboration among class members. Additionally, reciprocal teaching can help build students' confidence in their abilities to independently read and analyze challenging texts.

Activities Promoting Reading Comprehension

Before reading, teachers can set the purposes for reading and activate students' prior knowledge by making connections to what they already know. They can **preview** the texts and important vocabulary words and encourage students to make **predictions**.

During reading, teachers can model thinking aloud to demonstrate how they **monitor** their own understanding. They can check and revise predictions, make inferences, and form connections. They can provide students with guiding questions or graphic organizers to use as they read independently to encourage the same reading behaviors.

After reading, teachers can **model** summarizing, drawing conclusions, and evaluating the texts. They can also discuss how their thinking changed as they read and were presented with new evidence. They can encourage students to use the same strategies after reading independently by setting up literature circles, creating written response activities, and designing other reading response projects.

Types of Connections Readers Can Make to Texts

- Readers can make **text-to-text connections**. These are connections made between two or more different texts that have been read. Readers might make connections between the texts' events, characters, themes, or any other features. An example is when a reader identifies that characters in two different books both persisted to overcome challenges.
- **Text-to-self connections** refer to connections readers make between texts and their own personal experiences. An example is when a reader understands the sadness a character feels when losing a pet after having personally experienced the same thing.
- **Text-to-world connections** refer to connections readers make between events in texts and events that have happened in the real world. An example is when a reader makes connections between a text about an astronaut and news about a recent space launch.

To encourage readers to make these connections, teachers can model their own thinking during shared reading experiences. They can model thinking deeply about similarities rather than making surface connections. For example, rather than pointing out that two characters are both girls, they can compare their character traits. Teachers can also encourage the use of Venn diagrams to show the similarities and differences between two texts, people, or events.

Benefits of Comparing Different Books by the Same Author

When students read and compare multiple books by the same author, they use several reading strategies important for comprehension. They compare and contrast story elements between texts, such as characters, settings, problems, and solutions; they make text-to-text connections. They also consider how the author's life experiences may impact his or her writing style and content.

After completing multiple author studies, readers may also begin to identify favorite authors. These authors can serve as **mentors** for students, providing models of how to use language and incorporate story elements in their own writing. The connections readers feel to their favorite authors can boost engagement with reading and encourage them to seek out additional texts. Students can learn about the authors' lives and the paths they have taken as writers. They may be inspired by learning that people similar to themselves have become published authors.

Benefits of Learning About Topics Using Different Texts and/or Genres

Reading different texts on the same topic can give readers a more comprehensive understanding of the topic. Each text reflects the personal writing style and bias of the author. Reading multiple texts allows readers to hear different perspectives and form their own judgments.

Reading texts from **multiple genres** about the same topic is also beneficial. Each genre presents the information differently and serves unique purposes. Reading an **informational text** about the Civil War may provide readers with an understanding of the war's causes, events, and major figures. Reading a **historical fiction** book written from the perspective of a soldier may give readers a more personalized account of this period in time, engaging the readers and helping them form personal connections.

When reading multiple texts, readers also need to identify the important points from each and synthesize the information. They need to consider the authors' purposes for writing. These skills assist with reading comprehension.

Supporting Vocabulary Development

Encouraging Vocabulary Acquisition Through Reading and Writing Activities

If a new text contains unfamiliar vocabulary words that are central to the meaning and/or may be difficult to decode, a teacher may **preview** the words with the group. After introducing the topic of the text, the teacher may flip to the words, show students their spellings, and ask students to share what the words may mean based on prior knowledge and picture clues. Exposure to these words before reading will build readers' confidence and help them recognize and decode the words faster, maintaining fluency. Knowing the meanings in advance will also assist with comprehension.

When reading aloud to students, teachers may pause at new vocabulary words and model how to use context clues, prior knowledge, and picture support to decode and comprehend the new words. Students can be encouraged to use these strategies when reading independently.

Readers need repeated exposure to vocabulary words to develop automatic recognition and comprehension. Teachers may display classroom charts containing vocabulary words and their meanings, possibly using picture clues for young readers.

Students can also be encouraged to incorporate vocabulary words in their own writing. Word walls or charts containing the words can assist students with spelling and remembering the meanings of the words.

Helping Readers Explore the Meanings of Unknown Vocabulary Words

First, it is important for students to identify unknown vocabulary words when reading. Readers who are not monitoring their own comprehension may decode the words and continue reading, even if they do not understand their meanings. Teachers can model how to stop when they reach words they don't understand, even if they can decode them, and encourage students to do the same.

Next, readers need to determine which unknown words are central to the meanings of the text and worth exploring further. This is important because there may be many unknown words and, if readers stop extensively at each one, fluency and comprehension may be interrupted. Therefore, students can be encouraged to consider whether or not they can comprehend the sentences and overall meanings of the texts without devoting more energy to these particular unknown words.

If readers determine that the unknown words are central to the meaning of the text, they can be encouraged to use strategies such as using context clues, looking for known roots or affixes, or consulting dictionaries. Overall, readers should be encouraged to monitor their own reading and comprehension and determine when to apply known strategies.

Review Video: Acknowledging the Unknown When Reading
Visit mometrix.com/academy and enter code: 712339

Supporting Vocabulary Acquisition and Use Through Listening and Speaking

Young children begin their vocabulary development through listening well before they begin to read and write. Through listening to family members, caregivers, and others, children develop their meaning (oral) vocabularies. These are words that children understand when heard and eventually use in their own speech. These vocabularies can be developed by talking to the children frequently and for a variety of purposes, reading to them, exposing them to songs, rhymes, and poems, and many other language activities.

Children continue to build vocabulary through listening and speaking activities when they begin school. Teachers can read aloud to students often, varying the genres and purposes for listening. Engaging students in discussions about what was read aloud can give students a purpose for listening and opportunities to use text-related vocabulary in their own oral responses. Teachers can also incorporate key vocabulary words in class discussions.

Students should also have frequent opportunities to speak in the classroom. In addition to informal class discussions, students can present projects to classmates and explain their thinking during problem-solving. They should be encouraged to use content-specific vocabulary when appropriate.

Teaching Word Analysis Skills and Vocabulary to English Language Learners

Focusing on cognates is one way to help build word analysis skills and vocabulary for English language learners (ELLs). Cognates are words in different languages that share the same roots. For example, the English word *directions* and the Spanish word *direcciones* are cognates. ELLs can be encouraged to look for known parts of unfamiliar words. They can then use knowledge about the meanings in their native languages to determine the meanings of the English words. This strategy builds upon ELLs' prior knowledge. Explicitly teaching common roots and affixes can help ELLs quickly increase their vocabularies as well.

Scaffolding should also be provided when introducing ELLs to new words. This can be done using visuals that help demonstrate the meanings of the words. Real objects, pictures, and gestures can all be used. Graphic organizers can also be used to show how new words are related and how they connect to specific topics.

Teaching Word Analysis Skills to Struggling Readers

Struggling readers require consistent and explicit instruction, which often includes a combination of both whole-class instruction and targeted individual or small-group instruction daily. They also need frequent opportunities to manipulate words. Both building and breaking apart related words using letter tiles can help struggling readers develop understandings of patterns in the ways words are made.

Struggling readers can also benefit from explicit instruction on chunking words into component parts. Depending on the ages and prior knowledge of the students, this might include identifying syllable patterns, onsets and rimes, roots and affixes, or smaller sight words that are part of the larger words.

Struggling readers also need frequent opportunities to practice their word analysis skills using real texts. After explicit instruction on recognizing prefixes in words, for example, students can read texts that contain several prefixes. They can identify these words and their meanings. This will help them transfer their word analysis skills to realistic contexts. Scaffolding can be provided through anchor charts, graphic organizers, and teacher support during these independent reading experiences to provide reminders of known strategies.

Teaching Word Analysis Skills to Highly Proficient Readers

Proficient readers still have a need for differentiated reading instruction, even if they are meeting or exceeding grade-level expectations. They can benefit from developing the same word analysis skills as other readers, such as looking for known parts in unfamiliar vocabulary words, breaking words into components, and finding relationships between the meanings and spellings of different words. These strategies should be presented using materials and interactions that are both engaging and appropriately challenging for proficient readers. Use of texts that have some unfamiliar words will ensure that readers have opportunities to apply these strategies and continue to increase their vocabularies. Using assessments to determine reading levels or teaching readers to self-select appropriate texts can help ensure that the selected materials offer some challenges and learning opportunities for proficient readers.

Because proficient readers often devote less energy to decoding words than struggling readers, they are able to allocate more energy to reading comprehension, analysis, and reflection. Proficient readers can be asked to evaluate authors' word choices and discuss the effect that certain words have on the meaning or tone of the texts.

Understanding Graphophonics, Syntax, and Semantics

Reading strategies can be used and applied to different situations as needed. The types of text a student reads may differ greatly in terms of vocabulary, quality of context clues, picture support, and connections to the reader's prior knowledge. Therefore, the strategies that work to determine an unknown word in any one sentence or text may not work as well in another. These strategies are often unreliable. Instead, teachers should encourage readers to use phonics knowledge to decode unknown words. Proficient and skilled readers do not rely on cues when identifying an unknown word.

While these reading strategies are not recommended for instructional purposes, it is important to know the difference between strategies a reader may be using. Decoding words using graphophonic clues is a strategy where readers consider the letter-sound relationships in the word. Another strategy is to consider syntax, or how the word sounds in the sentence and fits into the overall sentence structure. A third strategy is to consider semantics, or the meaning of the text, to guess the unknown word. Basically, the reader is trying to determine if the unknown word looks right (graphophonics), sounds right (syntax), and makes sense (semantics).

When it comes to reading unknown words, it is best practice for students to use phonetic knowledge to decode words. Students who lack a basic understanding of phonics may rely on cues while reading unknown words. Thus, explicit and systematic phonics instruction is necessary in order to develop proficient readers.

Helping Students Use Context Clues

Teachers should explicitly introduce students to different types of context clues, including definition, antonym, synonym, and inference clues. Examples of sentences containing each type can be provided, and students can be asked to mark the clues, label each type, and explain the meanings of the unknown words. They can also be asked to find examples of each of these types of context clues in other texts. An anchor chart listing the different types of context clues and examples of each can also be posted in the classroom.

Students can also be given sets of words that are related in some way, such as pairs of synonyms or antonyms. They can be asked to write sentences that incorporate the word pairs, creating context clues for other readers. The students can then share their sentences with peers, asking them to identify the context clues and meanings of the unknown words.

Review Video: Reading Comprehension: Using Context Clues
Visit mometrix.com/academy and enter code: 613660

Importance of Knowing Latin and Greek Roots

Many English words are formed from Latin and Greek **roots**. Therefore, recognizing these roots and knowing their meanings can help readers with both decoding and comprehending.

When readers automatically recognize Latin and Greek roots, they will be able to quickly decode the main parts of words that contain them. If they automatically recognize the affixes as well, they will be able to break words into parts and decode them effortlessly. This will allow the readers to maintain speed and fluency while reading.

The roots also hold most of the meaning in words and form the bases of entire word families. Knowing the meanings of these roots will help readers quickly determine the meanings of many newly encountered words, especially if they also know the meanings of any attached affixes. For example, if readers know that the Latin root *port* means to carry, they will have clues about the meanings of the words *transport*, *transportation*, *import*, and *export* as well.

Helping Readers Identify Latin and Greek Roots in Unfamiliar Words

When teaching readers about Latin and Greek roots in English words, one strategy is to help them see the relationships between words in the same word families. This can be done by creating charts or other visual representations of word families and their meanings. For example, a root and its meaning can be written in the middle of a web, and words containing the root and their meanings can be written in circles branching off from the root.

Another strategy is to create three sets of cards, including prefixes, suffixes, and roots. Students can experiment with combining the sets of cards to try to form real words. When real words are created, students can explain their meanings. Students can also be given words containing prefixes, roots, and suffixes. They can be asked to break the words into their components and identify the meanings of each part.

Additionally, students can be encouraged to locate words containing Latin and Greek roots in the texts they read independently. They can use their knowledge of the roots to define the words.

Approaches to Vocabulary Learning

- A **definitional approach** to vocabulary learning is the most traditional. Students are either provided definitions of words or look them up in a dictionary, and they are drilled until they commit the meanings to memory.
- A **structural approach** to vocabulary learning emphasizes the morphological features of words—the roots, prefixes, and suffixes. Once students learn the recurring morphemes in English, they can deduce the meaning of a word in isolation without relying on its context.
- A **contextual approach** to vocabulary learning provides the students with multiple examples of a word used in realistic contexts, allowing them to infer the meaning without resorting to a dictionary or an explicit definition.
- A **categorical approach** to vocabulary learning groups words into categories based on a semantic similarity. For example, a student might be given a list of words associated with driving a car, such as "steering wheel," "to brake," "to accelerate," and "gear shift."
- A **mnemonic approach** to vocabulary learning builds associations between target words and mental images so that hearing a target word evokes the image, facilitating recall of the word's meaning.

Review Video: Types of Vocabulary Learning (Broad and Specific)
Visit mometrix.com/academy and enter code: 258753

Role of Non-Contextual Strategies in Vocabulary Development

Non-contextual strategies are used when new vocabulary is learned without seeing or hearing the words in context. For example, teachers may give students lists of new vocabulary words they have not yet encountered in texts. The teachers may ask students to define the words, use them in sentences, and memorize them. Quizzes may then be given in which students must match the words to their definitions or provide examples of the terms.

There are times teachers may use non-contextual vocabulary strategies, such as when students are learning content-specific words that are not often found naturally in texts. When studying parts of speech, for example, teachers may have students memorize the definitions of *noun*, *verb*, and *adjective*. These words are important for students' understanding of sentence structure, yet students are not likely to encounter these words written in texts with contextual clues. However, it is recommended that teachers do use contextual strategies whenever possible.

Students can be taught to use tools such as dictionaries to define unknown words when contextual clues are not available. They can be prompted to draw pictures to explain word meanings or use graphic organizers to show the relationships among words.

Role of Contextual Strategies in Vocabulary Development

Contextual strategies are used to determine the meanings of unknown vocabulary words when they are encountered in context. The ability to use these strategies to quickly determine word meanings is important for both reading fluency and comprehension. Because words can have multiple meanings, readers also need to use contextual strategies to determine which meaning makes sense in a given sentence.

Teachers can explicitly teach students about the different types of contextual clues often found in sentences. They can encourage students to highlight the words and phrases that provide clues about meanings of the vocabulary words.

Contextual clues often include synonyms or antonyms for the unknown vocabulary words. Therefore, when introducing new words, teachers can assist students with creating lists of synonyms and antonyms. Teachers can also ask students to solve analogies or determine which word does not belong when given a group of related words. These activities will help students recognize synonyms and antonyms and understand relationships among words when they are encountered in context.

Criteria for Selecting Vocabulary Words for Instruction

Vocabulary words can be divided into three tiers. Teachers should consider these tiers when determining which words to focus on during instruction.

- **Tier one words** are common words used in everyday speech. They are typically learned by the early grades through normal conversation. Explicit instruction on the meanings of these words is seldom needed.
- **Tier two words** are found in both fiction and nonfiction texts and are common enough that readers will likely encounter them in multiple texts. Tier two words carry a lot of meaning and can negatively affect comprehension if they are not understood by readers. When deciding which tier two words to focus on, teachers should consider how the words affect the overall meanings of the texts and their morphologies. They should consider if students will be able to form connections between these words and other words, helping them understand unfamiliar words encountered in the future.
- **Tier three words** are mostly found in nonfiction texts and are domain-specific. These words are important for understanding the texts and their domains. Because students are unlikely to have encountered these words before, explicit instruction is needed. This often includes pre-teaching the words and analyzing them in context.

Chapter Quiz

Ready to see how well you retained what you just read? Scan the QR code to go directly to the chapter quiz interface for this study guide. If you're using a computer, simply visit the online resources page at **mometrix.com/resources719/mtelreadsp62** and click the Chapter Quizzes link.

Literacy Assessment and Evaluation

Assessment Methodology

Assessment Methods

Effective teaching requires multiple methods of assessment to evaluate student comprehension and instructional effectiveness. Assessments are typically categorized as diagnostic, formative, summative, and benchmark and are applicable at varying stages of instruction. **Diagnostic** assessments are administered before instruction and indicate students' prior knowledge and areas of misunderstanding to determine the path of instruction. **Formative** assessments occur continuously to measure student engagement, comprehension, and instructional effectiveness. These assessments indicate instructional strategies that require adjustment to meet students' needs in facilitating successful learning and include strategies like checking for understanding, observations, total participation activities, and exit tickets. **Summative** assessments are given at the end of a lesson or unit to evaluate student progress in reaching learning targets and identify areas of misconception for reteaching. Such assessments can be given in the form of exams and quizzes or be project-based activities in which students demonstrate their learning through hands-on, personalized methods. Additionally, portfolios serve as valuable summative assessments in allowing students to demonstrate their progress over time and provide insight regarding individual achievement. **Benchmark** assessments occur less frequently and encompass large portions of curriculum. These assessments are intended to evaluate the progress of groups of students in achieving state and district academic standards.

Assessment Types

- **Diagnostic:** These assessments can either be formal or informal and are intended to provide teachers with information regarding students' level of understanding prior to beginning a unit of instruction. Examples include pretests, KWL charts, anticipation guides, and brainstorming activities. Digital resources, such as online polls, surveys, and quizzes are also valuable resources for gathering diagnostic feedback.
- **Formative:** These assessments occur throughout instruction to provide the teacher with feedback regarding student understanding. Examples include warm-up and closure activities, checking frequently for understanding, student reflection activities, and providing students with color-coded cards to indicate their level of understanding. Short quizzes and total participation activities, such as four corners, are also valuable formative assessments. Numerous digital resources, including polls, surveys, and review games, are also beneficial in providing teachers with formative feedback to indicate instructional effectiveness.
- **Summative:** Summative assessments are intended to indicate students' levels of mastery and progress toward reaching academic learning standards. These assessments may take the form of written or digital exams and include multiple choice, short answer, or long answer questions. Examples also include projects, final essays, presentations, or portfolios to demonstrate student progress over time.

- **Benchmark:** Benchmark assessments measure students' progress in achieving academic standards. These assessments are typically standardized to ensure uniformity, objectivity, and accuracy. Benchmark assessments are typically given as a written multiple choice or short answer exam, or as a digital exam in which students answer questions on the computer.

Review Video: Formative and Summative Assessments
Visit mometrix.com/academy and enter code: 804991

Determining Appropriate Assessment Strategies

As varying assessment methods provide different information regarding student performance and achievement, the teacher must consider the most applicable and effective assessment strategy in each stage of instruction. This includes determining the **desired outcomes** of assessment as well as the information the teacher intends to ascertain and how they will apply the results to further instruction. **Age-** and **grade-level-**appropriateness must be considered when selecting which assessment strategies will enable students to successfully demonstrate their learning. Additionally, the teacher must be cognizant of students' individual differences and learning needs to determine which assessment model is most **accommodating** and reflective of their progress. It is also important that teachers consider the practicality of assessment strategies and methods they will use to implement the assessment for maximized feedback regarding individual and whole-class progress in achieving learning goals.

Assessments That Reflect Real-World Applications

Assessments that reflect **real-world applications** enhance relevancy and students' ability to establish personal connections to learning that deepen understanding. Implementing such assessments provides authenticity and enhances engagement by defining a clear and practical purpose for learning. These assessments often allow for hands-on opportunities for demonstrating learning and can be adjusted to accommodate students' varying learning styles and needs while measuring individual progress; however, assessments that focus on real-world applications can be subjective, thus making it difficult to extract concrete data and quantify student progress to guide future instructional decisions. In addition, teachers may have difficulty analyzing assessment results on a large scale and comparing student performance with other schools and districts, as individual assessments may vary.

Diagnostic Tests

Diagnostic tests are integral to planning and delivering effective instruction. These tests are typically administered prior to beginning a unit or lesson and provide valuable feedback for guiding and planning instruction. Diagnostic tests provide **preliminary information** regarding students' levels of understanding and prior knowledge. This serves as a baseline for instructional planning that connects and builds upon students' background knowledge and experiences to enhance success in learning. Diagnostic tests allow the teacher to identify and clarify areas of student misconception prior to engaging in instruction to ensure continued comprehension and avoid the need for remediation. They indicate areas of student strength and need as well as individual instructional aids that may need to be incorporated into lessons to support student achievement. In addition, these tests enable the teacher to determine which instructional strategies, activities, groupings, and materials will be most valuable in maximizing engagement and learning. Diagnostic tests can be **formal** or **informal** and include pre-tests, pre-reading activities, surveys, vocabulary inventories, and graphic organizers (such as KWL charts). These tests are used to assess student understanding prior to engaging in learning. Diagnostic tests are generally not graded, as there is little expectation that all students in a class possess the same baseline of proficiency at the start of a unit.

Formative Assessments

Formative assessments are any assessments that take place in the **middle of a unit of instruction**. The goals of formative assessments are to help teachers understand where a student is in his or her progress toward **mastering** the current unit's content and to provide the students with **ongoing feedback** throughout the unit. The advantage of relying heavily on formative assessments in instruction is that it allows the teacher to continuously **check for comprehension** and adjust instruction as needed to ensure that the whole class is adequately prepared to proceed at the end of the unit. To understand formative assessments well, teachers need to understand that any interaction that can provide information about the student's comprehension is a type of formative assessment which can be used to inform future instruction.

Formative assessments are often a mixture of formal and informal assessments. **Formal formative assessments** often include classwork, homework, and quizzes. Examples of **informal formative assessments** include simple comprehension checks during instruction, class-wide discussions of the current topic, and exit slips, which are written questions posed by teachers at the end of class, which helps the teacher quickly review which students are struggling with the concepts.

Summative Assessments

Summative assessment refers to an evaluation at the end of a discrete unit of instruction, such as the end of a course, unit, or semester. Classic examples of summative assessments include end-of-course assessments, final exams, or even qualifying standardized tests such as the SAT or ACT. Most summative assessments are created to measure student mastery of particular **academic standards**. Whereas formative assessment generally informs current instruction, summative assessments are used to objectively demonstrate that each individual has achieved adequate mastery of the standards in question. If a student has not met the benchmark, he or she may need extra instruction or may need to repeat the course.

These assessments usually take the form of **tests** or formal portfolios with rubrics and clearly defined goals. Summative assessments are usually high-stakes, heavily-weighted, and they should always be formally graded. These types of assessments often feature a narrower range of question types, such as multiple choice, short answer, and essay questions to help with systematic grading.

Project-based assessments are beneficial in evaluating achievement, as they incorporate several elements of instruction and highlight real-world applications of learning. This allows students to demonstrate understanding through a hands-on, individualized approach that reinforces connections to learning and increases retainment. **Portfolios** of student work over time serve as a valuable method for assessing individual progress toward reaching learning targets. Summative assessments provide insight regarding overall instructional effectiveness and are necessary for guiding future instruction in subsequent years but are not usually used to modify current instruction.

Review Video: Assessment Reliability and Validity
Visit mometrix.com/academy and enter code: 424680

Benchmark Assessments

Benchmark assessments are intended to quantify, evaluate, and compare individual and groups of students' achievement of school-wide, district, and state **academic standards.** They are typically administered in specific intervals throughout the school year and encompass entire or large units of curriculum to determine student mastery and readiness for academic advancement. Benchmark assessments provide data that enable the teacher to determine students' progress toward reaching academic goals to guide current and continued instruction. This data can be utilized by the school and individual teachers to create learning goals and objectives aligned with academic standards. It can also be used to plan instructional strategies, activities, and assessments to support students in achieving these academic standards. In addition, benchmark assessments provide feedback regarding understanding and the potential need for remediation to allow the teacher to instill necessary supports in future instruction that prepare students for success in achieving learning targets.

Alignment of Assessments with Instructional Goals and Objectives

To effectively monitor student progress, assessments must align with **instructional goals** and **objectives**. This allows the teacher to determine whether students are advancing at an appropriate pace to achieve state and district academic standards. When assessments are aligned with specific learning targets, the teacher ensures that students are learning relevant material to establish a foundation of knowledge necessary for growth and academic achievement. To achieve this, teachers must determine which instructional goals and objectives their students must achieve and derive instruction, content, and activities from these specifications. Instruction must reflect and reinforce learning targets, and the teacher must select the most effective strategies for addressing students' needs as they work to achieve them. Assessments must be reflective of content instruction to ensure they are aligned with learning goals and objectives, as well as to enable the teacher to evaluate student progress in mastering them. The teacher must clearly communicate learning goals and objectives throughout all stages of instruction to provide students with clarity on expectations. This establishes a clear purpose and focus for learning that enhances relevancy and strengthens connections to support student achievement.

Clearly Communicating Assessment Criteria and Standards

Students must be clear on the purpose of learning throughout all stages of instruction to enhance understanding and facilitate success. When assessment **criteria** and **standards** are clearly communicated, the purpose of learning is established, and students are able to effectively connect instructional activities to learning goals and criteria for assessment. Communicating assessment criteria and standards provides students with clarity on tasks and learning goals they are expected to accomplish as they prepare themselves for assessment. This allows for more **focused instruction** and engagement in learning, as it enhances relevancy and student motivation. Utilizing appropriate forms of **rubrics** is an effective strategy in specifying assessment criteria and standards, as it informs students about learning goals they are working toward, the quality of work they are expected to achieve, and skills they must master to succeed on the assessment. Rubrics indicate to students exactly how they will be evaluated, thus supporting their understanding and focus as they engage in learning to promote academic success.

Rubrics for Communicating Standards

The following are varying styles of rubrics that can be used to communicate criteria and standards:

- **Analytic:** Analytic rubrics break down criteria for an assignment into several categories and provide an explanation of the varying levels of performance in each one. This style of rubric is beneficial for detailing the characteristics of quality work as well as providing students with feedback regarding specific components of their performance. Analytic rubrics are most effective when used for summative assessments, such as long-term projects or essays.

- **Holistic:** Holistic rubrics evaluate the quality of the student's assignment as a whole rather than scoring individual components. Students' scores are determined based upon their performance across multiple performance indicators. This style of rubric is beneficial for providing a comprehensive evaluation but limits the amount of feedback that students receive regarding their performance in specific areas.
- **Single-point:** Single-point rubrics outline criteria for assignments into several categories. Rather than providing a numeric score to each category, however, the teacher provides written feedback regarding the students' strengths and ways in which they can improve their performance. This style of rubric is beneficial in providing student-centered feedback that focuses on their overall progress.
- **Checklist:** Checklists typically outline a set of criteria that is scored using a binary approach based upon completion of each component. This style increases the efficiency of grading assignments and is often easy for students to comprehend but does not provide detailed feedback. This method of grading should generally be reserved for shorter assignments.

Communicating High Academic Expectations in Assessments

The attitudes and behaviors exhibited by the teacher are highly influential on students' attitudes toward learning. Teachers demonstrate belief in students' abilities to be successful in learning when they communicate **high academic expectations**. This promotes students' **self-concept** and establishes a **growth mindset** to create confident, empowered learners that are motivated to achieve. High expectations for assessments and reaching academic standards communicates to students the quality of work that is expected of them and encourages them to overcome obstacles as they engage in learning. When communicating expectations for student achievement, it is important that the teacher is aware of students' individual learning needs to provide the necessary support that establishes equitable opportunities for success in meeting assessment criteria and standards. Setting high expectations through assessment criteria and standards while supporting students in their learning enhances overall achievement and establishes a foundation for continuous academic success.

Effective Communication and Impact on Student Learning

Communicating high academic expectations enhances students' self-concept and increases personal motivation for success in learning. To maximize student achievement, it is important that the teacher set high academic expectations that are **clearly** communicated through **age-appropriate** terms and consistently reinforced. Expectations must be reflected through learning goals and objectives and must be **visible** at all times to ensure student awareness. Teachers must be **specific** in communicating what they want students to accomplish and clearly detail necessary steps for achievement while assuming the role of facilitator to guide learning and provide support. Providing constructive **feedback** throughout instruction is integral in reminding students of academic expectations and ensuring they are making adequate progress toward reaching learning goals. When high academic expectations are communicated and reinforced, students are empowered with a sense of confidence and self-responsibility for their own learning that promotes their desire to learn. This ultimately enhances achievement and equips them with the tools necessary for future academic success.

Analyzing and Interpreting Assessment Data

Teachers can utilize multiple techniques to effectively analyze and interpret assessment data. This typically involves creating charts and graphs outlining different data subsets. They can list each learning standard that was assessed, determine how many students overall demonstrated proficiency on the standard, and identify individual students who did not demonstrate proficiency on each standard. This information can be used to differentiate instruction. Additionally, they can track individual student performance and progress on each standard over time.

Teachers can take note of overall patterns and trends in assessment data. For example, they can determine if any subgroups of students did not meet expectations. They can consider whether the data confirms or challenges any existing beliefs, implications this may have on instructional planning and what, if any, conclusions can be drawn from this data.

Analyzing and interpreting assessment data may raise new questions for educators, so they can also determine if additional data collection is needed.

Using Assessment Data to Differentiate Instruction for Individual Learners

By analyzing and interpreting assessment data, teachers can determine if there are any specific learning standards that need to be retaught to their entire classes. This may be necessary if the data shows that all students struggled in these specific areas. Teachers may consider reteaching these standards using different methods if the initial methods were unsuccessful.

Teachers can also form groups of students who did not demonstrate proficiency on the same learning standards. Targeted instruction can be planned for these groups to help them make progress in these areas. Interventions can also be planned for individual students who did not show proficiency in certain areas. If interventions have already been in place and have not led to increased learning outcomes, the interventions may be redesigned. If interventions have been in place and assessment data now shows proficiency, the interventions may be discontinued.

If assessment data shows that certain students have met or exceeded expectations in certain areas, enrichment activities can be planned to challenge these students and meet their learning needs.

Aligning Assessments with Instructional Goals and Objectives

Assessments that are congruent to instructional goals and objectives provide a **clear purpose** for learning that enhances student understanding and motivation. When learning targets are reflected in assessments, instructional activities and materials become more **relevant**, as they are derived from these specifications. Such clarity in purpose allows for more focus and productivity as students engage in instruction and fosters connections that strengthen overall understanding for maximized success in learning. Aligning assessments with instructional goals and objectives ensures that students are learning material that is relevant to the curriculum and academic standards to ensure **preparedness** as they advance in their academic careers. In addition, it enables the teacher to evaluate and monitor student progress to determine whether they are progressing at an ideal pace for achieving academic standards. With this information, the teacher can effectively modify instruction as necessary to support students' needs in reaching desired learning outcomes.

Norm-Referenced Tests

On **norm-referenced tests**, students' performances are compared to the performances of sample groups of similar students. Norm-referenced tests identify students who score above and below the average. To ensure reliability, the tests must be given in a standardized manner to all students.

Norm-referenced tests usually cover a broad range of skills, such as the entire grade-level curriculum for a subject. They typically contain a few questions per skill. Whereas scores in component areas of the tests may be calculated, usually overall test scores are reported. Scores are often reported using percentile ranks, which indicate what percentage of test takers scored lower than the student being assessed. For example, a student's score in the 75th percentile means the student scored better than 75% of other test takers. Other times, scores may be reported using grade-level equivalency.

One advantage of norm-referenced tests is their objectivity. They also allow educators to compare large groups of students at once. This may be helpful for making decisions regarding class placements and groupings. A disadvantage of norm-referenced tests is that they only indicate how well students perform in comparison to one another. They do not indicate whether or not students have mastered certain skills.

Criterion-Referenced Tests

Criterion-referenced tests measure how well students perform on certain skills or standards. The goal of these tests is to indicate whether or not students have mastered certain skills and which skills require additional instruction. Scores are typically reported using the percentage of questions answered correctly or students' performance levels. Performance levels are outlined using terms such as *below expectations*, *met expectations*, and *exceeded expectations*.

One advantage of criterion-referenced tests is that they provide teachers with useful information to guide instruction. They can identify which specific skills students have mastered and which skills need additional practice. Teachers can use this information to plan whole-class, small-group, and individualized instruction. Analyzing results of criterion-referenced tests over time can also help teachers track student progress on certain skills. A disadvantage of criterion-referenced tests is that they do not allow educators to compare students' performances to samples of their peers.

Ways That Standardized Test Results Are Reported

- **Raw scores** are sometimes reported and indicate how many questions students answered correctly on a test. By themselves, they do not provide much useful information. They do not indicate how students performed in comparison to other students or to grade-level expectations.
- **Grade-level equivalents** are also sometimes reported. A grade-level equivalent score of 3.4 indicates that a student performed as well as an average third grader in the fourth month of school. It can indicate whether a student is performing above or below grade-level expectations, but it does not indicate that the student should be moved to a different grade level.
- **Standard scores** are used to compare students' performances on tests to standardized samples of their peers. Standard deviation refers to the amount that a set of scores differs from the mean score on a test.
- **Percentile ranks** are used on criterion-referenced tests to indicate what percentage of test takers scored lower than the student whose score is being reported.
- **Cutoff scores** refer to predetermined scores students must obtain in order to be considered proficient in certain areas. Scores below the cutoff level indicate improvement is needed and may result in interventions or instructional changes.

Formal and Informal Assessments

Assessments are any method a teacher uses to gather information about student comprehension of curriculum, including improvised questions for the class and highly-structured tests. **Formal assessments** are assessments that have **clearly defined standards and methodology** and which are applied consistently to all students. Formal tests should be objective and scrutinized for validity and reliability since they tend to carry higher weight for the student. Summative assessments, such as end-of-unit tests, lend themselves to being formal tests because it is necessary that a teacher test the comprehension of all students in a consistent and thorough way.

Although formal assessments can provide useful data about student performance and progress, they can be costly and time-consuming to implement. Administering formal assessments often interrupts classroom instruction and may cause testing anxiety.

Informal assessments are assessments that do not adhere to formal objectives, and they do not have to be administered consistently to all students. As a result, they do not have to be scored or recorded as a grade and generally act as a **subjective measure** of class comprehension. Informal assessments can be as simple as asking the students to raise their hands if they are ready to proceed to the next step or asking a particular question of an individual student.

Informal assessments do not provide objective data for analysis, but they can be implemented quickly and inexpensively. Informal assessments can also be incorporated into regular classroom instruction and activities, making them more authentic and less stressful for students.

Using Various Assessments

The goal of **assessment** in education is to gather data that, when evaluated, can be used to further student learning and achievement. **Standardized tests** are helpful for placement purposes and to reflect student progress toward goals set by a school district or state. If a textbook is chosen to align with district learning standards, the textbook assessments can provide teachers with convenient, small-scale, regular checks of student knowledge against the target standard.

In order be effective, teachers must know where their students are in the learning process. Teachers use a multitude of **formal and informal assessment methods** to do this. Posing differentiated discussion questions is an example of an informal assessment method that allows teachers to gauge individual student progress rather than their standing in relation to a universal benchmark.

Effective teachers employ a variety of assessments, as different formats assess different skills, promote different learning experiences, and appeal to different learners. A portfolio is an example of an assessment that gauges student progress in multiple skills and through multiple media. Teachers can use authentic or performance-based assessments to stimulate student interest and provide visible connections between language-learning and the real world.

Assessment Reliability

Assessment reliability refers to how well an assessment is constructed and is made up of a variety of measures. An assessment is generally considered **reliable** if it yields similar results across multiple administrations of the assessment. A test should perform similarly with different test administrators, graders, test-takers, and over multiple iterations. Factors that affect reliability include the day-to-day wellbeing of the student (students can sometimes underperform), the physical environment of the test, the way it is administered, and the subjectivity of the scorer (with written-response assessments).

Perhaps the most important threat to assessment reliability is the nature of the **exam questions** themselves. An assessment question is designed to test knowledge of a certain construct. A question is reliable in this sense if students who understand the content answer the question correctly. Statisticians look for patterns in student marks, both within the single test and over multiple tests, as a way of measuring reliability. Teachers should watch out for circumstances in which a student or students answer correctly a series of questions about a given concept (demonstrating their understanding) but then answer a related question incorrectly. The latter question may be an unreliable indicator of concept knowledge.

Measures of Assessment Reliability

- **Test-retest reliability** refers to an assessment's consistency of results with the same test-taker over multiple retests. If one student shows inconsistent results over time, the test is not considered to have test-retest reliability.
- **Intertester reliability** refers to an assessment's consistency of results between multiple test-takers at the same level. Students at similar levels of proficiency should show similar results.
- **Inter-rater reliability** refers to an assessment's consistency of results between different administrators of the test. This plays an especially critical role in tests with interactive or subjective responses, such as Likert-scales, cloze tests, and short answer tests. Different raters of the same test need to have a consistent means of evaluating the test-takers' performance. Clear rubrics can help keep two or more raters consistent in scoring.
- **Intra-rater reliability** refers to an assessment's consistency of results with one rater over time. One test rater should be able to score different students objectively to rate subjective test formats fairly.
- **Parallel-forms reliability** refers to an assessment's consistency between multiple different forms. For instance, end-of-course assessments may have many distinctive test forms, with different questions or question orders. If the different forms of a test do not provide the same results, the test is said to be lacking in parallel-forms reliability.
- **Internal consistency reliability** refers to the consistency of results of similar questions on a particular assessment. If there are two or more questions targeted at the same standard and at the same level, they should show the same results across each question.

Assessment Validity

Assessment validity is a measure of the relevancy that an assessment has to the skill or ability being evaluated and the degree to which students' performance is representative of their mastery of the topic of assessment. In other words, a teacher should ask how well an assessment's results correlate to what it is looking to assess. Assessments should be evaluated for validity on both the **individual question** level and as a **test overall**. This can be especially helpful in refining tests for future classes. The overall validity of an assessment is determined by several types of validity measures.

An assessment is considered **valid** if it measures what it is intended to measure. One common error that can reduce the validity of a test (or a question on a test) occurs if the instructions are written at a reading level the students can't understand. In this case, it is not valid to take the student's failed answer as a true indication of his or her knowledge of the subject. Factors internal to the student might also affect exam validity: anxiety and a lack of self-esteem often lower assessments results, reducing their validity as a measure of student knowledge.

An assessment has content validity if it includes all the **relevant aspects** of the subject being tested—if it is comprehensive, in other words. An assessment has **predictive validity** if a score on the test is an accurate predictor of future success in the same domain. For example, SAT exams purport to have validity in predicting student success in a college. An assessment has construct validity if it accurately measures student knowledge of the subject being tested.

Measures of Assessment Validity

- **Face validity** refers to the initial impression of whether an assessment seems to be fit for the task. As this method is subjective to interpretation and unquantifiable, it should not be used singularly as a measurement of validity.

- **Construct validity** asks if an assessment actually assesses what it is intended to assess. Some topics are more straightforward, such as assessing if a student can perform two-digit multiplication. This can be directly tested, which gives the assessment a strong content validity. Other measures, such as a person's overall happiness, must be measured indirectly. If an assessment asserted that a person is generally happy if he or she smiles frequently, it would be fair to question the construct validity of that assessment because smiling is unlikely to be a consistent measure of all peoples' general happiness.
- **Content validity** indicates whether the assessment is comprehensive of all aspects of the content being assessed. If a test leaves out an important topic, then the teacher will not have a full picture as a result of the assessment.
- **Criterion validity** refers to whether the results of an assessment can be used to **predict** a related value, known as **criterion**. An example of this is the hypothesis that IQ tests would predict a person's success later in life, but many critics believe that IQ tests are not valid predictors of success because intelligence is not the only predictor of success in life. IQ tests have shown validity toward predicting academic success, however. The measure of an assessment's criterion validity depends on how closely related the criterion is.
- **Discriminant validity** refers to how well an assessment tests only that which it is intended to test and successfully discriminates one piece of information from another. For instance, a student who is exceptional in mathematics should not be able to put that information into use on a science test and gain an unfair advantage. If the student is able to score well due to his or her mathematics knowledge, the science test did not adequately discriminate science knowledge from mathematics knowledge.
- **Convergent validity** is related to discriminant validity, but takes into account that two measures may be distinct but correlated. For instance, a personality test should distinguish self-esteem from extraversion so that they can be measured independently, but if an assessment has convergent validity, it should show a correlation between related measures.

Practicality

An assessment is **practical** if it uses an appropriate amount of human and budgetary resources. A practical exam doesn't take very long to design or score, nor does it take students very long to complete in relation to other learning objectives and priorities. Teachers often need to balance a desire to construct comprehensive or content-valid tests with a need for practicality: lengthy exams consume large amounts of instruction time and may return unreliable results if students become tired and lose focus.

Assessment Bias

An assessment is considered biased if it disadvantages a certain group of students, such as students of a certain gender, race, cultural background, or socioeconomic class. A **content bias** exists when the subject matter of a question or assessment is familiar to one group and not another. For example, a reading comprehension passage that discusses an event in American history would be biased against students new to the country. An **attitudinal bias** exists when a teacher has a pre-conceived idea about the likely success of an assessment of a particular individual or group. A **method bias** arises when the format of an assessment is unfamiliar to a given group of students. **Language bias** occurs when an assessment utilizes idioms, collocations, or cultural references unfamiliar to a group of students. Finally, **translation bias** may arise when educators attempt to translate content-area assessments into a student's native language—rough or hurried translations often result in a loss of nuance important for accurate assessment.

Authentic Assessments

An authentic assessment is an assessment designed to closely resemble something that a student does, or will do, in the real world. For example, students will never encounter a multiple-choice test requiring them to choose the right tense of a verb, but they will encounter contexts in which they have to write a narration of an event that has antecedents and consequents spread out in time—like narrating their version of what caused a traffic accident. The latter is an example of a potential **authentic assessment**.

Well-designed authentic assessments require a student to exercise **advanced cognitive skills** (e.g., solving problems, integrating information, performing deductions), integrate **background knowledge**, and confront **ambiguity**. Research has demonstrated that mere language proficiency is not predictive of future language success—learning how to utilize knowledge in a complex context is an essential additional skill.

The terms "authentic" and "performance-based" are often used interchangeably when describing assessments; however, a performance-based assessment doesn't necessarily have to be grounded in a possible authentic experience.

Performance-Based Assessments

A performance-based assessment is one in which students demonstrate their learning by performing a **task** rather than by answering questions in a traditional test format. Proponents of **performance-based assessments** argue that they lead students to use **high-level cognitive skills** since they focus on how to put their knowledge to use and plan a sequence of stages in an activity or presentation. They also allow students more opportunities to individualize their presentations or responses based on preferred learning styles. Research suggests that students welcome the chance to put their knowledge to use in real-world scenarios.

Advocates of performance-based assessments suggest that they avoid many of the problems of language or cultural bias present in traditional assessments, allowing more accurate assessment of how well students learned the underlying concepts. In discussions regarding English as a second language, they argue that performance assessments come closer to replicating what should be the true goal of language learning—the effective use of language in real contexts—than do more traditional exams. Critics point out that performance assessments are difficult and time-consuming for teachers to construct and for students to perform. Finally, performative assessments are difficult to grade in the absence of a well-constructed and detailed rubric.

Technology-Based Assessments

Technology-based assessments provide teachers with multiple resources for evaluating student progress to guide instruction. They are applicable in most formal and informal instructional settings and can be utilized as formative and summative assessments. Technology-based assessments simplify and enhance the efficiency of determining comprehension and instructional effectiveness, as they quickly present the teacher with information regarding student progress. This data enables the teacher to make necessary adjustments to facilitate student learning and growth. Implementing this assessment format simplifies the process of aligning them to school and district academic standards. This establishes objectivity and uniformity for comparing results and progress among students. It also helps ensure that all students are held to the same academic expectations. While technology-based assessments are beneficial, there are some shortcomings to consider. This format may not be entirely effective for all learning styles in demonstrating understanding, as individualization in technology-based assessment can be limited. These assessments may not illustrate individual students' growth over time but rather their mastery of an academic standard, thus hindering the ability to evaluate overall achievement. As technology-based evaluation limits hands-on opportunities, the real-world application and relevancy of the assessment may be unapparent to students.

Advantages and Disadvantages of Technology-Based Assessments

Technology-based assessments can have many advantages. They can be given to large numbers of students at once, limited only by the amounts of technological equipment schools possess. Many types of technology-based assessments are instantly scored, and feedback is provided quickly. Students are sometimes able to view their results and feedback at the conclusion of their testing sessions. Data can be quickly compiled and reported in easy-to-understand formats. Technology-based assessments can also often track student progress over time.

Technology-based assessments can have some disadvantages as well. Glitches and system errors can interfere with the assessment process or score reporting. Students must also have the necessary prerequisite technological skills to take the assessments, or the results may not measure the content they are designed to measure. For example, if students take timed, computer-based writing tests, they should have proficient typing skills. Otherwise, they may perform poorly on the tests despite strong writing abilities. Other prerequisite skills include knowing how to use a keyboard and mouse and understanding how to locate necessary information on the screen.

Portfolio Assessments

A **portfolio** is a collection of student work in multiple forms and media gathered over time. Teachers may assess the portfolio both for evidence of progress over time or in its end state as a demonstration of the achievement of certain proficiency levels.

One advantage of **portfolio assessments** is their breadth. Unlike traditional assessments, which focus on one or two language skills, portfolios may contain work in multiple forms, such as writing samples, pictures, and graphs designed for content courses, video and audio clips, student reflections, teacher observations, and student exams. A second advantage is that they allow a student to develop work in authentic contexts, including in other classrooms and at home.

In order for portfolios to function as an objective assessment tool, teachers should negotiate with students in advance of what genres of work will be included and outline a grading rubric that makes clear what will be assessed, such as linguistic proficiency, use of English in academic contexts, and demonstrated use of target cognitive skills.

Curriculum-Based Assessments

Curriculum-based assessments, also known as **curriculum-based measurements (CBM)**, are short, frequent assessments designed to measure student progress toward meeting curriculum **benchmarks**.

Teachers implement CBMs by designing **probes**, or short assessments that target specific skills. For example, a teacher might design a spelling probe, administered weekly, that requires students to spell 10 unfamiliar but level-appropriate words. The data from these assessments can be tracked over time to measure student progress toward defined grade-level goals.

CBM has several clear advantages. If structured well, the probes have high reliability and validity. Furthermore, they provide clear and objective evidence of student progress—a welcome outcome for students and parents who often grapple with less-clear and subjective evidence. Used correctly, CBMs also motivate students and provide them with evidence of their own progress; however, while CBMs are helpful in identifying areas of student weaknesses, they do not identify the causes of those weaknesses or provide teachers with strategies for improving instruction.

Textbook Assessments

Textbook assessments are the assessments provided at the end of a chapter or unit in an approved textbook. **Textbook assessments** present several advantages for a teacher: they are already made; they are likely to be accurate representations of the chapter or unit materials; and, if the textbook has been prescribed or recommended by the state, it is likely to correspond closely to Common Core or other tested standards.

Textbook assessments can be limiting for students who lag in the comprehension of academic English or whose preferred learning style is not verbal. While textbooks may come with DVDs or recommended audio links, ESOL teachers will likely need to supplement these assessment materials with some of their own findings. Finally, textbook assessments are unlikely to represent the range of assessment types used in the modern classroom, such as a portfolio or performance-based assessments.

Peer Assessment

A peer assessment is when students grade one another's work based on a teacher-provided framework. **Peer assessments** are promoted as a means of saving teacher time and building student metacognitive skills. They are typically used as **formative** rather than summative assessments, given concerns about the reliability of student scoring and the tensions that can result if student scores contribute to overall grades. Peer assessments are used most often to grade essay-type written work or presentations. Proponents point out that peer assessments require students to apply metacognition, build cooperative work and interpersonal skills, and broaden the sense that the student is accountable to peers and not just the teacher. Even advocates of the practice agree that students need detailed rubrics in order to succeed. Critics often argue that low-performing students have little to offer high-performing students in terms of valuable feedback—and this disparity may be more pronounced in ESOL classrooms or special education environments than in mainstream ones. One way to overcome this weakness is for the teacher to lead the evaluation exercise, guiding the students through a point-by-point framework of evaluation.

Cultural Influences on Language Development and Use

Role of Social Context in Language Development and Usage

Members of a group have a shared social identity that is formed by reading, writing, listening, and speaking with one another. Group members develop common expressions, mannerisms, and favorite stories that are understood by other members. For example, members of a professional group may use academic language specific to their field at conferences and work events. However, they will not likely use these terms while talking with people outside the field.

Additionally, **social context** plays a role in how people select the appropriate language to use. When asking a stranger for directions, a person would likely consider social norms and begin with an expression like "Excuse me." When talking with a good friend on the phone, a person might use an informal, joking tone. It is important for people to consider each situation and determine which approach to use.

Teachers can provide frequent opportunities for students to communicate with others for a variety of authentic purposes. This can include communicating with classmates, other students and adults within the school, family members, and community members.

Role of Cultural Context in Language Development and Use

Language involves not only the words people say but also the ways in which these words are interpreted by recipients. Differing backgrounds and cultures can affect how messages are received, so it is important for people to consider that others may view communications differently. For example, in some cultures, students are encouraged to ask questions and initiate discussions in class. In others, students are expected to defer to their instructors and not speak unless they are directly questioned. A student who tells an instructor that something doesn't make sense may be praised for using metacognitive strategies in one class while perceived as being rude in another.

Cultural context also affects how nonverbal communications are interpreted. For example, different cultures have their own norms about making eye contact while speaking or the use of gestures during greetings.

Teachers should be sensitive to these cultural differences and consider the roles they may play in student participation and communication. Additionally, teachers should help students view situations from multiple perspectives and consider how their attempts at communication may be perceived by others in various situations.

Interdependent Relationship Between Culture and Language

The ways that people use language and interpret language directed toward them is related to their cultures. Additionally, as cultures change over time, so do languages. Existing words can take on new meanings, and new words may be added to languages. These changes sometimes occur as a result of popular culture, including television, video games, and music. As people with different cultural backgrounds interact, they must negotiate these differences to make meaning.

Because culture and language are so intertwined, understanding the cultural contexts in which language is used is an important part of learning any new language. English language learners should be taught English skills in context, helping them understand how the language is used in realistic social interactions. Additionally, it is important for teachers to understand the cultural backgrounds of ELLs and the roles their cultures may play in their language interactions and expectations. Teachers should incorporate a variety of teaching strategies and methods into their classrooms to meet the needs of all students.

Selecting Appropriately-Leveled Texts

Selecting Appropriate Texts to Support Diverse Learners

When selecting appropriate texts to support diverse learners, teachers should take several factors into consideration. First, they should consider students' reading levels and stages of reading development to determine how much text support is needed. For emergent and early readers, teachers should consider how much picture support is present, how many words are printed on each page, and the predictability of the text. They should also consider how easily students will be able to decode the words based on spelling patterns, text clues, and use of high-frequency words.

For transitional and fluent readers, teachers should consider text complexity. This includes the vocabulary, language use, and sentence structure used in the texts. They should also consider how the texts relate to students' prior knowledge and interests and whether the content supports learning objectives. If topics are unfamiliar to students, some scaffolding or pre-teaching may be needed.

Determining If Texts Are at Students' Independent Reading Levels

When determining reading levels, teachers typically consider both accuracy rate and comprehension. Different reading programs vary slightly in their cutoff levels, but texts are generally considered to be at the independent level if they are read with 95% to 100% accuracy. Additionally, responding correctly to 90% to 100% of comprehension questions may indicate that texts are at students' independent levels. Texts at the independent reading level can be read by students with no assistance.

Texts that students can read independently are good candidates for free choice reading time. They also can be used when practicing comprehension strategies, such as inferring and drawing conclusions. Because students do not struggle to decode words in these texts, they have the mental energy available to do more complex analysis. Additionally, students can repeatedly read favorite books at their independent reading levels for fluency practice. They can also read these books to partners or family members.

Determining If Texts Are at Students' Instructional Reading Levels

Different reading programs vary slightly in their cutoff levels, but texts are generally considered to be at the instructional level if they are read with 90% to 94% accuracy. Additionally, responding correctly to 70% to 89% of comprehension questions may indicate that texts are at students' instructional levels. These books present some challenges for readers, but they can still be read without frustration.

Texts at the instructional level are appropriate for use in guided reading groups. Students are able to decode most words, yet a few miscues may occur that can be used as teaching points. Teachers may analyze student errors and use this information to plan mini-lessons. Additionally, students are able to apply comprehension strategies to analyze and discuss these texts. Texts at the instructional level allow students to have successful and positive experiences with reading while learning from their challenges.

Determining If Texts Are at Students' Frustration Levels

Different reading programs vary slightly in their cutoff levels, but texts are generally considered to be at the frustration level if they are read with less than 90% accuracy. Additionally, responding correctly to less than 70% of comprehension questions may indicate that texts are at students' frustration levels. These books are considered difficult for students to read.

Texts at the frustration level are not good candidates for students to read independently during guided reading groups, when teachers need to observe students' reading and help them apply strategies. Students may become frustrated with too many unknown words or lose the meanings of the texts.

However, these texts can be used in other beneficial ways. Students may enjoy exploring difficult texts on topics of interest, which may help them develop a love of reading. Because these texts can provide valuable information that students cannot access independently, teachers can also read these texts aloud or provide digital versions with audio. Teachers can model using reading strategies with these difficult texts during shared reading experiences. Additionally, students can be encouraged to read these texts with family members.

Systems Used to Level Books

There are several different systems that are used to level books. **Lexile** measures consider both text complexity and word frequency to level books. Specialized assessments are used to determine students' Lexile levels, which can then be used to select appropriate books.

Irene Fountas and Gay Su Pinnell developed another system for leveling books based on their recommendations for guided reading groups. Their system, sometimes known as **guided reading levels**, considers several factors to assign book levels. These factors include word frequency, sentence complexity, vocabulary, and text features. Running records can help identify guided reading levels.

The **Developmental Reading Assessment (DRA)**, also provides a system for leveling books. Students can take the DRA to determine their instructional reading levels. Results can then be used to select books using the DRA system.

Because there are many different leveling systems, conversion charts are available online to help teachers and parents identify book levels using their preferred systems.

Assessment Methodology for Language Skills

Purposes of Literacy Assessment

Literacy assessments can serve many purposes. Assessments can be used to monitor the progress of students toward achieving district and state benchmarks as well as individualized goals. They can identify specific skills that students have mastered as well as those that need additional practice. They can also identify if students are making adequate yearly progress.

Additionally, assessments can be used to guide teacher instruction. By analyzing assessment results, teachers can determine which topics they should focus on for whole-class, small-group, and individualized instruction. This helps ensure that too much instructional time is not spent on topics students have already mastered while ignoring topics that need additional practice.

Assessments can also be used to evaluate the effectiveness of reading programs. By analyzing students' assessment data over time, districts can look for trends in student achievement and progress toward closing achievement gaps.

Advantages and Disadvantages of Group and Individual Literacy Assessments

Group literacy assessments are administered to groups of students at one time. Teachers explain the directions and then instruct all students to begin working, while they observe and answer questions. Assessments are scored after students finish and submit them. Examples of group literacy assessments include state-mandated standardized reading and writing tests. Using the group approach to literacy assessments is more efficient than individualized assessment, freeing up more time for classroom instruction. It also assists teachers with classroom management because all students are being assessed at once.

Individualized assessments are given to one student at a time. Teachers may listen to students read, observe strategy usage, or ask students to retell stories they have read. Dynamic Indicators of Basic Early Literacy Skills (DIBELS) and Developmental Reading Assessment (DRA) are examples of individual assessments. This approach allows teachers to closely observe the strategies each student uses. However, it is more time intensive, and the remaining students in the class must be engaged in other activities.

Using Progress Monitoring to Assess Students and Guide Instruction

Progress monitoring is used to track students' progress toward achieving certain performance goals over time. Teachers first identify students who may benefit from progress monitoring. This usually occurs as a result of assessment data. Students who score below expectations on certain components of criterion-referenced tests may be progressively monitored in those areas.

Teachers then set performance goals that can be measured and tracked over time. For example, if students are currently decoding five CVC words correctly in one minute, the goal may be for them to decode 15 words per minute. Interventions are put in place to help students with these skills. Teachers then repeat testing in these targeted areas on a regular basis, such as weekly or biweekly. Results are recorded, and teachers look for progress over time. Once students have mastered the initial goals, new goals are set, or progress monitoring is discontinued, depending on students' needs.

Progress monitoring can help teachers identify whether or not current interventions are successful or whether changes are needed. It can also help teachers identify when students have mastered certain skills.

Types of Formal Assessments Used to Assess Oral Language and Reading Skills

There are several types of formal assessments designed to assess readers. Some assessments assess knowledge of concepts of print. These are typically performance assessments. Students are asked to locate titles and authors' names, identify letters and words, track the direction of print, and more. Teachers observe students and mark their responses on recording sheets containing scoring criteria. Other formal assessments ask students to identify letter names, apply phonological and phonemic awareness skills, and decode words. Portions of the DIBELS assessment are examples of this type. Data gained from these assessments can be used to group students, plan differentiated instruction, and develop interventions.

Other formal assessments evaluate students' decoding abilities and reading fluency. Students may be asked to read short texts while being timed. They may also be asked to retell stories or answer comprehension questions. Both DIBELS and DRA are two examples of this type of assessment. State standardized tests often require students to read passages and answer comprehension questions. In addition to helping teachers group students and differentiate instruction, these assessments can also help teachers select appropriately leveled texts. There are also formal assessments that specifically assess students' vocabulary knowledge.

Formally Assessing Written Language

Students' writing is often formally assessed using teacher-created, district-mandated, and state-mandated assessments. These assessments typically provide students with specific writing prompts indicating the topics and text structures they are expected to use. Sometimes prompts are based on reading passages that are also contained in the assessments. For example, students may be asked to read two related texts and write responses that explain the common theme they share.

Students' written responses on formal assessments are usually scored using either analytic or holistic rubrics. These rubrics should contain clear criteria that reflect the performance expectations for students. Common criteria include development, organization, language use, conventions, and following the writing process. By analyzing students' performances on different rubric criteria, teachers can plan individualized instruction and develop interventions for struggling students. For example, if students are struggling with language use, teachers can help students analyze mentor texts that contain strong examples.

Informally Assessing Literacy Development

One type of informal assessment is **miscue analysis**, which occurs when teachers listen to students as they read and analyze their miscues. By looking for patterns in the miscues, teachers can determine which strategies students are using and which are lacking. This information can be used to guide instruction.

- **Informal reading inventories** require students to read leveled texts while teachers note errors and fluency. Students then respond to comprehension questions about the texts. Information gained from informal reading inventories can be used to select leveled texts, group students, and plan appropriate instruction.
- **Portfolios** are another type of informal assessment. Portfolios consist of collections of student work, which can be used to show progress over time.
- **Performance assessments** can also be used to assess students' literacy development while allowing students to complete authentic tasks. For example, students may research nutritional guidelines and read food labels to create healthy weekly meal plans.
- **Informal assessment** can also occur when teachers observe students engaged in literacy activities, ask them to explain their thinking, and note performance on assignments and homework. These methods can provide valuable information about students' knowledge and skills, which can be used to guide instruction.

Rubrics

Rubrics are evaluation tools used to assign scores to students' work. They explain the criteria used to assign scores for different levels of mastery. Rubrics can be given to students when projects are assigned to ensure they understand expectations. They can make evaluation more consistent because all students are evaluated using the same criteria. Rubrics can also be easily adapted to reflect different types of activities and assignments.

There are many ways rubrics can be used to evaluate literacy development. They can be used to assess students' reading fluency, with categories relating to speed, accuracy, and prosody. They can also be used to evaluate projects relating to analysis and comprehension.

Additionally, rubrics can be used to assess students' writing. Categories relating to development, use of language, conventions, and other topics can be included. The rubrics can be adapted to reflect the genres or text structures used.

Analytic vs. Holistic Rubrics

Analytic rubrics assign separate scores for each criterion being evaluated. For example, if a writing rubric has criteria for development, use of language, and conventions, each of these areas receives its own score. These scores are then added together to determine the overall score for the assignment. Analytic rubrics provide targeted feedback and help students understand their strengths and weaknesses. However, they can be time-consuming to create and adapt.

Holistic rubrics provide one overall score for the assignment rather than evaluating each criterion separately. They list varying levels of performance, and each level describes the characteristics of assignments earning that score. For example, a writing assignment might be assigned a score ranging from 1 to 4. Assignments earning a score of 4 would be well developed, have effective use of language, and have few or no errors with conventions. Holistic rubrics can be faster for teachers to create and adapt for different assignments. However, the feedback is less targeted than it is when using analytic rubrics, which evaluate each criterion separately.

Running Records

Running records are tools used to record students' behaviors and use of strategies during reading. To administer running records, teachers provide students with books in their developmental reading levels and ask them to read the books aloud. While students are reading, teachers record the words read correctly with check marks. They also note errors by recording the actual words in the texts and the words students substituted for them. Word repetitions, omissions, and self-corrections are also noted using special symbols.

While running records used to be considered best practice, new research has since denounced this tool. Running records are not efficient, and they do not act as a reliable indication of fundamental literacy skills. Educators are encouraged to use universal screenings to gather data to compose homogeneous skill-based groups. Another useful tool is a **decodable running record**. This defers from a normal running record because it assesses phonic and phonemic skills using a decodable text; whereas, a running record based off level generally assess reading behaviors and the use of cueing systems.

Behavior	Notation	Example
Correct response	Mark every word read correctly with a check mark.	✓ ✓ ✓ ✓ ✓ Can you see my eyes?
Substitution	Write the spoken word above the word in the text.	✓ ✓ the ✓ ✓ Can you see my eyes?
Omission	Place a dash above the word left out.	✓ ✓ ✓ — ✓ Can you see my eyes?
Insertion	Insert the added word and place a dash below it (or use a caret).	✓ ✓ ✓ ✓ big ✓ Can you see my eyes?
Attempt	Write each attempt above the word in the text.	✓ ✓ ✓ ✓ e-ey Can you see my eyes?
Repetition	Write R after the repeated word/phrase and draw an arrow back to the beginning of the repetition.	✓ ✓ ✓ ✓R ✓ Can you see my eyes?
Appeal* (asks for help)	Write A above the appealed word.	✓ ✓ ✓ A ✓ Can you see my eyes?
Told word	Write T beside the word supplied for the reader.	✓ ✓ ✓ — ✓ Can you see my T eyes?
Self-correction	Write SC after the corrected word.	✓ ✓ ✓ the/sc ✓ Can you see my eyes?

Role of Performance-Based Assessments in Literacy Assessment

Performance-based assessments require students to solve real-world problems and accomplish authentic tasks by applying literacy skills and strategies. An example of a performance-based assessment is writing a letter to a government official in support of a new law, citing evidence-based reasons for the position. Depending on the types of tasks involved, performance-based assessments may require students to synthesize information from multiple sources, defend positions with text evidence, write texts following the writing process, and create materials to convey information to others.

Performance-based assessments are open ended and do not contain right or wrong answers. Typically, there are multiple ways that students can approach the tasks. The assessments are evaluated using rubrics, with clear criteria determined and shared with students in advance.

An advantage of performance-based assessments is that they allow students opportunities to solve real-world problems, thereby increasing learner engagement. They also require higher-level thinking skills, such as analysis, application, synthesis, and creation. Additionally, they often allow students some choices in how they present their learning. A disadvantage is that performance-based assessments may be time-consuming to create and implement. Grading can also be subjective.

Role of Portfolios in Literacy Assessment

Portfolios are collections of students' projects and work gathered over time. They can serve many purposes in assessing literacy development. They can be used to track students' progress over time and check for mastery of certain skills, which is useful for planning differentiated instruction. Portfolios can also be passed along to students' future teachers, helping them determine students' instructional levels. Additionally, portfolios can be used to help students self-evaluate their own progress and set future goals.

If using portfolios, teachers must make several decisions. They must determine how the portfolios will be used, which will influence the criteria used to select portfolio entries. They also need to determine how entries will be selected. Will teachers or students select the entries, or will both play roles in the process? Teachers also need to decide if the portfolios will be graded. Checklists and rubrics are possible tools that can be used to grade portfolios.

Some advantages of portfolios include the ability to see concrete evidence of student progress over time and the possibility of having students actively involved in assessing their own progress. However, evaluating portfolios is subjective, and teachers may be unsure of how to use them to guide instruction.

Determining When to Respond to Student Miscues in Reading

Even proficient readers make errors at times. Fluent readers often read texts rapidly and may occasionally omit or substitute words without changing the meanings of the texts. For example, they may substitute "her house" for "the house" in a text. These types of errors do not impact meaning and, if occasional, can be ignored. Stopping to correct these types of minor errors can interrupt fluency and comprehension.

Readers in the emergent and early stages of development may make frequent errors and become frustrated if corrected each time. Overcorrection may interfere with confidence and reading enjoyment. Teachers should strategically choose which types of errors to respond to during each reading session. One approach is to focus on a single type of error each time, such as errors where syntax cues are ignored. Another approach is to intervene only when errors affect the meaning of the text. Minor errors can be ignored to build fluency and confidence.

Supporting Advanced Readers

Characteristics of Advanced Readers

Advanced readers can display many different characteristics. They are sometimes identified by above-average scores on standardized reading assessments. Other times, observed reading behaviors and performances on classroom assignments can provide clues.

Advanced readers typically read fluently and have strong word recognition and decoding abilities. They are also able to flexibly apply a variety of reading strategies to figure out unknown words and meanings.

Advanced readers may also have well-developed vocabularies and incorporate varied words into their speech and writing. They may show a strong interest in reading and get deeply immersed in the texts they have selected. Advanced readers often love to talk with others about the books they have read, and they may make connections between the texts and themselves, other texts, and real-world events. Additionally, they are often able to analyze texts using high-level comprehension skills, such as evaluating and drawing conclusions.

Challenging/Engaging High-Achieving Readers

Collaborative Learning Opportunities

High-achieving readers can often benefit from participating in collaborative, project-based learning opportunities that allow them to apply higher-level reading and writing skills with others. Collaborative projects draw upon the strengths and unique problem-solving abilities of all group members and allow high-achieving readers to work with others to solve realistic problems. The projects allow students to share ideas and receive feedback from others of all skill levels, including other high-achieving students who may enjoy analyzing and discussing the same types of complex texts that they do.

High-achieving readers can benefit from forming collaborative relationships with teachers. They can be taught to use metacognitive strategies to self-monitor their own reading and set realistic but challenging goals for their own reading and writing development. They can collaborate with teachers to select literacy projects that pertain to their interests. This involvement in the learning process can help high-achieving readers stay interested and engaged in literacy instruction.

Open-Ended Assignments and Projects

High-achieving readers often benefit from having some choices about what and how they learn. This can include choices about the types and topics of texts they explore. For example, if classes are learning about persuasive writing, students may choose the texts they will analyze from a range of genres and topics.

Students can also have some choices about the complexity of the projects they complete, with options to delve deeper into topics if desired. For example, if students in a class are identifying characteristics of fairy tales, some students may choose to compare and contrast multiple versions of the same tale and note identifying features.

High-achieving readers may also benefit from having choices about the formats of their projects. Possible project ideas include creating multimedia presentations, writing alternative endings to texts, creating three-dimensional artistic representations of story events, and more. These options also accommodate different learning modalities. Teachers may create a menu of options for students to choose from or encourage them to come up with their own ideas.

Although students may be directing some of their own learning, teachers should still conference with high-achieving readers frequently to assess progress and collaborate on ideas.

Issues and Frustrations of High-Achieving Readers

High-achieving readers are sometimes required to read the same texts as the other students in their classes during reading instruction and in other content areas. Because these texts are often designed for on-level readers, they may be easy for high-achieving readers to decode and comprehend. Without any challenges in the texts, high-achieving readers may **finish quick**ly and possibly become bored.

High-achieving readers are also sometimes given extra work to complete when they finish their on-level work early. They may view this extra work as a punishment, and the new work may not be challenging for these students either. **Boredom** and **frustration** may then occur.

Additionally, high-achieving readers may become bored during whole-class lessons on concepts they have already mastered. For example, readers who are successfully decoding complex multisyllabic words will likely become bored during lessons on CVCe spelling patterns.

These high-achieving readers may sometimes appear disengaged, resist coming to school, or have behavior issues within the classroom. To prevent these issues from occurring, teachers can **differentiate instruction** and provide high-achieving readers with opportunities to read texts within their **instructional levels**. These students can also be encouraged to complete alternate assignments that are more challenging.

Screening for Reading and Language Delays

Screening vs. Diagnostic Assessments

Screening assessments are used to identify students who may be at risk for future academic difficulties. Information gained from these assessments can be used to determine which students would likely benefit from specialized interventions to help prevent academic difficulties in the future.

Adequate literacy screening is important in young children. Studies have shown that literacy difficulties are harder to remedy through intervention after third grade. By identifying these students early and providing appropriate interventions, these difficulties can be prevented or lessened. For example, phonemic awareness screenings are frequently given to early childhood students because phonemic awareness is a key indicator of future reading success.

Review Video: Developmental Screening Strategies
Visit mometrix.com/academy and enter code: 100353

Diagnostic assessments are used to identify students' existing knowledge and skills before beginning instruction. For example, students may complete diagnostic assessments focused on using comprehension strategies to understand nonfiction texts. Data from diagnostic assessments can be used to help teachers plan differentiated instruction to meet students' individual needs.

Identifying Students Who Have Not Met Standards

It is important to identify concerns with literacy development early to prevent future academic difficulties. Reading, writing, listening, and speaking affect performance across all content areas. Therefore, students who struggle with literacy may struggle in all academic areas.

- **Early screening** is one way to identify students who are not meeting standards and may have literacy difficulties. Depending on the ages of the students, screening can be given on a range of topics, including alphabetic principle, phonological and phonemic awareness, decoding strategies, fluency, and comprehension.
- The results of **criterion** and **norm-referenced formal assessments** can also be used to identify students who have not met standards. Teachers can look for specific skills and standard areas that students struggled with on these formal assessments. They can also look for indications that students are not meeting their adequate yearly progress goals.
- Additionally, **informal assessments** can be used to identify students who are not meeting standards. Classroom observations, running records, responses during literature circles, and other informal assessments are helpful tools for teachers to use.

All of these data points can be considered when determining which students may benefit from targeted interventions.

Determining Whether Students Have Reading or Language Delays

Generally, teachers should collect multiple data points over time before requesting that students be evaluated for potential delays or disabilities. Students may perform below expectations on assessments for a variety of reasons, including illness and fatigue. Therefore, no one assessment score should be used as the basis for an evaluation. However, if students perform similarly on multiple assessments over time, further investigation may be warranted. Assessment data can also be combined with classroom observations for supplementary information. Additionally, interventions can be attempted first to determine if achievement gaps can be closed through targeted instruction.

Parents sometimes request that their children be evaluated. Parents are often the first to notice potential issues because they observe their children's progress from year to year and witness the challenges firsthand. Parents can submit their requests for evaluations in writing to classroom teachers, reading specialists, administrators, or other school officials for consideration.

Signs of Dyslexia

Dyslexia is a common disorder that affects reading. Students with **dyslexia** often have difficulties with phonological awareness, accurate word recognition, decoding, and reading fluency. As a result, they may also have difficulties comprehending what they have read. Spelling may also be affected. Teachers may notice that students struggle to decode words and read fluently, and students may become anxious or frustrated when asked to read. Dyslexia does not affect intelligence and is marked by a gap between students' abilities and achievements.

Although there is no cure for dyslexia, targeted interventions are often successful. A multisensory approach to reading instruction is often helpful, along with systematic and explicit instruction in reading skills and sight word recognition. The Orton-Gillingham method is one commonly used approach. Teachers should also maintain supportive classroom environments and not rush students or force them to read aloud. Students with dyslexia may also benefit from some accommodations, such as extra time on tests, increased wait time when responding to questions, and access to audio versions of texts.

Review Video: Understanding Learning Disability Needs of Students
Visit mometrix.com/academy and enter code: 662775

Review Video: Disorders that Impair Reading Comprehension
Visit mometrix.com/academy and enter code: 306758

Signs of Dysgraphia

Dysgraphia is a disorder that affects written expression. Students with dysgraphia may have difficulties holding pencils correctly, forming letters, writing on lines, putting thoughts into written words, and organizing writing in meaningful ways. Handwriting and spelling are also commonly difficult for students. Students with dysgraphia may become frustrated or anxious if asked to write, and they may try to avoid writing when possible.

There are many ways teachers can assist students with dysgraphia. To assist with spelling, explicit instruction on sound-symbol relationships and spelling patterns may be helpful. Graphic organizers can be provided to assist students with written organization. Additionally, students may qualify for occupational therapy to assist with developing coordination and motor skills. Students with dysgraphia may also benefit from some accommodations, such as being allowed to type responses or answer questions orally. They may benefit from receiving extra time to complete assignments and tests.

Signs of Dyspraxia

Dyspraxia is a disorder that makes it difficult for the body to coordinate movement. Students with dyspraxia may have difficulties with balance and coordination, and they may have trouble performing tasks that require motor skills. Students with dyspraxia may also be sensitive to noise or touch in addition to spatial or perceptual difficulties, all of which might affect reading and writing. Some types of dyspraxia may also affect language, especially enunciation.

In the classroom, teachers can break large, multistep tasks into smaller chunks. If activities require movement, teachers can begin with simple movements first, and gradually increase the difficulty. Teachers can also provide extra processing time when giving directions and extra wait time when asking questions. Some students with dyspraxia may qualify for occupational therapy services. Students with dyspraxia may benefit from certain accommodations, such as seating that is free from noise and distractions.

Characteristics of Reading Comprehension Deficiencies

Students with **reading comprehension deficiencies** have difficulty understanding and responding to what they have read. They may have difficulty summarizing texts, making inferences, differentiating between main ideas and supporting details, and more. They often have issues with reading fluency as well, especially with phrasing and prosody. Students with comprehension deficiencies can often decode words efficiently, yet they struggle with comprehending the texts' meanings. However, some students may struggle with both decoding and comprehension.

To assist students with comprehension deficiencies, teachers can provide advance organizers that offer overviews of the text structures and story events. They can also preview texts or conduct picture walks to familiarize students with the topics. Before reading, they can instruct students to pay attention to specific key information within the texts. Additionally, teachers can model their use of comprehension strategies during think-alouds and shared reading experiences.

Characteristics of Reading Retention Deficiencies

Students with **reading retention deficiencies** have difficulties remembering what they have read. This may include difficulties summarizing texts, ordering story events, and making text connections after reading. Retention deficiencies may occur due to difficulties transferring information to short- or long-term memory or with difficulties retrieving information that has been previously stored in long-term memory.

To assist students with retention difficulties, teachers can provide students with graphic organizers that they can complete while reading. Story maps and sequencing charts are examples of graphic organizers that may be helpful. Teachers can also provide notes and text summaries to assist students with remembering important concepts and details. Additionally, students can be taught to use specific strategies to activate memory, such as visualizing as they read. They can also be taught to annotate texts by highlighting key phrases and taking notes, making it easier to locate important information in the future.

Effective Literacy Interventions

Components of Effective Literacy Interventions

Literacy interventions should be targeted to students' individual needs and based upon assessment data. Interventions can be delivered either individually or in small groups, if multiple students can benefit from the same interventions.

If commercial intervention programs are used, they should be carefully evaluated to ensure they are research-based. Interventions should be based upon clear objectives. They should also incorporate ways to measure students' progress to evaluate if the interventions are successful. Pre-tests are commonly given when interventions are implemented, and the results are used to set goals. Student progress is then monitored regularly to determine if progress is being made toward the performance goals.

Research has shown that frequent interventions are more effective than infrequent interventions, even if they occur for shorter blocks of time. For example, teachers may conduct small-group interventions daily, for 15 minutes each time. Students need frequent opportunities to practice and apply new skills. Interventions should include a mixture of systematic and explicit instruction and guided practice with feedback.

Although students benefit from interventions with classroom teachers and literacy specialists, some carefully selected computer-based interventions may also be used.

Evaluating the Effectiveness of Literacy Interventions

Literacy interventions are planned for students based upon assessment data. This initial data is used to set performance goals, and progress toward goals is measured using progress monitoring and intervention post-tests. If students make regular progress and achieve their performance goals within the expected time frames, the interventions are usually considered effective. If students make minimal or no progress toward their goals despite receiving interventions, the interventions may be considered ineffective, unless additional factors are impeding success.

However, interventions must be implemented with fidelity to determine their effectiveness. Teachers must use the agreed-upon strategies and instructional methods and meet with students consistently according to their intervention schedules. They must also ensure that the interventions are not interrupted. If issues occur in these areas, lack of student progress may not be the result of ineffective intervention planning. The interventions may have the potential to be successful, but the implementation and delivery methods may need improvement.

Reading Strategies vs. Reading Interventions

Reading strategies and reading interventions are often used interchangeably, but there are some key differences between the two. Reading strategies are methods teachers use to help students learn reading skills. To teach students to comprehend texts, teachers may encourage them to make predictions and inferences. Strategies are taught during regular classroom instruction and may be reinforced individually or in small groups. Meeting informally with a student to review and practice how to make predictions during one class session is not a formal intervention as no set improvement plan, regular meeting schedule, or progress monitoring assessment is involved.

Interventions are specific plans to help students make progress in targeted areas. They are based on assessment data, and they are scheduled for regular, set periods of time. Students' progress is monitored through frequent assessments to look for improvement. Reading strategies may be taught and practiced as part of formal intervention plans.

Reading Specialist's Role in Professional Development

Reading Specialists Support of Classroom Teachers

Reading specialists often play a variety of roles within their schools. Some reading specialists serve as intervention teachers. These specialists directly provide targeted intervention services to students who are struggling with reading, often in areas including phonemic awareness, decoding, sight word recognition, and comprehension. They may go into students' classrooms to provide intervention services, or they may pull students out for a set number of minutes each week.

Reading specialists can also provide professional development opportunities for classroom teachers. In small or large-group sessions, they often model how to use instructional strategies that are supported by research. They compile literature and resources related to literacy instruction and make these resources available to teachers. They may also work with individual teachers to develop instructional plans or overcome difficulties with literacy instruction.

Reading specialists may also oversee standardized literacy assessments for their schools and train teachers in testing procedures. They work with teachers to analyze assessment data, track students' progress over time, and use the results to plan or change appropriate interventions.

Professional Development Opportunities

Reading specialists provide professional development opportunities for teachers on a wide range of topics. For early childhood teachers, reading specialists may offer training about modeling concepts of print, planning phonological and phonemic awareness activities, creating print-rich environments, and designing effective literacy centers. Other topics may include types of reading and writing experiences and using multisensory approaches to reading and writing instruction.

- Professional development for elementary teachers may include topics such as incorporating reading and writing across content areas, using interactive word walls, using assessment data to guide instruction, modeling comprehension strategies, and designing effective literature circles.
- For middle and high school teachers, professional development topics may include teaching academic vocabulary, incorporating reading and writing across content areas, teaching text structures, and using higher-level comprehension strategies.

Reading specialists may also provide professional development opportunities on specialized topics, such as meeting the needs of students with disabilities and teaching reading strategies to ELLs.

Chapter Quiz

Ready to see how well you retained what you just read? Scan the QR code to go directly to the chapter quiz interface for this study guide. If you're using a computer, simply visit the online resources page at **mometrix.com/resources719/mtelreadsp62** and click the Chapter Quizzes link.

Theoretical, Professional, and Language Foundations

Reading Development

Typical Progression of Reading Development

Readers typically progress through four stages of reading development. The first stage of reading development is known as **emergent reading**. It is the stage in which readers develop pre-reading behaviors and begin understanding concepts of print. The second stage is called **early reading**. Early readers begin to use a combination of reading strategies and cueing systems to decode and comprehend simple texts. The third stage is called **transitional reading**. Transitional readers use a wide range of reading strategies to support comprehension of more complex texts. Rapid word recognition combined with effective use of strategies allows readers to read at an increased pace. **Fluent reading** is the last stage of reading development. Fluent readers confidently read and comprehend a wide range of complex texts independently.

Students' individual differences and prior experiences can affect at what ages and rates they progress through the stages.

Review Video: Stages of Reading Development
Visit mometrix.com/academy and enter code: 121184

Characteristics of the Emergent Stage of Reading

Emergent reading skills are strong predictors of future reading success. In the emergent stage, readers display **pre-reading behaviors**. They begin interacting with texts without actually reading the words. They learn the concepts of print, such as learning how to correctly hold books and understanding that print holds meaning. They begin to identify capital and lowercase letters, and they understand the predictable relationships between letters and sounds. They begin to understand that letters are combined to form words and words are combined to form sentences.

Readers in the **emergent stage** also develop oral language skills. This includes phonological awareness skills, such as rhyming and alliteration. They develop phonemic awareness skills, including the ability to blend, segment, and manipulate phonemes within words.

Emergent readers enjoy having others read to them. They respond to texts that are read aloud by making predictions, retelling events, and other activities. They react to illustrations and use them to make sense of the texts.

Instructional Strategies Used in the Emergent Stage

Teachers should read aloud to students in the emergent stage often, choosing from a range of genres. When reading, teachers should model concepts of print and how to make predictions, retell story events, and other reading strategies. Concepts of print should be explored in environmental print within the classrooms and the schools. Teachers should create print-rich environments containing several different types of texts for students to explore. Students should be given multiple opportunities to interact with different types of texts daily, both with others and independently.

Teachers should also plan **explicit instruction** on letter identification and letter-sound correspondence and give readers opportunities to practice recognizing and forming both capital and lowercase letters.

Additionally, teachers should plan classroom activities to build emergent readers' phonological awareness and phonemic awareness skills. This includes opportunities to practice rhyming, alliteration, onset and rime manipulation, and phoneme manipulation.

Characteristics of Texts Designed for Emergent Readers

Texts designed for emergent readers should have **pictures** or **illustrations** that strongly support the print. They should have a limited amount of text on each page and use **repetitive words** and phrases. They should include several high-frequency and easily decodable words, and the text should be placed in predictable places on each page. Simple sentence structure should be used.

Additionally, books for emergent readers should be focused on familiar objects and topics that will activate readers' prior knowledge. This assists readers with comprehension and making connections and allows them to focus on print concepts. The vocabulary should also be familiar. Print should be large and contain wide spaces between letters and lines of text.

Some emergent texts follow a pattern in which only the last word in each sentence changes. For example, each page of a text might say, "I like to ____." The missing word could be easily guessed based upon picture support.

Characteristics of the Early Reading Stage of Reading Development

In the early reading stage of development, readers increasingly use strategies to figure out unknown words and make meaning from texts. They begin to self-monitor their reading and self-correct if they realize that errors have been made. They expand their vocabularies and their automatic recognition of high-frequency words. They use picture clues, knowledge of letter-sound relationships, and repetition to decode unknown words in longer and more complex texts.

Early readers also continue developing comprehension strategies, such as predicting and summarizing. They use a combination of these comprehension strategies to make meaning from what they have read. They begin to read silently and no longer need to point to each word while reading.

Characteristics of Texts for Readers in the Early Reading Stage

Texts for **early readers** contain more print than those for emergent readers. They include longer sentences, more sentences per page, and more pages per book. The texts also contain more complex and **varied sentence structure**. There is less reliance on picture clues than in books for emergent readers, with the print carrying most of the meaning. More complex and content-specific vocabulary words are included. Multiple spelling patterns are used, requiring readers to use a combination of decoding strategies. There is less repetition, or longer and more complex phrases are repeated than those in emergent texts.

Texts for early readers also frequently focus on more complex story lines. Descriptive language is often included. The content of these books is still typically familiar to readers.

Readers in the early stage understand a variety of genres and purposes for reading. Therefore, texts for this stage are varied in genre and purpose.

Instructional Strategies Used with Readers in the Early Reading Stage

Students in the early reading stage are beginning to increase their reading rates and build fluency. Teachers need to provide systematic and explicit phonics instruction during this time. Teachers can provide decodable text based off phonics instruction that has already been taught. Teachers can also provide students with opportunities to frequently read and reread favorite books, which will help them build fluency. Teachers can prompt students to decode words using previously taught phonics instruction.

Early readers also benefit from activities that focus on advanced phonemic awareness skills, such as phoneme substitution. Additionally, students benefit from instruction on complex vocabulary words and spelling patterns. Teachers can also provide students with frequent opportunities to read varied text types and genres that incorporate more sophisticated vocabulary words and sentence structures than emergent texts.

Characteristics of Readers in the Transitional Stage of Reading Development

Readers in the transitional stage of reading development are able to engage in sustained, quiet reading for extended periods of time. They are able to read and comprehend longer, more advanced texts and can automatically identify a large number of high-frequency words. They have knowledge of complex spelling patterns, which they use to independently decode most unknown words, including multisyllabic words. They are also continuing to increase their fluency and reading rates.

Transitional readers utilize more strategies to assist with comprehension than early readers. They have an awareness of text structures and can gather and synthesize information from multiple text features, including print, graphs, charts, and sidebars. They rely more on the print than the pictures for meaning and can identify story elements, such as characters, setting, problem, and solution. Additionally, they develop higher-level comprehension skills, such as making inferences and drawing conclusions.

Characteristics of Texts for Readers in the Transitional Reading Stage

Students in the transitional reading phase are able to read more difficult texts than early readers. This includes both fiction and nonfiction texts covering a wide range of genres. It also includes both beginning chapter books and challenging picture books. Nonfiction texts may utilize multiple text structures and include features like graphs, charts, photographs, sidebars, and more. The topics may be either familiar or unfamiliar to readers. Some challenging and unknown vocabulary words may be included along with many high-frequency words. Story elements may be described in detail, using descriptive words and phrases. There are numerous chapter book series designed for transitional readers.

Books written for transitional readers have several lines of text per page. Some pages may be composed entirely of text, as in chapter books. The books have many pages with clearly defined spaces between lines of text.

Instructional Strategies Used with Readers in the Transitional Stage

Because **transitional readers** are beginning to read more complicated texts of different genres, it is helpful to teach about text structures. Understanding text structures and where to look for main ideas can assist transitional readers with comprehension. Teachers can also teach strategies to determine the meanings of **unknown vocabulary** words by analyzing word morphology. This includes recognizing and analyzing both affixes and roots.

Teachers can plan several opportunities for students to build reading fluency by rereading texts for meaningful purposes. They can also model advanced analysis and comprehension strategies during shared reading experiences, such as making inferences and drawing conclusions. They can provide students with tools like graphic organizers to assist with comprehension during independent reading. Additionally, they can encourage readers to support responses with text evidence.

Teachers can also assist transitional readers with selecting appropriately challenging texts for independent reading.

Characteristics of Readers in the Fluent Stage of Reading Development

Readers in the **fluent stage** of reading development read complex texts both **quickly** and **accurately**. They read with appropriate expression. They automatically recognize high-frequency words and efficiently use multiple strategies to determine unknown words they encounter. These strategies include using cueing systems, context clues, and substitutions.

Fluent readers are able to comprehend a wide range of complex fiction and nonfiction texts. They understand content-specific and technical vocabulary words or use strategies and tools to determine their meanings. They have a strong understanding of different types of text structures and know how to efficiently use text features to locate key information. They understand multiple purposes for reading and writing and are able to understand texts from multiple points of view. Additionally, fluent readers use **high-level thinking skills** to comprehend what they have read. They are able to evaluate texts and argue points using text evidence for support.

Characteristics of Texts for Readers in the Fluent Reading Stage

Texts for readers in the fluent reading stage are complex, varied, and sometimes abstract. Complex text structures are often used. For example, they may use flashbacks or weave back and forth while comparing and contrasting two things. Fictional texts for fluent readers contain highly developed plots and character development. They often use descriptive and figurative language. Additionally, these texts may have multiple themes or layers that require deep analysis. Content-specific and technical vocabulary words are commonly used. Topics may be either familiar or unfamiliar to readers.

Texts for fluent readers rely mostly on the print to convey meaning. Photos or illustrations are mainly included to convey important information that may be difficult to explain in print. For example, photographs of animals may be included in biology texts. Illustrations may be included in historical fiction texts where the settings or characters may be unfamiliar to readers.

Instructional Strategies Used with Readers in the Fluent Reading Stage

Readers in the fluent stage often read texts about new and **unfamiliar topics**. Therefore, teachers can instruct them to activate related prior knowledge that may assist them with making sense of the new texts. They can also model how to efficiently use **research tools** to learn more about unfamiliar topics.

Teachers can also model and encourage readers to use close reading techniques to deeply analyze texts. This process includes rereading texts multiple times to analyze different layers each time. It also includes evaluating, comparing and contrasting, making connections, and using other high-level comprehension strategies. Teachers can encourage readers to analyze texts from multiple perspectives, using text evidence to support their responses.

Because readers in this stage will frequently encounter content-specific and technical vocabulary words, teachers can continue to model word analysis skills, such as analyzing affixes and roots.

Academic Literacy

Academic literacy refers to the knowledge and skills necessary to communicate effectively in academic situations. It includes content-specific knowledge and vocabulary, such as mathematical terms. It also includes general knowledge and vocabulary used across all content areas, such as the terms *synthesize*, *summarize*, and *evaluate*. Additionally, it refers to the ability to communicate effectively in academic situations through reading, writing, listening, and speaking.

Academic literacy helps students flexibly adapt their use of reading strategies according to the types of text used and the purposes for reading. It helps them acquire content-specific vocabulary needed to comprehend academic texts and effectively communicate their learning using a variety of response types. It helps them summarize, evaluate, and make connections among content acquired from multiple sources and across content areas. Academic literacy also encourages students to effectively communicate and collaborate with others to construct meaning.

Types of Knowledge Commonly Used in Education

There are many types of knowledge commonly used in education.

- **Social** knowledge is knowledge about social conventions passed down within members of a community. It includes conventions related to expected greetings, manners, and conversational behavior.
- **Procedural** knowledge refers to the knowledge applied to carry out procedural tasks. An example is solving a complex math problem using a multistep algorithm.
- **Physical** knowledge refers to knowledge learned by observing the features of something. When students discuss the physical properties of rock samples, they are using physical knowledge.
- **Domain** knowledge refers to the knowledge and skills used by experts in a particular field. For example, a student explaining how she completed a division problem using the terms *dividend*, *divisor*, and *quotient* is using domain knowledge.
- **Empirical** knowledge refers to knowledge obtained from scientific experimentation and data collection. Determining the boiling points of different liquids as part of a science experiment is an example of empirical knowledge.

Role of Literacy in Different Types of Knowledge

Literacy plays a large role in the development and application of different types of knowledge in the classroom. Social knowledge is passed down through oral language and written texts. Students learn about social norms through the actions of characters in stories and through discussing texts with others. For example, children learn about solving conflict with friends by reading about characters who work through conflict. They also learn how to listen attentively and take turns through participation in literature circles.

- When students read nonfiction **procedural texts**, they develop procedural knowledge that can be used to accomplish tasks. Procedural texts also provide models of text structures students can use when explaining procedures to others.
- Reading texts containing **academic language** helps students develop and apply physical, domain, and empirical knowledge. Developing their academic vocabularies can assist students with expressing their observations and conclusions using academic language.

ACADEMIC READING VS. READING FOR ENTERTAINMENT

- **Academic reading** refers to thoughtfully reading and analyzing academic texts as part of content area studies. Readers usually have specific purposes in mind before beginning academic reading. For example, an entomology student may consult a field guide to correctly classify an insect found during a nature hike. Another student may read a social studies textbook to identify some major causes of the Revolutionary War for an essay assignment.
- **Reading for entertainment** refers to reading for fun. A student may select a fictional book from a favorite series to read on a rainy day.

When completing academic reading, readers often pay special attention to text structures and features to efficiently **locate needed information**. They may skim or skip around in the texts. They may stop to look up the meanings of **unfamiliar vocabulary words**. They may also read more slowly or reread passages multiple times to make sense of unfamiliar content.

When reading for entertainment, proficient readers still self-monitor their comprehension, but they have more freedom about which text elements they wish to respond to and analyze. They may also read at a quicker pace and choose to reread favorite parts for fun.

Development of Reading Fluency

COMPONENTS OF FLUENCY

Reading fluency is made up of several elements including rate, accuracy, and prosody.

- **Rate** refers to reading speed. Proficient readers adjust their reading speed flexibly depending on their purposes for reading. For example, they may read scientific textbooks containing technical vocabulary more slowly than graphic novels they are reading for entertainment. Rate is important for comprehension. If readers read too slowly, they may forget what they have already read and lose the overall meanings of the texts. If readers read too quickly, important points may be overlooked.
- **Accuracy** is another component of fluency. It refers to decoding words correctly without errors. Fluent readers automatically recognize many high-frequency words and use multiple strategies to decode unknown words. Accuracy is important because frequent errors may affect comprehension, especially if errors are made on words central to the meaning of the text.
- **Prosody** is another component of fluency. It refers to reading expression, including phrasing and intonation. Prosody affects the ways texts are understood. For example, readers should pause appropriately at commas to emphasize certain phrases. Using the correct intonation associated with each punctuation mark affects the tone of the texts.

PROGRESSION OF FLUENCY DEVELOPMENT IN READERS

- **Early readers** devote most of their mental energy to decoding words. In this stage of reading, the focus is on developing reading accuracy, which is one component of fluency. Early readers practice high-frequency words and learn strategies to decode words with simple spelling patterns. Rate and prosody play lesser roles but are still practiced with scaffolding.

- In the **transitional reading stage**, readers automatically recognize many high-frequency words and more efficiently use strategies to decode unknown words. There is still a focus on accuracy as readers encounter more complex vocabulary and spelling patterns. However, transitional readers increase their reading rates and begin to read independently with prosody. As readers gain confidence with familiar texts, their fluency increases.
- By the time they reach the **fluent stage**, readers are able to flexibly adapt their reading rates based upon their purposes for reading. Automatic recognition of most words results in reading accuracy. Fluent readers read with prosody, and they appropriately match their expressions to the texts.

Developing Fluency in Early Readers

When teaching early readers, the main focus is on developing **accuracy**. This is done through activities to develop automatic recognition of high-frequency sight words and explicit phonics instruction that teaches strategies to decode words with common spelling patterns.

To assist early readers with developing **speed and prosody**, teachers can encourage repeated readings of favorite texts. As readers develop more confidence with the texts through these repeated readings, their reading rates will increase. Because readers already know how to decode the words in these familiar texts, they have more energy available to focus on expression.

Teachers should frequently **model fluent reading**. This includes reading with appropriate speed, phrasing, and intonation. Teachers can also model disfluent reading, such as reading texts without expression, and ask students to explain the effects it has on comprehension. Choral reading of shared texts can also assist students with developing fluency.

Review Video: Fluency
Visit mometrix.com/academy and enter code: 531179

Maintaining Fluency in On-Level Readers

Like struggling readers, on-level readers can benefit from frequent teacher modeling of fluent reading, choral reading, and opportunities to reread familiar texts. Additionally, they can benefit from partner reading. Partner reading allows students to hear fluent reading modeled by classmates and reread texts repeatedly while receiving feedback. Students should first be taught procedures for how to listen attentively to their partners' reading and provide effective and encouraging feedback. Teachers should always be mindful of individual needs when pairing students.

Reader's theater is another strategy to assist on-level readers with fluency. In **reader's theater**, students read scripts from appropriately leveled texts to perform for classmates. Through rehearsing and performing, students have multiple opportunities to reread the scripts. They must also practice reading with appropriate expression for their characters and reading with appropriate speeds so they can be understood by their audiences. Additionally, reader's theater allows students in the audience to hear models of fluent reading. In reader's theater, the focus is on the reading, and few or no props are used.

Interventions to Use Assisting Readers Who Are Struggling with Fluency

Readers who are struggling with fluency can benefit from frequent modeling of fluent reading. As teachers reread familiar texts, students can join in and read chorally, matching their phrasing, speed, and expression to the teachers' reading. Students can also listen to audio recordings of texts.

Readers who struggle with fluency can also benefit from repeated readings of texts. After initial readings, teachers can give feedback to students and help them set goals for rereading. For example, they may encourage readers to pause at the periods between sentences. It is important that readers are given passages within their instructional reading levels. Reading texts far below their instructional levels will not challenge the readers. Reading texts that are too difficult will result in readers stopping frequently to decode unknown words, which interrupts fluency and causes frustration. Encouraging repeated readings of texts with rhyming and repetition, including poetry, can assist readers who are struggling with fluency.

Although teachers may monitor students' reading fluency over time, it is also important to create encouraging environments for readers. Continuously timing readers or forcing disfluent readers to read aloud in front of others may have negative effects.

Historical and Theoretical Background of Reading Programs

History of Reading Education in America

In colonial and early America, reading education focused on **memorization**. Students were expected to memorize the alphabet, syllables, words, verses, and poems. The poems and verses were recited in front of others for fluency practice.

In the 1800s, a more systematic approach to reading instruction was introduced. This included systematic phonics, sight word instruction, and reading across content areas. McGuffey Readers were a series of leveled primers commonly used for reading instruction. In the late 1800s, the idea of reading for meaning began to be promoted.

In the early 1900s, the focus continued to be on reading for **meaning** and **purpose**. Explicit and systematic phonics instruction was common. In the mid-1900s, basal readers became commonplace in schools. Basal readers contained leveled stories that were followed by comprehension questions, with separate phonics skill and drill activities.

In the 1980s, whole language was promoted. Proponents believed children would learn to read by being **immersed** in reading and writing experiences rather than using explicit phonics instruction. By the mid-1990s, a balanced approach to literacy instruction was common. **Balanced literacy** includes a combination of explicit and systematic phonics instruction and immersion in authentic reading and writing experiences.

Currently, best practices are connected to the **Science of Reading**. This term was first used in educational literature in the mid-20th century, but it was not until the beginning of the 21st century that the term reemerged. It took close to two decades before the Science of Reading began to be implemented across the nation. Based on this research, the five main components that make up effective teaching of reading are: **phonemic awareness, phonics, fluency, vocabulary, and comprehension**. The term **structured literacy** also stems from the Science of Reading.

Evolution of Literacy Instruction over the Years

Beliefs about the best ways to teach reading have evolved over the years. It was once believed that children are passive receivers of knowledge, and memorization and skill-and-drill approaches to reading instruction were common. Later, theorists suggested that children are active learners who construct their own meaning through scaffolded problem-solving. Literacy instruction then transitioned to focusing on reading and writing for authentic purposes. In most recent years, it focuses on phonemic awareness, phonics, fluency, vocabulary, and comprehension. This belief still acknowledges that students learn best when they are actively involved in the learning process, but there are specific methodologies to help teachers teach reading.

Current research supports the idea that students are actively involved in the learning process. They should receive a structured literacy approach to reading. Research also indicates that although children progress through typical stages of literacy development, learning is an individualized process. Differing prior knowledge and learning styles can affect the paths children take to becoming proficient readers and writers. Assessment is viewed as an important tool for helping ensure that learning is differentiated and individual student needs are met. Additionally, research indicates that language and literacy development have social components, and students benefit from opportunities to interact and collaborate with others for a variety of purposes.

Tenets of Behaviorism

The theory of **behaviorism** was shaped by several individuals, including Ivan Pavlov and B. F. Skinner. Popular in the early to mid-1900s, it centers around the belief that learners respond to external stimuli. If behaviors are reinforced, they will continue. **Reinforcement** may be positive, which occurs when stimuli are added after desired behaviors are demonstrated. Rewards and praise for completing assignments are examples of positive reinforcement. Reinforcement may also be negative, which occurs when stimuli are removed after desired behaviors are demonstrated. When teachers stop giving stern reminders to students after they begin their independent reading, **negative reinforcement** has occurred.

According to behaviorism, **punishments** are used to decrease undesirable behaviors. Taking away manipulatives from students who are misusing them is an example of using punishment to decrease undesirable behaviors.

Learning theory has evolved over time, and research now indicates that students are more actively involved in constructing meaning than suggested by behaviorism. Yet some tenets can still be applied to reading instruction. Teachers should be careful not to criticize or punish students for errors made during reading. Effort and use of reading strategies should be supported and encouraged.

Tenets of Cognitivism

Cognitivism became popular in the 1960s after the rise of behaviorism. Rather than believing that children are passive receivers of knowledge, **cognitivism** argued that there are many internal processes that affect learning. When students are confronted with new information, they attempt to make sense of it based on prior knowledge and other factors. Information that catches students' attention may proceed from sensory memory to short-term memory, where it must be processed and encoded to be transferred to long-term memory.

Cognitivism has many implications for reading instruction. Teachers should remember that learning to read is an active process. To facilitate memory transfer, students should have prior knowledge activated before reading. Attention must also be drawn to key information. This may be done using advance organizers, bolded text, or other cueing techniques. Information should also be broken into manageable chunks, and students should have opportunities to repeatedly practice new knowledge and skills. If too much information is presented at once, cognitive overload may occur. If students do not have opportunities to practice newly learned knowledge or skills, it may be forgotten. Teachers should ensure that they allow adequate opportunities for guided practice and feedback.

Piaget's Theory of Cognitive Development

Piaget's theory suggests that all children go through the same four stages of cognitive development, yet the rate at which they proceed through the stages may vary somewhat.

- From birth until about two years of age, children are in the **sensorimotor** stage. Children in this stage explore the world around them using their senses, including grabbing and chewing objects. At first, children's behaviors are caused by reflexes. Gradually, they learn that their behaviors can influence their environments, and they begin experimenting with different behaviors. They learn object permanence, meaning they understand that things still exist even when they are not visible.
- The **preoperational** stage lasts from age two until about age seven. In this stage, children begin thinking symbolically. They engage in symbolic play and begin using words to represent what they want. Children in this stage are egocentric and have trouble seeing other people's perspectives.
- The **concrete operational** stage lasts from age seven until about age twelve. In this stage, children begin to think logically but may still struggle with abstract ideas. They begin becoming less egocentric.
- In the **formal operational** stage, which begins around age 12 and continues into adulthood, people are capable of abstract and logical thoughts.

Review Video: Piaget's Cognitive Development Theory
Visit mometrix.com/academy and enter code: 100376

Applying Piaget's Theory of Cognitive Development to Reading Instruction

- Young children in the **sensorimotor stage** of cognitive development benefit from exploring types of books designed for this age group. This includes board books and cloth books containing different textures and materials to manipulate. By exploring these books using their senses, children will enjoy their first reading experiences.
- Children in the **preoperational stage** begin to think **symbolically**. The alphabetic principle can be explored in this stage. Children can also explore the purposes of punctuation marks and illustrations included in texts. They can explore using different types of texts to accomplish different purposes, such as writing letters to communicate with friends.
- Children in the **concrete operational stage** begin to think **logically**. Students in this stage can explore literary elements and text structures. They can also analyze texts deeply and comprehend relationships like cause and effect.
- By the **formal operational stage**, students should be reading and analyzing a variety of complex texts for personal and academic reasons.

Schema Theory

Schema theory suggests that when people learn new concepts, the new knowledge gets organized into units called **schemata**. These schemata include all of the information that is known about the concepts. For example, a young child's schema about cars might include knowing that they are used for transportation, they have four wheels and one steering wheel, and they are painted a variety of colors. These schemata are connected to one another when knowledge overlaps. For example, the child's schema about cars may be connected to his or her schema about motorcycles, which the child knows also have wheels and are used for transportation. When encountering new information, people look to existing schemata to make sense of the new knowledge.

Schema theory has several implications for reading instruction. It demonstrates the importance of activating prior knowledge before reading. Students can be asked what they already know about the topics of new texts. They can also complete **know**, **want**, and **learn** (KWL) charts to identify what they already know and want to learn about the topics. Additionally, students can be encouraged to make text connections. This may include text-to-self, text-to-text, and text-to-world connections.

Assimilation and Accommodation in Piaget's Theory of Cognitive Development

According to Piaget, people have existing schemata, or units of knowledge, about concepts they have learned. They look to these existing schemata to make sense of new information they encounter.

Sometimes the newly encountered information fits within an existing schema and is added to it. For example, if a student has an existing schema about baseball and learns a new rule he or she did not previously know, he or she may add this new information to the schema. This is known as **assimilation**. However, sometimes the newly encountered information challenges the existing schema. If this occurs, the existing schema must be altered. For example, a student may have an existing schema about a historical figure based on readings he or she has done from one person's perspective. Based on these prior readings, he or she may view the figure as a hero. However, the student may then read a book about the figure written from a different perspective, which highlights the negative impacts of the figure's actions on others. This new knowledge may challenge the student's existing schema and cause him or her to alter it. This is known as **accommodation**.

Teachers should model and encourage evaluating texts and consider how they affirm or challenge existing beliefs.

Tenets of Lev Vygotsky's Social Development Theory

Lev Vygotsky played a leading role in the development of the **constructivist learning theory**. According to Vygotsky, children interact in social and cultural contexts. Through their social interactions with others in these contexts, cognitive development takes place. Therefore, social interaction plays a large role in learning. Teachers can consider how to incorporate social learning experiences into reading instruction. This may include shared and interactive reading and writing experiences, collaborative projects, reader's theater, and literature circles.

Vygotsky also suggested that learning takes place when students are engaged in activities in their zones of proximal development. These are activities that students are almost able to complete independently, but they require some scaffolding or collaboration. Vygotsky explained that scaffolding should be provided by others who have higher abilities in the tasks being completed. These individuals might be teachers, parents, or other classmates. Teachers can differentiate learning activities to ensure they are within students' zones of proximal development rather than being too easy or too difficult. For example, they can select books in students' instructional reading levels for guided reading groups. Teachers can use assessments to determine how to differentiate instruction for each student.

> **Review Video: Zone of Proximal Development (ZPD)**
> Visit mometrix.com/academy and enter code: 555594

Tenets of Constructivism

The constructivist theory was influenced by several people, including John Dewey, Jean Piaget, and Lev Vygotsky. **Constructivism** suggests that learning is an active process. Rather than passively receiving knowledge from their teachers, students actively construct their own meaning through learning experiences. Meaning may differ among individual students because they each have unique prior knowledge and experiences. According to constructivism, students learn by solving real-world problems; gathering, synthesizing, and evaluating information; and testing ideas.

Constructivism plays an important role in reading instruction. When analyzing texts, teachers can encourage students to draw upon prior knowledge, consider if any existing assumptions have been challenged, and share their unique understandings with others. Teachers can also encourage students to use reading to solve realistic problems through problem-based learning activities. They can also give students some choices regarding the activities and methods used. Rather than directing all phases of assignments, teachers can instead use more collaborative approaches and provide scaffolding to students as needed.

Marie Clay's Literacy Processing Theory

While Marie Clay's **literacy processing theory** is not supported anymore due to updated research, it is important to understand what her theory suggests since it is still used throughout some schools. It suggests that all children approach learning to read with different background knowledge and experiences, which results in students taking different paths to becoming proficient readers and writers. It also suggests that reading and writing are complex and interrelated experiences, and children must read and write authentic texts to learn. Additionally, it suggests that learning to read and write are active processes, and children help create their own meanings.

Early childhood teachers should consider that all students have unique prior knowledge and experiences. Teachers can assess students' skills and build upon their existing strengths. Additionally, if students are struggling with specific literacy skills, interventions can be implemented to address students' needs. However, some tools that Marie Clay promoted are not considered to be best practice anymore. For example, she promoted the use of running records as one tool that can be used to identify strategy deficits and plan interventions, but this tool focuses on cueing systems rather than decoding words through phonics rules. Thus, teachers are now encouraged to not use running records.

John Dewey's Contributions to Theories of Reading Instruction

John Dewey greatly influenced the **constructivist theory** of education. Dewey believed that people are active learners who learn by **doing** rather than passively receiving knowledge. He believed that valuable instructional time is wasted in schools by attempts to passively transmit knowledge. Additionally, he believed that for the teaching of symbolic concepts to be effective, students need opportunities to explore the symbols in context.

Dewey's beliefs have shaped the way reading instruction occurs today. Students are expected to be active learners who complete word work activities, problem-solve to decode and encode texts, and critically analyze a variety of text types. Children are commonly engaged in guided reading groups in which they must apply strategies to decode and comprehend real stories. They are also asked to construct their own meaning from texts by activating prior knowledge and making personal connections. When teaching symbolic relationships like the alphabetic principle, students are given opportunities to explore these relationships using real words and texts.

David Perkins' Theory of Learnable Intelligence

David Perkins theorized that humans have three types of intelligence. **Neural intelligence** is determined by genetics and cannot be changed. It is sometimes measured using IQ tests. **Experiential intelligence** is developed by the types of experiences one has. For example, a child who grows up in a big city may have knowledge of how to read subway maps and bus schedules. Having diverse experiences increases experiential intelligence. **Reflective intelligence** refers to a person's ability to problem-solve and reason. It also involves self-awareness and the use of metacognitive strategies. Unlike neural intelligence, experiential and reflective intelligence can be grown and developed over time.

Teachers can consider this theory when planning reading instruction. They can create literacy-rich environments using varied activities and types of texts. These varied experiences can help students develop experiential knowledge. Print, digital texts, and media can be used to help students experience things that are distant from their own communities. Teachers can also model and encourage the use of metacognitive and problem-solving strategies.

Howard Gardner's Theory of Multiple Intelligences

Howard Gardner theorized that there are multiple types of intelligences. According to his theory, people have different strengths and prefer to represent knowledge in different ways. He outlined eight different types of intelligences.

- **Visual-spatial** intelligence includes the ability to visualize things easily, such as charts and maps.
- **Linguistic-verbal** intelligence refers to strength in using language for reading, writing, listening, and speaking.
- **Logical-mathematical** intelligence refers to the ability to reason, solve problems, and recognize patterns, often with numbers.
- **Bodily-kinesthetic** intelligence refers to skilled coordination and movement.
- **Musical** intelligence refers to the ability to recognize rhythm, sound, beat, and other musical elements.
- **Interpersonal** intelligence refers to the ability to interact effectively with others.
- **Intrapersonal** intelligence refers to strong self-awareness.
- **Naturalistic** intelligence refers to a strong understanding of nature. Gardner explained that each person may demonstrate characteristics of multiple types of intelligence.

Teachers can consider Gardner's theory when planning instruction. They can use a multisensory approach to literacy instruction and also incorporate music, art, movement, problem-solving, collaboration, and other experiences. They can allow students choices in the topics they read and write about and allow them to present their learning in different ways.

Louise Rosenblatt's Transactional Theory of the Literary Work

Rosenblatt's **Transactional Theory of the Literary Work** suggests that reading involves a **transaction** between the reader and the text. Each reader brings unique prior knowledge and experiences to the reading experience. These differences affect how the text is interpreted and the meaning that is made. Different readers may make different meaning from the same texts. Therefore, there is no one fixed meaning in any text. Instead, the meaning is determined by the reader's transaction with the text.

This theory suggests that readers must be active participants in the reading process to make meaning. For example, they should be encouraged to activate prior knowledge, self-monitor understanding, and make connections before, during, and after reading. They should be encouraged to analyze texts deeply, and the close reading process may assist with this goal. Because different students may interpret texts differently, literature circles and other opportunities to discuss meaning can be beneficial. Students can be encouraged to share what prior experiences and text clues helped guide their interpretations.

Kenneth Goodman's Socio-Psycholinguistic Theory of Reading Instruction

Kenneth Goodman explained that reading involves the interaction between thinking and language. Beginning readers do not approach new texts already knowing how to read all of the words. Instead, they combine their thinking with available language clues to guess what the words say. The **socio-psycholinguistic theory** supports the use of running records to record reading behaviors and miscues. The results of the running records can be used to provide targeted instruction in using specific cueing systems. Teachers can identify if students are using or ignoring the graphophonic, syntactic, and semantic cueing systems. Goodman also explained that teachers should observe students' reading behaviors to gain further insight into the reasons for their miscues.

In more recent studies, research has proven that the use of the cueing systems and running records are not considered to be best practice for reading instruction. Running records and cueing systems are not reliable indicators of fundamental literacy skills. Research promotes the teaching of systematic and explicit phonics instruction paired with decodable texts. This allows the teacher to encourage the students to decode words rather than guess.

Myers-Briggs Type Indicator Personality Types

There are many different theories of personality that attempt to explain differences in the ways people perceive the world and interact with those around them. One common tool to assess personality type is the Myers-Briggs Type Indicator. Based on Carl Jung's personality theory, the **Myers-Briggs Type Indicator** outlines four different scales that affect personality.

The first scale ranges from introversion to extroversion. **Introverts** gain energy from time alone and quiet reflection, whereas **extroverts** gain energy from interacting with others. The second scale ranges from sensing to intuition. People on the **sensing** side of the scale learn from interacting with their senses, whereas people on the **intuition** side rely on instincts. The third scale ranges from thinking to feeling. People on the **thinking** side apply logic and questioning to make decisions, whereas people on the **feeling** side rely more on their emotions and values. The fourth scale ranges from judging to perceiving. People on the **judging** side of the scale prefer routine and order, whereas those on the **perceiving** side prefer a more laid-back approach.

Effect of Personality Types on Literacy Instruction

Teachers should consider the role that **personality types** play in how students learn and interact with others. Information observed about students' personality types can help teachers plan differentiated instruction that meets the needs of all students.

Classes typically include students on a range of the introversion-extroversion scale. Students who are more introverted may not enjoy reading instruction if they are continually asked to read aloud or perform in groups. However, students who are more extroverted may not enjoy reading instruction if only given opportunities to read independently and complete individual assignments.

Additionally, some students think logically and may instinctively turn to text evidence for support of answers. They may have more difficulties responding personally to texts. On the other hand, students who rely more on feeling may respond to texts emotionally yet need encouragement to support answers with evidence.

Personality type can also affect how students perceive classroom routines and procedures. Some students may prefer detailed routines for reading groups and centers, whereas others may prefer more laid-back approaches. Being aware of students' personalities can help teachers plan a mixture of activity types and give students the support they need to succeed in situations outside of their comfort zones.

Learning Behaviors

There are several **learning behaviors** applicable to all subject areas that support literacy learning. Some of these behaviors include following oral and written directions, interacting appropriately with other learners, displaying curiosity and asking questions, attempting to solve complex problems, reasoning, and focusing on learning tasks. These learning behaviors support literacy development by encouraging students to seek information to answer questions and solve realistic problems. They also support the collaboration needed to participate in shared problem-based learning activities and analysis of texts in literature circles. Focus on learning tasks also helps students develop reading stamina and the ability to complete literacy-related projects. Additionally, students who attempt to reason independently may find it easier to comprehend complex texts without assistance.

Age-appropriate reading, writing, listening, and speaking behaviors also help students convey and understand meaning. These behaviors include listening purposefully, organizing thoughts before writing and speaking, and monitoring understanding.

Bloom's Taxonomy

Benjamin Bloom outlined a hierarchy of skills in each of three learning domains, including the cognitive, affective, and psychomotor domains. The domain most often applied to classroom instruction is the cognitive domain. In the **cognitive domain**, skills are ranked in the following order: knowledge, comprehension, application, analysis, synthesis, and evaluation. Knowledge is the lowest-level skill, whereas evaluation is the highest.

Reading specialists and classroom teachers should consider **Bloom's Taxonomy** while designing instruction and assessments. Learning objectives should include specific verbs in the taxonomy that accurately describe what students are expected to be able to do at the end of instruction. Objectives should include skills in all levels of Bloom's Taxonomy, not just the lower levels. When reading nonfiction texts, for example, students may answer some basic recall questions. However, they may also be asked to evaluate authors' claims and support their evaluations with evidence. Higher-level thinking skills are important for close reading activities, and they help students more deeply comprehend their reading.

Review Video: Bloom's Taxonomy
Visit mometrix.com/academy and enter code: 755020

Review Video: Learning Objectives
Visit mometrix.com/academy and enter code: 528458

Components of Balanced Literacy Programs

Balanced literacy programs teach students a variety of reading skills and strategies that can be used to decode and comprehend texts. They include a mixture of systematic and explicit skills instruction and opportunities to read and write texts for authentic purposes. However, balanced literacy programs are not supported by the science of reading since these programs encourage teachers to instruct students to use cueing systems to figure out unknown words while reading.

Balanced literacy programs include instruction in phonological awareness. This is important because phonological awareness abilities are key indicators of future reading success. Systematic and explicit phonics instruction is also an important part of balanced literacy programs. Phonics skills are used to help students both decode and encode texts. Reading fluency is also modeled and practiced in balanced literacy programs. Additionally, vocabulary is another component. Students receive explicit instruction in using context and morphological clues to figure out the meanings of unknown words. They also build connections among meanings of related words. Comprehension strategies are also taught and practiced as part of balanced literacy programs.

Phonics-Based, Whole Language, and Structured Literacy Approaches

Phonics-based reading programs use a bottom-up approach to instruction. Proponents of this approach believe that children learn best when instruction progresses from part to whole. They first teach children to identify letters and letter sounds. Next, they progress to teaching students to decode single words. Later, they decode sentences and longer texts.

Whole language reading programs use a top-down approach. Proponents of this approach believe children learn best from being immersed in authentic texts. They believe that by exploring these texts, children gradually learn the rules and patterns of language.

Structured literacy approaches are explicit, systematic, cumulative, diagnostic, and responsive. Evidence suggests that this approach is most effective for all kinds of readers. The basic elements of structured literacy instruction are: phonology, sound-symbol association, syllable instruction, morphology, syntax, and semantics. This approach can work with models like **Scarborough's Reading Rope**. This model was designed by Dr. Hollis Scarborough, and it demonstrates how different reading skills are woven together to develop proficient readers. Readers gain skills over years of instructional practice from the two main strands in Scarborough's Reading Rope, language comprehension and word recognition.

Implementing a Reading Program

Implementing Reading Programs

Implementing reading programs with **fidelity** means using them as the program developers intended. This includes following the intended pacing guides, incorporating all recommended instructional components, using the materials as intended, and more. Fidelity is necessary if reading programs are to be effectively evaluated after implementation. If not implemented with fidelity, unfavorable results may be due to causes unrelated to the quality of the programs. For example, students' comprehension scores may decline if teachers repeatedly skip the recommended comprehension components due to time constraints. Additionally, implementing the programs with fidelity helps ensure that students receive the research-based instruction promised by the programs. Presenting lessons out of sequence, omitting portions of instruction, and other changes may negatively affect the quality of instruction.

However, teachers sometimes have concerns with using reading programs exactly as intended. They may believe that some lessons are ineffective for their students, based on what they know about their students' prior knowledge and existing skills. Logistical issues, such as available time and resources, may also interfere with implementing programs with fidelity. When making instructional decisions, teachers and administrators must carefully weigh the program recommendations with their own beliefs about their students and best teaching practices.

Considerations When Selecting Reading Programs

There are numerous reading programs available, so educators should take several factors into consideration when determining which programs are best for their districts and schools. The selected programs should be based on reliable and valid research about how students learn best. Information should be provided about the research and educational philosophies the programs are based upon. Additionally, the selected programs should address all components of structured literacy instruction, including phonemic awareness, phonics, fluency, vocabulary, and comprehension. Teacher guides should be available, with plans for systematic instruction using developmentally appropriate pacing guides. Frequent opportunities for explicit instruction, guided practice, and extension activities should be included in the instructional plans.

Reading programs should also contain plans and materials to help teachers differentiate instruction. The programs should offer support for struggling, on-level, and advanced readers as well as ELLs. Leveled texts and tips for differentiating lesson plans may be included.

Selected reading programs should offer adequate professional development opportunities to help teachers use the programs successfully.

Evaluating Effectiveness of Reading Programs After Implementation

Before selecting and implementing new reading programs, districts should consider the instructional and performance gaps they hope to address. By analyzing current performance data and identifying areas in need of improvement, districts can establish specific and measurable goals for their reading instruction. These goals can be used to select appropriate programs and to evaluate their effectiveness over time. By comparing data related to the goals from both before and after the new programs are implemented, districts can determine if the gaps are shrinking.

For example, a district may determine that many of its elementary students are not meeting grade-level expectations for reading fluency on standardized state tests. They may determine that one goal for their new reading program is to increase the percentage of elementary students who meet grade-level expectations for fluency by a certain amount over the next two years. They may then select a reading program that features daily fluency instruction and leveled texts for fluency practice. The district can then analyze the data from the same tests over the next few years to determine if the percentage of students who met grade-level expectations for fluency increased by the expected amount.

Increasing Positive Results When Implementing New Reading Programs

Strategic planning and ongoing support are both necessary for new program implementation to be successful. Rushing the process initially or tapering off support too soon can lead to frustration and poor results.

It is important to have trusted reading specialists, administrators, or other educators who are well trained in the programs before they are introduced to teachers. These specialists should be available to address concerns and anxiety about the changes. These specialists should also share the research supporting the new programs and the district objectives they are designed to support.

Districts should provide opportunities within teachers' workdays to learn how to use the new programs rather than requiring them to explore the programs on their own time. The trainings should be carefully planned to maximize the use of teachers' limited time. Teachers should have opportunities to observe other teachers who are already using the programs effectively.

It is also important to provide frequent support throughout the duration of each program rather than tapering off support after the initial training period. Educators should have ongoing opportunities to share successful strategies and discuss concerns with others. Support specialists should also be easily accessible when needed.

Incorporating Literacy Centers in Literacy Programs

Literacy centers are important components of literacy programs. They allow students to practice literacy skills on a regular basis while also allowing teachers time to work with small groups for reading instruction. Teachers typically create routines that allow students to rotate through some or all of the centers each day. Sometimes they are given choices over which centers to visit. Other times, teachers may direct students to proceed through the centers in predetermined orders for management purposes.

There are several common centers in literacy-rich classrooms. **Independent reading centers** include several texts of various genres for students to read by themselves, usually in relaxing and comfortable environments. **Listening centers** contain digital texts and headphones. **Technology centers** contain computers and/or tablets for literacy games, digital presentations, research, and more. **Word work centers** contain activities and manipulatives that allow students to explore how words and sentences are put together. **Writing centers** contain paper, dictionaries, and other materials students can use for writing. **Partner reading centers** provide places for students to read with one another. Early childhood classrooms may also contain **sensory and dramatic play centers**. Additionally, classrooms contain designated areas where teachers can meet with small reading groups.

Classroom Management Strategies for Effective Literacy Centers

It is important to establish clear routines and expectations for literacy centers at the beginning of each school year. If several literacy centers will be included, they should be gradually introduced a few at a time, especially for younger students. When introducing each center, teachers should discuss and model expected center behavior. This includes explaining whether or not group work is allowed, how the materials should be properly used, and how to correctly complete the center activities. Each center's materials should be clearly labeled and be housed in designated locations.

Clear procedures should be in place for how students should rotate through the centers, minimizing confusion and overcrowding at each location. Countdown timers can be clearly displayed on projectors while students are working, providing warnings when it is time to clean up and rotate. Both auditory and visual clues can be provided to assist with transitions.

Teachers can also occasionally rotate center activities to allow students to practice newly learned skills and prevent boredom. However, teachers should model how to complete the new activities before asking students to do them independently during center time. This is especially important for young students who may not be able to read directions independently.

Record Keeping Strategies Useful in Literacy Instruction

Record keeping can assist teachers with assessing students' progress over time and differentiating instruction. Some teachers prefer to keep separate folders for each student. These folders may contain assessment data and work samples from throughout the year. Other teachers prefer to keep separate folders for each topic. For example, a teacher may have one guided reading folder that contains a list of students' current instructional reading levels and the skills that have been highlighted in each guided reading mini-lesson.

There are many types of records that may be useful. Copies of running records can be used to indicate students' growth in the use of reading strategies over time. Anecdotal records can provide information about observed reading behaviors and areas that need further instruction. Lists of students' reading levels and flexible grouping charts can assist teachers with planning guided reading groups. Writing portfolios can be used to demonstrate progress in writing, and they may be organized by genre, chronology, or other means. Dating each writing piece can assist teachers and students with observing growth.

Teachers may also keep records of literacy center schedules to ensure that students have opportunities to rotate through each center regularly.

Qualitative vs. Quantitative Research

Qualitative research is usually used to gather subjective information about people's opinions or understandings about things. **Qualitative research** can often be used to answer the questions what and why. Information may be gathered through focus groups, interviews, and observations. Researchers gather information in a neutral manner to ensure they do not influence the opinions of the subjects. Qualitative research could be used to determine reasons why teachers have abandoned a particular reading program, for example. This information could be used to revise the program to better meet teachers' needs and address concerns.

Quantitative research is used to gather numerical data that can be used to identify patterns and relationships. It can also be used to form generalizations and draw conclusions. For example, quantitative research could be used to identify if specific literacy interventions are leading to increased standardized test scores.

Characteristics of Valid Reading Research

With the ease with which people are able to post things on the Internet, abundant and often contradictory information about best practices in education can be found. Much of this information is not reliably tested. However, there are some characteristics that identify **valid reading research**, which teachers should use when making instructional decisions.

Reading research should be **reliable**. This means that other researchers should be able to replicate the research studies and get the same results. Research that relies on qualitative responses are more subjective and may be less likely to be replicated with the same results. This reliability should be taken into consideration when evaluating research. Reading research should also be **valid**, meaning the instruments should be designed to measure what they are supposed to measure. The research should also be **credible**. This means the research uses appropriate methodology, data collection, and analysis.

Sources of Valid Reading Research

There are many sources of valid reading research available. This research is sometimes available for free. Other times, paid subscriptions or enrollment in academic institutions is required to access the information.

The US Department of Education provides information about reading research and statistics on its website. This includes information related to current reading programs, literacy progress, and more.

There are also many education-related journals that contain information about reading research. Peer-reviewed journals help ensure that the research is reliable and valid. Examples include *Language Arts*, published by the National Council of Teachers of English, and the *Harvard Educational Review*, published by the Harvard Graduate School of Education. Many of these journals are available online and are sometimes also available in print form.

There are also multiple databases containing reading research. One example is the Education Resources Information Center (ERIC). These databases are available online and are also commonly available in the libraries of educational institutions.

Role of the Reading Specialist

The Goals of Schools' Reading Programs to Parents and Family Members

Although it is common for classroom teachers to communicate with family members about reading development, reading specialists also play important roles in promoting literacy at home. Reading specialists may conduct family surveys to learn more about home literacy behaviors and to assess parents' literacy-related needs and concerns. They may help organize school- or district-wide family literacy events. These events offer hands-on literacy activities appropriate for different grade levels that family members can complete with their children and take home for additional practice. They also feature interactive read-alouds that model ways parents can encourage reading behaviors with their children at home.

Additionally, reading specialists might be involved in organizing book fairs or lending libraries that supplement their schools' traditional libraries. They may provide families with information about reading goals and interventions or summer reading programs.

Promoting Collaboration Among Teachers and Other Colleagues

One role of a reading specialist is to promote collaboration among colleagues. A collaborative approach allows colleagues to develop and work toward shared goals. It can increase motivation to implement reading programs with fidelity and help colleagues share strategies to address common problems and concerns.

In addition to attending staff meetings, reading specialists can attend grade-level team meetings. Reading specialists can help grade-level teams analyze assessment data to identify areas in need of improvement. Together, the teams can create performance goals that will be used to drive reading instruction. They can collaboratively develop instructional plans and activities to help reach the shared goals. This type of collaborative approach can encourage motivation and accountability.

Reading specialists may also look for each colleague's strengths and note strong examples of research-based reading instruction. They can encourage these colleagues to share their strategies and allow others to observe their teaching. Teachers may also be encouraged to share problems they are having with reading instruction, and colleagues can work together to develop solutions to these problems.

Role in Improving Schools' Reading Curricula

Reading specialists typically have access to assessment data from multiple grade levels and time periods. They can lead data analysis teams that look for trends that may indicate gaps in their schools' reading curricula. Once these gaps are identified, reading specialists can work with teachers to revise curricula and instructional methods to better address these needs and improve student performance. Reading specialists often also serve on committees to evaluate and select potential reading programs to supplement or replace existing ones. Reading specialists can share their knowledge of research-based approaches to literacy instruction and use this knowledge to evaluate the potential reading programs.

Reading specialists also identify external professional development opportunities that may be beneficial for teachers based on their schools' instructional gaps. They advocate for opportunities for teachers to attend these sessions and share what they have learned with colleagues.

Additionally, reading specialists can recruit teachers who are willing to apply and model specific research-based instructional strategies while receiving coaching and support. For example, reading specialists can recruit teachers willing to try interactive word walls or literature circles.

Building Consensus Among Colleagues When Making Instructional Decisions

Reading specialists often deal with conflict in their roles. **Conflict** may occur when introducing new reading programs or helping teachers decide upon new instructional strategies and goals. One role of a reading specialist is to help establish a **consensus among the different stakeholders** involved, including teachers, administrators, board members, and other school staff.

To do so, reading specialists need to be seen as leaders who are respected in their area of expertise but also **flexible** and willing to listen to new ideas. By listening to suggestions and concerns while also explaining literacy-related research and best practices, reading specialists can help their teams develop shared visions for school reading instruction. They can help other stakeholders understand their roles in achieving these visions by outlining specific but attainable goals and defining the responsibilities of everyone involved. Other stakeholders will be more likely to cooperate with the plans if they understand the role they will play in accomplishing the shared goals.

Resolving Conflict Among Colleagues Regarding Reading Instruction

Instructional decisions have lasting effects on teachers and students. This is especially true when major decisions are made, such as selecting new reading programs. Conflict about instructional strategies and ways to implement change can lead to interpersonal conflict. Therefore, reading specialists who are facilitating these changes must often assist with conflict resolution.

- Reading specialists can first acknowledge the issues rather than ignore them, recognizing that conflict can be healthy when it leads to open discussions and sharing of ideas. They can then look for the root causes of the conflict. Although the conflicts may be based on personality differences, they may also be based on other issues, such as concerns about adequate time or resources and differing prior experiences. Helping highlight the true issues may lead to discussions about how the concerns can be alleviated.
- Reading specialists can also bring the discussions back to shared performance goals. Colleagues can be asked to restate the shared goals and the reasons behind them, reminding everyone involved that student success is the focus. Colleagues can then collaborate to find solutions that incorporate the ideas while still addressing the concerns of all parties involved.

Advocating for Public Support of Reading Education

It is important for reading specialists to be aware of policies that affect literacy education at the local, state, and national levels. This includes awareness of school board, state government, and US Department of Education policies. Attending local school board meetings and joining professional organizations that track impending legislation are two ways to assist with this goal. Reading specialists can share their knowledge with colleagues and community members and advocate for legislation and policies that support effective reading instruction. Additionally, they can interpret existing legislation for their colleagues and ensure that they understand the implications it has on their classroom instruction.

Reading specialists can assist their school districts with writing grants and educational proposals that can positively impact literacy instruction. This may include proposals for funding that can be used to purchase new materials or hire additional reading specialists.

Chapter Quiz

Ready to see how well you retained what you just read? Scan the QR code to go directly to the chapter quiz interface for this study guide. If you're using a computer, simply visit the online resources page at **mometrix.com/resources719/mtelreadsp62** and click the Chapter Quizzes link.

MTEL Practice Test

Want to take this practice test in an online interactive format?
Check out the online resources page, which includes interactive practice questions and much more: **mometrix.com/resources719/mtelreadsp62**

Multiple Choice Questions

1. The pairs of words *sea* and *see*, *fair* and *fare*, are called:

a. Homophones
b. Antonyms
c. Homographs
d. Twin words

2. Another name for a persuasive essay is:

a. Dynamic essay
b. Convincing essay
c. Argumentative essay
d. Position paper

3. A teacher is working with a group of third graders at the same reading level. Her goal is to improve reading fluency. She asks each child in turn to read a page from a book about mammal young. She asks the children to read with expression. She also reminds them they don't need to stop between each word; they should read as quickly as they comfortably can. She cautions them, however, not to read so quickly that they leave out or misread a word. The teacher knows the components of reading fluency are:

a. Speed, drama, and comprehension
b. Cohesion, rate, and prosody
c. Understanding, rate, and prosody
d. Rate, accuracy, and prosody

4. "Language load" refers to:

a. The basic vocabulary words a first grader has committed to memory.
b. The number of unrecognizable words an English language learner encounters when reading a passage or listening to a teacher.
c. The damage that carrying a pile of heavy books could cause to a child's physique.
d. The number of different languages a person has mastered

5. A syllable must contain:

a. A vowel
b. A consonant
c. Both a vowel and a consonant
d. A meaning

6. A third-grade teacher has several students reading above grade level. Most of the remaining students are reading at grade level. There are also a few students reading below grade level. She decides to experiment. Her hypothesis is that by giving the entire class a chapter book above grade level, high-level readers will be satisfied, grade-level readers will be challenged in a positive way, and students reading below grade level will be inspired to improve. Her method is most likely to:

a. Succeed, producing students reading at an Instructional reading level. High-level readers will be happy to be given material appropriate to their reading level. Grade-level readers will challenge themselves to improve reading strategies in order to master the text. Because only a few of the students are reading below grade level, the other students, who feel happy and energized, will inspire the slower readers by modeling success.
b. Succeed, producing students reading at an Independent reading level. High-level readers will independently help grade-level readers who will, in turn, independently help those below grade level.
c. Fail, producing students at a Frustration reading level. Those reading below grade level are likely to give up entirely. Those reading at grade level are likely to get frustrated and form habits that will actually slow down their development.
d. Fail, producing students reading at a Chaotic reading level. By nature, children are highly competitive. The teacher has not taken into consideration multiple learning styles. The children who are at grade level will either become bitter and angry at those whose reading level is above grade level or simply give up. The children reading below grade level will not be able to keep up and will in all likelihood act out their frustration or completely shut down.

7. Of the three tiers of words, the most important words for direct instruction are:

a. Tier-one words
b. Common words
c. Tier-two words
d. Words with Latin roots

8. At the beginning of each month, Mr. Yi has Jade read a page or two from a book she hasn't seen before. He notes the total number of words in the section and the number of times she leaves out or misreads a word. If Jade reads the passage with less than 3% error, Mr. Yi is satisfied that Jade is:

a. Reading with full comprehension
b. Probably bored and should try a more difficult book
c. Reading at her independent reading level
d. Comfortable with the syntactical meaning

9. The purpose of corrective feedback is:

a. To provide students with methods for explaining to the teacher or classmates what a passage was about
b. To correct an error in reading a student has made, specifically clarifying where and how the error was made so that the student can avoid similar errors in the future
c. To provide a mental framework that will help the student correctly organize new information
d. To remind students that error is essential in order to truly understand and that it is not something to be ashamed of

Refer to the following for question 10:

A third-grade science teacher gives her students one hour to read an article about penguins, take notes on important information, and use the notes to write a three-paragraph expository essay. Before they begin, the teacher writes the words *Spheniscidae*, *plumage*, and *Aptenodytes forsteri* on the board. She explains the meaning of each word. At the end of the hour, one student, Joshua, only has his notes completed. The teacher examines his notes, part of which are shown below.

> Penguins are animals that live in the Southern Hemisphere.
> Many people believe that penguins live in the Arctic, but that is not true.
> Penguins in Antarctica huddle together to stay warm. They take turns standing on the outside of the huddle, where it is colder.
> Penguins' feathers help protect them from the water and cold air.
> Penguins live in groups called colonies.

10. The words written by the teacher on the board are examples of:

a. Academic words
b. Alliteration
c. Content-specific words
d. Ionization

11. Which of the following best explains the importance prior knowledge brings to the act of reading?

a. Prior knowledge is information the student gets through researching a topic prior to reading the text. A student who is well-prepared through such research is better able to decode a text and retain its meaning.
b. Prior knowledge is knowledge the student brings from previous life or learning experiences to the act of reading. It is not possible for a student to fully comprehend new knowledge without first integrating it with prior knowledge.
c. Prior knowledge is predictive. It motivates the student to look for contextual clues in the reading and predict what is likely to happen next.
d. Prior knowledge is not important to any degree to the act of reading, because every text is self-contained and therefore seamless. Prior knowledge is irrelevant in this application.

12. A cloze test evaluates a student's:

a. Reading fluency
b. Understanding of context and vocabulary
c. Phonemic skills
d. Ability to apply the alphabetic principle to previously unknown material

13. Sight words are:

a. Common words with irregular spelling
b. Words that can easily be found on educational websites
c. Any word that can be seen, including text words, words on signs, brochures, banners, and so forth
d. There is no such thing; because oral language is learned before written language, all words are ultimately based on sound. The correct term is sound words and includes all words necessary to decode a particular text.

14. *Phone, they, church.* The underlined letters in these words are examples of:

a. Consonant blend
b. Consonant shift
c. Continental shift
d. Consonant digraph

15. Phonemic awareness is a type of:

a. Phonological awareness. Phonemic awareness is the ability to recognize sounds within words.
b. Phonics. It is a teaching technique whereby readers learn the relationship between letters and sounds.
c. Alphabetization. Unless a reader knows the alphabet, phonemic awareness is useless.
d. Syntactical awareness. Understanding the underlying structure of a sentence is key to understanding meaning.

16. Early in the school year, all members of a group of kindergarten students are able to chant the alphabet. The teacher is now teaching the students what the alphabet looks like in written form. The teacher points to a letter, and the students vocalize the corresponding sound. Alternatively, the teacher vocalizes a phoneme and a student points to it on the alphabet chart. The teacher is using _____________ in her instruction.

a. letter–sound correspondence
b. rote memorization
c. predictive analysis
d. segmentation

17. A fourth-grade teacher is preparing her students for a reading test in which a number of words have been replaced with blanks. The test will be multiple-choice; there are three possible answers given for each blank. The teacher instructs the children to read all the possible answers and cross out any answer that obviously doesn't fit. Next, the students should "plug in" the remaining choices and eliminate any that are grammatically incorrect or illogical. Finally, the student should consider contextual clues in order to select the best answer. This in an example of:

a. Strategy instruction
b. Diagnostic instruction
c. Skills instruction
d. Multiple-choice instruction

18. The term "common words" means:

a. One-syllable words with fewer than three letters. Some examples are *it, an, a, I, go, to,* and *in*. They are the first words an emergent writer learns.
b. One-syllable words with fewer than five letters. Some examples include *sing, goes, sit, rock, walk,* and *took*.
c. Words that are ordinary or unexceptional; because they tend to flatten a piece of writing, they should be avoided.
d. Familiar, frequently used words that do not need to be taught beyond primary grades.

19. Which is greater, the number of English phonemes or the number of letters in the alphabet?

a. The number of letters in the alphabet, because they can be combined to create phonemes.
b. The number of phonemes. A phoneme is the smallest measure of language sound.
c. They are identical; each letter "owns" a correspondent sound.
d. Neither. Phonemes and alphabet letters are completely unrelated.

20. *Train, brain, spring.* The underlined letters are examples of:

a. Consonant digraph
b. Consonant blend
c. Consonant shift
d. Continental shift

21. It is the beginning of the school year. To determine which second-grade students might need support, the reading teacher wants to identify those who are reading below grade level. She works with students one at a time. She gives each child a book at a second-grade reading level and asks the child to read out loud for two minutes. Which students will need reading support?

a. Only students who read fewer than 100 words in the time given
b. All students who read fewer than 200 words in the time given
c. All students who read more than 100 words in the time given
d. Only students who read more than 200 words in the time given

22. The most effective strategy for decoding irregular sight words is:

a. Segmenting sight words into syllables. Beginning readers are understandably nervous when encountering a long word that isn't familiar. Blocking off all but a single syllable at a time renders a word manageable and allows the reader a sense of control over the act of reading.
b. Word families. By grouping the sight word with similar words, patterns emerge.
c. A phonemic approach. When students understand the connection between individual words and their sounds, they will be able to sound out any sight word they encounter.
d. None; irregular sight words cannot be decoded. Readers must learn to recognize these as whole words on sight.

23. Which of the following choices will be most important when designing a reading activity or lesson for students?

a. Selecting a text
b. Determining the number of students participating
c. Analyzing the point in the school year at which the lesson is given
d. Determining a purpose for instruction

24. "Decoding" is also called:

a. Remediation
b. Deciphering
c. Alphabetic principle
d. Deconstruction

25. Which text(s) are likely to foster the greatest enthusiasm for reading and literature among students?

a. Free choice of reading texts, provided that students complete class assignments, projects, and discussions
b. An all-in-one textbook that includes all reading material for the year, study guides, and sample test questions
c. A variety of texts, including books, magazines, newspapers, stories from oral traditions, poetry, music, and films
d. A small selection of current best-selling books for children, some of which the children may already have read and liked

26. Phonological awareness activities are:

a. Oral
b. Visual
c. Tactile
d. Semantically based

27. A student is able to:

- apply strategies to comprehend the meanings of unfamiliar words
- supply definitions for words with several meanings such as *crucial, criticism,* and *witness*
- reflect on her background knowledge in order to decipher a word's meaning

These features of effective reading belong to which category?

a. Word recognition
b. Vocabulary
c. Content
d. Comprehension

28. A reading teacher is assessing an eighth grader to determine her reading level. Timed at a minute, the student reads with 93% accuracy. She misreads an average of seven words out of 100. What is her reading level?

a. She is reading at a Frustration level.
b. She is reading at a Listening level.
c. She is reading at an Instructional level.
d. She is reading at an Independent level.

29. When should students learn how to decode?

a. Decoding is the most basic and essential strategy to becoming a successful reader. It should be introduced to kindergartners during the first two weeks of school.
b. Decoding is not a teachable skill. It is an unconscious act and is natural to all learners.
c. Decoding should be taught only after children have mastered every letter–sound relationship as well as every consonant digraph and consonant blend. They should also be able to recognize and say the 40 phonemes common to English words and be able to recognize at least a dozen of the most common sight words.
d. Decoding depends on an understanding of letter–sound relationships. As soon as a child understands enough letters and their correspondent sounds to read a few words, decoding should be introduced.

30. ***Since, therefore,* and *accordingly* are examples of which type of signal words?**

a. Common, or basic, signal words
b. Compare/contrast words
c. Cause–effect words
d. Temporal sequencing words

31. A class is reading *The Heart Is a Lonely Hunter*. The teacher asks students to write a short paper explaining the story's resolution. She is asking them to locate and discuss the story's:

a. Outcome
b. Highest or most dramatic moment
c. Plot
d. Lowest point

32. A student encounters a multisyllabic word. She's not sure if she's seen it before. What should she do first? What should she do next?

a. Locate familiar word parts, then locate the consonants
b. Locate the consonants, then locate the vowels
c. Locate the vowels, then locate familiar word parts
d. Look it up in the dictionary, then write down the meaning

Refer to the following for questions 33–36:

A teacher is concerned about three of her students. While they are enthusiastic about writing, they do not always recognize letters, confusing *b*, *d*, and *p*, or *e* and *o*. They do, however, know which sounds go with certain letters when they are orally drilled. When they write, they appear to be attempting letter–sound associations.

"Now I'm writing *M*," the teacher heard one boy say as he scripted a large *N* in the upper right corner of his paper. He studied it for a moment and added, "Nope, it needs another leg." The student then wrote an *I* beside the *N*. "There," he said. "Now you are an *M*. I can write the word *man* because now I have *M*." The child then moved to the lower left corner of the paper. "M-A-N," he said to himself, slowly pronouncing each sound. "I already have that *M*. Here is where the rest of the word goes." He turned the paper sideways and wrote *N*.

The second child sang to herself as she gripped the crayon and scribbled lines here and there on her paper. Some of the lines resembled letters, but few actually were. Others were scribbles. As she "wrote," she seemed to be making up a story and seemed to believe she was writing the story down.

The third child didn't vocalize at all while he worked. He gripped the paper and carefully wrote the same letter over and over and over. Sometimes the letter was large, sometimes tiny. He turned the paper in every direction so that sometimes the letter was sideways or upside down. Sometimes he flipped it backward. "What are you writing?" the teacher asked him. "My name," the child told her. The teacher then realized the letter was, indeed, the first letter of his name. She gently told him he had done a fine job of writing the first letter of his name. Did he want her to help him write the rest of it? "Nope," he cheerfully told her, "it's all here." He pointed at one of the letters and "read" his full name. He pointed at another letter and again seemed to believe it represented all the sounds of his name.

33. The kindergarten teacher isn't certain if these children are exhibiting signs of a reading disability or other special needs. What should the teacher do?

a. Nothing. These children are simply at an early stage in the reading/writing process.
b. Nothing. She doesn't want to have to tell the parents that their children are sub-par in terms of intelligence. They are perfectly nice children and can contribute to society in other ways. She resolves to give them extra attention in other areas to help them build confidence.
c. She should recommend that the parents take the children to be tested for a number of reading disorders, including dyslexia.
d. She should arrange a meeting between herself, the school psychologist, and the reading specialist to discuss the matter and resolve it using a three-pronged approach.

34. In the above example, the emergent writers are demonstrating their understanding that letters symbolize predictable sounds, that words begin with an initial sound/letter, and that by "writing," they are empowering themselves by offering a reader access to their thoughts and ideas. The next three stages the emergent writers will pass through in order will most likely be:

a. Scripting the end-sound to a word (KT=cat), leaving space between words, writing from the top left to the top right of the page and top to bottom
b. Scripting the end-sound to a word (KT=cat), writing from the top left to the top right of the page and from top to bottom, separating the words from one another with a space between
c. Leaving space between the initial letters that represent words, writing from the top left to the top right of the page and from top to bottom, scripting the final sound of each word as well as the initial sound (KT=cat)
d. Drawing a picture beside each of the initial sounds to represent the entire word, scripting the end-sound to a word (KT=cat), scripting the interior sounds that compose the entire word (KAT=cat)

35. The teacher might best encourage the three students in the above example by:

a. Suggesting they write an entire book rather than just a single page. This will build confidence, teach them sequencing, and encourage the young writers to delve deeper into their ideas.
b. Ask the students to read their stories to her. Suggest they visit other children in the class and read to each of them.
c. Contact the local newspaper and invite a reporter to visit her class and write a story about her emergent writers. In this way, they are sure to see themselves as "real writers" and will more fully apply themselves to the task.
d. Invite all the parents to visit the class the following week. This will give all classmates, regardless of where they are on the learning spectrum, time to memorize their stories. The children will be very excited and will begin to see themselves as "real writers."

36. At what point should the kindergarten teacher in the above example offer the three children picture books and ask them to read to her?

a. When the three children are all able to script initial sounds, end sounds, and interior sounds.
b. As each child reaches the stage in which he or she can script initial sounds, end sounds, and interior sounds, the teacher should ask only that child to read to her.
c. As each child reaches the stage in which he habitually writes from the top to the bottom of the page, moving left to right.
d. From the first day of school onward

37. Which of the following statements regarding the acquisition of language is FALSE?

a. Young children often have the ability to comprehend written language just as early as they can comprehend or reproduce oral language when given appropriate instruction.
b. Oral language typically develops before a child understands the relationship between spoken and written words.
c. Most young children are first exposed to written language when an adult reads aloud.
d. A child's ability to speak, read, and write depends on a variety of physiological factors, as well as environmental factors.

38. A teacher is teaching students using rime analogies to support reading comprehension. Which of the following skills best relates to the use of rime analogies?

a. Students will be able to identify and use metaphors and similes.
b. Students will be able to identify and use similar sounding words.
c. Students will be able to identify and use similarly spelled words.
d. Students will be able to identify and use figures of speech.

Refer to the following for questions 39–40:

> A reading teacher is working with a student who has just moved to Texas from Korea. The child knows very few words in English. The teacher offers her a picture book of Korean folk tales. Using words and gestures, the teacher asks her to "read" one folk tale. The child "reads" the familiar tale in Korean. The teacher then writes key English words on the board and asks the child to find those words in the book. When the child finds the words, they read them together.

39. The strategy used in this situation is:

a. Useful. The child will feel more confident because the story is already familiar. She will also feel that the lesson is a conversation of sorts, and that she is communicating successfully. She will be motivated to learn the English words because they are meaningful and highly charged.
b. Useful. The teacher is learning as much as the child is. The teacher is learning about Korean culture and language, and she can apply this knowledge when teaching future Korean students.
c. Not very useful. The child needs to be exposed to as much American culture as possible. Encouraging her to remember her own culture will make her sad and will limit her curiosity about her new home.
d. Not very useful. The first things the child should learn are the letters of the alphabet and associative sounds. Only then can she begin to decipher an unfamiliar language.

40. By using this strategy, the teacher is taking care to consider what type of load?

a. Language load
b. Cognitive load
c. Bilingual load
d. Cultural load

41. Using brain imaging, researchers have discovered that dyslexic readers use the ___________ side(s) of their brains, while non-dyslexic readers use the ___________ side(s) of their brains.

a. left; right
b. right; left
c. right and left; left
d. right; left and right

42. A fifth-grader has prepared a report on reptiles, which is something he knows a great deal about. He rereads his report and decides to make a number of changes. He moves a sentence from the top to the last paragraph. He crosses out several words and replaces them with more specific words. He circles key information and draws an arrow to show another place the information could logically be placed. He is engaged in:

a. Editing
b. Revising
c. First editing, then revising
d. Reviewing

43. *Bi, re,* and *un* are:

a. Suffixes, appearing at the beginning of base words to change their meaning
b. Suffixes, appearing at the end of base words to enhance their meaning
c. Prefixes, appearing at the beginning of base words to emphasize their meaning
d. Prefixes, appearing at the beginning of base words to change their meanings

44. Examples of CVC words include:

a. Add, pad, mad
b. Cat, tack, act
c. Elephant, piano, examine
d. Dog, sit, leg

45. A teacher is working with a student who is struggling with reading. The teacher gives him a story with key words missing:

> The boy wanted to take the dog for a walk. The boy opened the door. The ____ ran out. The ___ looked for the dog. When he found the dog, he was very ______.

The student is able to fill in the blanks by considering:

a. Syntax. Oftentimes, word order gives enough clues that a reader can predict what happens next.
b. Pretext. By previewing the story, the student can deduce the missing words.
c. Context. By considering the other words in the story, the student can determine the missing words.
d. Sequencing. By putting the ideas in logical order, the student can determine the missing words.

46. Which of the following choices is NOT an element of metacognition?

a. A reader's awareness of themselves as a learner
b. A reader's understanding of a variety of reading strategies
c. A reader who is conscious about remembering what has been read
d. A reader who can read with prosody

47. Collaborative Strategic Reading (CSR) is a teaching technique that depends on two teaching practices. These practices are:

a. Cooperative learning and reading comprehension
b. Cooperative reading and metacognition
c. Reading comprehension and metacognition
d. Cooperative learning and metacognition

48. Context clues are useful in:

a. Predicting future action
b. Understanding the meaning of words that are not familiar
c. Understanding character motivation
d. Reflecting on a text's theme

49. A teacher has a child who does not volunteer in class. When the teacher asks the student a question the student can answer, she does so with as few words as possible. The teacher isn't sure how to best help the child. She should:

a. Leave the child alone. She is clearly very shy and will be embarrassed by having attention drawn to her. She is learning in her own way.
b. Ask two or three highly social children to include this girl in their activities. She is shy, and she probably won't approach them on her own.
c. Observe the child over the course of a week or two. Draw her into conversation and determine if her vocabulary is limited, if she displays emotional problems, or if her reticence could have another cause. Note how the child interacts with others in the class. Does she ever initiate conversation? If another child initiates, does she respond?
d. Refer her to the school counselor immediately. It is clear the child is suffering from either a low IQ or serious problems at home.

50. For their monthly project, a group of students can choose to read and respond to one book on a list supplied by their teacher. The books are grouped according to genre. Most students choose books listed under the genre that is described as "modern-day stories that are not true, but seem as though they could really happen." Which genre did most of the students choose from?

a. Historical fiction
b. Autobiography
c. Realistic fiction
d. Fantasy

51. A high school class reads an essay about the possible effects of sexual activity on teens. The author's position is very clear: she believes young people should avoid sex because they aren't mature enough to take the necessary steps to remain safe. The author cites facts, research studies, and statistics to strengthen her position. This type of writing is called:

a. Expository
b. Narrative
c. Persuasive
d. Didactic

52. A reading teacher feels that some of his strategies aren't effective. He has asked a specialist to observe him and make suggestions as to how he can improve. The reading specialist should suggest that first:

a. The teacher should set up a video camera and record several sessions with different students for the specialist to review. The presence of an observer changes the outcome; if the specialist is in the room, it will negatively affect the students' ability to read.
b. The teacher should reflect on his strategies himself. Which seem to work? Which don't? Can the teacher figure out why? It is always best to encourage teachers to find their own solutions so that they can handle future issues themselves.
c. They should meet to discuss areas the teacher is most concerned about and decide on the teacher's goals.
d. The specialist should arrive unannounced to observe the teacher interacting with students. This will prevent the teacher from unconsciously over-preparing.

53. A kindergarten teacher pronounces a series of word pairs for her students. The students repeat the pairs. Some of the pairs rhyme (*see/bee)* and some of the pairs share initial sounds but do not rhyme (*sit, sun).* The students help her separate the word pairs into pairs that rhyme and pairs that do not. Once the students are able to distinguish between two words that rhyme and two words that do not, the teacher says a word and asks them to provide a rhyme. When she says *cat* a child responds with *fat.* When she says *sing* a child offers *thing.* How does this strictly oral activity contribute to the children's ability to read?

a. It doesn't. Oral activities must have a written component to be useful to emergent readers.
b. It is helpful in that it demonstrates how different sounds are made with different letters.
c. It actually discourages children from reading. By emphasizing orality over literacy, the teacher is suggesting to the children that reading is not an important skill.
d. Being able to identify rhyme is an important element of phonological awareness.

54. Syllable types include:

a. Closed, open, silent *e*, vowel team, vowel-*r*, and consonant-*le*
b. Closed, open, silent, double-vowel, *r*, and *le*
c. Closed, midway, open, emphasized, prefixed, and suffixed
d. Stressed, unstressed, and silent

55. A student is able to decode most words fluently and has a borderline/acceptable vocabulary, but his reading comprehension is quite low. He can be helped with instructional focus on:

a. Strategies to increase comprehension and to build vocabulary
b. Strategies to increase comprehension and to be able to identify correct syntactical usage
c. Strategies to improve his understanding of both content and context
d. Strategies to build vocabulary and to improve his understanding of both content and context

56. How can reading comprehension and vocabulary best be assessed?

a. They should be assessed with brief interviews and tests every two months to determine how much learning has taken place. Students learn in spurts, and in-depth assessments of comprehension and vocabulary are a waste of time.
b. They should be assessed by a rough combination of standardized testing, informal teacher observations, attention to grades, objective-linked assessments, and systematized charting of data over time.
c. They should be assessed by giving students weekly self-assessment rubrics to keep them constantly aware of and invested in their own progress.
d. They should be assessed by having students retell a story or summarize the content of an informational piece of writing. The degree to which the material was comprehended, and the richness or paucity of vocabulary used in such work, provides efficient and thorough assessment.

57. An ORF is:

a. An Oral Reading Fluency assessment
b. An Occasional Reading Function assessment
c. An Oscar Reynolds Feinstein assessment
d. An Overt Reading Failure assessment

58. Round-robin reading refers to the practice of allowing children to take turns reading portions of a text aloud to the rest of the group during class. Which of the following statements is LEAST true about this practice?

a. Students have the chance to practice reading aloud with this strategy.
b. This practice is ineffective in its use of time, leaving students who are not reading aloud to become bored or daydream.
c. Round-robin reading lacks the creativity or engaging qualities that will interest students in building literacy skills.
d. This practice helps students feel comfortable with reading aloud due to continuous practice and encouragement from the teacher and peers.

59. Word-recognition ability is:

a. Equally important to all readers
b. Used only by fluent readers
c. Another term for "word attack"
d. Especially important to English language learners and students with reading disabilities

60. Research indicates that developing oral language proficiency in emergent readers is important because:

a. Proficiency with oral language enhances students' phonemic awareness and increases vocabulary.
b. The more verbally expressive emergent readers are, the more confident they become. Such students will embrace both Academic and Independent reading levels.
c. It encourages curiosity about others. With strong oral language skills, students begin to question the world around them. The more they ask, the richer their background knowledge.
d. It demonstrates to students that their ideas are important and worth sharing.

Refer to the following for questions 61–62:

In preparation for writing a paper, a class has been instructed to skim a number of internet and print documents.

61. The students are being asked to:

a. Read the documents several times, skimming to a deeper level of understanding each time.
b. Read the documents quickly, looking for those that offer the most basic, general information.
c. Read the documents quickly, looking for key words in order to gather the basic premise of each.
d. Read the documents carefully, looking for those that offer the most in-depth information.

62. The students are most likely preparing to write a(n) __________ essay:

a. personal
b. expository
c. literary
d. narrative

Refer to the following for questions 63–65:

A teacher has given the first paragraph of an essay to her students to analyze and discuss.

Americans have struggled with cigarettes far too long. Until now, it has been a personal choice to smoke (or not), but the time for change is rapidly approaching. Local legislation has already begun for schools, restaurants, arenas, and other public places to be smoke-free. Years ago, cigarette smoking was presented by the media as being fashionable, even sexy. In magazines, movies, and later in television, celebrities would indulge themselves with a smoke and even be paid to endorse a brand. As recently as 1975, it was common for talk show hosts like Tom Snyder and Johnny Carson to keep a cigarette burning. Cigarette smoking in America has persisted in spite of frightening concerns like lung cancer and emphysema. Over the years, the tobacco industry has sought to diffuse strong evidence that smoking is harmful. However, the myth of "safe cigarettes," questions about nicotine addiction, and denials about the dangers of secondhand smoke have proven to be propaganda and lies.

63. This is a(n) ____________ essay:

a. compare/contrast
b. persuasive
c. narrative
d. analytic

64. The thesis statement is:

a. However, the myth of "safe cigarettes," questions about nicotine addiction, and denials about the dangers of secondhand smoke have proven to be propaganda and lies.
b. Americans have struggled with cigarettes far too long.
c. Until now, it has been a personal choice to smoke (or not), but the time for change is rapidly approaching.
d. In magazines, movies, and later in television, celebrities would indulge themselves with a smoke and even be paid to endorse a brand.

65. The next three paragraphs in the essay will most likely address:

a. Smoking as a personal choice, changes in local legislation, and how fashionable smoking once was
b. How fashionable smoking once was, talk show hosts smoking on air, the myth of "safe cigarettes"
c. Propaganda and lies, the myth of "safe cigarettes," and how long Americans have struggled with cigarettes
d. The myth of "safe cigarettes," questions about nicotine addiction, and the dangers of secondhand smoke

66. The teacher and her students brainstorm a list of talents, skills, and specialized knowledge belonging to members of the class. Some of the items on the list include how to make a soufflé, how to juggle, and how to teach a dog to do tricks. One student knows a great deal about spiders, and another knows about motorcycles. The teacher asks the students to each write an essay about something they are good at or know a great deal about. What kind of essay is she asking the students to produce?

a. Cause and effect
b. Compare/contrast
c. Expository
d. Argumentative

67. *Carat, carrot, to, two,* and *too* share something in common. They are:

a. Nouns
b. Monosyllabic
c. Homophones
d. Diphthongs

Refer to the following for questions 68–70:

A class will visit an assisted living facility to interview residents about their lives. Each group of three has selected a theme such as love, work, or personal accomplishment and written several questions around that theme. Next each group practices interviewing one another. The teacher then asks all the students to discuss the questions that caused them to respond most thoughtfully, as well as those they were less inspired by. The students decided the questions that were easiest to respond to were those that asked for very specific information; for example, one inspiring question was, "Please tell me about something you learned to do as a child that affected the direction of your life." Those that were uninspiring were too broad, for example, "Please tell me about your happiest memory."

68. After they interview the residents, each group of three students will work together to write a piece about the resident. This kind of approach is called:

a. Collaborative learning
b. Companion learning
c. Bonded learning
d. Group learning

69. The genre the teacher expects is:

a. Memoir
b. Historical fiction
c. Biography
d. Autobiography

70. The teacher wants the students to apply what they've learned across content areas. Which of the following strategies would be most effective?

a. Students will interview a family member, asking the same questions.
b. Students will write a personal piece in which they address the same questions.
c. Students will do online research about the cultural, economic, or political events that were occurring during the specific time about which they've written.
d. Students pretend to be the interviewee and rewrite the piece from a first-person point of view.

Refer to the following for questions 71–73:

A seventh-grade teacher asks the reading teacher to suggest a lesson that students will find simultaneously challenging and fun. The reading teacher suggests the class read fairy tales from both Hans Christian Anderson and the Brothers Grimm and have a rapid-paced, energetic discussion about the many similarities and differences between the two while the teacher lists them on the board.

71. The individual strategies the students will employ are:

a. Collaborative learning and genre
b. Brainstorming and a compare/contrast strategy
c. Collaborative learning and brainstorming
d. Analyzing and genre

72. The lesson is asking the students to consider two different:

a. Learning styles
b. Genres
c. Writing styles
d. Reading styles

73. The primary benefit of this exercise is that it promotes students':

a. Vocabulary
b. Comprehension
c. Fluency
d. Word identification

74. The students enjoyed the assignment so much that the teacher suggested they select one fairy tale and modernize it without changing the basic structure. Evil kings and queens could become corrupt politicians, pumpkins could turn into Hummers, and romantic princes might reveal themselves as rock stars. The teacher believes this assignment will most effectively demonstrate to the students:

a. The importance of setting to meaning
b. The importance of characters to meaning
c. The importance of culture to meaning
d. The importance of creativity to meaning

75. The first-grade teacher wants her class to understand that stories have a certain order. She reads them a story, then orally reviews how each event that happened in the story caused the next event to happen. To reinforce the lesson, the teacher should:

a. Give each child a piece of drawing paper that has been folded in half and then in half again, creating four boxes, along with a piece that has not been folded. The teacher should then ask the students to draw a cartoon about the story. Each of the first four boxes will show the events in order. The second page is to show how the story ends.
b. Give each child a piece of drawing paper and ask the students to draw the most important scene.
c. Give each child a piece of drawing paper and ask the students to draw the story's beginning on the front of the page and ending on the back.
d. Give each child a piece of drawing paper that has been folded in half and then in half again, creating four boxes, along with a piece that has not been folded. The teacher should then ask the students to draw a cartoon about anything they want. She reminds them to put their story cartoons in proper order.

Refer to the following for question 76:

For a poetry unit, a class is reading a 14-line poem in iambic pentameter. There are three stanzas of four lines each, and a two-line couplet at the end. Words at the end of each line rhyme with another word in the same stanza. After the first week of this unit, the teacher wants to determine if the instructional methods she is using are successful. If students are meeting the objectives introduced so far, she will continue with the strategies she is currently using. If students are struggling to meet the objectives, she will reteach them using a different approach. For the assessment, she plans to ask students to identify the literary devices she has introduced in sample poems.

76. The class is reading a:

a. Sonnet
b. Villanelle
c. Sestina
d. Limerick

77. A teacher is working with a group of English language learners. She asks them to take two pieces of paper. At the top of the first paper, they are to write *SAME*, and at the top of the other, *DIFFERENT*. Each child will consider what his native country and the United States have in common, and what distinct features each country possesses. The children are using which method in organizing their ideas?

a. Hunt and peck
b. Consider and persuade
c. Evaluate and contrast
d. Compare and contrast

78. Which student is most likely to need referral to a reading specialist for assessment, special instruction, or intervention?

a. Annabel: a second-grade student who tends to skip over words or phrases when she reads, affecting her comprehension of the text.
b. Cliff: a kindergarten student who is already reading simple chapter books with his parents at home or in class.
c. Noelle: a first grader who avoids any activity in which she must read, both aloud or silently, preferring to ask an adult to read the text for her first.
d. Barrett: a third grader who often confuses the sounds of certain letters, such as /b/ and /d/ or /v/ and /u/.

79. Which assessment will determine a student's ability to identify initial, medial, blended, final, segmented, and manipulated "units"?

a. Phonological awareness assessment
b. High-frequency word assessment
c. Reading fluency assessment
d. Comprehension quick-check

80. A third grader knows he needs to write from left to right and from top to bottom on the page. He knows what sounds are associated with specific letters. He can recognize individual letters and can hear word families. He correctly identifies prefixes, suffixes, and homonyms, and his reading comprehension is very good. However, when he is asked to write, he becomes very upset. He has trouble holding a pencil, his letters are very primitively executed, and his written work is not legible. He most likely has:

a. Dysgraphia
b. Dyslexia
c. Dyspraxia
d. Nonverbal learning disorder

81. The phrase "pretty as a picture" is best described as a:

a. Metaphor
b. Simile
c. Synecdoche
d. Paradox

82. A fourth-grade teacher had her students write haiku in order to promote the students' __________.

a. reading comprehension
b. vocabulary
c. word identification skills
d. confidence

83. A second-grade teacher wants to help her students enrich their vocabulary. She's noticed that their writing journals are filled with serviceable but unexciting verbs such as "said" and "went," and general rather than specific nouns. The most effective lesson would involve:

a. Suggesting students use a thesaurus to replace common words with more unusual words
b. Suggesting students add an adjective to each noun
c. Brainstorming a list of verbs that mean ways of talking or ways of going, then adding them to the word wall along with some nouns that specify common topics
d. Suggesting students look up the meanings of boring words and consider another way to express them

84. Using graphic organizers, activating prior knowledge, and shared reading are examples of what type of instructional concept?

a. Modeling
b. Scaffolding
c. Assessing
d. Inspiring

85. Examples of onomatopoeia are:

a. Sink, drink, mink, link
b. Their, there, they're
c. Drip, chirp, splash, giggle
d. Think, in, thin, ink

86. "Code knowledge" facilitates reading fluency because:

a. It brings the entirety of the student's previous experience to bear on decoding a text.
b. It offers a framework for organizing new information by assigning code words to sets of ideas.
c. There is no such thing as "code knowledge." The correct term is "core knowledge."
d. It offers a systematic approach to untangling the wide variety of vowel sounds when an unfamiliar word is encountered.

87. What is the purpose of targeted instruction?

a. Deliver instructions that are precise, clear, and direct so that students understand exactly what is expected.
b. Accurately rank a group of learners from low achievers to high achievers so that the teacher knows from the beginning of the school year which students have less ability and will therefore need support.
c. Teach students how to take information from a text and reorganize it into bulleted lists.
d. Assess and target areas needing improvement as well as areas of greatest strength for each student to ensure that all members of a class are receiving instruction tailored to their specific needs.

88. Components of explicit instruction include:

a. Clarifying the goal, modeling strategies, and offering explanations geared to a student's level of understanding
b. Determining the goal, offering strategies, and asking questions designed to ascertain whether understanding has been reached
c. Reassessing the goal, developing strategies, and determining whether further reassessing of the goal is required
d. Objectifying the goal, assessing strategies, and offering explanations geared toward a student's level of understanding

89. A teacher has challenged a student with a book about Antarctica that is just beyond the high end of the student's Instructional level. The teacher points out that the student already knows quite a bit about penguins because the class studied them earlier in the year. He reminds the student that she's recently seen a television show about the seals that also live in Antarctic waters. The teacher gives the student a list of words she's likely to find in the text, and they discuss what those words might mean. The student begins to read, but stops to ask the teacher what *circumpolar* means. The teacher is also unfamiliar with the word, but reminds her that *circum* is a prefix. The student recalls that it means "about or around" and deduces that circumpolar most likely refers to something found around or in a polar region. This instructional approach is called:

a. Modular instruction
b. Scaffolding
c. Linking
d. Transmutation

90. Which of the following linguistic domains does NOT play a role in decoding unfamiliar words when reading?

a. Syntactic
b. Semantic
c. Graphophonic
d. Pragmatic

91. An understanding of the meanings of prefixes and suffixes such as *dis, mis, un, re, able,* and *ment* is important primarily for:

a. Reading comprehension
b. Word recognition
c. Vocabulary building
d. Reading fluency

92. VC, CVC, CCVC, CVCC, and CCVCC are among the types of:

a. Homophones
b. Closed syllables
c. Monosyllabic words
d. Polyglotal indicators

93. A student is taking a reading test. The teacher has blocked out a number of words. Each blank is assigned a set of three possible words. The student must select the correct word from each set so that the text makes sense. The student is taking:

a. A cloze test
b. A maze test
c. A multiple-choice quiz
d. A vocabulary test

94. When working with English language learners, the teacher should:

a. Avoid idioms and slang, involve students in hands-on activities, reference students' prior knowledge, and speak slowly.
b. Speak slowly, use monosyllabic words whenever possible, repeat each sentence three times before moving to the next sentence, and employ idioms but not slang.
c. Use monosyllabic words whenever possible, repeat key instructions three times but not in a row, reference students' prior knowledge, and have students keep a journal of new vocabulary.
d. Have students keep a journal of new vocabulary, reference students' prior knowledge, speak slowly, and involve students in hands-on activities.

95. Editing involves:

a. Correcting surface features such as sentence fragments, spelling, and punctuation
b. Fine-tuning the underlying structure of the piece to make the theme stand out
c. Reconsidering ideas, adding or subtracting information, and changing the underlying structure
d. Adding illustrations, charts, and other useful addenda

96. A seventh grader has never had much success with reading. Her ability to decode is rudimentary; she stops and starts when reading, frequently loses her place, or misreads an important word. She doesn't seem aware of where errors occur, or she does not attempt to correct them. When asked about what she's read, her comprehension is minimal. To help her, instructional focus on which of the following would be most useful?

a. Carefully organized lessons in decoding, sight words, vocabulary, and comprehension at least three to five times a week. These mini-lessons must be extremely clear, with the parts broken down to the lowest common denominator. The more tightly interwoven and systematized the instruction, the better chance this student will have.
b. A weekly lesson focusing on one aspect of reading. This student will be overwhelmed if too many strategies are offered at once. The instruction should focus first on recognizing sight words, then letter–sound association. Next, the girl needs an understanding of the rules of syntax.
c. The student isn't trying. Her instruction should be aimed at helping her learn to be self-motivated and disciplined in her approach to learning.
d. Comprehension strategies will help her grasp the overall meaning of a text. From there she can begin to drill down until she's able to combine various approaches that, working together, will enable her to read.

97. Silent reading fluency can best be assessed by:

a. Having the student retell or summarize the material to determine how much was understood.
b. Giving a written test that covers plot, theme, character development, sequence of events, rising action, climax, falling action, and outcome. A student must test at a 95% accuracy rate to be considered fluent at silent reading.
c. Giving a three-minute Test of Silent Contextual Reading Fluency four times a year. The student is presented with text in which spaces between words and all punctuation have been removed. The student must divide one word from another with slash marks, as in the example: The/little/sailboat/bobbed/so/far/in/the/distance/it/looked/like/a/toy. The more words a student accurately separates, the higher the silent reading fluency score.
d. Silent reading fluency cannot be assessed. It is a private act between the reader and the text and does not invite critique.

98. A teacher has given her students an assignment to write a non-rhyming poem of three lines. The first and last lines each contain five syllables, and the middle line contains seven syllables. The students are writing a:

a. Limerick
b. Metaphor
c. Villanelle
d. Haiku

99. "Verbal dyspraxia" refers to:

a. Trouble with the motor skills involved in speaking
b. Confusing word or sentence order while speaking
c. Misplacement of letters within words
d. An inability to process verbal information

100. Coarticulation affects:

a. Blending awareness
b. Phonemic awareness
c. Sequencing
d. Aural awareness

Constructed Response

1. Instructions

Review the sample below and identify at least one of the student's strengths and at least one of the student's weaknesses in reading fluency. Provide a recommendation for how to target the student's needs in future instruction relying on your knowledge of language and reading comprehension, including phonics, word structure, context-clues, and vocabulary acquisition.

Scenario

Ally, a third-grade student, reads an excerpt from the Tortoise and the Hare. Ally was primed on the words "Hare" and "Tortoise" prior to reading the passage. After reading the passage aloud, a short quiz assessed her comprehension of what she had just read. Ally normally scores well on reading retention, but struggled to remember particular details about what she had just read. Below is the notation of Ally's oral reading performance. Ally's reading was highly accurate, but very slow and included pauses throughout. Ally's reading performance did not include much verbal inflection to indicate the sentence type and breaks in her speech were relatively pervasive.

Sample Text

The Hare and the Tortoise

Aesop's Fables

A Hare was making fun of the Tortoise one day for being so slow.

"Do you ever get anywhere?" he asked with a mocking laugh.

"Yes," replied the Tortoise, "and I get there sooner than you think. I'll run you a race and prove it."

The Hare was much amused at the idea of running a race with the Tortoise, but for the fun of the thing he agreed. So the Fox, who had consented to act as judge, marked the distance and started the runners off.

The Hare was soon far out of sight, and to make the Tortoise feel very deeply how ridiculous it was for him to try a race with a Hare, he lay down beside the course to take a nap until the Tortoise should catch up.

The Tortoise meanwhile kept going slowly but steadily, and, after a time, passed the place where the Hare was sleeping. But the Hare slept on very peacefully; and when at last he did wake up, the Tortoise was near the goal. The Hare now ran his swiftest, but he could not overtake the Tortoise in time.

The race is not always to the swift.

Key:

◯	deletion	|	short pause	←	repetition	©self-correction
^	insertion	||	long pause	cat/cow	substitution	

2. Instructions

Review the following briefing of a student's writing sample. Identify one type of grammatical deficit student's sample, citing specific examples of the deficiency. Provide one instructional strategy that can help the student achieve in the area of difficulty. Provide sufficient theoretical or research-based support for the proposed instructional strategy, explaining why it is appropriate and targeted to the particular needs of the student.

Scenario

Adrian recently immigrated to America and is being placed in general 6th grade classes as he scored well on an English placement test. He spoke English in his home country as a school language and still struggles with certain common grammatical forms. Adrian occasionally has points taken off on some of his assignments due to these grammatical errors.

Sample of the Student's Journaling Assignment

Write about one of your favorite activities you get to do at school this year. Describe what has been the best part and the most difficult part about that activity. Think about the future and describe how you hope your activity will develop by 8th grade and by 12th grade.

> January 27
>
> This year I got to join the cross country team and run outside. The best part about the running is that I get to go out into the sun every day and be with friend on the team. Since this is my first year doing this running, I'm not fast and have a hard time finish the run when it is a longer one. The hard part is having to keep going after I'm tired already. We usually run 2 to 3 mile before we stop, but at first, I could only run 1 mile. My teammate encouraged me and helped me get better at running, and I am glad they have become my friend. When my dad picks me from school, he can usually tell how much fun I had with my group of friend. He is glad I want to stay on the team and practices running with me on the weekend. My hope for the future is that I can run in a 5k race by 8th grade and place in my age group. I hope to keep to push my limits and eventually run a half-marathon before I graduate high school and can go on to run in college.

3. Read the following scenario and provide an analysis of the teaching method, taking into account the class's assessment results. Provide at least two critiques of the instruction methodology and identify targeted recommendations on how to improve the teacher's instructional practices in areas of student deficits. Be sure to support your recommendations with your knowledge of language acquisition and reading development.

Scenario

Mrs. Johnson is reading a challenging fictional passage to her 2rd grade class with new vocabulary words used throughout. She uses a projector to allow the students to follow along as she reads the text. Periodically through the text, Mrs. Johnson switches to recall questions about the plot and characters of the story. She usually waits until about a third of the class has their hands raised before asking a student to provide the answer to the question. The classroom is alphabetically arranged and is set up in groups of four for a project in another subject. The teacher reads the story aloud to the class and is generally able to mediate classroom disruptions.

Assessment Results

Mrs. Johnson provides an individual assessment to the students to determine if they learned the key vocabulary words and remember the plot and characters of the story. The assessment format was fill-in-the-blank, with an answer bank provided for the vocabulary portion. She found that students' scores showed a fairly normal distribution of scores regarding the vocabulary words, but that there was a steep divide in the results regarding comprehension of the plot and recognition of the characters. Some students performed as expected and were able to recognize the plot with confidence, whereas other students left questions blank or clearly guessed at the questions.

Answer Key and Explanations

Multiple Choice Questions

1. A: Homophones. Homophones are a type of homonym that sound alike but are spelled differently and have different meanings. Other examples are *two, to,* and *too* and *their, they're,* and *there.*

2. C: The goal of a persuasive essay is to convince the reader that the author's position or opinion on a topic is correct. That opinion or position is called the argument. A persuasive essay argues a series of points that are supported by facts and evidence.

3. D: Fluent readers are able to read smoothly and comfortably at a steady pace (rate). The more quickly a child reads, the greater the chance of leaving out a word or substituting one word for another (for example, *sink* instead of *shrink*). Fluent readers are able to maintain accuracy without sacrificing rate. Fluent readers also stress important words in a text, group words into rhythmic phrases, and read with intonation (prosody).

4. B: Language load is the number of unrecognizable words an English language learner encounters when reading a passage or listening to a teacher. Language load is one of the barriers English language learners face. To lighten this load, a teacher can rephrase, eliminate unnecessary words, divide complex sentences into smaller units, and teach essential vocabulary before the student begins the lesson.

5. A: A syllable is a minimal sound unit arranged around a vowel. For example, *academic* has four syllables: *a/ca/dem/ic.* It is possible for a syllable to be a single vowel, as in the above example. It is not possible for a syllable to be a single consonant.

6. C: This method is likely to fail, producing students at a Frustration reading level. Those reading below grade level are likely to give up entirely. Those reading at grade level are likely to get frustrated and form habits that will actually slow down their development. Giving students texts that are too far beyond their reach produces frustrated readers. In an effort to succeed, frustrated readers are likely to apply strategies that have worked for them in the past but cannot work in this case because the text is simply beyond them. Looking for contextual clues to understand the meaning of unfamiliar words requires that most of the words in the passage are familiar. Breaking unfamiliar words into individual phonemes or syllables can be effective, but not if the number of such words is excessive. In this case, students below reading level and students at reading level will become frustrated when the skills that have worked for them in the past now fail.

7. C: Tier-two words are words that are used with high frequency across a variety of disciplines or words with multiple meanings. They are characteristic of mature language users. Knowing these words is crucial to attaining an acceptable level of reading comprehension and communication skills.

8. C: When reading independently, students are at the correct level if they read with at least 97% accuracy.

9. B: A reading teacher offers corrective feedback to a student in order to explain why a particular error in reading is, in fact, an error. Corrective feedback is specific; it locates where and how the student went astray so that similar errors can be avoided in future reading.

10. C: These are content-specific words. Because these words are specific to penguins, it's unlikely the students know their meanings. Without understanding what these words mean, the students would not be able to understand the content of the passage they were about to read.

11. B: Prior knowledge, which rises from experience and previous learning, provides a framework by which new knowledge gained from the act of reading can be integrated. Every act of reading enriches a student's store of prior knowledge and increases that student's future ability to comprehend more fully any new knowledge acquired through reading.

12. B: In a cloze test, a reader is given a text with certain words blocked out. The reader must be able to determine probable missing words based on contextual clues. In order to supply these words, the reader must already know them.

13. A: Sight words occur in many types of writing; they are high-frequency words. Sight words are also words with irregular spelling. Some examples of sight words include *talk, some,* and *the.* Fluent readers need to recognize these words visually.

14. D: A consonant digraph is group of consonants in which all letters represent a single sound.

15. A: Phonemic awareness is the ability to recognize sounds within words, so it is a type of phonological awareness. Segmenting words and blending sounds are components of phonemic awareness. Phonological awareness includes an understanding of multiple components of spoken language. The ability to hear individual words within a vocalized stream and the ability to identify spoken syllables are types of phonological awareness.

16. A: Letter–sound correspondence relies on the relationship between a spoken sound or group of sounds and the letters conventionally used in English to write them.

17. A: Strategic instruction involves teaching a methodic approach to solving a reading problem. It consists of strategies done in steps which aid the reader in eliminating incorrect responses.

18. D: Common words are familiar, frequently used words that do not need to be taught beyond primary grades. Common or basic words are the first tier of three-tier words. These words are widely used across the spoken and written spectrum. Some examples are *walk, go, wish, the, look, happy,* and *always.* This essential vocabulary is taught early in a reader's instruction, and beyond that, it need not be taught.

19. B: A phoneme is the smallest measure of language sound. English language phonemes, about 40 in number, are composed of individual letters as well as letter combinations. A number of letters have more than one associated sound. For example, "c" can be pronounced as a hard "c" (cake) or a soft "c" (Cynthia). Vowels in particular have a number of possible pronunciations.

20. B: Consonant blend refers to a group of consonants in which each letter represents a separate sound.

21. A: At the beginning of the school year, second-grade students should be able to read 50–80 words per minute. By the time they are well into the school year, second-grade level reading is tracked at 85 words per minute.

22. D: None; irregular sight words cannot generally be decoded. Readers must learn to recognize these as whole words on sight. They either have irregular spelling or do not follow typical phonic patterns, so an attempt at decoding may ultimately mislead the reader. Segmenting them into syllables or using a phonemic approach are ineffective strategies to aid a reader in recognizing a sight word because these approaches depend on rules a sight word doesn't follow. Word families group words that share common patterns of consonants and vowels. The spelling of those words is, therefore, regular because they follow a predictable pattern. Sight words that are irregular, do not follow a predictable pattern, and must be instantaneously recognized for writing fluency. Decoding is not useful.

23. D: It is impossible to include every text desired into the language curriculum—there are simply too many good books, stories, poems, speeches, and media available. Teachers must first think about what skills their students need to acquire, as well as what skills they have already mastered. In designing activities for class, a good teacher will start first with the purpose for instruction. For example, purposes of reading can include: reading for information, reading for enjoyment, understanding a message, identifying main or supporting ideas, or developing an appreciation for artistic expression/perception. Once the purpose or intended learning outcome has been identified, the teacher will have a much better idea of which texts, strategies, and activities will support that purpose.

24. C: The act of decoding involves first recognizing the sounds individual letters and letter groups make and then blending the sounds to read the word. A child decoding the word *spin*, for example, would first pronounce *sp/i/n* as individual sound units. She then would repeat the sounds, smoothly blending them. Because decoding involves understanding letters and their sounds, it is sometimes known as the alphabetic principle.

25. C: Students can easily become bored or disinterested in reading if they are not exposed to a variety of reading texts. Also, reading can be overwhelming or frustrating for students who are still learning to read fluently or to comprehend what they read. By incorporating media, oral stories, and various types of print, students of all ability levels can build both fluency and comprehension skills. This approach also enables the teacher and students to discuss the relationship between all aspects of literacy—including speaking, listening, thinking, viewing, and reading.

26. A: Phonological awareness refers to an understanding of the sounds a word makes. While phonological awareness leads to fluent reading skills, activities designed to develop an awareness of word sounds are, by definition, oral.

27. B: Strategizing in order to understand the meaning of a word, knowing multiple meanings of a single word, and applying background knowledge to glean a word's meaning are all ways in which an effective reader enhances vocabulary. Other skills include an awareness of word parts and word origins, the ability to apply word meanings in a variety of content areas, and a delight in learning the meanings of unfamiliar words.

28. C: In one minute, a student who misreads one or less than one word per twenty words, or with 95%–100% accuracy, is at an Independent reading level. A student who misreads one or less than one word per ten words, or with 90%–95% accuracy, is at an Instructional level. A student misreading more than one word out of ten, or with less than 90% accuracy, is at a Frustration level.

29. D: Decoding depends on an understanding of letter–sound relationships. As soon as a child understands enough letters and their correspondent sounds to read a few words, decoding should be introduced. The act of decoding involves first recognizing the sounds individual letters and letter groups in a word make and then blending the sounds to read the word.

30. C: Signal words give the reader hints about the purpose of a particular passage. Some signal words are concerned with comparing/contrasting, some with cause and effect, some with temporal sequencing, some with physical location, and some with a problem and its solution. The words since, therefore, and accordingly are words used when describing an outcome; outcomes have causes.

31. A: Story action can be analyzed in terms of rising action, story climax, falling action, and resolution. Rising action consists of those events that occur before and lead up to the story's most dramatic moment, or climax. The climax occurs toward the end of the book, but rarely, if ever, right at the end. Following the climax, the consequences of that dramatic moment are termed "falling action." The story reaches resolution with the outcome of the falling action.

32. C: She should locate the vowels, then locate familiar word parts. Syllables are organized around vowels. In order to determine the syllables, this student should begin by locating the vowels. It's possible to have a syllable that is a single vowel (*a/gain)*. It isn't possible to have a syllable that is a single consonant. Once the word has been broken into its component syllables the reader is able to study the syllables to find ones that are familiar and might give her a clue as to the word's meaning, such as certain prefixes or suffixes.

33. A: This teacher doesn't need to do anything. These children are simply at an early stage in the reading/writing process. When emergent readers become aware of the connections between letters and sounds, and between reading and writing, they want to practice the skills they see proficient readers use. While a proficient writer knows that letters are grouped into words and that words are constructed into sentences that move from left to right and from the top of the page to the bottom, an emergent reader/writer knows only that letters magically contain sounds that other people can read. It is necessary for children to pass through early stages in which they scribble-write and pretend they are scripting letters, which leads to a stage in which they actually do write the initial letter of a word all over the page. Next, the emergent reader/writer will write the initial letter of many of the words that belong in the sentence and will write them sequentially. KJM, for example, might mean *the cat chased a mouse.*

34. A: The next three stages are scripting the end-sound to a word (KT=cat), leaving space between words, and writing from the top left to the top right of the page and from top to bottom. Each of these steps is progressively more abstract. Scripting the end-sound to a word helps a young writer recognize that words have beginnings and endings. This naturally leads to the willingness to separate words with white space so that they stand as individual entities. Once this step is reached, the child realizes that in English, writing progresses from left to right and from the top of the page to the bottom.

35. B: She can ask the students to read their stories to her and suggest they visit other children in the class and read to each of them. The teacher should encourage these students by "reading" what they have written, even if what she reads is incorrect. She might misread KJM as *Kathy jumped rope with Mandy*. Most children will not be upset by this but will correct the teacher's misreading by reading what the letters really mean.

36. D: The teacher should encourage all students to "read" picture books from the first day of school. Talking about the pictures from page to page gives young readers the idea that books are arranged sequentially. Pictures also offer narrative coherence and contextual clues. Emergent readers who are encouraged to enjoy books will more readily embrace the act of reading. Holding a book and turning pages gives young readers a familiarity with them.

37. A: Most adults can understand the relationship between oral and written language: components of oral language have representational symbols that can be written and decoded. However, most normally-developing children acquire spoken language first and begin to develop reading and writing skills as they approach school-age. Many children are first exposed to the concept of written language when an adult introduces books or other written texts. However, a child's ability to read and write develops over time and is dependent on the development of physiological processes such as hearing, sight, and fine motor skills for writing. Written language development also typically requires direct instruction. Most children must be taught to read and write and rarely learn these skills simply by observing others.

38. C: Analogizing is based on recognizing the pattern of letters in words that share phonological and orthographical similarities. In phonology and in spelling, the initial sound of a word is called an *onset*, whereas the sounds that follow the onset are called the *rime*. The following words each have a different onset sound, but share the same rime: *rent*, *sent*, *bent*, and *dent*. Rime analogies are an explicit teaching method that helps draw attention to patterns in rime and onset spellings. As students become more familiar with these patterns, they should be able to decode common rime patterns in words faster and with greater accuracy, contributing to higher reading fluency.

39. A: The child will feel more confident because the story is already familiar, so this strategy is useful. She will also feel that the lesson is a conversation of sorts, and that she is communicating successfully. She will be motivated to learn the English words because they are meaningful and highly charged. As a newly arrived immigrant, the child feels overwhelmed. Presenting her with a book of folk tales from her country tells her that she needn't lose her culture in order to function in this one. It also comforts her by reminding her that her past and present are linked. Allowing her to speak in Korean helps her express herself without fear of judgment or failure. Presenting her with an English vocabulary that is meaningful ensures that she will eagerly embrace these words, her first words in her new language.

40. D: The teacher is considering the cultural load the student is facing. Cultural load is concerned with how the relationship between language and culture can help or hinder learning. By using the Korean folk tale, the teacher offered the child the opportunity to learn new words in a context that was culturally familiar. By demonstrating respect for her student's culture, she helped lighten the cultural load.

41. C: Researchers have discovered through brain imaging that a dyslexic reader uses both sides of the brain. Non-dyslexic readers use only the left side.

42. B: Revision (literally, *re+vision*) is the act of "seeing again." When revising, writers examine what they have written in order to improve the meaning of the work. Fine-tuning word choices, moving information to another location, and adding or deleting words are all acts of revision.

43. D: Suffixes appear at the end of words. Prefixes are attached to the beginning of words to change their meanings. *Un+happy, bi+monthly,* and *re+examine* are prefixes that, by definition, change the meanings of the words to which they are attached.

44. D: CVC words, like dog, sit, and leg, are composed of a consonant, a vowel, and a consonant. To learn to read them, students must be familiar with the letters used and their sounds. A teacher can present a word like *sit* to students who also know the consonants *b/f/h/p* and ask them to create a word family of other CVC words. The students will be able to read *bit, fit, hit,* and *pit* because they are similar to the word *sit* that they have just learned.

45. C: By considering the other words in the story, the student can determine the missing words. The student is depending on the information supplied by the rest of the story. This information puts the story into context.

46. D: Prosody is not an element of metacognition. Metacognition means a reader's awareness of their own reading processes as they improve reading comprehension. Other elements of metacognition include awareness of areas in the text that the reader does not comprehend and an understanding of how the text is structured.

47. D: Collaborative Strategic Reading (CSR) is a technique that largely depends on cooperative learning and practice of metacognition. In practice, this look slike putting students into groups and having them self-monitor their own reading comprehension using various reading strategies. One popular reading strategy that can be used includes "click and clunk," which is where students report which parts of the story *click* to them, or which makes sense without much difficulty, and which parts *clunk*, or are not easy to understand. Then the group would collaborate to resolve the clunks and ensure everyone understood the reading assignment. Other strategies can include use of context clues, rereading, or any other reading comprehension strategy, paired with group discussion.

48. B: Context clues offer insight into the probable meaning of unfamiliar words.

49. C: Until the teacher monitors the child's verbal abilities and habits, she cannot determine if the lack of interaction suggests a learning disability, an emotional problem, or simply a shy personality. The teacher should informally observe the child over a period of time, noting if and when she initiates or responds to oral language, if she is reading with apparent comprehension, if her vocabulary is limited, and the degree to which the child is interested in understanding.

50. C: There are many genres from which students can choose to read. The most elemental distinction between genres consists of fiction and non-fiction, the latter referring to stories or texts that are true, or factual. Fictional texts can fall into a variety of categories. Realistic fiction seems as though it could be true. These stories involve realistic characters and settings with which readers can often identify. This type of fiction can consist of different subjects, but it still must be relatable in nature.

51. C: The author is hoping to persuade or convince young readers to avoid sex by providing them with facts and using rhetorical devices, such as dispelling opposing arguments.

52. C: They should meet to discuss areas the teacher is most concerned about and decide on the teacher's goals. In order to best achieve goals, those goals must be understood and established.

53. D: Young children use language in a solely oral way. Oral language is composed of separate sounds that are represented in written form by the alphabet. In order to read, a child must first have a sense of the sounds that are used in English (phonological awareness). By helping children hear the difference between rhyming and non-rhyming words, the teacher is preparing them to make the transition to sound–letter association and word families.

54. A: Syllable types include closed, open, silent *e*, vowel team, vowel-*r*, and consonant-*le*. A closed syllable ends with a consonant, such as *cat*. Open syllables end with a vowel, such as *he*. Vowel team syllables contain two vowels working together, such as *main*. Vowel-*r* syllables such as *er* and *or* frequently occur as suffixes. Consonant-*le* syllables also typically occur as suffixes, such as *battle* or *terrible*.

55. A: The student should receive instruction focused on just the areas in which he is exhibiting difficulty, which are comprehension and vocabulary. Improved vocabulary will give him greater skill at comprehending the meaning of a particular text. Strategies focused on enhancing comprehension together with a stronger vocabulary will provide the greatest help.

56. B: Reading comprehension and vocabulary cannot be sufficiently assessed with occasional, brief assessments. Performing continuous observation, using high-stakes and standardized testing, paying attention to grades, and closely tracking the outcomes of objective-linked assessments are interrelated tools that, when systematically organized, offer a thorough understanding of students' strengths and weaknesses.

57. A: ORF stands for oral reading fluency. This assessment measures the words correct per minute (WCPM) by subtracting the number of errors made from the total number of words orally read in a one- to two-minute period of time. It is used to find a student's Instructional reading level, to identify readers who are having difficulties, and to track developing fluency and word recognition over time.

58. D: Round-robin reading is a common practice in language arts classes and has been for many years. In this process, students take turns reading aloud for their peers. Other students are asked to follow along silently in their texts while a peer is reading. This strategy does provide a way for students to read texts in class and include as many students as possible, which is often the intended outcome. However, this process often creates a boring atmosphere, since only one student at a time is actively engaged. While that student is reading, other students may become distracted by their own thoughts, other school work, or off-task interaction with each other. All of these issues subvert the intended outcome of the process. There is rarely enough time for each student to practice reading aloud to build students' reading fluency or comprehension in significant ways.

59. D: Word recognition is required for reading fluency and is important to all readers, but it is especially so to English Language Learners and students with reading disabilities. It can be effectively taught through precisely calibrated word study instruction designed to provide readers with reading and writing strategies for successful word analysis.

60. A: Proficiency with oral language enhances students' phonemic awareness and increases vocabulary. Understanding that words are scripted with specific letters representing specific sounds is essential to decoding a text. Students cannot effectively learn to read without the ability to decode. An enhanced vocabulary supports the act of reading; the larger an emergent reader's vocabulary, the more quickly he will learn to read. He will be able to decode more words, which he can organize into word families and use to decode unfamiliar words.

61. C: The students have been instructed to read the documents quickly, looking for key words in order to gather the basic premise of each. Skimming allows a reader to quickly gain a broad understanding of a piece of writing in order to determine if a more thorough reading is warranted. Skimming allows students who are researching a topic on the internet or in print to consider a substantial body of information in order to select only that of particular relevance.

62. B: The students are likely preparing to write an expository essay. Expository essays clarify an idea, explain an event, or interpret facts. The position the author takes is often supported with statistics, quotations, or other evidence researched from a variety of sources.

63. B: A persuasive essay takes a strong position about a controversial topic and offers factual evidence to support this position. The goal of a persuasive paper is to convince the audience that the claim is true based on the evidence provided.

64. A: In this case, the last sentence of the paragraph contains the thesis statement. A thesis statement offers a hypothesis or opinion that the remainder of the paper then sets out to prove. Oftentimes, the thesis statement also offers a clear road map of the paper, foreshadowing the focuses of the paragraphs that follow and the order in which they will appear.

65. D: The next three paragraphs will likely address the myth of "safe cigarettes," questions about nicotine addiction, and the dangers of secondhand smoke. These three foci are presented in the thesis statement in this order and will be fleshed out in the following three paragraphs as the body of the essay.

66. C: Expository essays are any type of essay in which the writer is providing meaningful information about a topic for the purpose of informing. Most of the topics listed in the example include informational tasks, explaining the process of doing something, such as baking or juggling. Expository essays can use various organizational schemes to help structure the information, such as by comparing and contrasting two things. An expository essay is different from an argumentative essay in that it is not trying to convince the reader of anything, but only trying to inform. Similarly, the purpose of a descriptive essay is to show detail, but not necessarily to inform about how something works.

67. C: Homophones are words that are pronounced the same but differ in meaning. For example, a bride wears a 2-carat ring, but a horse eats a carrot. These words are not all nouns or monosyllabic, and none of them are diphthongs. Diphthongs (D) are a single-syllable sound made up by combining two vowels, such as in the words *weird*, *applause*, and *boy*.

68. A: A group of students working together on a project are applying numerous learning strategies at once. Collaborative learning is a hands-on approach that actively involves students in the learning process. Students involved in collaborative learning typically retain the lesson better.

69. C: A biography relates information about part of the life of an individual. An autobiography is a biography about the writer's own life. A memoir is also autobiographical, but focuses on a theme. Historical fiction uses a setting or event based in historical fact as the background for characters and/or action that is invented.

70. C: Students will do online research about the cultural, economic, or political events that were occurring during the specific time about which they've written. By researching the historic setting that surrounded the events their interviewee discussed, students are simultaneously broadening their understanding of the context and working in a different content area.

71. B: The students will employ brainstorming and a compare/contrast strategy. Brainstorming is a prewriting activity in which an individual or group responds to a specific question by considering any and all responses that arise without editing, prioritizing, or selecting. Once the brainstorming session is complete, students look at the results and eliminate any responses that are not useful, then group and prioritize the remaining responses. In this example, the students are having a collaborative learning experience in that they are brainstorming together; however, collaborative learning is not a strategy per se, but is the outcome of a strategy. The students are also employing a compare/contrast strategy in that they are looking both at how the two writing styles share common elements and how they are distinct.

72. C: Both Anderson and the Grimms wrote in the same genre, that of fairy tales. Genre refers to types of writing. Mystery, romance, adventure, historical fiction, and fairy tales are some examples of genres. A genre can include many different authors and writing styles. These students are being asked to compare two distinct writing styles within a single genre in order to locate similarities and differences.

73. B: This exercise promotes students comprehension by requiring them to examine the authors' use of setting, plot, pacing, word choice, syntactical structures, narration, mood, metaphors, point of view, voice, and character development to find ways in which they are similar as well as different. In so doing, the students are discovering that language shapes meaning in ways both subtle and profound.

74. C: Authors make thousands of decisions in the act of writing: what point of view to take, how much weight to give an event, what to reveal about a character, what words will most effectively express the writer's intention, and more. While many of these decisions are consciously artistic choices, some are unconscious and imbedded in the cultural expectations of time and place in which the author has lived. To understand a text to the fullest degree possible, it is necessary to read it with an eye to the cultural framework it came from.

75. A: The teacher should give each child a piece of drawing paper that has been folded in half and then in half again, creating four boxes, along with a piece that has not been folded. The teacher should then ask the students to draw a cartoon about the story. Each of the first four boxes will show the events in order. The second page is to show how the story ends. When a child is able to visually see the way a familiar story has unfolded, that child can find causal or thematic connections in the action that increases her comprehension of the story overall. Asking the class to draw a single picture or to draw the beginning and end doesn't sufficiently demonstrate the importance of order to meaning. While some first-graders may be able to create their own cartoon stories that demonstrate a logical series of events, many first-graders are not yet ready to organize thought into a linear progression.

76. A: There are three primary types of sonnets. The Shakespearean sonnet is specifically what these students are reading. A Spenserian sonnet is also composed of three four-line stanzas followed by a two-line couplet; however, the rhymes are not contained within each stanza but spill from one stanza to the next (*abab bcbc cdcd ee).* A Petrarchan sonnet divides into an eight-line stanza and a six-line stanza.

77. D: Asking children to write a list provides them with a visual model that is a side-by-side comparison of the two countries. In creating that visual model, each student first has to organize his or her thoughts mentally, deciding whether each particular item under consideration is shared between both countries or is a difference between them.

78. D: Teachers will observe a variety of developmental arcs when teaching reading, since all students learn differently. It is very important to understand which instances are normal in the course of learning and which signal a learning difficulty. Barrett is still exhibiting confusion over certain letter-sounds, typically when the letters look similar. At his age, this difficulty could suggest that Barrett has an issue with reading that could be addressed by a reading specialist. The other three choices describe normal behaviors that are commonly exhibited by children when they are learning to read. Choice C, Noelle, may describe an instance in which a student is having a learning problem. However, the teacher will need more information about Noelle's reading skills besides her reluctance to read before making a determination about how to proceed.

79. A: The words in this question prompt are most often used to refer to *sounds* made while reading. Initial/onset, medial, and final sounds are decoded in the beginning, middle, and end of words. When a teacher needs to assess an emergent or struggling reader's ability to differentiate between sounds in words, he or she may use a phonological awareness assessment. This tool will provide the teacher with information about the student's current ability to decode or encode words.

80. A: Individuals with dysgraphia have difficulty with the physical act of writing. They find holding and manipulating a pencil problematic. Their letters are primitively formed, and their handwriting is illegible.

81. B: "Pretty as a picture" is a simile, which is a comparison of two unlike things using the words *like* or *as*. A metaphor is a similar comparison between two unlike things, but metaphors do not use the words *like* or *as*. Synecdoche is a phrase that uses a part to represent the whole of something. For instance, one might refer to "the crown" to refer to a royal family. Finally, a paradox is a statement that appears to contradict itself. All of these are considered figures of speech.

82. B: Writing haikus will promote students' vocabularies. The tightly controlled syllabic requirements will cause students to search for words outside their normal vocabularies that will fit the rigid framework and still express the writer's intended meanings. Often, students will rediscover a word whose meaning they know, but they don't often use.

83. C: The most effective lesson would be brainstorming a list of verbs that mean ways of talking or ways of going, then adding them to the word wall along with some nouns that specify common topics. Second graders aren't developmentally ready for a thesaurus; most will believe that any words in a particular list are interchangeable. For example, a student who wrote *my little sister walks like a baby* might find the verbs *strut, sidle,* and *amble* in the thesaurus. None of these verbs would be an appropriate substitution. Supplementing a noun with an adjective often results in flat writing: *There's a tree in my yard* might become *There's a nice tree in my big yard.* Adjectives such as *pretty, fun, cute, funny,* and so forth don't add much in terms of meaning, but they are the adjectives younger writers reach for first. A more specific noun is both more meaningful and more interesting. *There's a weeping willow in my yard* is evocative.

84. B: Scaffolding refers to any kind of special instruction designed to help students learn a new or challenging concept. There are countless forms of scaffolding techniques. The three techniques mentioned in the question prompt are all used to facilitate student understanding of a given text or a concept taught within the text. Scaffolding should not be confused with modeling strategies, which refer to the process of demonstrating how something should be done before a student tries it on his or her own.

85. C: The words drip, chirp, splash, giggle are examples of onomatopoeia. Onomatopoeia refers to words that sound like what they represent.

86. D: It offers a systematic approach to untangling the wide variety of vowel sounds when an unfamiliar word is encountered. Code knowledge, also called orthographic tendencies, is a helpful approach to decoding a word when multiple pronunciation possibilities exist. For example, in the words *toe, go, though,* and *low*, the long O sound is written in a variety of ways. A code knowledge approach teaches a reader to first try a short vowel sound. If that doesn't help, the reader should consider the different ways the vowel or vowel groups can be pronounced, based on what he knows about other words.

87. D: Targeted instruction is achieved by assessing areas needing improvement as well as areas of greatest strength for each student, and adjusting instruction to target those areas. This helps to ensure that all members of a class are receiving instruction tailored to their specific needs.

88. A: Explicit instruction involves clarifying the goal, modeling strategies, and offering explanations geared to a student's level of understanding. Explicit instruction is well organized and structured. It offers easily understood steps and depends in part on frequent reference to previously learned materials.

89. B: When using scaffolding, a teacher assigns a task that is just beyond the student's current level. The teacher encourages the student's attempts at comprehension by offering various supports that largely depend on prior knowledge, in order to develop the student's willingness to move forward into uncharted territory as a confident independent learner.

90. D: Decoding unfamiliar words when reading primarily involves understanding the structure, meaning, and the relationship between letters and sounds. Syntactic (e.g. syntax) refers to word order and sentence structure, which is necessary to interpret the meaning of phrases in context. Semantics refers to word meaning and has a very direct role in decoding meaning when encountering word roots. Graphophonic refers to written words and how the written form corresponds to the oral form of a word. To adequately read and recognize unfamiliar words, a reader needs to be able to sound out and possible recognize patterns that they have encountered elsewhere. With each of these systems activated, readers are able to succeed when encountering many unfamiliar words. However, the pragmatic domain, which deals with the use of language in social contexts and the rules for effective communication, does not directly contribute to the process of decoding written words.

91. A: Prefixes and suffixes are important for reading comprehension because they change the meanings of the root word to which they are attached. A student who understands that *un* means "not" will be able to decipher the meanings of words such as *unwanted, unhappy,* or *unreasonable.*

92. B: Closed syllables are those that end with a consonant. *At, dog, spit, duck,* and *pluck* are all examples of closed syllables.

93. B: A maze test is a specific type of cloze test. In a cloze test, words are deleted, and the reader must supply the missing words using contextual clues and vocabulary that is familiar. A maze test is essentially a multiple-choice application of a cloze test.

94. A: Teachers of English language learners should not employ idioms and slang in their instruction because these informal uses of speech are likely to confuse the students. Involving students in hands-on activities such as group reading and language play makes the experience both more meaningful and more immediate. New knowledge can only be absorbed by attaching it to prior knowledge; referencing what students already know is essential. Speaking slowly to English language learners is important, because they are processing what is being said at a slower rate than a native speaker.

95. A: Editing is the final step in the writing process and involves correcting surface features such as sentence fragments, spelling, and punctuation. The writer has already decided the ideas or events are in proper order, have been sufficiently described, and are clear. Now the writer turns his or her attention to surface features, "scrubbing" errors in spelling, punctuation, and syntax from the writing.

96. A: This student needs carefully organized lessons in decoding, sight words, vocabulary, and comprehension at least three to five times a week. These mini-lessons must be extremely clear, with the parts broken down to the lowest common denominator. The more tightly interwoven and systematized the instruction, the better chance this student will have. This type of learner needs, first and foremost, instruction that has been highly organized into a system that will make sense to her. If possible, she should receive private instruction on a daily basis. The instruction needs to focus on decoding, recognizing words, reading with increasing fluency, enhancing vocabulary, and comprehension. She should be working at the Instructional level, or with texts she can read with at least 90% accuracy.

97. C: Silent reading fluency can be monitored over time by giving the Test of Silent Contextual Reading Fluency (TSCRF) four times a year. A similar assessment tool is the Test of Silent Word Reading Fluency (TOSWRF), in which words of increasing complexity are given as a single, undifferentiated, and unpunctuated strand. As with the TSCRF, three minutes are given for the student to separate each word from the next. *Itwillcannotschoolbecomeagendaconsistentphilosophysuperfluous* is an example of such a strand.

98. D: Based on a Japanese form of poetry, haiku have become popular with students and teachers alike. Reading and writing haiku helps younger students become aware of syllables and helps older students learn about subtleties of vocabulary.

99. A: Verbal dyspraxia refers to trouble with accurately producing sounds due to oral motor functions. Verbal dyspraxia is a broad grouping of motor speech conditions and may present as inaccurate and inconsistent speech, slow speaking, and difficulty in producing sounds accurately in isolation or in typical speech.

100. B: Coarticulation affects phonemic awareness. Vocalizing words involves arranging a series of continuous, voiced, unvoiced, and stop sounds. As one sound is being uttered, the tongue and lips are already assuming the shape required by the next sound in the word. This process, which is not conscious, can distort individual sounds. One sound can slur into another, clip the end of the previous sound, or flatten or heighten a sound. For children who have difficulty hearing distinct phonemic sounds, individual instruction may be required.

Constructed Response

1. Sample Response:

Ally's oral reading performance sample showed few errors with actual phonic performance. She was capable of sounding out many longer words with relative success. The words she had the most difficulty with were words that she was less familiar with the spelling of, such as "Hare." Additionally, she would periodically skip multi-syllabic words that she struggled with. Ally seemed to have the most difficulty with maintaining the pace of her reading, which detracts from her actual reading fluency as she would frequently pause between roughly every three and four syllables. She seemed to have particularly long pauses before more difficult words and at the end of a line, where she would need to find the beginning of a new line. The segmentation of Ally's reading makes comprehension and expression difficult, as she is not reading the passage with natural inflections as it would be read by a more experienced reader. With Ally's high accuracy and lower reading speed in mind, one general recommendation would be to focus on facilitating opportunities for Ally to improve the areas hindering her overall fluency in reading. Fluency is functionally made up of accuracy, speed, expression, and comprehension. Ally's expression and comprehension are likely negatively impacted by her frequent pauses when reading. This pattern of pausing to ensure accuracy in pronunciation is likely a problem that will self-resolve with general practice, but targeting her speed in decoding complex words and improving her fluidity in reading sight words is likely to be more effective.

In response, a teacher can employ targeted practice by simply providing Ally with more opportunity to practice reading aloud. Ally will benefit from practicing reading aloud with passages high in sight words that do not require her to stop to decode larger chunks. If Ally continues to pace herself slowly so she does not make any mistakes, the teacher can tell Ally explicitly that the activity is about speed and not about making no mistakes. The teacher can also permit Ally to repeat a sentence that she struggled with to break down the tendency to pause when reading. This should help her practice reading more fluidly with room for proper stress and intonation in her speech with fewer unnatural pauses.

Ally can also benefit from reading more challenging passages, intentionally helping her encounter more difficult, multi-syllabic words. By learning larger vocabulary words and encountering them naturally in passages, she should have ample opportunity to practice sounding out difficult words faster. With one-on-one reading instruction, the teacher can effectively help Ally challenge herself with these new words by asking her to re-read the whole sentence if she does try to skip a difficult word.

In summary, Ally needs targeted practice to help her increase her overall reading fluency. She is strong in her accuracy, but needs to practice reducing her pauses in reading and become more comfortable with encountering larger words in reading practice.

2. Sample Response:

Adrian's journal entry had several grammar deficiencies, but one of the most frequent areas that Adrian could improve on is his omission of the plural -s to words such as "friends" and "miles." It is possible that Adrian's primary language does not use morphemes to indicate if a word is plural or not, so he may be experiencing primary language interference. One primary goal in helping Adrian address this grammar issue is to help him raise his own awareness of the grammatical form through direct teaching and then help Adrian employ the correct grammar form independently over time.

Krashen's monitor hypothesis asserts that in second language acquisition, a learner can only refine their language production by self-monitoring their output and working to correct their own mistakes. This requires that Adrian is aware of the correct grammar form as well as having the time and attention to focus on correcting his own grammar. With Krashen's theory in mind, the teacher should first try to assess if Adrian is able to successfully identify the correct grammar form on a targeted formative assessment without any prior instruction. Regardless of whether or not Adrian does successfully add plural -s indicators to plural words, he may need explicit instruction or reinforcement of the concept to make sure he understands it fully. If he is able to succeed on the initial assessment, he may just not be putting the effort into monitoring his own speech and needs to be coached.

A good way to start Adrian off on self-monitoring is to begin a targeted correction program. The teacher can discretely remind Adrian when he has made an error in omitting the plural -s. If this is to be effective and inclusive, the teacher needs to limit corrections to times that Adrian won't be put on display in front of the class. As Adrian improves, the teacher should make the cueing more subtle and only ask Adrian to repeat himself, implying that he can make a correction to what he said. Although directly helping Adrian monitor his own grammar is helpful, Adrian is more likely to encounter success if he is able to monitor and correct his grammar in non-school environments.

3. Sample Response:

Mrs. Johnson's class demonstrates an increased need for improved classroom organization, improved access to the materials during the instruction process, and better implementation of formative assessment during the instruction. Firstly, the divide in the students' assessment results is most likely indicative of distractions during the reading process. Students who were unable to focus on the story while it is being read aloud would inevitably have no knowledge with which to answer the fill-in-the-blank questions. Having the students move to an area circled around the teacher, rather than in groups of four, would be more helpful in gaining the student's attention and minimizing distractions throughout the reading portion of class.

A second factor is that this scenario allowed little time for students to re-read the passage for themselves. The use of a shared text via projector, rather than individual reference materials, is a natural impedance to a student's ability to read the text at their own pace. Displaying a text while reading it aloud can be a helpful way to provide scaffolding to some students, but many students at this age need to be able to re-read the text to remember important plot points.

Mrs. Johnson admirably employed the use of formative assessment throughout the reading-aloud portion of the class, but rather than only waiting for a portion of student hands to be raised, she should allow an appropriate amount of time for the students to review the text by verbally specifying when she will expect an answer ('I'll check back in with you for an answer in a minute and a half'). This time allotment should allow for the students to re-read the portion of the passage in question and think before responding. Then, rather than selecting students only based on who has raised their hand, she should employ a method to choose students who do not commonly answer to assess comprehension on a whole-class level rather than focusing on specific individuals.

In summary, Mrs. Johnson's class should be rearranged with a better setup for supporting students' attention during the reading process, along with employing assessment strategies with the whole class in mind. The students should also be given a copy of the passage and enough time to read it at their own pace.

How to Overcome Test Anxiety

Just the thought of taking a test is enough to make most people a little nervous. A test is an important event that can have a long-term impact on your future, so it's important to take it seriously and it's natural to feel anxious about performing well. But just because anxiety is normal, that doesn't mean that it's helpful in test taking, or that you should simply accept it as part of your life. Anxiety can have a variety of effects. These effects can be mild, like making you feel slightly nervous, or severe, like blocking your ability to focus or remember even a simple detail.

If you experience test anxiety—whether severe or mild—it's important to know how to beat it. To discover this, first you need to understand what causes test anxiety.

Causes of Test Anxiety

While we often think of anxiety as an uncontrollable emotional state, it can actually be caused by simple, practical things. One of the most common causes of test anxiety is that a person does not feel adequately prepared for their test. This feeling can be the result of many different issues such as poor study habits or lack of organization, but the most common culprit is time management. Starting to study too late, failing to organize your study time to cover all of the material, or being distracted while you study will mean that you're not well prepared for the test. This may lead to cramming the night before, which will cause you to be physically and mentally exhausted for the test. Poor time management also contributes to feelings of stress, fear, and hopelessness as you realize you are not well prepared but don't know what to do about it.

Other times, test anxiety is not related to your preparation for the test but comes from unresolved fear. This may be a past failure on a test, or poor performance on tests in general. It may come from comparing yourself to others who seem to be performing better or from the stress of living up to expectations. Anxiety may be driven by fears of the future—how failure on this test would affect your educational and career goals. These fears are often completely irrational, but they can still negatively impact your test performance.

Elements of Test Anxiety

As mentioned earlier, test anxiety is considered to be an emotional state, but it has physical and mental components as well. Sometimes you may not even realize that you are suffering from test anxiety until you notice the physical symptoms. These can include trembling hands, rapid heartbeat, sweating, nausea, and tense muscles. Extreme anxiety may lead to fainting or vomiting. Obviously, any of these symptoms can have a negative impact on testing. It is important to recognize them as soon as they begin to occur so that you can address the problem before it damages your performance.

The mental components of test anxiety include trouble focusing and inability to remember learned information. During a test, your mind is on high alert, which can help you recall information and stay focused for an extended period of time. However, anxiety interferes with your mind's natural processes, causing you to blank out, even on the questions you know well. The strain of testing during anxiety makes it difficult to stay focused, especially on a test that may take several hours. Extreme anxiety can take a huge mental toll, making it difficult not only to recall test information but even to understand the test questions or pull your thoughts together.

Effects of Test Anxiety

Test anxiety is like a disease—if left untreated, it will get progressively worse. Anxiety leads to poor performance, and this reinforces the feelings of fear and failure, which in turn lead to poor performances on subsequent tests. It can grow from a mild nervousness to a crippling condition. If allowed to progress, test anxiety can have a big impact on your schooling, and consequently on your future.

Test anxiety can spread to other parts of your life. Anxiety on tests can become anxiety in any stressful situation, and blanking on a test can turn into panicking in a job situation. But fortunately, you don't have to let anxiety rule your testing and determine your grades. There are a number of relatively simple steps you can take to move past anxiety and function normally on a test and in the rest of life.

Physical Steps for Beating Test Anxiety

While test anxiety is a serious problem, the good news is that it can be overcome. It doesn't have to control your ability to think and remember information. While it may take time, you can begin taking steps today to beat anxiety.

Just as your first hint that you may be struggling with anxiety comes from the physical symptoms, the first step to treating it is also physical. Rest is crucial for having a clear, strong mind. If you are tired, it is much easier to give in to anxiety. But if you establish good sleep habits, your body and mind will be ready to perform optimally, without the strain of exhaustion. Additionally, sleeping well helps you to retain information better, so you're more likely to recall the answers when you see the test questions.

Getting good sleep means more than going to bed on time. It's important to allow your brain time to relax. Take study breaks from time to time so it doesn't get overworked, and don't study right before bed. Take time to rest your mind before trying to rest your body, or you may find it difficult to fall asleep.

Along with sleep, other aspects of physical health are important in preparing for a test. Good nutrition is vital for good brain function. Sugary foods and drinks may give a burst of energy but this burst is followed by a crash, both physically and emotionally. Instead, fuel your body with protein and vitamin-rich foods.

Also, drink plenty of water. Dehydration can lead to headaches and exhaustion, especially if your brain is already under stress from the rigors of the test. Particularly if your test is a long one, drink water during the breaks. And if possible, take an energy-boosting snack to eat between sections.

Along with sleep and diet, a third important part of physical health is exercise. Maintaining a steady workout schedule is helpful, but even taking 5-minute study breaks to walk can help get your blood pumping faster and clear your head. Exercise also releases endorphins, which contribute to a positive feeling and can help combat test anxiety.

When you nurture your physical health, you are also contributing to your mental health. If your body is healthy, your mind is much more likely to be healthy as well. So take time to rest, nourish your body with healthy food and water, and get moving as much as possible. Taking these physical steps will make you stronger and more able to take the mental steps necessary to overcome test anxiety.

Mental Steps for Beating Test Anxiety

Working on the mental side of test anxiety can be more challenging, but as with the physical side, there are clear steps you can take to overcome it. As mentioned earlier, test anxiety often stems from lack of preparation, so the obvious solution is to prepare for the test. Effective studying may be the most important weapon you have for beating test anxiety, but you can and should employ several other mental tools to combat fear.

First, boost your confidence by reminding yourself of past success—tests or projects that you aced. If you're putting as much effort into preparing for this test as you did for those, there's no reason you should expect to fail here. Work hard to prepare; then trust your preparation.

Second, surround yourself with encouraging people. It can be helpful to find a study group, but be sure that the people you're around will encourage a positive attitude. If you spend time with others who are anxious or cynical, this will only contribute to your own anxiety. Look for others who are motivated to study hard from a desire to succeed, not from a fear of failure.

Third, reward yourself. A test is physically and mentally tiring, even without anxiety, and it can be helpful to have something to look forward to. Plan an activity following the test, regardless of the outcome, such as going to a movie or getting ice cream.

When you are taking the test, if you find yourself beginning to feel anxious, remind yourself that you know the material. Visualize successfully completing the test. Then take a few deep, relaxing breaths and return to it. Work through the questions carefully but with confidence, knowing that you are capable of succeeding.

Developing a healthy mental approach to test taking will also aid in other areas of life. Test anxiety affects more than just the actual test—it can be damaging to your mental health and even contribute to depression. It's important to beat test anxiety before it becomes a problem for more than testing.

Study Strategy

Being prepared for the test is necessary to combat anxiety, but what does being prepared look like? You may study for hours on end and still not feel prepared. What you need is a strategy for test prep. The next few pages outline our recommended steps to help you plan out and conquer the challenge of preparation.

Step 1: Scope Out the Test

Learn everything you can about the format (multiple choice, essay, etc.) and what will be on the test. Gather any study materials, course outlines, or sample exams that may be available. Not only will this help you to prepare, but knowing what to expect can help to alleviate test anxiety.

Step 2: Map Out the Material

Look through the textbook or study guide and make note of how many chapters or sections it has. Then divide these over the time you have. For example, if a book has 15 chapters and you have five days to study, you need to cover three chapters each day. Even better, if you have the time, leave an extra day at the end for overall review after you have gone through the material in depth.

If time is limited, you may need to prioritize the material. Look through it and make note of which sections you think you already have a good grasp on, and which need review. While you are studying, skim quickly through the familiar sections and take more time on the challenging parts.

Write out your plan so you don't get lost as you go. Having a written plan also helps you feel more in control of the study, so anxiety is less likely to arise from feeling overwhelmed at the amount to cover.

Step 3: Gather Your Tools

Decide what study method works best for you. Do you prefer to highlight in the book as you study and then go back over the highlighted portions? Or do you type out notes of the important information? Or is it helpful to make flashcards that you can carry with you? Assemble the pens, index cards, highlighters, post-it notes, and any other materials you may need so you won't be distracted by getting up to find things while you study.

If you're having a hard time retaining the information or organizing your notes, experiment with different methods. For example, try color-coding by subject with colored pens, highlighters, or post-it notes. If you learn better by hearing, try recording yourself reading your notes so you can listen while in the car, working out, or simply sitting at your desk. Ask a friend to quiz you from your flashcards, or try teaching someone the material to solidify it in your mind.

Step 4: Create Your Environment

It's important to avoid distractions while you study. This includes both the obvious distractions like visitors and the subtle distractions like an uncomfortable chair (or a too-comfortable couch that makes you want to fall asleep). Set up the best study environment possible: good lighting and a comfortable work area. If background music helps you focus, you may want to turn it on, but otherwise keep the room quiet. If you are using a computer to take notes, be sure you don't have any other windows open, especially applications like social media, games, or anything else that could distract you. Silence your phone and turn off notifications. Be sure to keep water close by so you stay hydrated while you study (but avoid unhealthy drinks and snacks).

Also, take into account the best time of day to study. Are you freshest first thing in the morning? Try to set aside some time then to work through the material. Is your mind clearer in the afternoon or evening? Schedule your study session then. Another method is to study at the same time of day that you will take the test, so that your brain gets used to working on the material at that time and will be ready to focus at test time.

Step 5: Study!

Once you have done all the study preparation, it's time to settle into the actual studying. Sit down, take a few moments to settle your mind so you can focus, and begin to follow your study plan. Don't give in to distractions or let yourself procrastinate. This is your time to prepare so you'll be ready to fearlessly approach the test. Make the most of the time and stay focused.

Of course, you don't want to burn out. If you study too long you may find that you're not retaining the information very well. Take regular study breaks. For example, taking five minutes out of every hour to walk briskly, breathing deeply and swinging your arms, can help your mind stay fresh.

As you get to the end of each chapter or section, it's a good idea to do a quick review. Remind yourself of what you learned and work on any difficult parts. When you feel that you've mastered the material, move on to the next part. At the end of your study session, briefly skim through your notes again.

But while review is helpful, cramming last minute is NOT. If at all possible, work ahead so that you won't need to fit all your study into the last day. Cramming overloads your brain with more information than it can process and retain, and your tired mind may struggle to recall even previously learned information when it is overwhelmed with last-minute study. Also, the urgent nature of cramming and the stress placed on your brain contribute to anxiety. You'll be more likely to go to the test feeling unprepared and having trouble thinking clearly.

So don't cram, and don't stay up late before the test, even just to review your notes at a leisurely pace. Your brain needs rest more than it needs to go over the information again. In fact, plan to finish your studies by noon or early afternoon the day before the test. Give your brain the rest of the day to relax or focus on other things, and get a good night's sleep. Then you will be fresh for the test and better able to recall what you've studied.

Step 6: Take a Practice Test

Many courses offer sample tests, either online or in the study materials. This is an excellent resource to check whether you have mastered the material, as well as to prepare for the test format and environment.

Check the test format ahead of time: the number of questions, the type (multiple choice, free response, etc.), and the time limit. Then create a plan for working through them. For example, if you have 30 minutes to take a 60-question test, your limit is 30 seconds per question. Spend less time on the questions you know well so that you can take more time on the difficult ones.

If you have time to take several practice tests, take the first one open book, with no time limit. Work through the questions at your own pace and make sure you fully understand them. Gradually work up to taking a test under test conditions: sit at a desk with all study materials put away and set a timer. Pace yourself to make sure you finish the test with time to spare and go back to check your answers if you have time.

After each test, check your answers. On the questions you missed, be sure you understand why you missed them. Did you misread the question (tests can use tricky wording)? Did you forget the information? Or was it something you hadn't learned? Go back and study any shaky areas that the practice tests reveal.

Taking these tests not only helps with your grade, but also aids in combating test anxiety. If you're already used to the test conditions, you're less likely to worry about it, and working through tests until you're scoring well gives you a confidence boost. Go through the practice tests until you feel comfortable, and then you can go into the test knowing that you're ready for it.

Test Tips

On test day, you should be confident, knowing that you've prepared well and are ready to answer the questions. But aside from preparation, there are several test day strategies you can employ to maximize your performance.

First, as stated before, get a good night's sleep the night before the test (and for several nights before that, if possible). Go into the test with a fresh, alert mind rather than staying up late to study.

Try not to change too much about your normal routine on the day of the test. It's important to eat a nutritious breakfast, but if you normally don't eat breakfast at all, consider eating just a protein bar. If you're a coffee drinker, go ahead and have your normal coffee. Just make sure you time it so that the caffeine doesn't wear off right in the middle of your test. Avoid sugary beverages, and drink enough water to stay hydrated but not so much that you need a restroom break 10 minutes into the test. If your test isn't first thing in the morning, consider going for a walk or doing a light workout before the test to get your blood flowing.

Allow yourself enough time to get ready, and leave for the test with plenty of time to spare so you won't have the anxiety of scrambling to arrive in time. Another reason to be early is to select a good seat. It's helpful to sit away from doors and windows, which can be distracting. Find a good seat, get out your supplies, and settle your mind before the test begins.

When the test begins, start by going over the instructions carefully, even if you already know what to expect. Make sure you avoid any careless mistakes by following the directions.

Then begin working through the questions, pacing yourself as you've practiced. If you're not sure on an answer, don't spend too much time on it, and don't let it shake your confidence. Either skip it and come back later, or eliminate as many wrong answers as possible and guess among the remaining ones. Don't dwell on these questions as you continue—put them out of your mind and focus on what lies ahead.

Be sure to read all of the answer choices, even if you're sure the first one is the right answer. Sometimes you'll find a better one if you keep reading. But don't second-guess yourself if you do immediately know the answer. Your gut instinct is usually right. Don't let test anxiety rob you of the information you know.

If you have time at the end of the test (and if the test format allows), go back and review your answers. Be cautious about changing any, since your first instinct tends to be correct, but make sure you didn't misread any of the questions or accidentally mark the wrong answer choice. Look over any you skipped and make an educated guess.

At the end, leave the test feeling confident. You've done your best, so don't waste time worrying about your performance or wishing you could change anything. Instead, celebrate the successful completion of this test. And finally, use this test to learn how to deal with anxiety even better next time.

Review Video: Test Anxiety
Visit mometrix.com/academy and enter code: 100340

Important Qualification

Not all anxiety is created equal. If your test anxiety is causing major issues in your life beyond the classroom or testing center, or if you are experiencing troubling physical symptoms related to your anxiety, it may be a sign of a serious physiological or psychological condition. If this sounds like your situation, we strongly encourage you to seek professional help.

Online Resources

Due to our efforts to try to keep this book to a manageable length, we've created a link that will give you access to all of your online resources:

mometrix.com/resources719/mtelreadsp62

It's Your Moment, Let's Celebrate It!

Share your story @mometrixtestpreparation